AR3

WID

THE FILMS
OF
SEAN CONNERY

THE FILMS OF

SEAN CONNERY

LEE PFEIFFER
and
PHILIP LISA

A CITADEL PRESS BOOK
Published by Carol Publishing Group

ACKNOWLEDGMENTS

The authors gratefully acknowledge the following companies: MGM/United Artists, Warner Brothers, Columbia Pictures, Hollywood Pictures, Walt Disney Productions, 20th Century–Fox, Paramount Pictures, Universal Pictures, Handmade Films, Cannon Films, Interstar Releasing, TriStar Pictures, UPI, and Worldwide.

Many thanks also to the following individuals: Mike Boldt, for his superb artwork; Walter Brinkman for his skilled photography; Ron Plesniarski, Barbara Lynch, and Bob Klepeis for providing rare research materials; Karen DeFelice; Jerry Ohlinger's Movie Memorabilia Store in New York City; Connery fans supreme Kevin Doherty and John Ewaniuk; Steve Schragis, Bruce Bender, Gary Fitzgerald, Chris Simon, Mike Lewis, Steven Brower, Don Davidson, Margaret Wolf, and Bill Wolfsthal of Citadel Press; and the usual heartfelt thanks to Janet and Nicole Pfeiffer, Phil and Mary Ann Lisa and Eileen Lisa for their patience and understanding regarding the long hours put into this project.

We are also thankful to the following individuals of journals which analyze Sean Connery's career: Dave Worrall of the James Bond Collector's Club, P.O.B. 1570, Christchurch, Dorset, BH23 5YH, England; Charles Helfenstein of *SPIES* magazine, P.O.B. 476, Frederick, MD 21701; The Ian Fleming Foundation, P.O.B. 6897, Santa Barbara, CA 93160; Jerome Nicod and Laurent Perriot of Club James Bond 007, 5 cours Emile Zola, 69100 Villeurbanne, France; and Graham Rye of the James Bond 007 Fan Club and Archive in England.

Special thanks to our good friend John Parkinson of Eon Productions for his kind permission to reprint the photos from the James Bond films.

In response to those who have requested information about obtaining collectibles from the films of Sean Connery, extensive catalogs of posters, novelties, books, toys, and records can be had by writing to: Spy Guise, Dept CB, P.O.B. 152, Dunellen, NJ 08812, USA.

A Citadel Press Book
Published by Carol Publishing Group
Citadel Press is a registered trademark of Carol Communications, Inc.
Editorial, sales and distribution, rights and permissions inquiries should be addressed to Carol Publishing Group, 120 Enterprise Avenue, Secaucus, N.J. 07094
In Canada: Canadian Manda Group, One Atlantic Avenue, Suite 105, Toronto, Ontario M6K 3E7
Carol Publishing Group books may be purchased in bulk at special discounts for sales promotion, fund-raising, or educational purposes. Special editions can be created to specifications. For details, contact Special Sales Department, 120 Enterprise Avenue, Secaucus, N.J. 07094.

Manufacturing in the United States of America

10 9 8 7 6 5 4 3 2 1

Designed by A. Christopher Simon

Library of Congress Cataloging-in-Publication Data

Pfeiffer, Lee.
    The films of Sean Connery / Lee Pfeiffer and Philip Lisa.—
Rev. and updated.
        p.   cm.
    "A Citadel Press book."
    ISBN 0-8065-1837-5 (pb)
    1. Connery, Sean.   I. Lisa, Philip.   II. Title.
PN2598.C76P44   1996
791.43'028'092—dc20   96-35942
                                                                CIP

To my mother-in-law,
Helen Plaza,
who personifies "wonderful."

—L.P.

To Eileen,
my "Pretty Irish Girl,"
for her endearing support, inspiration, and love.

—P.L.

CONTENTS

Through the years, Sean's films and personal appearances have been ratings hits on television.

SEAN CONNERY

A British secret agent finds himself strapped to a table, threatened with dissection from a laser beam. A Barbary pirate kidnaps an American woman and brings two great nations to the brink of war. A smooth-talking nineteenth-century con man stages "the crime of the century" by plotting "The Great Train Robbery." An English adventurer establishes himself as king of a lost civilization. A lone lawman on a distant planet confronts the ultimate terror. These diverse situations and characters from various popular films all share a common "bond" in the guise of the man who brought them to life on-screen: Sean Connery. Indeed, the actor's own life is almost as incredible as those of his cinematic alter egos.

Few actors have personified the Horatio Alger spirit more than Connery. He has overcome a poverty-stricken childhood, a variety of diverting career goals, a tempestuous first marriage, critical barbs aimed at his initial acting attempts (one critic said that he was "in no danger of growing old in the business"), and the fear of being typecast as the very character that made him a man of enormous wealth. Today, Connery is one of the few superstars whose popularity is not confined to a specific geographical region. Now in his sixties, he has entered a renaissance period in his life and is enjoying a surge of critical and popular acclaim not equaled since his James Bond heyday of the 1960s. To illustrate the impact his persona has had on international culture, one need only look at his experience in filming *The Man Who Would Be King* (1975) in Morocco. Clad in Arabic attire for the movie, he took a break and went for a spin in his Jeep, ending up in a remote mountain bypass surrounded

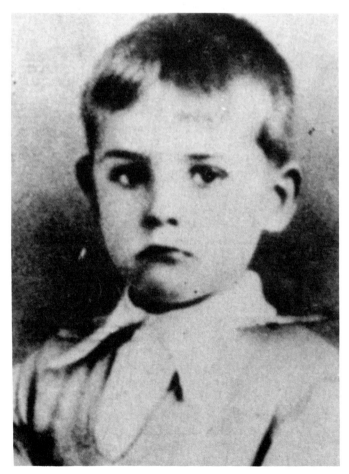

Little Tommy Connery, age four.

9

by gun-wielding rebels who forced him out of the vehicle and seemed prepared to do away with him. Fortunately, one of them recognized him from his films and let him go unharmed. It was probably one of the few times in his life that this intensely private man was happy to be recognized in public!

Connery's success would be impressive under any circumstances. However, when one examines his early life and socioeconomic background, it seems incredible that this poor Scots boy should ever have evolved into an internationally recognized actor of wealth and esteem. He was born on August 25, 1930, in Fountainbridge, Scotland. His parents—Joseph and Euphemia ("Effie")—were proud, hardworking people. Effie had been employed as a charlady when time permitted her to leave the sides of Sean and his younger brother, Neil. Joe Connery was the primary breadwinner in the family, working endless hours as a lorry driver to keep food on the table. "I wouldn't see him," reflected Sean. "There was no father in the sense of checking school grades and things like that. I don't think he knew what I did. One spent a terrific amount of time alone, on one's own. . . . I lacked self-confidence as a boy. . . . One's parents left one free to make one's own way."

"Making one's own way" in those days meant that a child would inevitably start to earn a living at the earliest possible moment. Connery was no exception. With Europe under Hitler's reign of terror, Sean's parents had dramatically decided to evacuate their son. "Fate is extraordinary," he later reflected. "In 1940, I was all set to sail to Australia as a war evacuee. Then a boat was sunk and I didn't go. But if I had, my whole life would probably have been different. If I'd gone on that boat and grown up, say in Sydney, I might well have become a tennis player, or a golfer, a clerk, or a waiter." As it was, his chances for obtaining a solid education rapidly diminished. He recalled, "I left school just before I was fourteen . . . I took what work I could. I wasn't about to be offered a chartered accountant's job. Scotland didn't have much to offer anyone who didn't have a proper education. When it came to the choice of French or metalwork in school, we took metalwork. Who did we know in France?" A bitterness can be found in Connery's statements—a bitterness reflecting his long intolerance of social systems that deprive young people of the education necessary for advancement. Perhaps for that reason, Connery founded the Scottish International Education Trust in the early 1970s. The organization is dedicated to providing academic training for underprivileged youth in Scotland. His total commitment to this fund was illustrated in 1971 when he donated his

entire salary for *Diamonds Are Forever* ($1.25 million) to the charity.

In his youth Connery was known to his parents as Tommy (his Christian name), but acquired several nicknames including Big Tam (the lad was quite tall for his age), Shane, and eventually Sean, the name he would adopt professionally. "I was called Sean long before I was an actor," he said in a 1964 interview. "I had an Irish buddy when I was twelve named Seamus—pronounced 'Sha-mus.' So they nicknamed us Shamus and Shawn and it stuck." Young Sean drifted from job to job, taking whatever employment might be extended to a little-educated, disillusioned boy. "I always paid my share of the rent," he would state years later. "The attitude in our home was the prevalent one in Scotland—you make your own bed and you have to lie on it. I didn't ask for advice and I didn't get it. I had to make it on my own, or not at all." Disgruntled with the lack of opportunity in Scotland, Connery followed many other young men who dreamed of seeing exotic lands and living daring adventures by joining the Royal Navy. This proved to be a regrettable move. Having signed on for a twelve-year hitch, Connery soon discovered that advancement in the Navy depended on discipline and education—two qualities that he sorely lacked. Instead of conforming, Sean waged a one-man war against the service—a war that, naturally, could not be won. His anxiety led him to develop duodenal ulcers, which in turn, mandated his release from the Navy. Although Connery was delighted to be free of the constraints of military life, he now faced the gloomy prospect of finding suitable employment in civilian life.

He moved back in with his family, but had little money to enjoy a vigorous social life. "I took girls out now and then," he conceded, "but I never brought a girl to my home, always a bit secretive about girls, I suppose. I'd come home in the evening—mother would have dinner ready prompt at six o'clock—I'd wash, shave, eat dinner, and be on my date by seven—usually I'd meet them at Benn's Corner in the west end of town. I was never in the position of being able to wine and dine a girl. I didn't have the right clothes anyway. Usually, I'd take a date to the cinema, to a dance, or on the old motorbike."

Under a grant for disabled seamen, Sean literally went into a "dying business" and took up the noble art of coffin polishing. He once recalled a memorable characteristic of the undertaker who employed him: "He was an extraordinary man. He had the dying business worked out to a T. He would go and see someone who was seriously ill and mentally measure them. . . . Suddenly a week or so later, the husband

Left: Sean, age nine, in his "Sunday best." Right: As an amateur soccer player, he was told he had professional potential.

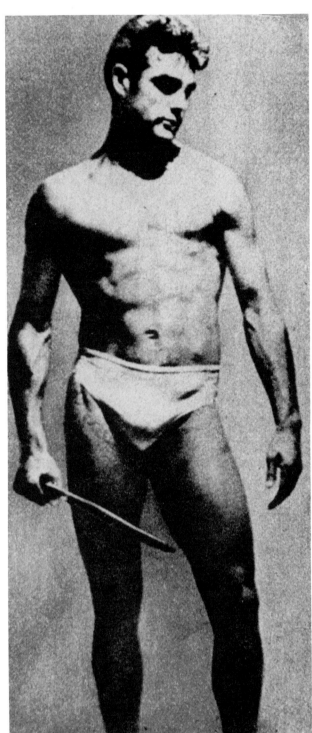

An early occupation of Sean's was posing as a model for art classes.

Striking a pose as Scotland's representative to the Mr. Universe contest.

Sean (second from right in second row from top) on the Fet-Lor amateur soccer team, circa 1950.

or wife would come in and he'd say, 'Oh, it just so happens that I have a coffin that would suit you!' " Yet, the thought of his hard work being buried with the dearly departed soon made him forsake this promising career. He became a laborer for a short time and then found temporary work as a lifeguard in one of London's largest public pools. He supplemented his income by using his excellent physique to pose as an (almost) nude model for art classes. These were lean times, indeed, for the future Oscar winner. Connery has always been somewhat haunted by his impoverished past, as though he cannot fathom how fate allowed him to gain wealth while his peers went on to largely working-class lives. Hard work had something to do with it, but as virtually everyone in his social group had worked hard, this was by no means a ticket to fame and fortune. As Connery would be the first to admit, his success was due not only to his drive but also to a remarkable string of circumstances compounded with good instincts and pure luck. Yet, he has never forgotten his roots. He has remained cautious about spending money, even in these times when wealth is not a concern. As with many individuals who had to overcome poverty, he seems somewhat insecure about his wealth and doesn't appear to take it for granted. Connery does not consider himself a cheap man, and this is evidenced by his stately homes in Marbella, Spain, and the Bahamas. Rather, he detests waste and flashiness. "I'm not stingy, but I'm careful with money. I don't throw it around," he remarked, "because money gives you power and freedom to operate as you want. I have a respect for its value, because I know how hard it is to earn and to keep. I come from a background where there was little money, and we had to be content with what there was. One doesn't forget a past like that. . . . Even today, when I have a big meal in a restaurant, I'm still conscious that the money I'm spending is equal to my dad's wages for a week."

Overspending was the least of Sean's concerns in the days when he was posing for art classes. Connery began to use his interest in physical fitness as an outlet for his frustrations. Before long, he had evolved into a professional bodybuilder and represented Scotland in the 1953 Mr. Universe contest, held in London. Sean placed third, but this did little to add to his income. Unbeknownst to him, however, fate was about to place him on the path of fame and fortune. He later recalled to Britain's *Films and Filming* how he strayed into the field of acting: "As it happened, several of the entrants in the Mr. Universe contest were in the *South Pacific* company, which was in the last three months of its run at the Drury Lane [theater]. After that, they were going on tour, and some cast replacements were coming up. So they told me about this, and I went to audition. Did some handsprings, and so on. I guess I could look like an American Marine, stripped to the waist. I couldn't sing, but I said I could and I joined in singing 'There Is Nothing Like a Dame' with the rest of them. The whole idea of traveling around the country in the musical appealed to me. I didn't seriously consider myself as an actor. But I was about

12

a year with *South Pacific,* all told. There was an American actor in the company, Robert Henderson, and he encouraged me to think about acting . . . That man I shall never forget—he changed my life. Every town I went to on the tour, I would go to see anything else that was playing at the matinees. I compiled this list of basic material that would give me a grounding in literature. And the work I did on that was very intense."

Through constant rehearsals, sometimes done in private at late hours, Connery began to feel confident about approaching acting as a profession. He continued to receive encouragement from Robert Henderson and has always acknowledged the importance this man played in inspiring him. He eventually landed minor roles in the stage productions *Witness for the Prosecution* (directed by Robert Henderson), *Point of Departure,* and *A Witch in Time.* His television acting debut occurred with a 1956 telecast of *The Escaper's Club,* which costarred Robert Shaw, who would later star with Connery in *From Russia With Love* and *Robin and Marian.* In 1957, he received a major career boost. The BBC was mounting a live production of Rod Serling's *Requiem for a Heavyweight,* a hard-hitting drama focusing on the rise and fall of a professional boxer. Jack Palance had received great acclaim for his performance in the American TV version, but was unavailable for this telecast. A talent hunt was undertaken to find a suitable replacement. Connery tested for the role and, to his amazement,

was accepted. Although he was paid only twenty-five pounds for the ninety-minute production (retitled *Blood Money* for U.K. broadcast), the acclaim he received was worth a fortune. Critics' praise of the young actor caused film offers to materialize with regularity.

Unfortunately, the films Connery appeared in did little to add to the prestige of his television work. Capable but unremarkable low-budget titles such as *No Road Back* (filmed before *Heavyweight*), *Hell Drivers,* and *Timelock* offered him limited exposure, but at least he was building his acting abilities. In a 1957 TV production of *Anna Christie,* Sean costarred with an aspiring young actress named Diane Cilento. Cilento was married with a daughter, but the twenty-four-year-old actress was living apart from her husband. Sean was instantly attracted to the beautiful and self-reliant daughter of an Australian family of aristocrats. Diane was slower to reciprocate, but the two strong-willed individuals began an intense relationship that would last for years. Around this time, Sean was signed to a long-term contract by 20th Century-Fox—a deal that netted him the sizable income of 120 pounds per week, regardless of whether he worked or not. His hopes that the studio would use its star-making power creatively on his behalf were quickly dashed. He was constantly told he was too tall or burly for most of the interesting roles. The studio did lend him out to MGM for a mediocre adventure called *Action of the Tiger* (directed by future 007 helmsman

5. After going to sea and working at many jobs, Sean tried acting. Here he is as he appeared in the play, Anna Christie.

6. In 1958 he starred in Rediffusion's TV drama, The Square Ring.

7. Next came the role of Julien in Colombe for the BBC.

8. He played Hotspur in the Shakespeare TV serial, An Age Of Kings.

9. In yet another BBC production, he played the lead in Anna Karenina.

10. With Alfred Burke in a scene from The Crucible.

16 Magazine paid tribute to Sean's early career in film with this 1965 article.

13

Terence Young), and *Tarzan's Greatest Adventure*, one of the better entries in that series. Neither, however, provided a role that would "click" with the public.

Sean became increasingly disgruntled, and the rumor mill had it that Fox was considering dropping his contract. However, Paramount borrowed him to star opposite Lana Turner in a turgid World War II romance titled *Another Time, Another Place*. While on the set, Sean and Lana became fast friends and socialized quite a bit, much to the consternation of Lana's then beau, reputed gangster Johnny Stompanato. The latter warned Sean to cease his off-camera activities with his leading lady, and when tempers flared, Connery responded to the threats by punching the bargain-basement "godfather" in the face. Sean finished the film and moved on to his next assignment—a trip to the States (on loan once again) to film *Darby O'Gill and the Little People* for Disney. Meanwhile, one of Hollywood's more notorious scandals erupted when the fiery-tempered Stompanato got into a fall-down fight with Turner in her Los Angeles home. Acting to save her mother's life, Turner's fourteen-year-old daughter, Cheryl, impolitely buried a butcher knife in Mr. Stompanato, causing his death. Sean received word of all this while on location and was advised that Stompanato's gangland crony Mickey Cohen was seeking revenge on the actor, convinced that somehow Sean was responsible for the deadly fight. For once Connery kept a low profile and reluctantly moved to a dingy motel in the San Fernando Valley. He completed his work with Disney and returned to the safety of Britain, leaving Cohen and his "boys" holding an empty bag. As one writer stated, this was probably the last time anyone would come close to pushing around Sean Connery.

Another Time, Another Place was a critical and commercial dud, and Connery did not gain much from it except for prominent billing. This allowed him to sign for a starring role in *The Frightened City*, a British "kitchen sink" drama with some moments of action that let Sean build his reputation as a leading man. Once again on loan, he moved onto *Operation Snafu*, a low-budget military farce designed primarily to promote Connery's costar, British comedian Alfie Lynch. Neither film represented the big break Sean was looking for. *Darby O'Gill* had proven a hit, but his performance was overshadowed by special effects and singing Leprechauns. At last Fox gave Connery a film assignment—a cameo role in the studio's all-star production of *The Longest Day*. Connery was to receive equal alphabetical star billing—along with forty-two other actors! The film, of course, proved to be a success, but Sean's role allowed for little impact as

the shadows of such giants as Wayne, Mitchum, Fonda, and Burton blurred his contribution. Disgruntled, Connery felt as though his talents would never be fully utilized.

Simultaneously, producer Albert R. ("Cubby") Broccoli had recently ended a partnership with Irving Allen that had resulted in a string of successful action/adventure epics. Broccoli was determined to buy the screen rights to Ian Fleming's James Bond novels, which had been somewhat of a mini-sensation since the character's literary debut in 1954. However, Broccoli learned that fellow producer Harry Saltzman held an option on the rights, but couldn't get the necessary financing. He refused Cubby's offer to buy him out, wisely insisting upon a joint-production deal. Leery of getting into another partnership, Broccoli reluctantly accepted. After being refused by every studio in town, they concluded a deal with Arthur Krim of United Artists to produce the first 007 film, *Dr. No*, on a $1-million budget. With the financing in place, they still had a key assignment—casting the role of James Bond. They knew that if the audience rejected or was indifferent to the actor, Bond would both begin and end his cinematic career with *Dr. No*.

Dozens of stories have been circulated about who was responsible for recognizing Sean's potential as Bond. While it is true that a London newspaper poll did bring him the majority of votes, Broccoli and Saltzman had already been aware of Sean. Future Bond editor and director Peter Hunt had sent some reels of *Operation Snafu* to Saltzman to scrutinize, on the basis that Sean had a good screen presence. However, the key to the casting of Connery resided with Cubby's wife, Dana. The couple had screened *Darby O'Gill*, and when Broccoli asked his wife what she thought of Connery, she replied, "He's a very sexy guy." Cubby was skeptical, as it took a trained eye to envision Sean in an after-six formal. The role in *Darby O'Gill* was that of a farmer and a country bumpkin. Dana's instinct allowed her to look beyond that, and she convinced Cubby and Harry to screen-test the actor.

Amazingly, Connery was ballsy enough to refuse to test, although the producers tricked him into doing some "rehearsals" on-camera with several actresses. Sean has always said that the legend about his being arrogant in front of the producers and pounding the desk was a lot of malarkey. He confessed to "putting on a bit of a show" but insists he was not overly temperamental. He recently recalled, "I used strong and commanding movements, not with weight, but to show how Bond is in control of a scene." Broccoli and Saltzman were impressed by his confidence and overlooked his disheveled appearance. They soon signed him for the role that, for better or worse, would be viewed as his on-screen alter ego for decades to come. In doing so, Connery beat out other prospective candidates such as Richard Johnson, who was reluctant to star in a series; Patrick Mc-Goohan, who declined due to the violent nature of the role, and Roger Moore, Ian Fleming's first choice. Moore was rejected because he was already appearing as "The Saint" on television. (Ironically, all of these men would capitalize on the Bondian success in 007-inspired vehicles in the years to come. Moore, of course, was destined to play the role himself.)

Production on *Dr. No* was slated to begin in 1962—the same year Diane Cilento divorced her husband and almost immediately married Connery in a small civil ceremony in Gibraltar. They honeymooned briefly in Costa del Sol before embarking on a whirlwind ride of fame and fortune, all courtesy of Agent 007. Diane became pregnant with the couple's son, Jason, but Sean was forced to occupy his time preparing for the filming of the first Bond epic. *Dr. No* is one of those rare phenomena in the cinema—a film in which virtually everything went right: the cast, the direction, the technicians, and the production values. The producers felt they had a winner, but the studio did not know what to make of this ground-breaking mixture of sex and humorous violence.

Uncertain of its reception in this country, United Artists opened the film unceremoniously in hundreds of theaters simultaneously, making *Dr. No* in effect one of the first movies from a major studio to open on saturation booking, which has long since become standard practice. This, despite the enthusiastic reception the film received in its British debut several months earlier. Eventually, word of the movie's success reached America, and it proved to have as much "staying power" on-screen as its hero did in the boudoir. Quickly, *Dr. No* became *the* film to see in early 1963.

Ironically, Connery had mixed reactions to the large grosses the movie was pulling in internationally. From day one, he confessed, he was nervous about assuming the mantle of 007: "Well, after I got over my surprise [of being signed for the role] and really began to consider it, I didn't want to do it because I could see that, properly made, it would have to be the first in a series, and I wasn't sure if I wanted to get involved with that and the contract that would go with it. Contracts choke you, and I wanted to be free. . . . However, I did see this would be a start—a marvelous opening. Although I must admit

in all honesty, I didn't think it would take off as it did." To be sure, the films proved to be "properly made." Broccoli and Saltzman's company, Eon Productions, showed a unique ability to hire the best and the brightest people, and their efforts gave the Bond films a professional polish that has stayed with the series through the present time. James Bond would not just become a cinematic hero, he would also emerge as an international phenomenon.

Connery was paid a mere $16,000 for *Dr. No,* but it seemed like a fair deal at the time. The producers had a limited budget, and Sean was hardly a household name. However, tensions arose immediately when Connery asked Saltzman to pay him a two hundred-pound allowance for living expenses, which Sean claimed had been part of a verbal agreement. Saltzman balked, but eventually paid. The reluctance on Harry's part made the actor distrust the producer throughout the years to come. Though Sean may have had mixed emotions about the success of 007, he nevertheless enjoyed the inevitable rewards. He completed work on the second Bond film, *From Russia With Love,* and used his increased paycheck to buy a three-story mansion in Acton Park outside of London. At the same time, Diane was progressing well with her acting career and was generally viewed as a "star of tomorrow."

From Russia With Love was a greater hit than anyone had hoped for and James Bond—thanks to an endorsement from Pres. John F. Kennedy—became the most promising screen hero since Tarzan. Yet, Sean was becoming increasingly nervous about being viewed as a "one-trick pony." Although his contract with Eon allowed him to do non-007 films, it required him to do so for Broccoli and Saltzman. The men were determined to strike while the Bond bandwagon was hot and were preoccupied with preparing the third installment in the series, *Goldfinger.* Connery complained, and Broccoli and Saltzman amended the contract, allowing Sean to do non-Bond films for other producers. The first of these, *Woman of Straw,* was generally dismissed as bargain-basement Hitchcock. Ironically, his next film, Hitchcock's *Marnie,* was also dismissed as bargain-basement Hitchcock, although it has acquired a cult following. Connery was excellent in both of these underrated films, but the public clamored for him as Bond. It was a tense Connery who began work on *Goldfinger.* United Artists had now increased the budget to allow for state-of-the-art sets and special effects, but Sean found it increasingly difficult to welcome strapping on 007's shoulder holster while his non-Bondian efforts sank like anchors.

Goldfinger was more than a success—it was an international phenomenon and spawned a cottage industry of James Bond products and toys that exists even today. As an action thriller, it is as good as movies get, but Sean seemed annoyed at the increasing popularity of his cinematic alter ego. He sought seclusion and shunned the spotlight. He only reluctantly granted interviews and made it clear that questions regarding his personal life were off-limits. He became impatient and irritable, and one influential columnist wrote, "Sean has absolutely no sense of humor." This was untrue, of course, as Sean's friends and confidants found him to be a warm and witty man in private. According to close friend Michael Caine, just as the press had to avoid discussing Sean's family life, friends knew that dwelling on the Bond films was also verboten. "If you were his friend, you just didn't mention it in those days," recalled Caine. Connery grumbled in an interview, "I find that fame

"From rags to riches": Sean and wife Diane Cilento are greeted by Princess Margaret at a royal premiere.

Sean visits Diane on the set of *The Agony and the Ecstasy*, 1965.

tends to turn one from an actor and a human being into piece of merchandise, a public institution. Well, I don't intend to undergo that metamorphosis. This is why I fight so tenaciously to protect my privacy, to keep interviews like this to a minimum, to fend off prying photographers who want to follow me around and publicize my every step and breath. The absolute sanctum is my home, which is and will continue to be only for me, my wife, my family, and my friends. I do not and shall not have business meetings there. When I work, I work my full stint, but I must insist that my private life remain my own. I don't think that's too much to ask." Perhaps not, but the press and the public didn't care, and intrusions upon Sean's personal life only increased as the Bond bonanza boomed. In any event, to this day Connery has refused to go the usual star route and hire a publicist.

Friends felt that the Connerys were becoming somewhat resentful of each other. There was still genuine emotion in the marriage, but Diane, while tending to regard the 007 films as so much rubbish, envied Sean's international fame and fortune. Connery, however, was allegedly envious of his wife's acceptance as a "serious" actress—a label only reinforced by her 1964 Oscar nomination for *Tom Jones*. Michael Caine recalled the tension in the Connery household: "I remember once I was with them in Nassau. Diane was cooking lunch, and Sean and I went out. Of course, we got out and one thing led to another, you know, and we got back for lunch two hours later. Well, we opened the door and Sean said, 'Darling, we're home!'—and all the food she'd cooked came flying through the air at us. I remember the two of us standing there covered in gravy and green beans." Not that Connery lacked support from the press for his acting skills. When *Goldfinger* had wrapped, Sean plunged into Sidney Lumet's *The Hill,* a gritty film set inside a British military prison. It was shown at the Cannes Film Festival, where it received an award for its screenplay, and Sean had every reason to believe this one would be a hit on its own merits. Critics raved that his performance was worthy of an Oscar, but such praise had to suffice. *The Hill* was a box-office flop.

Yet, the Bond juggernaut continued. *Thunderball,* filmed in 1965, promised to be "The Biggest Bond of All." With a budget of $5.5 million, it did not disappoint. However, even the simple pleasure of enacting Bond was becoming an annoyance to Connery as the character increasingly took a backseat to the gadgetry. *Thunderball* was not just a film, it was an event—one of the decade's most heavily promoted movies. By this time, the actor's pay had soared to $500,000—a sum his parents could not even relate

A light moment with Hitchcock on the ill-fated *Marnie,* 1964.

Sean indulges in his favorite pastime on the set of *Thunderball* in the Bahamas, 1965.

17

SMART GETS BOND!

We saw it with our own eyes... "Get Smart's" Don Adams came face to face with Sean Connery and Jumped right into action!

Turn the page for an exclusive interview with Master Agent Maxwell Smart...alias Don Adams

Sean meets the competition via the fan magazines—with Don (*Get Smart*) Adams at a party, 1965.

JACKIE: Hurt Again And Again By Close Friends

SYBIL: To Spite Burt She Marries Young B

PHOTOPLAY

Sean Connery   Robert Vaughn

BEDROOM SPY VS LIVING ROOM SP

The Undercover Facts: Who Is More Of A Ma

Connery vs. Man From U.N.C.L.E. Robert Vaughn in *Photoplay*'s virility contest, 1965.

A very rare shot of Sean and U.N.C.L.E.'s David McCallum at the 1966 Emmy Awards. Mai Britt is the lucky lady.

to. Connery looked after his family in Scotland and would periodically visit them, as if to remind himself that a real world existed outside the sphere of Agent 007. He publicly acknowledged that he was "eternally grateful" for the wealth the role had brought him, but reiterated, "I don't want to be eternally bound by Bond!" While all of this was going on, Broccoli and Saltzman were having serious disputes of their own. Connery cynically noted, "They are not exactly enamored of each other. Probably because they're both sitting on fifty million dollars and looking across the desk at each other thinking, 'That bugger's got half of what should be all mine!' " In actuality, the disputes were caused by creative, not financial, differences, but the resulting conflicts never affected the quality of product. James Bond kept getting bigger and more popular. *Thunderball* was one of the highest-grossing films of all time.

During this time, Connery and Cilento had survived a brief separation and had reconciled. He continued to plug away at establishing a new on-screen persona, but his role as a wild poet in the offbeat comedy *A Fine Madness* went the same way as *The Hill*—good personal reviews, poor box-office business. By the time Sean reported to Japan for filming of the next 007, *You Only Live Twice,* he had succeeded in once more amending his contract, making this his last Bond movie. It also proved to be the least pleasant to film. The usually quiet and dignified Japanese went into hysterics at the prospect of mingling with Connery. The Japanese paparazzi proved to be every bit as ruthless as their international counterparts, and the fans mobbed Sean wherever he went. He later recalled, "It was completely swamping . . . there were people crowded into hotel lobbies and on the street corners, just waiting to get a look at me. It became a terrible pressure, like living in a goldfish bowl. And I'm really a secretive person. I don't have a press representative. So the papers and magazines don't get fed the sort of things about me that they're supposed to get fed about film actors. If you do that, you have to virtually take on someone who is living with you in order to represent you. . . . I like freedom of movement, which the claustrophobic pressures of being a movie star don't allow. That was part of the reason why I wanted to be finished with Bond. Also, I was becoming very identified with it and it was becoming wearying and boring."

By this point the Bond rage had spawned numerous imitators of varying quality. As "spy mania" swept the world, even Connery's family was not exempt from trying to capitalize on the phenomenon: his younger brother, Neil, was talked into making an ill-fated low-budget exploitation flick titled *Operation*

Sean admires a sculpture honoring his role in *Dr. No.*

Kid Brother, which has since become legendary among lovers of bad movies. The ad campaign stressed that Neil's character was supposed to be the brother of agent-you-know-who, and the producers succeeded in signing Bond veterans Lois Maxwell, Bernard Lee, Anthony Dawson, Daniela Bianchi, and Adolfo Celi—only to waste their talents. Sean angrily denounced the film, stating: "Neil is a plasterer, not an actor. Still, they put him in a film over in Rome—gave him the lead, too! It's a typical example of the way some people do things. It doesn't matter whether the person can act or not. What matters is one happens to be one's brother." Fortunately, Neil never quit his day job and returned to the world of plastering. (Eight years Sean's junior, Neil still lives modestly in Edinburgh. He gave up his plastering career in 1982 after suffering from a fall, but still dabbles in acting. He says, "I've always looked up to Sean. . . . [He] lives out of suitcase, but I'm happy here in Edinburgh. I like having roots and knowing exactly where I am.")

Connery spurned Eon's temptations of more money and fatter deals to continue as 007. He adamantly refused and announced he would spend more time with his family, concentrate on his marriage, and indulge in one of his few passions: golf. Broccoli and Saltzman signed Australian model George La-

19

NEIL CONNERY IS TOO MUCH

"OPERATION KID BROTHER" IS TOO MUCH FOR ONE MOTHER!

TECHNICOLOR · TECHNISCOPE ·

Lobby card for Neil Connery's screen debut in the exploitation film *Operation Kid Brother* (1967). Bernard Lee (left) looks as though he is reacting to the reviews.

zenby for the Bond role in *On Her Majesty's Secret Service,* and Sean went off to Spain to star in producer Euan Lloyd's big-budget western, *Shalako.* Despite his costarring with Brigitte Bardot, the film was another flop. Prestigious epics such as *The Molly Maguires* and *The Red Tent* continued his downward slide at the box office. Connery's detractors ignored the good personal notices he was receiving in these films and speculated that the audience was rejecting the man. In retrospect, however, these were not the most commercial films, and the rejections certainly had nothing to do with Sean's capabilities as an actor. Nevertheless, the strain of failing to find acceptance outside the Eon empire only worsened the tensions at home.

To the surprise of the entertainment industry, Connery was lured back into "Bondage" by Broccoli and Saltzman for the 1971 *Diamonds Are Forever.* The agreement was hardly based on sentimentality on anyone's part, but more out of business necessity. Connery had recently established the Scottish International Education Trust, a charity to help the underprivileged in Scotland. Of course, it did not hurt if

Diamonds helped rejuvenate Connery at the box office. Broccoli and Saltzman had their own troubles with George Lazenby, when the actor "retired" as Bond after his one appearance in the role. *On Her Majesty's Secret Service* is generally regarded as one of the best films of the series, but its grosses were lower than the standard to which Eon had become accustomed. The word went out: get Connery at any price. Sean repeatedly spurned the offers, until United Artists handed him what was then the biggest salary in film history along with a percentage of the gross.

Film fans rejoiced in the return of their reluctant idol in the role he had sought to leave behind. The strategy worked and Sean once again became a "hot property." (Ironically, while he was making *Diamonds,* his latest film, *The Anderson Tapes,* was released to good reviews and box office. If Sean had known this, perhaps he would not have been enticed back into the Bond role.) Less enthused about enduring Sean's worldwide publicity was Diane Cilento. She sued for divorce. Not surprisingly, Connery was loath to comment on this, but he did state philosophically: "One is always reluctant to admit failure. A

Getting a technical view of things on the set of *The Anderson Tapes* in 1971.

On location for *Diamonds Are Forever* in Las Vegas, Sean is reminded that it's impossible to keep a low profile, as evidenced by the marquee.

Back in Bondage, Sean chats with producer Cubby Broccoli on the set of *Diamonds Are Forever* in 1971.

marriage that goes wrong is as bad as anything can be, I suppose. What we had to do was step back and see just what we were doing to each other, to our lives and to our children's lives. Our careers were incompatible, not us. You are offered a part and you want to do it, but suddenly there are a hundred questions to ask: What is she doing? What is he doing? Who will look after the kids? Can they come? Who will take care of the house? Interminable. . . . It's not my way of living at all. So we finally had to come to terms with what we had gotten ourselves into. The children,

fortunately, know the situation and they're great. And it's all coming to some kind of civilized understanding and agreement now."

Sean had been psychologically prepared for the end of his marriage—these things rarely arise as surprises to either party. Shortly before the divorce, he had been playing in a golf tournament in Morocco, when he met thirty-eight-year-old French artist Micheline Roquebrune, who was playing in the competition. Sean ended up winning the men's tournament and Micheline the women's. Micheline later recalled, "In the morning we played golf. Then we were introduced. In the afternoon, we did something else. . . . I think I was madly in love with him from first look." Micheline was not very familiar with Connery's work and was unimpressed by his fame. She recalled being drawn to him because of his eyes. Unsurprisingly, Connery was grateful that this beautiful woman was not interested in his celebrity status, and a relationship ensued.

Depressed over the disintegration of their marriage, Connery and Diane never let the situation get ugly, and neither denounced the other in the tabloids. Connery did not emerge suddenly on the party circuit, dating starlets. Friends said he had always been a family man at heart and was far more prone to lasting relationships than one-night stands. The affair with Micheline intensified. Meantime, Sean had to cope with the devastating loss of his father to cancer. The death came suddenly, and Sean felt a sense of helplessness as even his fame and wealth could do nothing to ease the pain of his suffering father. Connery's family visits had to be limited, as British tax laws prohibited him from working more than ninety days a year in England or Scotland. Perhaps it was because of his inability to return "home" as often as he would have liked that he took the news of his father's illness as a terrible blow. Joe Connery's death had a devastating impact on Sean and caused him to reevaluate many aspects of his life.

Professionally, Connery plunged into an art-house film called *The Offence*, his third for Sidney Lumet. A low-budget movie, it was financed by United Artists as part of his *Diamonds* contract and was a brilliantly enacted but depressing tale. Those few who saw it once again predicated an Oscar nomination for Sean. Sadly, the studio gave the movie a token opening in a few art houses, where it died quickly. As the old adage goes, "It wasn't released, it escaped." Connery waded through the audience-alienating effort *Zardoz* and reached rock bottom with *The Terrorists* in 1974 (it premiered at the bottom of a double bill). He was back in the pre-*Diamonds* doldrums, as the return to 007 granted him only a brief resurgence in popularity.

At least his personal life was on the upswing. Micheline proved to be the perfect match for Connery: beautiful, patient, humorous, and sensitive. In 1975, the couple married and took up residence in Marbella, Spain. (Connery still lives there but also has houses in Monaco and the Bahamas.) His exodus from Great Britain was primarily driven by the punitive laws whereby Sean was in the 98 percent tax bracket. Through marriage, Sean had legally inherited a new family member, Micheline's son, Stefan,

by her first husband. The Connery household now consisted of Micheline, Stefan, and Sean's son, Jason, a teenager with budding acting ambitions. His daughter, Giovanna, had continued to reside with Diane. By all accounts, the marriage has made Sean a more peaceful man, and a little less sensitive about dealing with his private life in public. (Selected journalists are now even allowed into his home!)

Perhaps coincidentally, Sean's career rebounded as well, following "a whole period where I made some dumb choices." The trilogy of *The Wind and the Lion, The Man Who Would Be King,* and *Robin and Marian* brought him international acclaim, and for the first time entire reviews of his films were written without any reference to James Bond. Sean enjoyed making these movies and still feels that they represent some of his best screen work. He became more relaxed and spent as much time playing his beloved game of golf as time would allow. He commented, "Golf should be mandatory in every school. You see, it's the only sport that teaches you that when you cheat, you cheat yourself." He also became increasingly selective about his film roles, although many promising projects fell apart at the seams. There were artistic successes such as *A Bridge Too Far* and *The Great Train Robbery,* as well as such notorious flops as *The Next Man, Cuba,* and the terribly misguided *Meteor.*

With the exception of his cameo appearance in *Time Bandits* in 1981, Connery's career between 1978 and 1982 was in danger of experiencing another decline. He made some good films: *Outland, Five Days One Summer, Wrong Is Right.* However, none clicked at the box office, and the latter two were financial disasters. For any number of reasons, he decided to once more do what many felt would be an impossibility: return as James Bond in independent producer Jack Schwartzman's 1983 film, *Never Say Never Again,* the title of which is a sly wink at Sean's oft-stated vow not to play the role beyond certain points in time. In fact, the movie was a complicated culmination of a legal process that had begun a decade before involving another producer, Kevin McClory, and his consistently thwarted plans to capitalize on his right to remake *Thunderball.* (McClory had won a plagiarism suit against Ian Fleming in 1961.) The press went into high gear speculating whether Sean was too old to pull off the part. Sean didn't think so, but felt that pushing the role beyond this point would be impractical. He stated, "I'm fifty-four, and that's about as old as the character should be. I think Bond should be somewhere around thirty-five—old enough to be as experienced as he's supposed to be and to have done all those things." Reminded that Roger Moore, who was film-

En route for a rare stage appearance with Audrey Hepburn at
the Radio City Music Hall premier of *Robin and Marian* in 1976.

ing the competing 007 epic, *Octopussy,* was slightly more mature than Connery, Sean laughingly said of his friend, "Someone should tell him he's too old, too!"

Never Say Never Again was described by Connery as "a nightmare" to film. He had anticipated that his return to the role would be a happy experience, but the opposite was true. He had fall outs with Schwartzman and ended up bringing the producer to court in an attempt to recoup monies he claimed had been withheld from him. (In 1985, Connery continued his battles with Cubby Broccoli and sued the producer for $225 million for alleged missing monies from the Eon Bond films. Broccoli called his allegations "unfounded" and claimed, "The only thing I have done to Mr. Connery was to place him in the role of 007, which became the most successful film series in the world and made him an extremely wealthy and important film personality.") Despite the legalities and technical problems, *Never* was a smash at the box office, and Connery underwent yet another career renaissance. He took a gamble and became the first major client for aspiring agent Mike Ovitz, who today is the most powerful player in the industry. According to 007 director Terence Young, "the best decision Sean ever made was to return Michael Ovitz's call. . . . Believe me, Michael Ovitz is the most important man in Sean's life."

Lucrative film roles soon resumed, under Ovitz's guidance. *Highlander* and *The Name of the Rose* were domestic flops but sizable hits in the international market. The latter film brought Connery a British Academy Award, as well as a slew of other European honors. His big American comeback occurred in 1987 with the release of *The Untouchables.* The Brian De Palma big-screen version of the classic television series surprised everyone by becoming a huge hit. Sean was singled out for the most ecstatic praise and received several prominent awards from critics' societies as well as a Golden Globe.

In February 1988 he was nominated for an Oscar as Best Supporting Actor. The man who had been so consistently ignored by his peers was finally getting his moment in the sun. Intimates speculated that he would not attend the ceremony, but on the big evening, there was Sean looking debonair as ever escorting Micheline. His competition consisted of Albert Brooks for *Broadcast News,* Morgan Freeman for the little-seen *Street Smart,* Vincent Gardenia for the hit *Moonstruck,* and Denzel Washington for *Cry Freedom.* Many had pegged Connery the favorite, but he was clearly an outsider to Hollywood and had basically thumbed his nose at the establishment over the years. However, he made a spectacular entrance onstage earlier to present an award for special effects. Walking out of a mist, he introduced himself: "The name's Connery: Sean Connery." The thunderous ovation he received eliminated any doubt in most viewers' minds, and later his name was announced as the winner for Best Supporting Actor. Sean seemed stunned at the honor, but confessed that just as the envelope was being opened, he thought to himself, "I think I just might win." He gave a short, gracious speech and returned to his seat following his standing ovation, making only one faux pas—he never kissed Micheline before walking to the podium!

With Oscar firmly in hand, Connery almost immediately graduated from the role of respected actor to

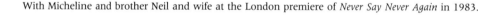

With Micheline and brother Neil and wife at the London premiere of *Never Say Never Again* in 1983.

A still from *Sean Connery's Edinburgh*, a film funded by Sean to promote tourism in his native Scotland.

when I wrote out what I wanted to say, half the people would take the pen and write their answers back! You realize very quickly that the world is full of idiots!"

Connery made a full recovery from this potentially life-threatening illness and immediately went back to work. In between his hits have been a few misses: the underrated *Family Business,* the overrated and interminably boring *Russia House,* a time-killing cameo in *Highlander II: The Quickening,* and *Medicine Man,* his first film as executive producer. The last received largely negative reviews and proved to be one of his most grueling movies, with the sixty-year-old actor required to do most of his own stunts in the oppressive jungles of Mexico. Audiences seemed to appreciate the film, and it was a fair-sized hit—proof of Sean's drawing power at the box office when he is cast in an action-adventure role.

On the home front, Sean remains happily married to Micheline. With the children grown, the Connerys enjoy a somewhat low-key lifestyle and generally shun the party circuit. For them, an enjoyable day is being able to share their passion for golf. Sean's son Jason has successfully followed in his dad's footsteps, portraying Robin Hood in the British TV series of the late eighties and ironically landing the role of James Bond's creator in *The Secret Life of Ian Fleming.* Increasingly comfortable in dealing with the press, Sean

international icon. His services were always in demand, and the few forgettable films he did in the late eighties (*The Presidio, Family Business*) were more than offset by such hits as *Indiana Jones and the Last Crusade* and *The Hunt for Red October.* The film version of *Rosencrantz and Guilderstern Are Dead* was to have included Connery, who agreed to work for $70,000. However, a major health scare caused him to drop out. Through an ironic set of circumstances, he ended up having to pay $300,000 in damages to the producers. He ruefully commented, "I've been in court cases for twenty-five or thirty years, and I've never lost one. I've put lawyers' kids through school. And I wouldn't have lost this one, but life is too short." The scare consisted of the discovery of some polyps in Sean's throat that might have been cancerous. Fortunately, they were not, but the resulting operation caused Sean to refrain from speaking for an entire month—a torturous experience for an actor! He recounted, "I had this pen which I wore around my neck, and every time I wanted to say something, I wrote it down on the backs of old scripts. . . . I printed up cards saying 'I'm sorry, I cannot speak. I have a problem with my throat. Thank you.' And ten out of ten would look at the card and say, 'Why? What's the matter?' And

Despite the press's efforts to play up a rivalry, Sean and his 007 successor, Roger Moore, have maintained a close friendship dating back to the 1960s.

still shies away from personal questions—they always seem to backfire. A recent interview with Barbara Walters reopened some ancient wounds when Sean tried to defend a 1965 comment he had made about situations in which slapping a woman is justified. "A genuine case of lifting it out of context," claimed Sean, who merely meant that depriving one of one's dignity through psychological manipulation can be even worse than physical abuse. Nevertheless, there were the usual "chauvinist pig" comments in the press. Despite this, in 1989 he was named by *People* magazine as "The Sexiest Man Alive"–quite an honor for a man approaching senior citizenship. What did Sean think of the honor? "Well, there aren't many sexy *dead* men!" he quips, but still maintains he was flattered by the honor.

Sean has been politically active and has given some controversial support to the Scottish Nationalist Party, which strives for total independence from England for Connery's native land. His critics fire back that Sean has turned his back on Scotland and should stay out of the nation's politics. This enrages Connery, who growls, "I'm not allowed to have a place in Scotland, otherwise I would have. Once you move out, you can't have a place where you can sleep, otherwise it's a residence. It's absurd . . . and they don't differentiate between your visits for work and your visits for pleasure. . . . They don't encourage you to bring work into this country!" In the late seventies, Sean took Micheline, his children, and his elderly mother on a tour of the old neighborhood in Fountainbridge, immediately before his old house was to fall victim to the wrecking ball. Micheline was aghast at the poverty that still remained, but for Sean and Effie it was a bittersweet occasion that allowed him to realize his good fortune.

Distrustful of most strangers ("Why should he trust them?" wonders friend Michael Caine), Sean now oversees most aspects of his business deals himself. He's convinced that the average movie studio or business associate will be tempted to take advantage of him, if left unchecked. He still doesn't give a damn about public opinion and is not shy about alienating his potential adversaries or future employers. (He claims to have sued every movie studio to date, except Paramount.) The fact that he is growing older also doesn't seem to preoccupy him, and along with Clint Eastwood, he remains one of the few superstars in their "golden years" not to immerse themselves in vain attempts to recapture their youth. Sean explains: "I'm dealing with maturity all right. I'm much more interested in keeping enthusiastic than anything else. In my movie roles, I'm acknowledging and accepting aging. I suppose perennial face-lifts, hairpieces, and

nips and tucks are a way of trying to deny that it's actually happening—the aging that's en route to death. As much as one would like to postpone death, it's inevitable—the only sure thing in life."

Other topics on which Sean has recently espoused his philosophies:

- *On his international appeal:* "I have a very strong *international* foundation. Outside the United States, there isn't an actor who gets better exposure or success ratios in any country than me."

- *On the pitfalls of growing up in poverty:* "As a kid, you're not concerned about life's unfairness or how disadvantaged you are. You just do what you have to do."

- *On James Bond:* "I never disliked Bond, as some have thought. Creating a character like that does take a certain craft. It's simply that when one is a trained actor, it's natural to seek other roles."

- *On his successors in the role:* (On Roger Moore) "There was no element of danger and suspense when they discarded the reality. It became more interested in hardware. And that's when it lost its impetus for me." (On Timothy Dalton) "I think Timothy Dalton in *The Living Daylights* and *Licence to Kill* is very good. He's around the right age and is first class with the action scenes. . . . I'm quite pleased to see the series get better. I think old Ian would have approved!"

- *On his sexiest costar:* "Of them all, I'd have to say the sexiest and most lovely was my costar from *The Man Who Would Be King:* Michael Caine!"

Since this book was initially published in 1993, Connery has kept more active than most men half his age. He starred in the controversial 1993 screen adaptation of Michael Crichton's best-seller *Rising Sun.* The result was not a box-office blockbuster, but the international grosses were solid enough for him to retain his stature as one of the top male stars currently working in the cinema. It was in the summer of 1993 that Connery must have felt a sense of déjà vu regarding a health scare. He was admitted to a London hospital for a period of weeks to battle a mysterious ailment. When it was learned the hospital specialized in cancer treatment, the rumor mill went wild for the second time in four years with renewed speculation that Connery was battling throat cancer.

In fact, Connery *was* having renewed problems with polyps in his throat—the same affliction he was treated for previously. He explained, "What happened was that I had polyps on my vocal cords for about six years. I had them lasered off each time. But then I had a little twinge of a problem while I was doing *Rising Sun*. I couldn't get the timbre of my voice right. I couldn't get the variation and the enunciation as comfortable as I wanted. So I went back to the doctor and he suggested radiation. I went for six weeks and didn't have any side effects or problems. Then I made the announcement that I had done radiation treatment. The publicists said not to do it, that it would set off an explosion. But I thought, If you do radiation and it's a success, why not speak about it?''

Connery soon found out why he shouldn't have spoken about it. The press had a field day with stories about ''poor Sean Connery on his deathbed.'' To complicate matters, he began getting phone calls inquiring about rumors that he had actually passed away. Supposedly, the rumors began the week that race car driver James Hunt and former Texas governor John Connelly died. The overseas wire services apparently mingled and mangled the two names and began to issue bulletins that Sean Connery, who played James Bond, had died. To stop the tidal wave of gossip, Connery took dramatic action and made an appearance on *The David Letterman Show* via jet-pack, à la *Thunderball*! The outrageous stunt was done to prove he was in fine health, and it became one of the more memorable TV moments of the year.

In 1994, Connery returned to work—fit as a fiddle—in the witty comedy *A Good Man in Africa*. The film was an underrated flop, but Connery did gain the lion's share of good notices. In early 1994, he received a Lifetime Achievement Award (the first award of several he would get from various organizations) from the National Board of Review, composed of the nation's leading film critics. In a touching moment, Joseph Wiseman took to the stage to pay tribute to the man with whom he had costarred in *Dr. No* and had not seen since. Then, as the audience applauded wildly, Connery and Wiseman sat back and watched a film clip of their classic first scene together.

Throughout this period, Connery was said to have been considering a number of projects, none of which ever materialized. He was to have played the charismatic spirit of a sea captain in a 20th Century-Fox remake of *The Ghost and Mrs. Muir*. Next, he bowed out of a film called *Smoke and Mirrors*, in which he would have played a charlatan who uses magic to colonize an African country. These projects remain in limbo. He also changed his mind about starring in *Assassins* for director Richard Donner. The film was eventually made with Sylvester Stallone and proved to be a disappointment.

Instead of these projects, Connery filmed two diverse movies, both released in 1995: the legal thriller *Just Cause*, and the megabudget period adventure *First Knight*. Both were worthy films, and the latter can be included among Connery's finest efforts. The grosses, however, were soft. Nevertheless, Connery seems to have no trouble retaining his icon-like status in the world film community. In fact, Connery received one of his most important honors to date in January 1996: the Cecil B. DeMille Lifetime Achievement Award from the Hollywood Foreign Press. Presented at the Golden Globe Awards, Connery looked on as a film retrospective of his career was shown (hiding his head when clips of a young, full-haired Sean was seen in *Another Time, Another Place*). Connery received a standing ovation that dwarfed that of his Oscar night win. He gave a lengthy, heartfelt, and very witty speech, indicating he was clearly moved.

Connery was seemingly everywhere in 1996. The sword-and-sorcery epic *Dragonheart* had Dennis Quaid top-billed. However, critics (who gave mixed reviews to this very underrated film) agreed that the scene-stealer was Sean Connery—who ironically does not even appear on-screen. Connery instead lent his voice for the lovable Draco, last of the noble dragons. The superb special effects team created a marvelous living, breathing mythical creature whose physical characteristics were based on Connery's own facial expressions. Sean's passionate intonation of the weary dragon's obsession with dying with dignity made this one of the most affecting performances of his career. Although Connery is never seen, such is his presence as a performer that he controls the entire narrative. The film was unwisely released in the early summer, when the box office was being dominated by *Twister* and *Mission: Impossible*, yet *Dragonheart* opened surprisingly strong but faded quickly. Had the film been released against less dramatic competition, it could have been a major hit.

Connery's other 1996 epic—released virtually simultaneously with *Dragonheart*—was *The Rock*, a $70-million thriller for the MTV generation that paired the former 007 with recent Oscar winner Nicholas Cage. There wasn't a tremendous amount of advance publicity for this film, which gave Connery his meatiest role in years—a criminal mastermind who is the only person ever to escape from Alcatraz and who must now break *in* to defeat a group of terrorists. The film opened to huge grosses and became the actor's biggest hit since *Indiana Jones and the Last Crusade*. Ironically, Connery—who defined action films before the core audience for *The Rock* was even born—is now a top box-office attraction with yet another generation.

It should be noted that 1995 marked the return of James Bond to theater screens with Pierce Brosnan's *GoldenEye*. Brosnan wisely refused to compare himself to Connery but did stress that as far as he was concerned Connery was *the* man for the role. (Brosnan had idolized Connery ever since he first saw *Goldfinger* in 1964.) Although Connery had nothing to do with the film, he was inevitably asked about the Bond legacy while the film was in production. Connery suggested that the series had to be totally reinvented to survive in the 1990s. He later said that he felt both Brosnan and the film succeeded admirably. Audiences agreed. The series which Connery played such a dramatic role in popularizing had its most successful entry yet: *GoldenEye* would gross over $350 million worldwide and revitalize the sagging MGM/United Artists empire. Reflecting on his own Bond films, Connery said recently, "I was going upstairs and I heard my own voice coming from one of the rooms. My grandchildren were watching *Goldfinger*. So I sat down with them and watched for a bit. It was interesting. There was a certain elegance, a certain assurance to it that was quite comforting. There was a leisureliness that made you not want to rush to the next scene." Ever the perfectionist, however, he added, "Of course, I also saw things that could have been improved. . . ." Asked if he ever watches his old Bond films, Connery said, "I have the videos and the grandchildren and my sons come and they sit down and they know all the lines. *I* don't remember the lines, but they all know the lines and say them before they come . . . It's kind of funny that it's retained that sort of . . . familiarity."

At an age when most men are looking forward to retirement, Sean Connery is at the peak of his career. Love him or hate him, there is no one quite like him working in films today. For those of us who grew up on Connery's films, there is something comforting about his continued success. He was among the top ten box-office attractions in the world back then and continues to remain in that elite group today. As long as Connery seems to transcend the ravages of time, we all feel a lot younger. He has survived the "hero du jour" philosophy in Hollywood to be an international icon. Along the way, he has made more than his share of enemies. Yet, he remains fiercely loyal to those he calls friends. He will not hesitate to sue anyone who he feels has exploited him. What is generally not known is that virtually all proceeds won from such suits are donated to his charity. Connery isn't as much motivated by the money as by the principle. As an actor, he continues to sharpen his skills with a wide diversity of roles. Significantly, even when his movies flop, he is generally the beneficiary of good personal notices. Longtime friend director Sidney Lumet attributes this to Sean's not taking his craft and talents for granted: "He has stayed hungry, and I think he always will."

He has received many international awards, in addition to the Oscar. The one that means the most to him is "The Freedom of Edinburgh," which has previously been awarded to Benjamin Franklin, Queen Victoria, Dwight Eisenhower, and Winston Churchill. When asked what he would like as an epitaph, Connery replied, "I'd just like to be an old man with a good face—like Picasso or Hitchcock." Perhaps the most fitting salute to Sean was offered by Steven Spielberg, who proclaimed, "There are seven genuine movie stars in the world today—and one of them is Sean Connery. . . . He will be remembered throughout recorded film history."

THE FILMS
OF
SEAN
CONNERY

NO ROAD BACK   This Belgian reissue poster deceptively
promoted Sean as the star: a film far removed from the world
of 007.

30

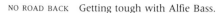
NO ROAD BACK   Getting tough with Alfie Bass.

NO ROAD BACK

1957

Released by RKO Pictures

CAST:

Railton: Skip Homeier; *Hayes:* Paul Carpenter; *Beth:* Patricia Dainton; *Inspector Harris:* Norman Wooland; *Mrs. Railton:* Margaret Rawlings; *Marguerite:* Eleanor Summerfield; *Rudge:* Alfie Bass; *Spike:* Sean Connery.

CREDITS:

Director: Montgomery Tully; *Producer:* Steve Pallos; *Screenplay:* Charles A. Leeds and Montgomery Tully; *Director of Photography:* Lionel Banes; *Editor:* James Cannock; *Music:* John Veale. *Running Time:* 83 minutes.

Although it is rumored that Sean Connery's first appearance on the big screen came as an extra in the 1954 Errol Flynn British musical, *Lilacs in the Spring* (U.S. title: *Let's Make Up*), *No Road Back* was his first opportunity to make an impression on audiences. Connery had won an audition for director Montgomery Tully, who had seen potential in the young actor after seeing some of his television work. This led to his being cast as Spike, a tight-lipped member of an underworld mob in this minor B movie.

NO ROAD BACK   Casing the joint with Paul Carpenter prior to breaking in.

The plot centers on the unexpected return to England of young medical student John Railton (Skip Homeier), who has completed his education in the United States. He is shocked to discover that both his mother (Margaret Rawlings) and fiancée, Beth (Patricia Dainton), have become key participants in an organized crime network that specializes in high-profile robberies. Railton is astonished to discover that proceeds from these crimes have been used to pay for his education. Planning to retire after one final haul from a jewelry store's safe, Mrs. Railton plans the heist with her right-hand man, Clem (Paul Carpenter). The meticulously planned heist goes awry, however, when a night watchman is killed. Railton delays informing the police until Clem can make good his escape. His loyalty is rewarded with the latter's attempt to pin the entire affair on him. Only Ma Railton's confession prevents the injustice from occurring.

The experience of working on a film seemed to appeal to Connery, who found that even as a minor player he got the attentions of the young ladies who lingered about the set. He was not immune to the practical jokes that actors play on each other, however. His costars told him to complain to director Montgomery Tully about his disappointment with his character's obvious speech impediment. Connery gullibly did so, only to realize that his director suffered from a similar handicap.

Filmed in the summer of 1956 at Pinewood Studios outside London, *No Road Back* was completed in six weeks. It's a surprisingly effective "crime meller," and Sean has a decent amount of screen time to make the most of his physical presence, even if his dialogue was rather light. If there's a fly in the ointment, it is the casting of forties and fifties flash in the pan Skip Homeier in the romantic lead. He's strictly a whitebread, "Oh my gosh" hero who appears as though he couldn't survive more than a few minutes beyond the range of his mother's apron, let alone become a success in America. Still, the film remains engrossing throughout and has a fair amount of suspense.

No Road Back did not launch Sean to stardom, but he recognized this as an opportunity to continue fine tuning his talents.

HELL DRIVERS

1957

Released by Rank

CAST:

Tom: Stanley Baker; *Gino:* Herbert Lom; *Lucy:* Peggy Cummins; *Red:* Patrick McGoohan; *Cartley:* William Hartnell; *Ed:* Wilfrid Lawson; *Dusty:* Sidney James; *Jill:* Jill Ireland; *Tinker:* Alfie Bass; *Scottie:* Gordon Jackson; *Jimmy:* David McCallum; *Johnny:* Sean Connery.

CREDITS:

Director: Cy Endfield; *Producer:* S. Benjamin Fisz; *Screenplay:* John Kruse and Cy Endfield; *Director of Photography:*

HELL DRIVERS Stanley Baker (center) finds he can't count on Sean's help in his struggle with Patrick McGoohan (right).

32

Geoffrey Unsworth; *Editor:* John D. Guthridge; *Music:* Hubert Clifford. *Running Time:* 108 minutes.

Based on his significant popularity and exposure in various stage and television productions, Sean Connery secured the services of a young, distinguished agent named Richard Hatton, who was instrumental in helping the actor land big-screen theatrical roles. Still, the work was sporadic at best. Sean later recalled, "I was too big or too square . . . or whatever. I just couldn't fit the parts they wanted me to fill." Director Cy Endfield gave Connery a small role in *Hell Drivers,* a low-budget actioner he was filming at Pinewood Studios outside London. (A few years later Sean would return to Pinewood in style as the James Bond films were to make their "home" there.)

Nearly an entire year went into researching a screenplay that realistically depicted the conflicts between the hard-bitten truck drivers who rush their vehicles between a gravel pit and a construction site. Leading man Stanley Baker ably portrays an ex-convict hired by William Hartnell, a deceitful foreman. Baker soon discovers that his new boss and a corrupt driver (Patrick McGoohan) are padding the payroll, resulting in punishing work schedules for those who must generate enough productivity to keep the head office convinced there are more employees on the job than there actually are. Naturally, Hartnell and McGoohan are pocketing the salaries for the "ghost workers." When Baker threatens to expose the scheme, his friend (Herbert Lom) is brutally killed. This leads to a climactic confrontation in which the villains' truck plunges over a cliff, leading to their fiery deaths.

Filming for *Hell Drivers* began in December 1956 amidst a serious oil shortage caused by the Suez crisis. The filmmakers were barely able to obtain enough fuel to prevent the production from closing down. Connery had a bit role with a few lines of dialogue, but did manage to register an imposing physical presence during a café brawl. It was dismissed as a B movie, with one critic noting that it would only be of interest to someone obsessed with learning the technicalities of the British trucking business. This was rather unfair because *Hell Drivers* was a fine film in almost every aspect. Sadly, it has not been seen in the United States in many years and is unavailable on video as of this writing.

The film did provide an early showcase for a remarkably talented pool of individuals, many of whom would find fame within the next few years. Director Cy Endfield would team with Stanley Baker for the brilliant *Zulu.* Cinematographer Geoffrey Uns-

worth would become a legend in his craft; writer John Kruse would contribute prominently to the smash hit TV series *The Saint;* Herbert Lom would find fame as Peter Sellers's long-suffering boss in the Pink Panther films; Jill Ireland would later wed costar David McCallum and embark on a successful acting career that would see her remarried to Charles Bronson; McCallum would find stardom in *The Man From U.N.C.L.E.;* and Patrick McGoohan would become famous as "Secret Agent" John Drake as well as through his classic television series *The Prisoner.* Thus, *Hell Drivers* provided a unique casting coup: the teaming of three of the screen's immortal "secret agents"—Connery, McCallum, and McGoohan (who would be on the short list of candidates to play James Bond in *Dr. No*).

For Connery, the release of *Hell Drivers* coincided with his signing a long-term contract with 20th Century-Fox. The studio promised to provide a publicity campaign to make Sean a star, but ended up lending him to other studios for largely unimpressive films. The road to Connery's ultimate success would be marked by obstructions and numerous disappointments. With few exceptions, Connery has had little regard for film studios, and his treatment by Fox sowed the early seeds of the discontent he feels to this day.

TIME LOCK

1957

Released by Independent Film Distributors/British Lion

CAST:

Pete Dawson: Robert Beatty; *Lucille:* Betty McDowall; *Steven Walker:* Vincent Winter; *Colin:* Lee Paterson. (Sean Connery is billed as *"2nd Welder"*.)

CREDITS:

Director: Gerald Thomas; *Producer:* Peter Rogers; *Screenplay:* Peter Rogers; *Director of Photography:* Peter Hennessey; *Editor:* John Trumper; *Music:* Stanley Black. *Running Time:* 73 minutes.

Sean Connery's third appearance on film occurred in this dramatic thriller based on a story by British television writer Arthur Halley. It was adapted for the

TIME LOCK Sean (left) races against time to save a boy locked within a bank vault.

screen by Peter Rogers, who, along with director Gerald Thomas, would popularize the *Carry On . . .* series of British satires that remain favorites today in the United Kingdom. The plot relies on the timeworn gimmick of placing a child in jeopardy. Here, the six-year-old son of a banker accidentally locks himself into a vault. It can only be opened via a time lock device that will not be activated for another forty-eight hours. With only ten hours of available oxygen, the youngster appears doomed as the nation is mobilized to free him. Connery has a minor but pivotal role, as a welder who ultimately succeeds in freeing the lad—unconscious and only moments from death.

Time Lock commenced filming in December 1956 at Beaconsfield Studios in Britain. Connery's role could be considered somewhat of a step back for the struggling young actor. In his previous two films he may have had minor roles, but at least he was quite visible in many key scenes. Here, although his character is instrumental in providing the upbeat ending, there was little in the way of dramatic challenge. In fact, throughout a good deal of his limited screen time, a welder's mask hides the face of the future James Bond! The film enjoyed a brief run in Britain, where it quickly faded from the mind of the public. It had a spotty theatrical release in the United States and has appeared on television occasionally. Today, it remains largely unseen—a fate unfortunately shared by several of Sean's earliest films.

ACTION OF THE TIGER

1957

Released by Metro-Goldwyn-Mayer

CAST:

Carson: Van Johnson; *Tracy:* Martine Carol; *Trifon:* Herbert Lom; *Henri:* Gustavo Rojo; *Security Officer:* Tony Dawson; *Mara:* Anna Gerber; *Katina:* Yvonne Warren; *Mike:* Sean Connery.

CREDITS:

Director: Terence Young; *Producer:* Kenneth Harper; *Screenplay:* Robert Carson, based on the novel by James Wellard; *Editor:* Frank Clarke; *Director of Photography:* Desmond Dickinson. *Running Time:* 93 minutes.

Sean Connery's next role was somewhat more substantial than his previous efforts, but far less in magnitude than some subsequent biographies would lead readers to believe. The film was *Action of the Tiger,* a grade B adventure flick toplining Van Johnson as a bargain-basement Bogart mixed up in intrigue within Communist Albania. Although it is commonly stated that Connery displayed enormous star quality here, this is not really the case. Sean's scenes amount to little more than token appearances, aside from a brief attempt at molesting leading lady Martine Carol.

Action of the Tiger was described by director Terence Young as "terrible . . . badly directed, very badly acted," and that harsh assessment seems largely accurate. The film was shot in Spain's Sierra Nevada, as well as the seaports of Málaga and Almuñécar, and the location work was often demanding. Over two hundred technicians were ultimately utilized to bring this rather minor epic to the screen. As was typical in the 1950s, the script largely consists of dated sexual innuendos, combined with Commie-bashing bravado. The pressbook informs us that "Albania today is a country riddled with fear, intrigue, and bestiality!" (Apparently, not even the livestock is safe from those culprits from the Kremlin!)

ACTION OF THE TIGER   Subdued by Van Johnson after a drunken assault on Martine Carol.

ACTION OF THE TIGER   Original pressbook advertisement.

Van Johnson is woefully miscast as a daring adventurer who is reluctantly persuaded by blond bombshell Martine Carol to smuggle her brother out from behind the Iron Curtain. Despite Van's moaning and groaning about the suicidal aspects of the mission, we all know immediately that he is a regular Joe who can't resist a damsel in distress. After numerous close calls, the two stars locate their man, only to discover he is now blind (thus making him the only person with an excuse for not recognizing this as a turkey after reading the script). Before you can say "Moses," Johnson is leading Carol and her sibling through the wilds of Albania to the Greek border, accompanied by a troop of children who their parents fear will be abused by the Commies. The real child abuse takes place when the kids are forced to endure Johnson making embarrassingly bad attempts to convey a tough-guy image. There's enough corn and ham on display to supply an Iowa barbecue.

For all its detriments, however, *Action of the Tiger* does display some impressive production values, including beautiful cinematography and color. While Johnson is a disaster, Carol does manage to display enough cleavage to keep the audience awake. Herbert Lom pops up late in the film with an amusing portrayal of a resistance fighter. He gets beaten up by Johnson, insulted by Carol, and finally mortally wounded by a hand grenade—all of which undoubtedly proved to be useful training for the abuse he

35

would take over the years from Peter Sellers in the Pink Panther films.

Connery appears briefly at the beginning of the film as Mike, the first mate of the boat on which Johnson lives. His scenes are limited to a few drunken brawls, but he is allowed to rescue everyone in the rather limp climax. Despite his limited screen time, those around him saw potential. Martine Carol said with some prophecy, "This boy should be playing the lead instead of Van Johnson. This man has star quality." Of greater significance is the fact that Terence Young agreed with her assessment, recalling later, "He was a rough diamond. But already he had a rough animal force. Like a younger Burt Lancaster or Kirk Douglas." When Connery asked him if he would ever be a star, Young replied with characteristic candor, "Not after this picture, you're not. But can you swim? If you can, you'd better get a job swimming until I can get you a proper job, and I'll make up for what I did to you this time." Five years later, Young kept true to his word by directing Connery in *Dr. No.* (Incidentally, 007 trivia buffs will recognize Anthony Dawson in *Action of the Tiger*, wherein he is billed as Tony Dawson. He would later appear opposite Connery as the evil Professor Dent in *Dr. No.*)

Action of the Tiger proved to be second-feature material and did not elicit much interest from either critics or audiences. Connery later dismissed the flick as "pretty rotten," but did state his admiration for director Young. Although James Bond was still five years away, Sean was about to receive the star treatment in a film opposite the legendary Lana Turner.

However, he would quickly discover the meaning of the old warning, "Be careful what you wish for. You just may get it!"

ANOTHER TIME, ANOTHER PLACE

1958

Released by Paramount Pictures

CAST:

Sara Scott: Lana Turner; *Carter Reynolds:* Barry Sullivan; *Kay Trevor:* Glynis Johns; *Mark Trevor:* Sean Connery; *Jake Klein:* Sidney James; *Alan Thompson:* Terence Longdon.

CREDITS:

Director: Lewis Allen; *Producers:* Lewis Allen and Smedley Aston; *Screenplay:* Stanley Mann from the novel by Lenore Coffee; *Director of Photography:* Jack Hildyard; *Editor:* Geoffrey Foot; *Music:* Douglas Gamley. *Running Time:* 95 minutes.

Another Time, Another Place is remembered only as a routine black-and-white B tearjerker that became the centerpiece of an off-screen scandal involving

36

LANA TURNER · BARRY SULLIVAN · GLYNIS JOHNS

Another Time, Another Place

INTRODUCING SEAN CONNERY · JOSEPH KAUFMAN · LEWIS ALLEN · STANLEY MANN · LENORE COFFEE   VISTAVISION
A Lanturn Production · A Paramount Release

As this lobby card indicates, this film gave Sean his first prominent billing.

Lana Turner, murder, sex, the mob, and—reluctantly on his part—Sean Connery. Undoubtedly, the true-life shenanigans that disrupted the filming would have made for a more cinematic showcase for Sean's most prominent film appearance of that time. The relative newcomer to films would have a costarring role opposite legendary "sweater girl" Lana Turner, whose career decline was hastened by MGM's dropping her upon completion of an eighteen-year contract. Paramount used the opportunity to sign Turner at a reduced salary to star in this melodramatic love story set in England during the final days of World War II.

Still possessing enough clout to have casting approval written into her contract, Lana showed significant interest in the actor who would portray the pivotal role of her younger screen lover. On the basis of some tests, Turner insisted that Sean Connery be signed for what was to be his "breakthrough" role. Once again 20th Century-Fox prospered by loaning Sean to a rival studio, while doing virtually nothing in-house to develop the actor in any way. Although Connery would receive fourth billing, it would be highlighted in all print ads with the caption "Introducing Sean Connery" in bold letters. This was misleading the public to a certain degree, as Sean had

ANOTHER TIME, ANOTHER PLACE   Original pressbook advertisement.

37

ANOTHER TIME, ANOTHER PLACE   Covering the blitz with Lana Turner.

ANOTHER TIME, ANOTHER PLACE   As Mark Trevor.

already appeared in several minor films. *Another Time, Another Place,* however, would be his first to receive wide distribution in the United States.

Principal photography began in September 1957 in the quaint village of Palperro in Cornwall, a locale that was to serve as the hometown of Sean's on-screen character. In the film, Connery plays a BBC reporter who has a brief affair with Lana Turner, portraying a correspondent from the United States. Complicating matters is Sean's confession that he is married and his wife and child are awaiting his return. Connery was twenty-seven at the time; Turner was thirty-seven and Glynis Johns, who portrayed Sean's wife, was thirty-three. (Sean and Glynis, however, share no scenes together.) Recalled Connery, "In the film, I was supposed to be married to Glynis, but I was also having an affair with Lana and I died halfway through the picture. It was only when I was asked what it was like to make love to an older woman did I ever become aware of a woman's age."

The plot then thickens as Connery's confession about his marital status sends Turner into emotional turmoil. This is made worse by his character's death in a plane crash. The script takes a Turn(er) for the worse when Lana decides to visit Sean's hometown in the mistaken belief that being close to his home will help ease her emotional pain. Anyone with a brain the size of a dehydrated grape can predict what will happen next: Connery's wife and child innocently take in Lana as a boarder, unaware of her prior relationship with Sean—but not for long. As Glynis begins to suspect that all is not kosher, Lana decides to confess her sins to the widow. In real life this would undoubtedly result in Glynis plunking a flowerpot over Lana's cranium, but in "reel" life this proves to be the therapy everyone needs. Glynis soon winds up with Sean's best buddy (what are friends for?), and Turner becomes engaged to her publisher (Barry Sullivan) and, on the basis of her unusual methods of enhancing marital relations, presumably goes on to be marriage counselor to Elizabeth Taylor and Zsa Zsa Gabor.

Principal photography "wrapped" in January 1958, and Paramount sought to capitalize on subsequent headlines involving the stabbing death of Lana's gangland boyfriend, Johnny Stompanato, by her daughter, Cheryl, in the Hollywood scandal of the year. Sean gained unwanted publicity when he incurred Stompanato's wrath by escorting Lana to various events a few times too often for his taste. (Connery has always been closedmouthed regarding the nature of his relationship with Turner, but has recalled, "Lana is a lovely lady. We went around together during the filming, and sometimes I'd pick her up on my motor scooter, and she'd be all dressed up for the evening, but she'd hop on anyway. A good sport.") Stompanato proved to be somewhat less of a good sport, and Sean responded to his threats by belting him. This caused the actor to keep a low profile while in the States due to rumors of revenge plots being undertaken by some wiseguys who were friendly with Stompanato. The studio not so subtly rushed the film to theaters. It need not have bothered, as *Another Time, Another Place* was universally panned and proved to be a box-office dud—something a disgruntled Connery had known from seeing the final cut in advance. In fairness, Connery does dominate the film, although his appearance is limited to some twenty minutes. The movie starts on a promising note, and the initial affair is presented in a somewhat compelling manner with World War II England an engaging setting. However, the plot nosedives faster than the doomed plane carrying Connery's equally doomed character. Once Sean disappears from the screen, so does most of the film's charisma.

Turner still looks glamorous and is photographed beautifully by cinematographer Jack Hildyard. But she fails to ignite any sparks when they are needed most. Somewhat more successful is the likable performance of Glynis Johns. Connery later voiced his disappointment with the film for which he had such high hopes: "The script was not entirely satisfactory; they were rewriting as they were shooting so they started with the end first, and I was dead at the end . . . so by the time they led up to me, I was only a picture on a piano. The film wasn't very good—it was beautifully lit but dreadfully directed." Critics agreed, with one reviewer noting, "The BBC commentator is played by a newcomer to films called Sean Connery, who will not, I guess, grow old in the industry." Nevertheless, Connery's next big break would come from some very small characters commonly known as leprechauns!

DARBY O'GILL AND THE LITTLE PEOPLE

1959

Released by Buena Vista

CAST:
Darby O'Gill: Albert Sharpe; *Katie:* Janet Munro; *Michael McBride:* Sean Connery; *Pony:* Kieron Moore; *Sheelah:* Estelle Winwood; *King Brian Connors:* Jimmy O'Dea.

DARBY O'GILL AND THE LITTLE PEOPLE   Lobby card for 1969 reissue.

DARBY O'GILL AND THE LITTLE PEOPLE   With Albert Sharpe.

DARBY O'GILL AND THE LITTLE PEOPLE   On the set with Janet Munro.

CREDITS:

Director: Robert Stevenson; *Producer:* Walt Disney; *Screenplay:* Lawrence Edward Watkin, suggested by stories by H. T. Kavanagh; *Director of Photography:* Winton C. Hoch; *Editor:* Stanley Johnson; *Music:* Oliver Wallace. *Running Time:* 89 minutes.

Prior to its general release, *Another Time, Another Place* was screened for a group of Walt Disney executives who were in England for preproduction work on *Darby O'Gill and the Little People.* Disney was searching for capable actors whose salaries would be modest enough to allow the bulk of the budget to be spent on elaborate special effects. Disney's people were astute enough to recognize Sean Connery's screen presence and offered him the romantic lead in *Darby O'Gill.* As with the Lana Turner picture, 20th Century-Fox found it more lucrative to loan out the contracted Connery than use him in its own films.

Securing any kind of work with the powerhouse Disney organization was a dream come true for aspiring thespians in the late 1950s. Arriving in Hollywood, Sean lost no time in soaking up the atmosphere and admiring the abundance of beautiful women. He used some of his hard-earned money to rent a sports car and would "down a few" regularly with the largely Irish cast. His costars later recalled that Connery was even then the consummate professional, however, and no amount of "elbow bending" the night before precluded him from being on the set ready, willing, and able to work. It's a policy he's always practiced, and he does not tolerate unprofessional, egotistic behavior.

Walt Disney had planned to do a project about leprechauns since 1947, when a trip to Ireland inspired him. His original concept was to do a series of cartoons, but plans remained fragmented until he decided to do a live-action feature film. The shooting lasted fifteen weeks with virtually all scenes filmed on studio property. An elaborate re-creation of a small turn-of-the-century Irish village had been meticulously built. The special effects department contributed some convincing matte paintings that were seamlessly blended into the film in a successful attempt to provide the feel of genuine Irish locales. Connery's costars included popular Irish entertainer Albert Sharpe in the title role of the rascally Darby O'Gill. Sharpe had won praise for his leading role in the Broadway production of *Finian's Rainbow,* but had retired until lured back by Disney. The female lead was Janet Munro, whom Walt signed to a long-term contract that never did lead to stardom for this likable performer. The cast also included noted actress Estelle Winwood, who was the wife of Sean's friend and mentor, Robert Henderson.

While there was a genuine feeling of fraternity among the cast, they were somewhat critical of director Robert Stevenson's methods. Some felt Stevenson was more interested in the technicalities than the people in the story. He had predetermined ideas for directing and rarely improvised or wavered from the script and storyboards. He would also insist upon numerous retakes until a scene was exactly right. This caused some tempers to flare, as many actors were impatient about working in the heat for long hours while wearing heavy makeup and costumes. Stevenson, director of Disney's highly successful *Old Yeller,* later muted any criticism of his creativity with his spectacularly profitable *Mary Poppins.*

Walt Disney took a great deal of interest in the production and frequently visited the set. It is doubtful he had been aware of Sean's link to the Lana Turner–Johnny Stompanato scandal when the young actor had been brought to Hollywood. With Disney's obsession with fostering a squeaky-clean image, it might have cost Connery his pivotal role. Undoubtedly, Walt did learn of Sean's troubles after production began, but he said nothing and remained supportive of his grateful leading man. (Tipped off by friends that he might be targeted by some of Stompanato's alleged mob buddies, the usually stubborn Connery agreed that the better part of valor would be to reside in the Hollywood suburbs during filming. Here he could keep a lower profile.)

As for the movie itself, *Darby O'Gill* is one of Disney's least seen or discussed film in recent years. This is somewhat puzzling because this is an enchanting work on every level and stands with the best of Disney's live-action achievements. It also succeeds in delivering special effects that are impressive by today's standards without sacrificing characterizations. The plot is an agreeable confection centering on a lovable teller-of-tall-tales, Darby O'Gill (Albert Sharpe), who plays a continuous game of cat and mouse with his friendly adversary, Brian Connors, king of the leprechauns (Jimmy O'Dea). Seems that if one succeeds in capturing the pint-size monarch, one will get three wishes granted. As in all such cases, Darby—a mere mortal—continually squanders his wishes through the trickery of King Brian. Interwoven with the magical shenanigans is a love story involving Darby's daughter, Katie (Janet Munro), and a local handyman named Michael (Sean Connery). The engaging screenplay jumps all over the place, but consistently holds one's interest through

DARBY O'GILL AND THE LITTLE PEOPLE Receiving a nocturnal visit from leprechaun King Brian (Jimmy O'Dea).

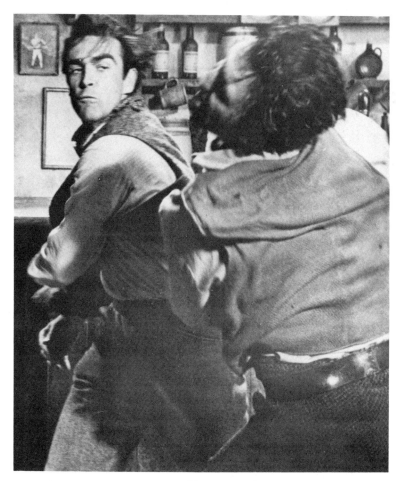

DARBY O'GILL AND THE LITTLE PEOPLE Duking it out with Kieron Moore in the pub.

41

DARBY O'GILL AND THE LITTLE PEOPLE   Sean's rendition of "Pretty Irish Girl" resulted in a 45 RPM record in England.

The real star of *Darby O'Gill,* however, is the special effects team. The sets are wonderfully realistic; the matte work was exceptional for its day, and Winton C. Hoch's photography is superb. (Hardly surprising as Hoch's work on *The Searchers* in 1956 remains one of the finest achievements in cinematography the industry has seen.) A sequence featuring a spectacular dance and horse race within the leprechaun kingdom is outstanding in every way. Impressive special effects work is also apparent in the climax, wherein Darby is terrorized by banshees and other harbingers of doom. The musical interludes are most welcome, as they are logically worked into the story and do not bring the action to an implausible halt.

The film was greeted with lukewarm reviews, but performed well at the box office. It was successfully reissued in 1969 with an ad campaign that—unsurprisingly—played up Sean Connery's presence. (Sean's likeness barely appeared in the original advertisements.) It is occasionally shown on television, is available on video, and is coming to be regarded as a Disney classic. Its box-office clout in 1959 provided the young Sean Connery with his first bona fide hit.

Prior to the film's release, a Hollywood producer and his wife attended a preview at the Disney studio. After watching Connery's performance for a short while, the producer asked his spouse what she thought of the young actor. The wife had the foresight to look through the country-bumpkin role assigned to Sean and said she felt this man had true sex appeal. This ordinarily inconsequential comment was noted with great interest by the producer, who filed it away in his mind. The man's name was Albert R. Broccoli, and the opinion of his wife, Dana, would ultimately lead to Connery's being the central figure in one of the greatest phenomena in motion picture history.

the final frames when the seemingly inevitable tragic ending turns upbeat due to a clever plot twist.

The performances are all admirable, with Sharpe and O'Dea particularly enjoyable. The best sequences have these two marvelous hams trying to outwit each other through inventive mind games and drinking bouts. Munro and Connery are a saccharine-sweet couple, but the soft-spoken Connery does show glimpses of an underlying, if (Disney) repressed, sexuality. He even gets to sing a couple of songs, and the results were good enough for a 45 rpm record ("Pretty Irish Girl") to have been cut for distribution in England. While it's doubtful Sinatra has been losing sleep over any plans Connery might have about pursuing a singing career, the future Agent 007 acquits himself rather well.

TARZAN'S GREATEST ADVENTURE

1959

Released by Paramount Pictures

CAST:

Tarzan: Gordon Scott; *Slade:* Anthony Quayle; *Angie:* Sara

Shane; *Toni:* Scilla Gabel; *O'Bannion:* Sean Connery; *Kruger:* Niall MacGinnis; *Dino:* Al Mulock.

CREDITS:

Director: John Guillermin; *Producers:* Sy Weintraub and Harvey Hayutin; *Screenplay:* Berne Giler and John Guillermin, based on a story by Les Crutchfield; *Director of Photography:* Ted Sciafe; *Editor:* Bert Rule; *Music:* Douglas Gamley. *Running Time:* 90 minutes.

Following prominent roles in *Another Time, Another Place* and *Darby O'Gill and the Little People,* Sean Connery took what some felt was a step backward, accepting a relatively minor role in a low budget Tarzan adventure. While probably unenthused about the vehicle, Connery viewed this as paying his dues in order to gain a foothold in the Hollywood community.

Tarzan's Greatest Adventure was the umpteenth cinematic adventure of Edgar Rice Burroughs's legendary hero. By this time every actor with a biceps larger than Don Knotts's seemed to have tried the role, most without putting a dent in the image created by Johnny Weissmuller. The ape man du jour this go-round was Gordon Scott, who parlayed the role

TARZAN'S GREATEST ADVENTURE   With Anthony Quayle.

into a successful career in several Tarzan "epics." Scott played the King of the Jungle in a one-note manner that did not elicit much excitement, but he at least took the proceedings seriously. Unlike the hokey Weissmuller performance, Scott's underplaying is quite refreshing and lends a genuine air of mystery to the intriguing persona of Tarzan.

The razor-thin plot finds a gang of murderous hoodlums led by Slade (Anthony Quayle) on an expedition to exploit a hidden diamond mine. The group kills some innocent bystanders, prompting Tarzan to swing into action to preserve truth, justice, and the American . . . wait a minute, that's that *other* guy. Along the way, there are the obligatory jungle bimbos. Tarzan's "babe" is Angie (Sara Shane), a buxom blond pilot whose plane crashes in a river exactly where the loin-clothed hero is out for a Sunday paddle. Naturally, she stays safely inside the wreckage of the plane until she is certain the waters are properly infested with man-eating crocodiles— *then* she attempts to swim to shore. This causes Tarzan to strangle the poor croc, who seemed to have far more appreciation for female companionship than the famed Ape Man. (At least the croc tries to nibble her, while Tarzan seems close only to the ever-present Cheetah.) A predictable *African Queen*–type relationship ensues, but of course ol' Tarzan keeps his loincloth firmly in place.

Meanwhile, Slade is having problems with a double-crossing partner named Kruger (well played by

TARZAN'S GREATEST ADVENTURE   As the evil O'Bannion.

43

TARZAN'S GREATEST ADVENTURE Disguised as natives, Sean and Anthony Quayle discuss their plot with Scilla Gabel.

Niall MacGinnis), two feuding henchmen (Sean Connery and Al Mulock), and Kruger's possessive bimbette (Scilla Gabel). Despite being mired in the midst of the jungle, the latter naturally sports the latest in fashionable swimwear, cosmetics, and hairdos. Inevitably, this band of scoundrels tangles with Tarzan when our hero tries to avenge the murders of the innocents.

As Tarzan flicks go, this one is substantially above average, due in no small part to the (relatively) inspired direction of John Guillermin, who later made such topflight action films as *The Bridge at Remagen* and *The Towering Inferno*. Like the best of the Bond films, this episode in the Tarzan canon is most enjoyable because it doesn't seem embarrassed by the scenario and refuses to play for slapstick. The other major attribute is the sterling cast. In addition to Gordon Scott's notable presence, the always excellent Anthony Quayle gives psychological shadings to his villainous character that separate him from most of the boring bad guys found in similar tales. Sara Shane is occasionally amusing as the would-be Jane, and Connery makes his presence felt in the relatively minor role of the evil O'Bannion, a slow-witted and wild-spirited crook who meets an untimely end, courtesy of Tarzan's arrow. The film culminates in a well-directed fight to the death between Tarzan and Slade atop a mammoth rock from which one of the participants falls to his doom.

TARZAN'S GREATEST ADVENTURE Anthony Quayle hunts Tarzan, as Connery lies dying.

This Tarzan film also boasts relatively impressive production values, and the prerequisite stock footage of stampeding animals intercut with Scott walking through the studio back lot is mercifully minimal. Additionally, our man in the fur lined jockstrap only swings on a vine a single time, and forestalls his famous yell until immediately preceding his battle with Slade.

Not surprisingly, *Tarzan's Greatest Adventure* was not dissected at length by critics, although a few perceptive souls did acknowledge its attempt to appeal to mature audiences. The British *Monthly Film Bulletin* noted "the production values are above average and the villains are suitably larger than life; Jane is nonexistent, the natives and the chimpanzee comedy element are restricted to one short scene, and a literate and grammatical Tarzan gives vent to his famous war cry only at the finish." *Variety* was also relatively kind, calling the film "a furious affair, with an exciting chase or two. . . . Scott puts little emotion into his greatest adventure, but he swings neatly from tree to tree, takes good care of a crocodile even if it does appear dead from the start . . . and more than anything else looks the part. Quayle is excellent, MacGinnis is equally fine. Sean Connery and Al Mulock, the two other male members of the expedition, are okay." Although this was hardly the type of notice to bring Connery's abilities to the attention of cinemagoers, one can see that even in this minor role, the actor tended to dominate each of his scenes. His talents were reminiscent of the proverbial bull in the china shop—bursting to break out of the confines of mediocre films into a meaningful project.

THE FRIGHTENED CITY

1961

Released by Anglo Amalgamated Films (Allied Artists in U.S.)

CAST:

Waldo Zhernikov: Herbert Lom; *Inspector Sayers:* John Gregson; *Paddy Damion:* Sean Connery; *Harry:* Alfred Marks; *Anya:* Yvonne Romain; *Sadie:* Olive McFarland.

CREDITS:

Director: John Lemont; *Producers:* John Lemont and Leigh Vance; *Screenplay:* Leigh Vance from an original story by Vance and Lemont; *Director of Photography:* Desmond Dickinson; *Editor:* Bernard Gribble; *Music:* Norrie Paramor. *Running Time:* 97 minutes.

Sean Connery's irritation with 20th Century-Fox's handling of his career was increasing with each day. Despite promises to the contrary, the big star-making project the studio had originally promised him had yet to materialize. Each time a prestigious production

began to roll, Sean was left at the starting gate while other actors were signed. Fox continued to lend his talents to other studios in return for fees, but none of these films catapulted him to a "name" in the industry. Rumors began to circulate that Fox was mulling dropping Sean's contract. However, an independent British film company was suitably impressed with his talent and inquired about Sean's availability for a leading role in *The Frightened City,* a gritty black-and-white exposé of the London underworld. Connery liked the script and the "able cast" and agreed to do the movie.

Sean had a key role as a rugged hood who also has an eye for the ladies—a sort of James Bond from the other side of the tracks. *The Frightened City* marked Connery's reemergence to the big screen following a year's layoff during which he continued to polish his skills through television and stage appearances. (He had been approached about a supporting role in *El Cid* but chose to pass on it to star opposite future wife Diane Cilento in a play at Oxford.) Production on the film began in December 1960 at Shepperton Studios and concluded eight weeks later. To inject a sense of authenticity, producer-writer Leigh Vance frequented some of London's seedier nightspots wherein criminals abounded. The theme of the script was to show the frustration of modern lawmen in combating crime while being restricted by nineteenth-century legislation.

In the story, the inhabitants of a major city are increasingly victimized by brutal extortionists, who are running rampant. The clashes between the hoods and the cops are less severe than the intergang warfare depicted. Six main gangs exist in the city, with the protection racket split between them. It occurs to mastermind Herbert Lom that the gangs should form an alliance, thus making their combined power virtually unstoppable. The scheme works until a gangland chief opposes one of Lom's directives, resulting in the murder of the former at the hands of thug Alfred Marks. This infuriates gang member Sean Connery, who was the victim's best friend. Sean sets out for revenge, engaging in fistfights and sexual hanky-panky—all in the line of duty, of course. (The traits are similar to those Sean would later exude as a certain British secret agent.) Ultimately, Connery kills Marks and through a plea bargain with the authorities succeeds in bringing down the entire crime syndicate in an ending that ties up the loose ends perhaps a bit too neatly.

The Frightened City was not a particular hit with critics or audiences, although it gave Sean much needed exposure and moved his name up to third

THE FRIGHTENED CITY   Original U.S. lobby card depicting Connery eavesdropping on Alfred Marks (center) and Herbert Lom.

THE FRIGHTENED CITY
The climactic struggle
with Alfred Marks.

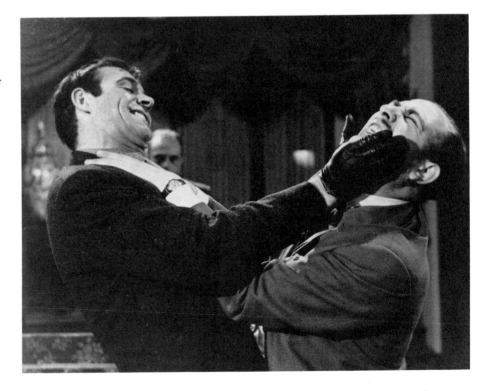

46

THE FRIGHTENED CITY   Tangling with Alfred Marks.

THE FRIGHTENED CITY   Getting the drop on Herbert Lom.

billing. Astute viewers could sense the underlying talent waiting to be discovered in this intense young actor. The movie's publicist recalled Sean's being enthused about the film: "Sean gave the impression of being pleased with the movie, and he was terribly professional. Our goal was [to release] a better than average thriller, and Sean went along with that fully." *The Frightened City* afforded Connery his most significant role to date, but even better things were awaiting him in the near future, for in his next film, Sean would be the star.

OPERATION SNAFU

U.K. TITLE: *ON THE FIDDLE*

1961

Released by American International

CAST:

Horace: Alfred Lynch; *Pedlar:* Sean Connery; *Bascombe:* Cecil Parker; *Cooksley:* Stanley Holloway; *Buzzer:* Alan King; *Doctor:* Eric Barker; *Trowbridge:* Wilfrid Hyde-White.

CREDITS:

Director: Cyril Frankel; *Producer:* S. Benjamin Fisz; *Screenplay:* Harold Buchman; *Based on the novel* Stop at a Winner *by R. F. Delderfield; *Director of Photography:* Edward Scaife;

Editor: Peter Hunt; *Music:* Malcolm Arnold. *Running Time:* 89 minutes.

Sean Connery followed his prominent role in *The Frightened City* with an undistinguished British comedy titled *Operation Snafu.* Released as *On the Fiddle* in England, the film helped keep Sean's name near the top of the billing, but did little to impress critics. The story casts Connery and Alfred Lynch as the Newman-Redford team of the 1940s. Each man is a reluctant World War II enlistee in the British army. The ultraslick and conniving Lynch has been forced to join the service to avoid a scandal. Connery, cast as a brawny but dim-witted Gypsy, has found a haven in the army from a brood of sex-starved women at home. (Could this really be the future 007?) The men find they complement each other and a friendship ensues based upon one common desire: avoiding the battleground at any cost.

The men initiate all kinds of productive scams, but fall into trouble when Lynch is forced to propose to a local girl he has bedded. Connery helps him out of the dilemma—by arranging for a transfer for both men to the battle zones. Managing to sidestep action, they take over a local bar and make it a financial success by hiring voluptuous barmaids. However, when American sergeant Alan King takes over the operation, he has Lynch and Connery transferred to the front. Predictably, the two become reluctant heroes when confronted with the enemy and return to England to receive decorations from the Allies. The film's sting-in-the-tail ending finds the con men once more in command of their bar when Lynch's "fiancée" unexpectedly shows up—with his newborn in her arms.

OPERATION SNAFU
Reluctant heroes: Sean Connery and Alfred Lynch.

OPERATION SNAFU This 1965 U.S. lobby card tried to promote Connery's image as 007—despite the film having been made before he assumed that role.

OPERATION SNAFU Connery and Lynch get some grim news from Sgt. Alan King.

OPERATION SNAFU   Sean and Alfred Lynch trying their best to stay out of the line of fire.

While undoubtedly tame by today's standards, *Operation Snafu* was considered somewhat risqué at the time. The film was largely ignored by critics and public alike, although it did bring Connery to the attention of agent Dennis Selinger, who would later represent the actor throughout some of the most prosperous years of his career. The movie remained largely unseen in the United States until Sean hit paydirt as James Bond. In 1964, it was released with a deceptive ad campaign that downplayed the fact this was a broad British farce. The oafish-looking Connery of the film was replaced in the print ads with a still from the 007 series, and Connery's name now towered above the title with tag lines that shouted, "From Boudoir to Battlefield . . . It's SEAN CONNERY . . . Mixing Dames and Danger as Only He Can!" Pressbook articles complemented the deceit with one story headlined

SEAN CONNERY FLIRTS AGAIN WITH DANGER AND WOMEN
IN EXCITING "OPERATION SNAFU" ADVENTURE

The ruse met with only modest success at the box office. The film joins several other Connery movies that have all but vanished from sight in the United States. Occasionally shown on television in the sixties and seventies, *Operation Snafu* has not been broadcast in recent years, nor has it yet to appear on video.

Trivia note: Operation Snafu was distinguished by Connery's first association with several individuals with whom he would interact later. The film's editor, Peter Hunt, would mastermind the brilliant editing techniques in the James Bond films and would become a successful director. The movie also allowed Sean to costar with Alfred Lynch, with whom he would later team for *The Hill,* and Alan King, who would costar with him in *The Anderson Tapes.*

THE LONGEST DAY

1962

Released by 20th Century-Fox

50

SALUTING THE 20th ANNIVERSARY OF D-DAY
THE INTERNATIONALLY ACCLAIMED HIT!
FIRST TIME AT POPULAR PRICES!
Continuous Performances! Every Thrilling Scene Exactly As Shown In The Roadshow Version!

DARRYL F. ZANUCK'S **THE LONGEST DAY**
WITH 42 INTERNATIONAL STARS!
Based on the Book by CORNELIUS RYAN
Released by **20**th Century-Fox

THE LONGEST DAY   The poster for *The Longest Day* capitalized on the all-star cast.

CAST:

Vandervoort: John Wayne; *Cota:* Robert Mitchum; *Roosevelt:* Henry Fonda; *Gavin:* Robert Ryan; *Bluemtritt:* Curt Jurgens; *RAF Pilot:* Richard Burton; *Steele:* Red Buttons; *Lovat:* Peter Lawford; *Martini:* Sal Mineo; *Fuller:* Jeffrey Hunter; *Flanagan:* Sean Connery; *Schultz:* Richard Beymer; *U.S. Rangers:* Paul Anka, Robert Wagner.

CREDITS:

Directors: Ken Annakin, Andrew Marton, and Bernhard Wicki and Gerd Oswald. *Producer:* Darryl F. Zanuck. *Screenplay:* Cornelius Ryan, based on his book. *Directors of Photography:* Henri Persin, Walter Wottitz, Pierre Levent, and Jean Bourgoin; *Editors:* Marie-Louise Barberot and Samuel E. Beetley; *Music:* Maurice Jarre. *Running Time:* 180 minutes.

   Still technically under contract to 20th Century-Fox, Sean Connery was becoming increasingly incensed at the studio's unwillingness to find a suitable "star" vehicle for him. Promising projects for which he was loaned to other studios had been disappointments at the box office, save for *Darby O'Gill.* Prior to his contract's expiring with Fox, the studio decided to have Sean appear in the much ballyhooed production

THE LONGEST DAY   As Private Flanagan.

51

THE LONGEST DAY
Getting some last minute advice from a fellow combatant.

THE LONGEST DAY   Leading the D-Day assault on Normandy Beach.

of *The Longest Day,* producer Darryl F. Zanuck's epic re-creation of the D-day invasion.

Zanuck, the controversial supermogul, was returning to Fox after a long absence to take over the reins as president. His inaugural project was gigantic in scope and carried a then megabudget of $10 million. (If the studio was nervous about *this* budget, the $40 million cost of the in-development *Cleopatra* would make the Zanuck project expenditure look like pocket change.) Zanuck had a passion to film Cornelius Ryan's classic recounting of that fateful day June 6, 1944, and he spared no expense to insure the technical details were reproduced with precise accuracy. Three international directors helmed this massive undertaking, and Zanuck himself took a hand in directing certain sequences. Primary shooting took place on Normandy and Corsica, with studio work filmed in Paris. A total of thirty-one locations were ultimately used, and at one time, two full-scale units were shooting simultaneously in different regions. The logistics of bringing the story to the screen seemed to match those of the actual invasion, with armies of actors and technicians on the set.

A big spender when it came to the technicalities, Zanuck was also not shy about using his considerable clout to entice major stars to appear in the film for token fees. The idea was to have an army of well-known actors film extended cameos to appear throughout the story line. As this was *the* high-profile film of the new decade, he had little trouble convincing the desired thespians to waive their usually high salaries and sign up, if not in the desire to enhance their careers, then certainly out of patriotism. Ironically, the nation's leading patriot—John Wayne—had no desire to participate in the superstar "cattle call." Zanuck felt Wayne's presence was an absolute necessity and offered the Duke $30,000 for a few days' work. However, Wayne was still harboring a grudge from the prior year when Zanuck had made unkind remarks about Duke's directorial and starring chores on *The Alamo*. Making Zanuck sweat for weeks, Wayne relented after receiving a "slight" raise: $250,000 for four days' work with an option to leave the set if his pregnant wife, Pilar, gave birth during filming. The price was high, but Wayne's contribution to the film—a grand total of twelve minutes—added millions to the box-office coffers.

The Longest Day is an epic in every sense of the word. What could have been a disjointed, uneven mess flows seemlessly through the competence of the directors and editors. The film boasts some of the most impressive battle sequences ever to appear on the screen, but never loses sight of the human elements of the story. It is alternately suspenseful, frightening, humorous, and heartbreaking, and it is impossible to watch the events unfold without being reminded of the futility of war.

The film was nominated for many Oscars and received an abundance of international awards. It was a tremendous hit with audiences as well. Critics praised it as one of the most moving epics ever filmed. The *New York Times* exclaimed, "Stupendous! . . . There are no more worlds to conquer." *Variety* dubbed *The Longest Day* "a solid and stunning war epic. . . . The savage fury and sound of war are ably caught on film. It carries its three-hour length by the sheer tingle of the masses of manpower in action, peppered with little ironic, sad, silly actions that all add up to war. . . . The use of forty-three actual star names in bit and pivotal spots helps keep the aura of fictionalized documentary. . . . The battles take their place among some of the best ever put on the screen."

Connery had a minor role lasting less than a couple of minutes. His Private Flanagan is described in the program notes as "a tough and seasoned veteran soldier whose Irish temperament saw him through the landing at Sword Beach." The description is deceiving, as Sean's minimal screen time allows for little development of any personal characteristics. He has a couple of witticisms, but mostly just ducks the incoming shells. Nevertheless, he could certainly take

pride in sharing star billing with the likes of such genuine superstars as Wayne, Mitchum, and Fonda. As with the actual invasion of Normandy, the ultimate success of the project was not due to a few people, but the combined contributions of many. Besides, little could Connery realize he was soon to have a rendezvous with destiny—courtesy of Her Majesty's Secret Service.

Trivia note: Also featured in the film was Gert Frobe, who two years later would immortalize the title role in *Goldfinger*. In *The Longest Day*, however, Frobe and Connery do not share any scenes together.

DR. NO

1962

Released by United Artists

CAST:

James Bond: Sean Connery; *Honey:* Ursula Andress; *Dr. No:* Joseph Wiseman; *"M":* Bernard Lee; *Felix Leiter:* Jack Lord; *Professor Dent:* Anthony Dawson; *Moneypenny:* Lois Maxwell; *Quarrel:* John Kitzmiller; *Miss Taro:* Zena Marshall; *Sylvia Trench:* Eunice Gayson; *Major Boothroyd:* Peter Burton.

CREDITS:

Director: Terence Young; *Producers:* Albert R. Broccoli and Harry Saltzman; *Screenplay:* Richard Maibaum, Johanna Harwood, and Berkely Mather, based upon the novel by Ian Fleming; *Director of Photography:* Ted Moore; *Editor:* Peter Hunt; *Production Designer:* Ken Adam; *Music:* Monty Norman. *Running Time:* 105 minutes.

Despite having enjoyed a lucrative film career that is now spanning its fifth decade; having been cast in a wide diversity of roles from Robin Hood to the dad of Indiana Jones; having received universal praise for many unforgettable performances; and having been awarded the Oscar—it is *still* impossible to read even cursory coverage of Sean Connery's career without reference to him as the "ex–James Bond" or "former 007." Such is the colossal impact Sean has made on the minds of international moviegoers in the thirty years since he assumed the mantle of the deadly agent with a license to kill. The image of "Mr. Kiss-Kiss-Bang-Bang" (as Bond was known in Italy) would prove to be both a blessing and a curse for Connery, as

DR. NO   Original Spanish poster.

he enjoyed the fruits of the role while trying (initially with no success) to separate his off-screen persona from that of his cinematic part. Connery has mellowed in recent years regarding Bond and was actually persuaded to return to the role on two occasions. Contrary to belief, he holds a great deal of pride in the series and his performances, although the international fanfare that greeted the Bond films found the once poor Scot initially emotionally incapable of handling the drastic change in his fortunes.

The origins of the Bond films have been told on many occasions, usually with glaring discrepancies. This much is agreed: American producers Albert R. "Cubby" Broccoli and Harry Saltzman formed an uneasy alliance in their determination to bring Ian Fleming's notoriously naughty thrillers to the screen. The producers were initially rebuffed by most studios, but at United Artists, Arthur Krim showed his faith in the project with a deal cemented only by a handshake. The studio wanted a big name such as Cary Grant to portray Bond, but Grant, a close friend of Broccoli's, wouldn't consider becoming involved with a potential series. Ian Fleming suggested either David Niven or—prophetically—Roger Moore, but Broccoli and Saltzman wisely turned their attention to finding an actor who would be likely to sign on for "the long haul" in the unlikely event the low-budget ($1 million) adventure spawned sequels.

Nearly every actor in London seemed to test for the role of 007. *The Daily Express,* which ran comic-strip

DR. NO   Bond's first on-screen meeting with the crusty "M" (Bernard Lee).

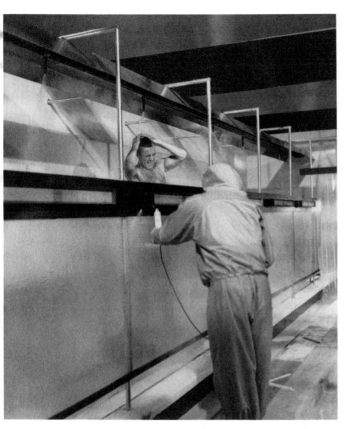

DR. NO Bond is decontaminated after being captured in Dr. No's uranium field.

Soon, Connery's name topped the short list of candidates that included Richard Johnson, future 007 stuntman Bob Simmons (who would double for Connery throughout much of his career), and Patrick McGoohan, who would later find fame as *Secret Agent*'s John Drake. During Sean's initial meeting with the producers, observers were shocked to see him in scruffy attire—a far cry from the ultra sophisticate he desired to portray on-screen. Broccoli remembered, "Sean came into the meeting with us wearing baggy trousers, a brown shirt, no tie, and suede shoes. He pounded the desk and told us what he wanted. What impressed us was that he had balls." Connery even refused to take a screen test—something almost unheard of for a little-known actor. The producers lured Sean into some tests under the guise of doing some experimental camera setups with actresses. As Connery left, Broccoli recalled, "He walked like he was Superman, and I believed we had to go along with him. The difference between him and the other young actors was like the difference between a still photo and film. We knew we had our Bond." Connery later confessed, "I was lucky when

versions of the Bond novels, initially suggested Connery as a candidate on the basis of a recent interview he had given to columnist Patricia Lewis, who was struck by the actor's personality. When the paper ran a readers poll, Sean's name appeared on a majority of the ballots. Simultaneously, at a screening of *Darby O'Gill and the Little People*, Cubby Broccoli's wife commented to him that Connery exuded the raw sexuality required for the role of Bond. This was reinforced when future 007 editor Peter Hunt sent reels from *Operation Snafu* to the producers with the recommendation of Sean for the role.

Sean recently recalled the experience: "Originally, they were considering all sorts of stars to play James Bond. Trevor Howard was one. Rex Harrison was another. The character was to be a shining example of British upper-crust elegance, but they couldn't afford a major name. Luckily, I was available at a price they could afford. The press at the time had a bit of fun with the notion of an ex–coffin polisher playing this silky Ian Fleming character. But Terence Young was quite an elegant man himself, so he took me to his shirtmaker, his tailor, his shoemaker, helped me learn the proper Eton manner. Everyone predicted disaster."

DR. NO. Between takes, Sean's calisthenics seem to impress Ursula Andress.

DR. NO.   Bond prefers a more discreet greeting upon his arrival in Jamaica.

from scratch—not even Fleming knew much about him at this time. I see Bond as a complete sensualist—his senses finely tuned and he's awake to everything. He is the invincible figure every man would like to imitate, every woman is excited by, and everyone's survival symbol."

Any doubt about Connery's suitability for the role was summarily dismissed with his first screen close-up (now a classic) wherein he identifies himself as "Bond. James Bond." He immediately captured the ability to alternately charm as the cultural sophisticate and kill as a cold, professional executioner. Bond was equally at ease juggling a bottle of Dom Pérignon and a Walther PPK. Yet, in *Dr. No*, 007 was not presented as the cinematic Superman he would later become. Bond's struggle with the title villain

Cubby Broccoli and Harry Saltzman approached me about *Dr. No*. It was like asking a boy who was crazy about cars if he'd mind having a Jaguar as a present."

Initial studio reaction about the choice of Connery was unenthused at best. ("See if you can do better," demanded one executive.) Even Ian Fleming expressed disappointment by understating, "He is not exactly what I envisaged." (Fleming later amended the statement with the notation, "But he would be if I wrote the books over again.") The task of grooming the hard-edged Scot into a British sophisticate fell to director Terence Young, with whom Sean had previously filmed *Action of the Tiger*. Curiously, although among the first to spot Sean's star potential on that movie, Young was initially opposed to casting him as 007. Nevertheless, he gamely went about helping Connery get the feel of 007, recalling, "I made him wear the clothes—dinner jackets and everything—for a month before he started shooting." Aside from having read Fleming's *Live and Let Die*, Sean did little research into the role. He later explained, "Bond sort of existed from nowhere and was born at age thirty-two if you read the books. I had to start playing Bond

DR. NO.   As part of a publicity stunt, Sean "breaks the bank" in an Italian casino.

and his army of accomplices mandates that he meets with agonizing torment while relying on his wits and fists to survive. (In future Bond epics, of course, an array of state-of-the-art gadgetry and weaponry would be at his disposal.)

Despite the intensity of the violence in *Dr. No,* the filmmakers realized they needed to distinguish the movie from the standard grade B action genre. The theory was to inject an element of self-spoofing humor in the form of droll, ironic double-entendre throwaway quips. These were designed to relieve the tension of an ultraviolent encounter by sending up audiences and making them laugh after experiencing a shock. With the ingredients of violence and danger expertly blended with wit and humor, *Dr. No* excelled as a glorious live-action comic strip for adults,

DR. NO. Comparing strategy with Felix Leiter (Jack Lord).

endearing James Bond as one of the great fictional figures of the screen.

The film benefited from a magnificent cast that would set the standard for Bond films to follow. Ursula Andress posed Venus-like in nearly every scene and became the dream girl not only of male audience members, but of bikini manufacturers as well. Her emergence from the surf in a then-daring two-piece swimsuit remains among the great screen entrances. The Swiss-born Andress accepted the role of survivalist nature girl Honey Rider primarily because she sought to see the Caribbean. She gave little thought to the film itself, dismissing it as just another bit of fluff. As the title villain, Joseph Wiseman is wonderfully frightful in a classic performance as the megalomaniacal madman who seeks to gain world domination through destruction of the U.S. space program. The cast was rounded out by future *Hawaii Five-O* star Jack Lord as the first—and perhaps best—of the series' Felix Leiters; Bernard Lee as the curmudgeonly "M," Bond's ill-tempered boss; Lois Maxwell as the sexiest old maid in film history, Miss Moneypenny; and a host of other intriguing actors.

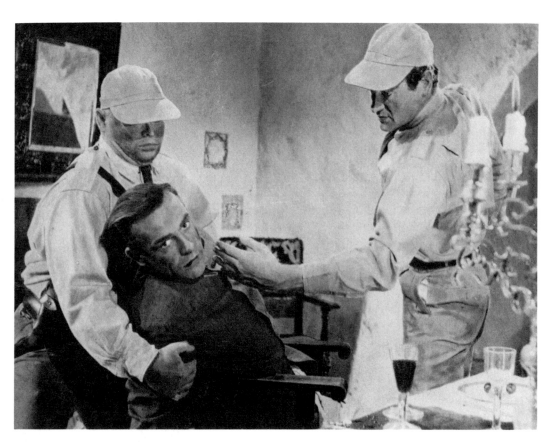

DR. NO. Bond gets a dose of Dr. No's "hospitality."

DR. NO. Catching a few winks between scenes in Jamaica.

While casting preparations were being undertaken in London, locations were being scouted in Jamaica to insure that the film captured the exotic beauty and intrigue of Bond's universe. One location was an estate named Laughing Water, which boasted two natural waterfalls, a beach of white sand, and abundant floral beauty. Other locales included the alleged place where *Bounty*'s Captain Bligh planted bread-fruit brought from Tahiti; Falmouth's eerie quagmire (where Bond battles Dr. No's deadly "dragon tank"); the streets of historic Kingston; the foothills of the Blue Mountains; and the intriguing scenery of Port Royal. Back in London's Pinewood Studios, magnificent sets were designed by Ken Adam, the production genius whose talent made *Dr. No* appear to have a budget ten times its actual cost. His incredible laboratory set contained enough scientific equipment to rival any NASA research center.

Outstanding contributions came from Terence Young's letter-perfect direction; Peter Hunt's ground-breaking achievement in lightning-fast editing techniques; and of course the introduction of the indelible "James Bond Theme." Much credit is also given to Broccoli and Saltzman for guiding this project every step of the way and taking a personal interest in insuring the seeds of the legendary series were sown with this very first 007 adventure. Incredibly, when the film went over budget by $100,000, the studio feared the movie would not be able to recoup its cost. Connery later recalled, "No one dared presume anything. I was an unknown, Cubby Broccoli was not an international name, and we were projecting an English secret agent as a superhero. We were conscious of how tight the budget was. I can remember Cubby in Jamaica digging sand at the edge of the sea so we could get in the last shot before darkness. . . . I'm sure he's not dug much sand since then."

In truth, no one associated with the series has dug much sand since then, foremost of all Sean Connery. The film quickly became an undeniable hit, and Connery and the "Bond team" became major names in the international cinema. These were heady times for all concerned, and enthusiasm for the inevitable sequel prevailed among the star and producers, and relations continued to be cordial. Connery, still trying to absorb his sudden fame, was not yet confident enough of his newfound stardom to worry about typecasting, and even Broccoli and Saltzman put aside creative differences long enough to congratulate themselves on the cinematic coup of the year. The winds of change would soon blow away this goodwill, and well-publicized infighting among the principals would soon dominate the gossip columns. For now, however, the world had found a new movie phenomenon, and a poor Scotsman who as a boy slept in a bureau drawer was about to embark upon a career of wealth and fortune he could only have fantasized about just months before.

FROM RUSSIA WITH LOVE

1964

Released by United Artists

CAST:

James Bond: Sean Connery; *Tatiana:* Daniela Bianchi; *Kerim Bey:* Pedro Armendariz; *Rosa Klebb:* Lotte Lenya; *Red Grant:* Robert Shaw; *"M":* Bernard Lee; *Moneypenny:* Lois Maxwell; *"Q":* Desmond Llewelyn; *Sylvia:* Eunice Gayson; *Morzeny:* Walter Gotell; *Kronsteen:* Vladek Sheybal.

FROM RUSSIA WITH LOVE   Japanese reissue poster.

CREDITS:

Director: Terence Young; *Producers:* Albert R. Broccoli and Harry Saltzman; *Screenplay:* Richard Maibaum and Johanna Harwood, based on the novel by Ian Fleming; *Director of Photography:* Ted Moore; *Editor:* Peter Hunt; *Art Director:* Syd Cain; *Music:* John Barry. *Running Time:* 116 minutes.

With international cash registers still ringing from the receipts of *Dr. No,* production started on the second James Bond adventure, *From Russia With Love,* in April 1963. This was a high-spirited time for those associated with the series—they were enjoying the realization that Broccoli and Saltzman's Eon Productions had the makings of a lucrative series that would enrich all involved. Success, however, was by no means assured. All too often promising film series have quickly fallen flat due to the desire to cash in on a "quickie" sequel. Cubby and Harry did not make that mistake. They used the success of *Dr. No* to

FROM RUSSIA WITH LOVE At the mercy of Red Grant (Robert Shaw).

FROM RUSSIA WITH LOVE The ferocious battle with Robert Shaw aboard the Orient Express—one of the screen's great fight sequences.

secure a $2-million budget for the next film—twice the cost of bringing Bond's introductory epic to the screen. From minute one, the producers displayed an uncanny knack for getting the most out of their dollar, and indeed, to this day Broccoli is a master of getting a dollar's worth of production value out of every penny. The Eon team worked wonders with their budget and managed to shoot extensively in such diverse locations as Istanbul, England, the hills of Scotland, Madrid, and Venice.

No one was more caught up in the excitement of newfound success than Sean Connery. Broccoli and Saltzman had wisely signed him to a multipicture deal, and Sean was every bit the producer's dream at this time. He granted the mandatory interviews, chatted with fans, and signed autographs. He posed happily with Cubby and Harry for the paparazzi and seemed genuinely astonished that he had become the center of international attention. Though it was not to last, for the moment things in the Eon empire could not have been better. Returning was director Terence Young, whose expertise behind the camera on *Dr. No* played no small part in that film's success. Much of the technical talent returned as well, most notably cinematographer Ted Moore, screenwriters Richard Maibaum and Johanna Harwood, editor Peter Hunt, and composer John Barry, who although uncredited for writing the famous James Bond theme for *Dr. No* is widely viewed as being the creative force behind this monumental signature piece. (Production designer Ken Adam was unavailable and was replaced by Syd Cain. Likewise, main title designer Maurice

Binder's protégé Trevor Bond took on the new assignment.) *From Russia With Love* marked the first joint appearance by the "office staff" with Bernard Lee and Lois Maxwell accompanied by Desmond Llewelyn in his debut as "Q"—replacing Peter Burton from the previous film.

During the sixteen-week shoot, the pace was absolutely frenetic and fraught with unforeseen problems. During a scene in which Bond is pursued on foot by a SPECTRE helicopter, the chopper very nearly finished Sean off as neatly as his on-screen enemies sought to. Connery wasn't afraid to do most of his stunts, but this time an inexperienced pilot came frighteningly close to the actor (although it does make for a realistic scene!). While scouting locations, Terence Young's helicopter crashed into the ocean and the director barely escaped with his life. Likewise, the climactic speedboat chase wherein Bond empties gasoline drums into the ocean and ignites them with a flare to destroy a fleet of SPECTRE pursuers proved to be a director's nightmare. The fire atop the gasoline-soaked ocean burst out of control, almost incinerating several stuntmen. Again, however, the on-screen results are terrifically exciting.

In his book *James Bond in the Cinema,* author John Brosnan perceptively notes that *From Russia With Love* is unique among the Bond films. Its tone and story line avoid the bombastic set pieces and special effects of the films that would follow, and for that matter *Dr. No* as well. The plot is quite down-to-earth, with 007 seducing a beautiful KGB agent, Tatiana Romanova (Daniela Bianchi), and having her assist him in steal-

FROM RUSSIA WITH LOVE   A publicity pose with Daniela Bianchi.

FROM RUSSIA WITH LOVE   On the set in Yugoslavia with Bond creator Ian Fleming.

ing a valuable Soviet decoding machine. What he doesn't know is that they are unwitting pawns of the apolitical but evil terrorist organization SPECTRE, which intends to ignite an East-West confrontation while stealing the device for themselves. The story follows Fleming's novel closely and stands apart as one of the most realistic Bond films to date, rivaled perhaps only by *Licence to Kill* (1989). The filmmakers capitalized on President Kennedy's fascination with the Bond mystique and the fact that he had listed *From Russia With Love* among his ten favorite books of all time.

The film is meticulously cast and populated by memorable characters and performances, most of which set the standard for the 007 epics to follow. Bianchi, a former Miss Universe contestant in her film debut, is properly sexy, naive, and bold—a perfect James Bond girl. Even more impressive is the supporting cast, headed by the great Lotte Lenya as the evil Rosa Klebb, a woman with the impolite habit of

61

FROM RUSSIA WITH LOVE Japanese record promo (left) and original Spanish poster.

FROM RUSSIA WITH LOVE Striking a deadly pose on the Orient Express set.

kicking her victims with a poison-coated knife extending from her shoe (there had to be *some* advantage to wearing those Soviet clodhoppers!). As her trained killer, bleach-blond Robert Shaw is nothing less than brilliant as Red Grant, the silent and menacing psychotic muscleman—a performance that ranks among the screen's most menacing portrayals. Pedro Armendariz is equally fine as Bond's larger than life ally, Kerim Bey, in a witty and inspired performance. (Armendariz was terminally ill during the production and barely completed his scenes. Tragically, he took his life shortly after the film wrapped.)

In *From Russia With Love* all the elements jelled perfectly to make this not only one of the best Bonds but also an undisputed classic of the action genre. From the eerie precredits sequence wherein Bond's double is stalked and brutally murdered, the audience is hopelessly hooked. The sex element—tame by today's standards—was shockingly graphic at the time, with hints of lesbianism (Klebb's attraction to Tania), threesomes (Bond's apparent dalliance with two Gypsy women simultaneously), and voyeurism (SPECTRE filming Bond and Tania making love) presented none too discreetly. Above all, the stunning action sequences kept audiences on the edge of their seats. Bond was not yet an institution, and there was an element of genuine suspense that would inevitably suffer in future films as 007's invincibility became more pronounced.

The film's highlights include the aforementioned helicopter chase, Bond's spectacular destruction of the SPECTRE fleet, and an all-out battle in a Gypsy camp. It boasts what is arguably the series' best sequence—the fistfight to the death between Bond and Grant in a compartment aboard the Orient Express. Superbly directed by Terence Young, the resulting brawl is a classic, made all the more tense by his insistence upon shooting it in a dim blue light. Both Connery and Shaw performed most of their own stunts over the three-day period in which the scene was filmed. Peter Hunt's editing is a textbook example of how to cut a sequence and should be shown to aspiring students in that field. (Hunt's lightning-fast editing would influence the style of action-adventure films for years to come.)

From Russia With Love had a lavish premiere in London that was attended by most of the principals, as well as Sean's parents, Joe and Effie, neither of whom could seem to acclimate to the world of fame and glitter that their son had entered—a world so far removed from their own. Critics loved the second 007 outing and praise was profuse throughout the world. Most accepted the film for what it was—a first-rate, tongue-in-cheek spoof of the espionage genre done on a large scale with a dizzying pace. As with *Dr. No*,

FROM RUSSIA WITH LOVE   Original U.S. art still.

FROM RUSSIA WITH LOVE   After killing Grant, 007 subdues the assassin's contact.

63

neither the filmmakers nor Connery made the mistake of overemphasizing the humor, as so many of the later Bonds would do. *From Russia With Love* gets laughs from the audience through a subtle wink of the eye, while films such as *Moonraker* preferred to do it through a pie in the face. The film became a box-office sensation. For the last time, Sean Connery, Cubby Broccoli, and Harry Saltzman would share a "bond"—an ecstatic appreciation of the extraordinary success they had recently found and had worked so hard to obtain. However, the young actor as well as his employers were to find out that the result of international fame and success was not always what it had originally seemed.

WOMAN OF STRAW

1964

Released by United Artists

CAST:

Maria: Gina Lollobrigida; *Anthony Richmond:* Sean Connery; *Charles Richmond:* Ralph Richardson; *Lomer:* Alexander Knox; *Thomas:* Johnny Sekka; *Baines:* Laurence Hardy; *Fenton:* Danny Daniels.

CREDITS:

Director: Basil Dearden; *Producer:* Michael Relph; *Screenplay:* Robert Muller and Stanley Mann, based on the novel by Catherine Arley; *Director of Photography:* Otto Heller; *Editor:* John B. Guthridge; *Production Designer:* Ken Adam; *Music:* Muir Mathieson. *Running Time:* 117 minutes.

Sean Connery had earned his paycheck on *From Russia With Love,* having endured grueling physical demands and an overrun in the filming schedule. He understood the trials and tribulations that had occurred in bringing the second Bond epic to the screen and was the ultimate professional in doing his part to insure the success of the film. He did, however, promise his wife, Diane, that he would take a lengthy holiday before embarking on a new project. This changed when director Basil Dearden offered him the male lead in *Woman of Straw,* a complex cat-and-mouse murder yarn that gave Sean two unique op-

portunities. The first was to play the role of a devious and unscrupulous playboy who, contrary to James Bond, had no redeeming values. The second was the chance to costar with Ralph Richardson, whom Connery had long admired and referred to as his favorite actor.

While Sean may have considered Richardson the ultimate costar, the *real* lead in the film was Italian bombshell Gina Lollobrigida, one of the reigning screen sex symbols of the 1960s. Richardson was assured of sharing "above-title billing," but the advertising campaign and publicity focused almost exclusively on the pairing of Lollobrigida with rising star Connery. Filming began in August 1963 with most of the location work done in Great Britain. A two-week shoot in Majorca allowed Connery to sample the local flavor of the nation he would later call home. To insure that the opulence of the lifestyles of the rich and famous were properly exhibited, the producers convinced wealthy financier Juan March to donate his $5-million estate and $2-million yacht for key sequences. Production designer Ken Adam, who played no small part in the initial success of the Bond films, recreated a gigantic Elizabethan manor, complete with priceless artifacts. The results were appropriately depressing. Said Adam, "I wanted to create a home which could create a simultaneous feeling of great size and great wealth coupled with loneliness and a kind of cold austerity. This was the character of the man we were trying to convey in the background of his home—someone who had spent large sums of money to bring together treasures from various faraway places yet had never succeeded in obtaining the mood of a 'home' as most persons like to think of it."

The atmosphere designer Ken Adam created was appropriate for the somber mood of the entire film. The plot shows Richardson as a cantankerous, stuffy old coot who rolls about the cavernous rooms of his mansion in his wheelchair, insulting and terrorizing the staff—a man who might be the offspring of a tryst between Ironside and Ma Barker. Despite his failing health, Richardson has enough vinegar in his veins to dispose of nurses like Kleenex. In the wings, playboy nephew Sean Connery impatiently awaits his uncle's death, gnawed by the knowledge that Richardson's hatred for him will eliminate him from inheriting the old man's empire, despite his being the only heir.

When nurse du jour Gina Lollobrigida arrives on the scene, her spunk prompts Connery to envision an elaborate plan to enlist her aid in insuring that Richardson's fortune makes its way into his hands. Connery convinces Lollobrigida to entice Richardson to marry her. With his uncle's death imminent, Gina is

IT'S SO EASY TO SET FIRE TO A WOMAN OF STRAW!

GINA LOLLOBRIGIDA
SEAN CONNERY
RALPH RICHARDSON

IN MICHAEL RELPH AND
BASIL DEARDEN'S PRODUCTION

"WOMAN OF STRAW"

FROM THE NOVEL BY CATHERINE ARLEY
ALSO
STARRING ALEXANDER KNOX
SCREENPLAY BY ROBERT MULLER AND STANLEY MANN
PRODUCED BY   DIRECTED BY
MICHAEL RELPH   BASIL DEARDEN
EASTMANCOLOR RELEASED THRU UNITED ARTISTS

T H E A T R E

WOMAN OF STRAW Pressbook advertisement

WOMAN OF STRAW With Gina Lollobrigida and Ralph Richardson.

WOMAN OF STRAW Looking quite Bondian as Anthony Richmond.

to inherit the kingdom and split the proceeds with Connery. Lollobrigida reluctantly sells out her morality and makes the plan a reality—all the while enduring Richardson's humiliating outbursts. Over time, however, she eventually falls for the old man, which is somewhat less plausible than Mother Teresa's hitting it off with Charles Manson. Nevertheless, Connery does not want any genuine emotion to develop and cause Gina to renege on her promise to split the wealth.

Connery poisons Richardson, and through an elaborate scheme, convinces Gina it was a natural death. He lies to her by telling her that for legal reasons the death must be covered up for several days in order for Richardson's will to be legally effective. In doing so, Lollobrigida unknowingly becomes a "woman of straw"—an Italian expression for a naive girl who allows herself to be the pawn of a manipulative schemer. Richardson is dressed and propped up in his wheelchair, and no one is the wiser. The sequence strains credibility somewhat, as it almost becomes a Hitchcockian version of *Weekend at Bernie's*. Gina soon finds herself framed by Connery for the murder, but a suspicious detective (Alexander Knox) pursues the case further. Through his efforts and the brave testimony of a black servant (Johnny Sekka) whom Lollobrigida befriended, Sean is exposed in a twist ending. In an ironic climax, his attempt to flee is thwarted when the servant hurls Richardson's

WOMAN OF STRAW   Lobby card depicting Connery's seduction of Lollobrigida.

WOMAN OF STRAW   The plot thickens as Connery and Lollobrigida try to disguise Richardson's death.

WOMAN OF STRAW
As Anthony Richmond.

WOMAN OF STRAW Sean endures his uncle's sarcastic remarks, while scheming to murder the old man.

wheelchair at him, causing Connery to fall to his death.

Woman of Straw met with tepid reviews from the international press. Typical was the critique from *Variety*, which complained, "The film gets bogged down by the stilted dialogue and the situations, which are high as the Empire State Building. . . . Richardson . . . manages to dominate the screen, even when he's a corpse. Lollobrigida, when not changing her high-class duds, is out of her depth in what must be a serious role if it's to jell, while the well-dressed Connery wanders around with the air of a man who can't wait to get back to being James Bond." Actually, nothing could have been further from the truth as Connery stated prior to filming: "I don't want to be Bond all the time. . . . It riles me when people call me Bond off the set. . . . That's why I'm making pictures like *Woman of Straw*, in the hope audiences will accept me in other parts." (Mind you, this was well *before* Bondmania reached its peak.) Yet, Sean was not much kinder to this film than the critics were. He complained, "I wasn't all that thrilled with *Woman of Straw*, although the problems were my own. I'd been working nonstop since goodness knows how long and [was] trying to suggest rewrites while making another film [*From Russia With Love*]. . . . I won't make that mistake again."

68

The mood on the set was far from amicable, with the press trying to play up reported tensions between Connery and Lollobrigida. When the latter showed a penchant for arriving late on the set, Connery snapped none too discreetly, "The trouble with a lot of stars is that they develop heads as big as their close-ups." On another occasion, when Lollobrigida took to "advising" Basil Dearden as to how a scene should be played, Sean rose to his defense, exclaiming to Gina, "Either he is directing the picture or you are. If it is you, I may not be in it." The paparazzi fed upon these tensions and later exaggerated an incident in which Sean accidentally slapped Lollobrigida too hard, causing the actress's mouth to bleed and sending her home to recuperate. Connery apologized, stating, "You only have to be an inch out in your calculation and I was," but gossip columnists absurdly theorized there might have been subliminal satisfaction on Sean's part.

While the film was generally dismissed as pseudo-Hitchcock, it remains popular with Connery fans, although it rarely shows up on television and is not available on video. Sean is mesmerizing as the cold-hearted yet charismatic murderer, and this remains the only time to date he has portrayed a character who is genuinely evil. In recent years, his popularity has precluded him from playing such roles. He can be irascible, dishonest, and a cad, but audiences would probably not respond to Connery in a downright villainous portrayal. His performance in *Woman of Straw* did indeed allow him to "stretch" as an actor, and he clearly carries most of the weight in the dramatic scenes with Lollobrigida. The latter, however, is suitably sultry when slinking about in her lingerie, and she and Connery do create some genuine sparks. As for Ralph Richardson, it goes without saying that this consummate professional does not disappoint, and his performance is never less than riveting.

Woman of Straw was a modest success at the box office. It has generally been ignored in discussions of the key films of Sean Connery's career. Yet, we submit, it is a gripping and satisfying thriller that keeps the audience in suspense throughout, without the benefit of violence or gratuitous nudity. If it were filmed today, it would probably star Mickey Rourke and some flash-in-the-pan starlet. It would also undoubtedly be unwatchable. *Real* sex symbols such as Connery and Lollobrigida evoke their sensuality from insinuation and never let the emphasis on passion detract from the central story. Nowhere is this more evident than with *Woman of Straw*, a fine film that will

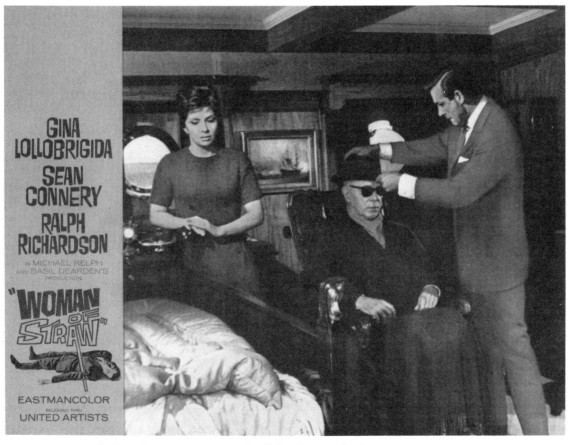

WOMAN OF STRAW   The deceit begins, as Connery and Lollobrigida use Richardson's body as the centerpiece of their plot to inherit his wealth.

hopefully be exposed to greater audiences in the future.

Trivia note: If Connery's white tuxedo in the opening shots of *Goldfinger* looks familiar, it's because it is the same one he wears in *Woman of Straw.* This amusing little anecdote was related by an astute reporter on the *Goldfinger* set who noticed that several of Sean's outfits bore the initials "A.R." His character's name in *Woman of Straw* was Anthony Richmond.

MARNIE

1964

Released by Universal Pictures

CAST:

Marnie Edgar: "Tippi" Hedren; *Mark Rutland:* Sean Connery; *Lil Mainwaring:* Diane Baker; *Sidney Strutt:* Martin Gabel; *Bernice Edgar:* Louise Latham; *Cousin Bob:* Bob Sweeney; *Mr. Rutland:* Alan Napier; *Sam Ward:* S. John Launer; *Susan:* Mariette Hartley; *Sailor:* Bruce Dern.

CREDITS:

Director: Alfred Hitchcock; *Screenplay:* Jay Presson Allen, based on the novel by Winston Graham; *Director of Photography:* Robert Burks; *Editor:* George Tomasini; *Production Designer:* Robert Boyle; *Pictorial Designer:* Albert Whitlock; *Music:* Bernard Herrmann. *Running Time:* 130 minutes.

Per his contract with Eon Productions, Sean Connery was also obligated to make a series of non–James Bond movies for Broccoli and Saltzman. However, as their star became increasingly irritated by the blurring of his real-life persona with that of 007, the producers relented and agreed that his contract would only extend to the Bond films. This made Sean available for work outside of the Eon realm. One of Connery's ambitions was to extend himself in high-profile films that had nothing to do with the world of espionage. He informed Cubby Broccoli that he very much wanted to make a picture for Alfred Hitchcock. Broccoli didn't know Hitch well, but through a conversation with Universal boss Lew Wasserman, he learned that the master director would consider Sean for the romantic lead in his next film, *Marnie.* For most actors, the opportunity to work with the legendary director would have been a humbling experience. As enthused as Connery was, however, he insisted

MARNIE   Connery tries to unravel the reasons behind Marnie's ("Tippi" Hedren) frigidity.

upon reading the script before committing to the project. This action shocked the industry. How dare a young upstart insist upon reviewing a Hitchcock script when even Cary Grant honored Hitch's aversion to showing his actors the story line up front? Connery's response: "I'm not Cary Grant."

Sean's rationale was that he did not want to portray a character in any way resembling Bond. Upon reading the script, Connery was satisfied and completely enthused about the project. Although he would get second billing to "Tippi" Hedren, Hitchcock's budding leading lady, he could console himself with a $400,000 paycheck. Additionally, Hitch was on a roll. His last three films—*North by Northwest, Psycho,* and *The Birds*—were all enormous hits. Anticipation for this next film was great, and Sean would be center

MARNIE   Hitchcock advising "Tippi"
Hedren, Diane Baker, and Sean on how
to play a key scene.

stage for the expected praise the movie was sure to
draw. Hitchcock was equally happy having the services of the one of the screen's most exciting new
leading men. He commented, "I wanted him for my
picture because the part requires a virile, aggressive
man with a lot of authority." On the set, actor and
director hit it off quite well. The cast and crew were so
enamored of Sean that at the wrap party, they presented him with an expensive watch. Hitch, likewise,
enjoyed Connery's presence so much that he gave
Sean a specially made clock that he said would ensure
he would return to the United States, where *Marnie*
was filmed. Connery did not understand the context
of the statement until he learned that the clock would
only operate properly in the U.S. time zone!

Alas, for all the goodwill and great expectations,
Marnie was a failure with both public and the critics,
who up to now had rarely panned a Hitchcock film.
Hitchcock had purchased the rights to Winston Gra-
ham's best-seller with the notion of making it Grace
Kelly's vehicle to return to films. However, her sub-

MARNIE   Mark and Marnie try to calmly confront a party guest
who knows of Marnie's criminal past.

MARNIE   Rehearsing with script supervisor Lois Thurman.

gious firms, then robbing them blind and disappearing into a new identity. This emotionally distraught person, however, cannot understand her own motives. She occasionally visits her puritanical mother (Louise Latham), who refuses to give Marnie any love or affection, despite her daughter's attempts to shower her with money and gifts. Additionally, under her mother's influence, Marnie has always distanced herself from men and is repelled by their touch. Not a lesbian, she is completely asexual and frigid. Moreover, she panics whenever she's in close contact with the color red and is paralyzed with fear during thunderstorms.

Marnie's secret, frustrated life is interrupted when she is caught stealing from her latest employer, prosperous publisher Mark Rutland (Sean Connery). Instead of prosecuting her, however, he becomes fascinated by her psychosis and forces her to marry him. The marriage is a cold, distanced one and Rutland fails to find the secrets behind Marnie's fears and motivations. Ultimately, however, he takes her to her mother's house where, in a devastating confrontation, he discovers her mother had been a prostitute. During a tryst with a sailor during a thunderstorm, the man became abusive and Marnie, then a little girl, murdered him in defense of her mother. The trauma forced her to forget the entire incident, and it explains

jects in Monaco made it quite clear to their serene highness that they looked with disdain on their royalty working for a living—even in a glamorous Hollywood production. Thus, Grace Kelly backed out, much to Hitchcock's dismay. Yet, the director's well-known fascination for blond "ice queens" led him to a suitable substitute—"Tippi" Hedren," a curvaceous beauty who physically resembled the classic Hitchcock heroines. Hedren had made her starring film debut the prior year in *The Birds* and was promptly signed by Hitch to a seven-year exclusive contract.

Unfortunately, Hitchcock became obsessed with the actress and tried to exert a Svengali-like influence over her. Hitch, who had admittedly been celibate for thirty years despite being married, began to gear the film to reflect his frustrations with Hedren, who refused to be seduced by the Master. The aloofness of the Marnie character was to many a thinly disguised enactment of Hitchcock's love-hate relationship with Hedren. When the director made a blatant sexual overture to Hedren, the actress became enraged. The two did not speak for the duration of the film, and Hitchcock gave his direction through assistants. The two never again worked together.

The plot of *Marnie* concentrates on the mysterious title character, a gorgeous woman who displays an admirable work ethic, becoming employed in presti-

MARNIE   Conducting some personal business beside Hitch's director's chair.

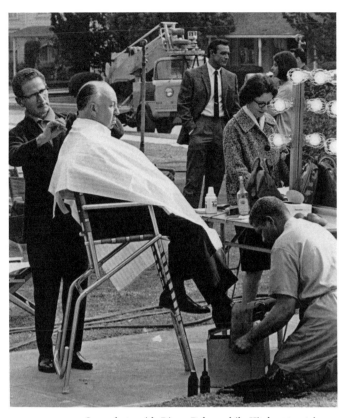

MARNIE   Sean chats with Diane Baker while Hitch gets a trim.

her aversion to storms and the color red (symbolizing the blood she spilled from the sailor).

Marnie is a curious film that, upon first glance, is a distinct disappointment having come from Hitchcock. Slow-moving and talky, it was shot almost entirely on studio sets, which might help to convey Marnie's claustrophobic life, but does little to breathe life into the film. Surrealistic, the movie often seems part nightmare, part fantasy. These elements are often intriguing, but the film goes on far too long, and the shock ending is not enough of a hook to justify the slow pace. *Marnie* suffers from some horrendous production values, as well. For example, the end of the street outside Marnie's home is a rather garish painting of a shipyard that is so blatantly phony, one must assume the device is intentional. Some say it is meant to represent the abundance of falsehoods in the heroine's life, but it ends up being merely laughably distracting.

Likewise, the film's use of amateurish rear-screen projection techniques is among the worst in memory. Even the sets seem phony, with Marnie's red-brick home more closely resembling a set from Mr. Rogers's neighborhood than an actual tenement. And Hitchcock uses some hokey plot devices and camera tricks. Thunderstorms arrive and depart at the most

appropriate times; when Marnie encounters any red object, the screen is bathed in a reddish hue to simulate her revulsion; and as she battles her conscience about seizing a pile of cash, Hitchcock actually resorts to using the zoom lens repeatedly—something excusable for a film school student but inconceivable for the master director. In his book *Hitchcock's Films*, author Robin Wood makes a convincing argument that all of these "shortcomings" are actually intentional and represent innovative filmmaking precisely because they are so patently fake. He concurs with many other of the director's apologists that *Marnie* is "one of Hitchcock's most fully achieved and mature masterpieces." However, Donald Spoto, in his landmark biography of Hitchcock, *The Dark Side of Genius*, dismisses this as nonsense and argues that Hitch was so distraught about Hedren's rebuff that he lost all interest in *Marnie*. In fact, he cites a later interview in which the director admits to the film's shortcomings and maintains he simply did not have the time to fix them properly. He apparently made no attempt to justify the existence of these flaws.

Marnie opened to poor reviews and did mediocre box office. Critics jumped the gun in true Hollywood tradition and immediately began to paint a picture of Hitchcock as washed-up and out of inspiration—despite the magnificent body of work that preceded this film. Universal used *Marnie*'s failure to justify aborting a film with supernatural overtones called *Mary Rose* that Hitchcock had dreamed of making. He later indicated that, despite his affection for Connery, casting him was perhaps a mistake and that the mature presence of Laurence Olivier might have helped the film. Hitchcock was clearly off the mark here, as *Marnie* benefits from an excellent performance by Connery and admirable work from Hedren, who is on-screen in virtually every shot, and who was all but assailed by the international press. Largely because of the cast, *Marnie* remains interesting throughout and undeserving of the critical thrashing it received. It is by no means Hitchcock at his most inspired, but had the film been released two decades earlier, it would likely have been a hit. For *Marnie* is clearly a 1940s film, with phony backdrops, a measured pace, and Bernard Herrmann's lushly romantic score.

Despite the disappointment of starring in one of Hitchcock's rare screen missteps, Connery had nothing but compliments for the Master and even today refuses to speculate on the inner frustrations of the director's mind. He told *Rolling Stone* in 1983, "I know that Hitch was intrigued by that blond Grace Kelly–type of woman, but I find it kind of sad to be looking for something like that against somebody as special as Hitch was. I'm not mad about that sort of Sherlock Holmes bit, you know?" He later added, "It's funny, but the film buffs at UCLA are constantly dissecting *Marnie* these days to see how it was done. When it was first released, there was a lot of criticism of Hitchcock because he used a studio set for the dockside scene. But the backdrop looked just like the port of Bristol—if not Baltimore, where it's supposed to be. I adored and enjoyed Hitchcock tremendously. He never lost his patience or composure on the set. And he never looked through the viewfinder because he had every frame of the movie in his head from that first day of shooting. . . . Hitchcock certainly wasn't an emotional basket case. He always had a most active mind, and he survived to eighty-one—pretty good for a man who never did any exercise, always weighed over two hundred fifty pounds, and had a fair whack at the booze."

Of the principals involved with *Marnie*, Hedren would most suffer. Her career as an above-the-title star would vanish, although she continues to act today and has had the satisfaction of seeing daughter Melanie Griffith become an international star. She has devoted a good deal of her time to preserving wildlife. She recently recalled working with Connery and called him "marvelous" while admitting she would have been romantically intrigued by him had she not been in another relationship. As for Hitch, he continued to suffer the slings of audience and critical indifference with his next films, *Torn Curtain* and *Topaz*. He stunned the industry in 1972 with the vintage Hitchcockian thriller *Frenzy*, which was a bona fide hit. And Sean Connery could chalk up the memorable experience of working with one of the world's greatest directors before embarking on the film that would turn Agent 007 from a hit into an international phenomenon—all courtesy of a rather disagreeable man named Auric Goldfinger.

GOLDFINGER

1964

Released by United Artists

CAST:

James Bond: Sean Connery; *Pussy Galore:* Honor Blackman; *Goldfinger:* Gert Frobe; *Jill Masterson:* Shirley Eaton; *Tilly Masterson:* Tania Mallet; *Oddjob:* Harold Sakata; *"M":* Bernard Lee; *Solo:* Martin Benson; *Moneypenny:* Lois Maxwell; *"Q":* Desmond Llewelyn; *Felix Leiter:* Cec Linder; *Simmons:* Austin Willis.

CREDITS:

Director: Guy Hamilton; *Producers:* Albert R. Broccoli and Harry Saltzman; *Screenplay:* Richard Maibaum and Paul Dehn, based on the novel by Ian Fleming; *Director of Photography:* Ted Moore; *Editor:* Peter Hunt; *Production Designer:* Ken Adam; *Music:* John Barry. *Running Time:* 109 minutes.

A recent study of the cinema indicated that more than 80 percent of the active moviegoing public has viewed *Goldfinger*. In 1964, it is safe to say that the two biggest international cultural phenomena were caused by the Beatles and this third epic in the 007 canon. The former were well on their way to becoming legends via their unstoppable hits on vinyl, coupled with the success of *A Hard Day's Night*. However, the release of *Goldfinger* easily catapulted James Bond into the same league as the Fab Four from Liverpool, making Sean Connery a box-office icon.

Until this point, the Bond films had concentrated on espionage and sex, with a dose of wry humor. Even though the producers would have been justified if they followed the old adage "If it ain't broke, don't fix it," *Goldfinger* introduced two characteristics to the series: an emphasis on high-tech hardware and a less subtle form of humor. Armed with their largest budget to date, Broccoli and Saltzman launched their screen hero into a world of quasi spy thrillers coupled with an element of science fiction. From this point on, Bond would always be on the cutting edge of technology and would employ state-of-the-art gadgetry to help combat his notorious enemies.

Originally, Terence Young was to return to direct, but he saw the possibility of *Goldfinger*'s turning into a box-office phenomenon and pressured the producers for a cut of the profits. They refused and replaced him with Guy Hamilton. One can only speculate what direction the film might have taken with the more measured Young, but Hamilton's vision of James Bond had success written all over it from the first day of shooting. The producers quickly dismissed any notion that the change in directors might harm the series. Hamilton knew well in advance exactly how he wanted scenes shot and left little room for improvisation. He also exerted a good deal of control over the casting and insisted upon hiring Honor Blackman as this film's femme fatale, Pussy Galore. Some pundits thought it was a mistake, as Blackman was

GOLDFINGER   Promotional poster from Finland.

technology. The end result works wonderfully well, and the love/hate relationship between "Q" and Bond continues to this day, despite the introduction of four different 007s! Equally important is the film's emphasis on large-scale production design, with original set designer Ken Adam outdoing himself with his magnificent replica of Fort Knox, where the climactic battle occurs. Denied access to the interior of the actual building for security reasons (not even the president of the United States is permitted inside!), Adam created his vision of what it should look like, while admitting the actual interior is probably quite dull. Stacked from floor to ceiling with glistening bricks of gold, the set is a masterwork of design and fully reinforces the "golden" aura about the entire film.

GOLDFINGER   The quintessential Bond—with martini and weapon in hand.

already mature by "Bond girl" standards. Hamilton, however, was impressed by her role as Cathy Gale, the leather-clad feminist hero of *The Avengers* television series, and felt she would be ideal for the hard-edged role of Miss Galore. The choice proved to be a wise one, as Blackman is definitely one of the most memorable characters in a Bond film. Hamilton may have erred, however, in not allowing Blackman to emphasize the overt lesbianism of her character as evidenced in the novel. Despite a few hints here and there, an opportunity was missed by not exploring this intriguing aspect.

Hamilton is also credited with shaping the key role of "Q," who gets his first big scene in this film when he introduces Bond to his infamous, gadget-laden Aston Martin. Desmond Llewelyn recalls he was going to play the role straight, as he did in *From Russia With Love*. Hamilton, however, instructed him to add an element of impatience and disdain toward Bond for his manhandling of Q branch's masterworks of

As for the character of Bond, some subtle changes were occurring, courtesy of screenwriters Richard Maibaum and Paul Dehn, as well as Sean Connery himself. *Goldfinger* found the actor completely maturing in the role to strike an impeccable balance between the supercool and stylishly sophisticated playboy and the deadly—and occasionally ruthless— agent of Her Majesty's Secret Service. Sean recognized his growth in the role, stating, "*Goldfinger* sort of demonstrates what I believe is a subtler, more discriminating Bond than in the earlier films. It's a process of development. At first it was I who had to model myself on the James Bond that Ian Fleming and the scriptwriters had shaped for me. But now I am making Bond more and more like me, instead of the other way around. I am trying to make Bond grow up a little in the same way that I am growing." Ironically, Connery's remarks seemed to promote the very notion that he was trying to dismiss: the blending of Bond/Connery into one entity.

In actuality, Sean was not in the best of dispositions when it was time to bring *Goldfinger* to the screen. He had boldly boasted that he could "cut the shackles [of Bond] free anytime I want to—they aren't made of steel chains, but of the smoothest silk." This was only partially true. He had certainly gone full steam into *Woman of Straw* and *Marnie*, but neither proved he had much of an audience at this time outside of the Bondian universe. For the first time, he began to realize that there might not be enough room in his career for "serious projects" while simultaneously being identified with 007. Behind the scenes at Eon, Broccoli and Saltzman were increasingly alienated from each other's creative ideas as well. Both strong willed, the producers each had very definite ideas on how to develop the series. When disagreements arose, progress would be halted until a compromise was reached. The partnership had always been tense, as Broccoli had originally wanted to buy Saltzman's option on the series and produce the films alone, and Saltzman had insisted on a partnership.

Once filming began, Connery seemed to get into the spirit of things, and those associated with the movie recall he was always the consummate professional who never let his frustrations compromise his performance. Connery would later lament that his acting abilities were often dismissed because the role fit him like a glove. Nowhere is this more evident than with *Goldfinger*. His performance is superb, but even when the ecstatic reviews came out, few critics acknowledged the inherent skill in his bringing the Bond persona to the screen. Like John Wayne, Sean was such a good actor, he made it all look too easy. Despite his initial appearance of enthusiasm on the

set, Connery's well-known temper flared on a few occasions. He disdained the continuous flow of journalists escorted to the set by studio publicity hacks who mandated he give repetitive interviews. When a female reporter asked who was portraying *Goldfinger*, Connery replied it was the noted German actor Gert Frobe. The lady responded that she had never heard of *her*, prompting Sean to storm off the set. Connery also became embittered by a back injury suffered in the fight sequence with Goldfinger's henchman Oddjob (Harold Sakata).

Goldfinger is one of a few films to approach cinematic perfection. Later 007 epics would divide movie buffs into pro and con camps, but it is safe to say virtually every filmgoer agrees that *Goldfinger* is sterling entertainment. The ambitious plot retained the flavor of Fleming's novel, but wisely updated the story line. Auric Goldfinger is a charming but sinister, megarich power broker with an unquenchable thirst for increasing his massive personal supply of bullion. He develops an audacious plan to obtain a nuclear bomb from the Red Chinese and detonate it within Fort Knox. This would insure the destruction of the U.S. gold supply and increase the value of his own holdings tenfold. Naturally, James Bond is the only

GOLDFINGER Two pop culture icons: Sean Connery and the famous Aston Martin DB5.

Door Panels Hail Bond's Return!

GOLDFINGER Theater door panels promoted Sean's latest Bond blockbuster.

GOLDFINGER The Fort Knox battle with Oddjob (Harold Sakata).

77

GOLDFINGER The ill-tempered gadgets genius "Q" (Desmond Llewelyn) introduces Bond to the Aston Martin DB5—and warns him to return it intact.

man who can stop him. The film trots the globe at a dizzying pace with memorable characters and scenes. Top of the list is Gert Frobe and his performance as the title character. Truly larger than life, Frobe's Auric Goldfinger alternates between being a witty, avuncular man of culture and a megalomaniac with a penchant for imaginative ways of torturing people. One gentleman is crushed to death inside his Cadillac, and in the film's most harrowing scene, Bond is almost split lengthwise by a laser beam. Frobe is more than complemented by Harold Sakata and his infamous portrayal of Oddjob, the mute Korean karate expert with a razor-brimmed derby. The sight of Goldfinger and Oddjob posing as formidable villains might be laughable in less capable hands, but the skill of the actors and filmmakers make them two of the screen's immortal bad guys.

The film also boasts an impressive supporting cast, with Bernard Lee, Lois Maxwell, and Desmond Llewelyn firmly establishing their respective personas as the Bond "stock company." Most enjoyable is the ability of Bernard Lee's "M" to quickly intimidate the otherwise fearless James Bond. Lois Maxwell is suitably sexy as Moneypenny, and Llewelyn works wonders with his brief appearance as "Q." Shirley Eaton has a short but famous stint as Bond's ill-fated lover

GOLDFINGER Rehearsing the film's final scene with Honor Blackman.

GOLDFINGER On the "Miami" set with a bevy of beauties.

Jill, whose betrayal of Goldfinger results in her being suffocated by a head-to-toe coating of gold paint. Eaton's golden-clad image was one of the most publicized of the 1960s and is still used extensively today in articles about the series.

It must be reiterated that the success of a James Bond film is due to the creative input from a community of people. The actors deserve their due and are generally the focal point of international attention. However, Broccoli and Saltzman—despite their differences—deserve praise for overcoming obstacles and ensuring that the series continued to grow in new directions. They never cheated their audience and made each film more elaborate than the last. One must also cite Guy Hamilton for his superb direction—every element of the film works well (save for some shoddy rear-projection techniques in the Miami sequence), and the climax is, in the words of the *New York Times,* "drenched in cliff-hanging suspense." Peter Hunt's deft editing continues to amaze, with the fight scenes in particular cut with astounding technique. There is nary a wasted or dull frame in the entire film. John Barry's score is one of the best of the series, and the title song (as belted out over the credits by Shirley Bassey) is a classic that soared to the top of the pop charts.

GOLDFINGER Posing in "Fort Knox" with Shirley Eaton, Honor Blackman, and Tania Mallet.

GOLDFINGER Grappling with Goldfinger
(Gert Frobe) aboard the hijacked jet in
the film's climactic fight scene.

Goldfinger premiered in September 1964 in London to near unanimous raves. A few critics complained there was too much emphasis on technology, but while this carping would be valid for later Bond films, most saw the technology at the time as an innovative and exciting ingredient. By the time the film opened in New York several months later, a massive and brilliantly constructed ad campaign had preceded it. *Goldfinger* became *the* movie to see, and it played throughout much of 1965, before being successfully reissued with other Bond films. Accompanying *Goldfinger* was the first barrage of 007 merchandise, led by Corgi's immortal toy replica of the Aston Martin. (Incredibly, new versions are still being produced!)

Most of these products were not created until the film proved to be a box-office bonanza. Within weeks, factories throughout the world began spewing forth Bond toys, games, records, and clothes. James Bond was no longer a film series, it was an entire industry. This did not please Sean Connery, who felt he should have not only a greater share of the profits (he was paid £50,000 for *Goldfinger*), but also a stake in the merchandise bearing his likeness. He made it clear he wanted to be a full partner with Broccoli and Saltzman, neither of whom were inclined to agree. Ironically, just as these individuals reached the epitome of success, the threads binding their relationship began to unravel.

Trivia Note: Connery has somewhat mellowed over the years toward the Bond series, and *Goldfinger* in particular. Amazingly, he claims to have seen the film only once—when it premiered. However, in 1990 he confessed that his granddaughter had recently requested that he watch a Bond film with her. Sean chose *Goldfinger* and admitted, "I liked it more this time!"

THE HILL

1965

Released by Metro-Goldwyn-Mayer

CAST:

Joe Roberts: Sean Connery; *RSM Wilson:* Harry Andrews; *Harris:* Ian Bannen; *Stevens:* Alfred Lynch; *King:* Ossie Davis; *Bartlett:* Roy Kinnear; *McGrath:* Jack Watson; *Williams:* Ian Hendry; *Medical Officer:* Sir Michael Redgrave.

CREDITS:

Director: Sidney Lumet; *Producer:* Kenneth Hyman; *Screenplay:* Ray Rigby, based upon his novel; *Director of Photography:* Oswald Morris; *Editor:* Thelma Connell. *Running Time:* 123 minutes.

"Some people think I couldn't make a go of it if there weren't romantic angles in my pictures. But they won't be able to say that about this picture—there isn't a single, solitary romantic moment in it!" This comment by Sean Connery coincided with the worldwide premiere of *Goldfinger*, which caused audiences to line up and cash registers to jingle from London to Beirut. "This picture" referred to Connery's most artistically demanding film to date—an adaptation of Ray Rigby's novel *The Hill*. Based in part on the author's experiences in a British prison camp, the movie would be as far removed from the world of 007 as Connery could hope to be. He would also be playing against type by portraying a rather tragic figure who epitomized the antiheroes who would become so predominant in the 1960s. To further insure distance between Bond and himself, he played the part sans toupee and with a mustache.

Connery had been approached to do *The Hill* previously, but had to decline due to his involvement with other projects. He became available when his plans to costar with Diane Cilento in Terence Young's *The Amorous Adventures of Moll Flanders* fell through. (The film was later made with Richard Johnson and Kim Novak.) Connery had several months to consider other projects before starting the next Bond thriller, *Thunderball*—ironically under Young's direction—in early 1965. *The Hill* was to be a small film in terms of scope and budget, but it would prove to be one of the most physically demanding. Connery was enthused about the project. The failure of his previous

non-Bond films had left him more insecure than ever that audiences only wanted to see him as an agent of Her Majesty's Secret Service. Yet, it was Sean's success as Bond that allowed him to be paid the then astronomical fee of £150,000. Connery admitted later, "It is only because of my reputation as Bond that the backers put up the money for *The Hill*. It's a marvelous movie with lots of good actors in it, but it's the sort of film that might have been considered a noncommercial art-house property if my name were not on it."

Connery relished the fact that the abbreviated shooting schedule left him time to intensify his preparations for his role. The director would be Sidney Lumet, who had made critically acclaimed films such as *12 Angry Men* and *Fail-Safe*. Lumet liked to work quickly and efficiently. He drove himself and his cast and crew hard, but within two weeks, he had forty-five minutes of usable footage "in the can." Shooting took place in Gabo de Gata, Spain, a desert location not far from Almería. Preparing the set proved to be unexpectedly arduous.

THE HILL   Original pressbook advertisement.

THE HILL   Ian Bannen subjects Connery to the torturous climb up the hill.

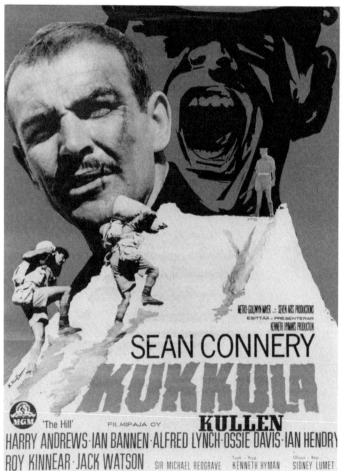

METRO-GOLDWYN-MAYER ... SEVEN ARTS PRODUCTIONS
ESITTÄÄ · PRESENTERAR
KENNETH HYMAN'S PRODUCTION

SEAN CONNERY

KUKKULA
KULLEN

'The Hill'   FILMIPAJA OY

HARRY ANDREWS · IAN BANNEN · ALFRED LYNCH · OSSIE DAVIS · IAN HENDRY
ROY KINNEAR · JACK WATSON   SIR MICHAEL REDGRAVE   Tuott. · Prod. KENNETH HYMAN   Ohjaus · Reg. SIDNEY LUMET

THE HILL   Danish theater poster.

The location was literally in the middle of the desert, and no resources were readily available. Problems arose immediately. Although sand was obviously plentiful, it was not the right texture to mix with cement. Ironically, one hundred tons of sand had to be transported to a desert location! Additionally, two thousand gallons of water were imported to create the mini-oasis that serves as the center of the prison. Although only two palm trees were required for this part of the set, they, too, had to be brought from distant locales. In all, five hundred tons of plaster and 250,000 feet of timber were used to build the residences of the prisoners and guards.

Topping it all off was the logistical nightmare of building "the hill" itself. On-screen, it is this imposing mountain of sand that is used to punish the prisoners, by having them scale it in the blazing sun with full backpacks. The crew felt no more fortunate than the hapless victims seen in the film. Five hundred workers labored for two months, using ten thousand feet of steel and sixty tons of lumber and stone to build the sand-laden monstrosity, which rose thirty-five feet, with a fifty-square-foot base. Additionally, twelve men had to rake and redress the sand daily.

Although temperatures routinely reached 115 degrees, Lumet refused to slow the pace. He shot for ten hours a day, six days a week, wrapping up the filming in only seven weeks. However, this tested the limits of the cast's physical and psychological capacities. Sickness and dehydration were common, and there was a

Sean Connery is the proud and defiant inmate of a British military prison located in a desert outpost

Metro-Goldwyn-Mayer and Seven Arts Productions present **"THE HILL"**

constant fear of sunstroke. The cast had agreed to do all the climbing without the benefit of doubles. Lumet also insisted on filming the climbs in continuous takes. He lamented, "Doing it in several takes would have been charity. The actors knew it would be difficult, but they are all rugged men and were able to fulfill what was expected of them." Lest Lumet sound too much like Captain Bligh, he set the example by scaling the hill himself.

For those involved, the effort expended on *The Hill* was well worth it. The script, written by Ray Rigby himself, spared none of his novel's grittiness and brutality. The plot centers on a British prison stockade in the North African desert during World War II. A desolate, depressing place even by prison standards, the camp is presided over by a weak-willed, ineffectual commandant. The real authority comes from RSM Wilson (Harry Andrews), a by-the-book career army man who views his mission as tearing down the prisoners' willpower, then rebuilding them into model soldiers. For years he has proudly professed a successful track record. However, fate is about to upset his world and every value he has stood for.

Wilson is assigned a new staff sergeant named Harris (Ian Bannen), a sadistic brute whose determination to gain power at the prisoners' expense borders on the psychotic. Harris takes particular delight

THE HILL   As Joe Roberts.

83

THE HILL   Nearing the breaking point.

in torturing a new group of prisoners consisting of Jocko King (Ossie Davis), a cynical black man whose patience with army prejudice is wearing thin; Mc-Grath (Jack Watson), a lifer who merely wants to do his time and return to active duty; Stevens (Alfred Lynch), a sensitive young man whose weakness attracts attacks from prisoners and guards alike; and Bartlett (Roy Kinnear), the archetypal jovial fat man who constantly pleads for mercy from one and all. Harris's most severe treatment is reserved for Joe Roberts (Sean Connery), a sergeant jailed for hitting an officer for ordering his men on a suicidal mission.

For days on end, Harris makes the men climb the hill in relentless heat, hoping to break them. Instead, he only gets rebellion from Connery, who incites the others to resist as well. When Stevens dies from a particularly brutal session on the hill, Harris and Wilson lie to cover up the crime. Nevertheless, a sympathetic staff sergeant (Ian Hendry) comes to Connery's aid after the latter has been severely beaten by Harris and some cronies. In an incredibly tense confrontation, Harris and Wilson attempt to black-mail the medical officer (Michael Redgrave) from validating the facts and requesting a court-martial. To Connery's shock, the medical officer refuses to be bullied and goes for help. Alone with Connery, Harris prepares to show his rage by continuing to beat the lame prisoner. Despite Connery's protests, however, his cellmates come to his aid and brutalize Harris. The film ends with Connery in tears, screaming for the

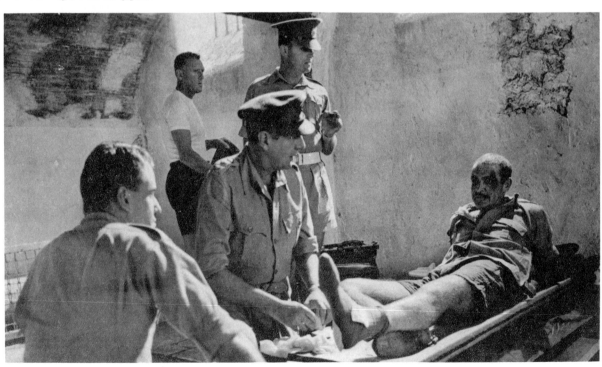

THE HILL   After inspecting Connery's injuries, the doctor (Michael Redgrave) attempts to put an end to Ian Bannen's tyrannical treatment of prisoners.

beating to stop, as he knows that by their pummeling Harris, the prisoner's case is totally undermined. The sight of the pain-wracked, helpless Connery sobbing to himself, "I won! I won!" in a vain attempt to change reality is not easy to forget.

The Hill is arguably the greatest film of Sean Connery's career. It succeeds on every level: the direction and script are first rate, and the acting is uniformly flawless. This is not a Sean Connery–starrer. Rather, it is an ensemble piece in which Connery plays a pivotal role, and he is superb as a man who would rather have died with the rest of his squad than be the lone survivor. It's a gutsy performance, with no vanity or attempts to chew the scenery at the expense of his costars, each of whom has his own moment to shine. Andrews is stunning as the old-line soldier who fails to see his subordinate is rapidly taking informal control of the camp. Ossie Davis provides the only laughs in the film, when he "resigns" from the King's army and parades about in his underwear to protest his treatment. Alfred Lynch (Connery's costar from Operation Snafu), Jack Watson, Roy Kinnear, Ian Hendry, and Michael Redgrave are all letter perfect. The scene-stealer, if there is one among all these glittering performers, is Ian Bannen. His Sergeant Harris is a textbook example of a little man trying to compensate for his insecurities through brutalizing others.

The Hill premiered as the British entry at the Cannes Film Festival, where it shared the award for Best Screenplay with France's Platoon 317. On its general release, Lumet's film garnered the kind of reviews studios can only dream of. Connery received his share of the praise, with Newsweek exclaiming, "[His] work is a revelation!" and Time predicting that "[he] may be the screen's new Clark Gable." Other critics echoed these sentiments. Variety called the movie "a harsh, sadistic, and brutal entertainment, superbly acted and made without any concessions to officialdom. . . . Connery gives an intelligently restrained study, carefully avoiding forced histrionics." Clearly, Sean had succeeded in convincing the critics he had talent beyond the boudoir appeal of James Bond. Sidney Lumet echoed the critical acclaim by stating, "Anyone who thinks Sean can't act is in for one hell of a surprise!"

The surprise, unfortunately, was on Lumet and Connery, as The Hill proved to be a box-office dud in the all-important American market. Connery's name above the title could not make fans warm to this ultra-British tale of depression and brutality. The language was unintelligible to many cinemagoers, and indeed, it takes repeated viewings to understand many key lines. In some prints, subtitles were actually used! Despite predictions of a wealth of Oscar nominations, the film—released early in 1965—had faded from memory by the time the Academy Awards rolled around. Tragically, The Hill failed to garner a single nomination. Ironically, Thunderball—released the same year—would not only be a box-office smash, but also win an Oscar. Connery's patience with Mr. Bond had run out.

To this day, however, Connery remains justifiably proud of this little-seen yet richly rewarding film that has inexplicably failed to appear on video in the U.S. (although it is shown frequently on cable television). Along with The Man Who Would Be King, Robin and Marian, The Name of the Rose, and The Untouchables, Connery feels The Hill is most representative of his finest work as an actor. It would be difficult for any objective critique of his career to differ.

THUNDERBALL

1965

Released by United Artists

CAST:

James Bond: Sean Connery; *Domino:* Claudine Auger; *Largo:* Adolfo Celi; *Fiona Volpe:* Luciana Paluzzi; *Felix Leiter:* Rik Van Nutter; *"M":* Bernard Lee; *Paula:* Martine Beswick; *Count Lippe:* Guy Doleman; *Patricia:* Molly Peters; *"Q":* Desmond Llewelyn; *Miss Moneypenny:* Lois Maxwell; *Foreign Secretary:* Roland Culver.

CREDITS:

Director: Terence Young; *Presented by:* Albert R. Broccoli and Harry Saltzman. *Producer:* Kevin McClory; *Screenplay:* Richard Maibaum and John Hopkins, based on the original story by Kevin McClory, Jack Whittingham, and Ian Fleming; *Director of Photography:* Ted Moore; *Editor:* Peter Hunt; *Production Designer:* Ken Adam; *Music:* John Barry. *Running Time:* 133 minutes.

It was a clearly reluctant Sean Connery who reported to the set of the fourth James Bond adventure, *Thunderball,* in March 1965. Inspired by his work on *The Hill,* Connery was counting the days remaining in "Bondage," enthused about the prospect of finding acceptance in other "serious" films. Despite having

THUNDERBALL   Original Japanese poster

THUNDERBALL   Practicing for the skeet shooting sequence while producer Cubby Broccoli (right) looks on.

cies, prided himself on being a traditional family man. By the time filming had commenced, the Bondian universe was larger in scope than anyone had envisioned, even given the success of *Goldfinger.* Connery himself predicted the series could not possibly last beyond five films, but any such thoughts were immediately dispelled when he encountered the circuslike atmosphere on the set.

By this point, Broccoli and Saltzman had been given a virtual blank check by United Artists, and the producers continued to use the money productively. *Thunderball* would boast the enormous (by 1965 standards) budget of $5.5 million. With Bondmania in full bloom, the press descended on the locations in the Bahamas in hopes of subjecting Sean to the usual round of largely inane interviews. This time, the star had enough clout to avoid as many reporters as possible, although he did give an insightful and controversial interview to *Playboy.* Still, he couldn't prevent the constant crowd of fans straining to see their idol at work. Connery tried to console himself by reconciling with Diane and having her and the children fly to the Bahamas while he was filming. Unfortunately, this was tantamount to placing two very private people on display in a Macy's window. The couple was followed and hounded mercilessly by the press, until Diane headed back to Europe, distraught from the effects of the Bond phenomenon.

Thunderball was a troubled project from day one. Broccoli and Saltzman originally envisioned this to be the first Bond film. However, in 1961, Ian Fleming

become a worldwide sex symbol, Connery in many ways envied his wife, Diane Cilento. The previous year, Mrs. Connery had received an Oscar nomination for 1963's *Tom Jones* and was preparing to shoot a key role in the prestigious production of *The Agony and the Ecstasy.* Friends speculated that this tension contributed to the well-publicized separation the couple agreed to before Sean went on location for *Thunderball.* The domestic problems worried Connery, who, despite his allegedly chauvinistic tenden-

THUNDERBALL   Attending the Paris premiere of *Goldfinger,* where he introduced his leading lady for *Thunderball,* Claudine Auger.

THUNDERBALL Sean and wife Diane Cilento find an unwelcome fan wants to drop in for a bite.

was sued for plagiarism by writer Kevin McClory for having used the discarded treatment of a screenplay the two had worked on years before as the basis of Fleming's *Thunderball* novel. The court sided with McClory and awarded him screen rights, while Fleming retained control of the book. McClory quickly made it known that he was shopping for an actor to portray 007 in his own independent production. (Richard Burton was reportedly interested.) Broccoli and Saltzman did not want a competing version of their series and signed McClory as producer of *Thunderball* when their film came to fruition in 1965. (Legal battles would continue over the years as McClory sought to remake the film.)

Director Terence Young returned, having reconciled his financial differences with Eon. Most of the original talent from the previous 007 films were also on board, but logistically, shooting *Thunderball* would be a Herculean task compared to the previous Bonds, largely because much of this one was shot underwater. The plot has SPECTRE hijacking two NATO nuclear bombs for international blackmail. When the plan goes awry, an evil army of scuba divers launch an underwater assault, intending to detonate the bombs off the coast of Miami. James Bond must race against the clock and seemingly insurmountable odds to stop them, relying on increasing numbers of gadgets from Q branch. While the scenes with Desmond Llewelyn's cantankerous Major Boothroyd are as amusing as ever, even the filmmakers wondered if the accent on technology

THUNDERBALL In action during the pre-credits scene.

THUNDERBALL Flirting with the always attentive Miss Moneypenny (Lois Maxwell).

was overshadowing the character of Bond. Connery remarked, "We have to be careful where we go next because I think with *Thunderball* we've reached the limit as far as size and gimmicks are concerned. . . . What is needed now is a change of course—more attention to character and better dialogue."

As usual, Sean was surrounded on-screen by a bevy of beauties, this time headed by Claudine Auger, a former Miss France, in the leading-lady role of Domino. The scene-stealer, however, is Luciana Paluzzi as a sensual but murderous Fiona Volpe, whose scenes with Connery are among the sexiest in the series. Bond has another good antagonist in the form of Emilio Largo, excellently played by Adolfo Celi in the typical Bondian villain custom: charming, witty, and totally ruthless. The film also featured a first for a Bond film—glimpses of nudity. Maurice Binder's superb main title sequence showed a bit of female breast, which caused censorship problems in Spain. Additionally, Connery as Bond has a fling with sexy Molly Peters in a scene in which her bare derriere is viewed pressed against a steam-room window.

Thunderball has suffered over the years from repeated complaints that its emphasis on technology destroyed the character of Bond for years to come. This is an overstatement, as the movie works superbly as pure entertainment. Granted, one wishes that the characterizations could have been dwelled upon longer, but under no circumstance could the film be

Photo of Sean Connery courtesy of United Artists and *Thunderball*. (The mask is ours.)

The Devil with James Bond!

Ian Fleming said he wrote for fun and money. *The Devil with James Bond!* contends that he made the statement tongue in cheek—and proceeds to reveal that underlying Bond's exploits was a carefully woven plot by Fleming to name and destroy exponents of today's seven deadlier sins, particularly apathy. Hidden among the girls, the guns, the wines, and the cars is Fleming's analysis of the relationship between the demonic and individual responsibility.

Intriguing and fast-paced like the spy thrillers themselves, this new look at Secret Agent 007 is sure to provoke heated discussions. And it went into a second printing—even before publication day.

John Knox Now at your bookstore

THUNDERBALL The release of *Thunderball* inspired this book which examined the controversial nature of the films.

89

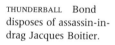
THUNDERBALL A "Social visit" to S.P.E.C.T.R.E. mastermind Largo's (Adolfo Celi) estate.

called dull. In the knockout precredits sequence, Bond battles and kills an assassin in drag, escapes via a jet pack, then utilizes his famed Aston Martin to thwart his pursuers—and all of this occurs before the opening titles! There's also a well-staged scene wherein Bond is stalked by SPECTRE as he darts among hundreds of participants in the Bahamian Junkanoo—a local Mardi Gras. (Terence Young staged this entire event for the film, enlisting scores of local residents as extras.) *Thunderball*'s underwater sequences are lushly filmed by cinematographers Lamar Boren and Ted Moore, though Terence Young has spoken of his dissatisfaction with this emphasis on underwater action. He claims this necessitated a slowdown in the action, particularly the climactic battle beneath the sea. This is somewhat true earlier in the film, when the bombs are kidnapped by SPECTRE, but is an unfair assessment of the final reel. Thanks to Young's inspired direction, Peter Hunt's wonderful editing, and John Barry's thundering score, the sequence is a marvel to behold. Likewise, the final fight aboard the speeding hydrofoil is excellently staged, marred only by the too rapid back-screen projection.

Thunderball opened as United Artists' big Christmas release for 1965. A massive publicity campaign had preceded it for many months, with cover stories in such publications as *Life* and *Esquire*. In November, *The Incredible World of James Bond* aired on NBC,

THUNDERBALL Bond disposes of assassin-in-drag Jacques Boitier.

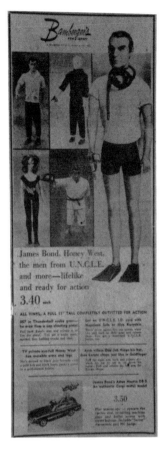

THUNDERBALL *Thunderball* spawned a cottage industry of 007 toys—like this doll displayed here with other popular spy toys of the day. (The doll now retails for $150.)

films and gushing, "The best of the lot. Funny and pretty, too. It is filled with such underwater action as would delight Cousteau. An assortment of girls in the barest of bare bikinis is a measure of the splendor of the film. Connery is at his peak of coolness and nonchalance." Less enthused was the New York *Daily News*, which, though favorable to the film, noted, "Nonacting is the ticket in a Bond thriller. Now that he and Bond are practically synonymous, Sean Connery looks bored. Not that it matters, for the key to his success is his effortless approach." While it is undeniable that Sean may not have appeared as inspired as he did in previous films, this was largely due to the technology-laden script. Many reviews exemplified the unfair criticism Connery was subject to and what led him to loath the media's blending of actor and character. His frustrations were heightened by the lukewarm reception the public had previously given *The Hill*. While the world rejoiced in Bondmania, Connery quickly sought to immerse himself in unrelated projects, complaining of the series, "I am fighting for money and time. . . . And I want to do them in as little time as possible, so I can fit in other things that mean more to me. These Bond pictures can take six months of my time, working every day." Quite to his dismay, however, audience acceptance for his non-Bond films was still years away.

honoring the entire series, but in actuality serving as a plug for the new film. (Connery could not be persuaded to act as host of the program.) Unlike the case with *Goldfinger,* manufacturers had plenty of time to gear up for an avalanche of 007-related merchandise. Indeed, the pressbook for *Thunderball* was an oversize, unwieldy publication depicting dozens of toys, games, and health and beauty items, all bearing the Connery image. Professing disdain for it all, he commented "The whole thing has become a Frankenstein's monster—the merchandising, the promotion, the pirating—they're thoroughly distasteful. . . . It's a lot of rubbish!" Nevertheless, Bond was big business, and woe to the parents who did not ensure their child had an ample number of 007 toys under the tree that Christmas morning. By this point, the entire world was spy crazy. The 007 films had also inspired an amazing number of takeoffs on film and television—the most successful being *The Man from U.N.C.L.E., Get Smart,* and *I Spy.*

Thunderball premiered to the anticipated pandemonium and dominated the box office for months, routinely being held over in many theaters for what seemed to be an eternity, as Bond fans flocked to see it again and again. Critics were generally ecstatic, with the *New York Times* naming it as one of the year's best

A FINE MADNESS

1966

Released by Warner Bros.

CAST:

Samson Shillitoe: Sean Connery; *Rhoda Shillitoe:* Joanne Woodward; *Lydia West:* Jean Seberg; *Dr. Oliver West:*

A FINE MADNESS Samson acts up atop the Brooklyn Bridge.

A FINE MADNESS   Original art still.

Patrick O'Neal; *Dr. Vera Kropotkin:* Colleen Dewhurst; *Dr. Menken:* Clive Revill; *Dr. Vorbeck:* Werner Peters; *Daniel K. Papp:* John Fielder; *Mrs. Fish:* Kay Medford; *Mr. Fitzgerald:* Jackie Coogan.

CREDITS:

Director: Irvin Kershner; *Producer:* Jerome Hellman; *Screenplay:* Elliot Baker, based on his novel; *Director of Photography:* Ted McCord; *Editor:* William Ziegler; *Music:* John Addison. *Running Time:* 103 minutes.

Now, ladies and gentlemen—
The first revolutionary laugh discovery since the
feather!
A Fine Madness!!!
With Sean Connery as the extrastrength laugh
ingredient.
Tested with amazing results!!!
Don't ask—Demand—*A Fine Madness!* It's
guaranteed!!!

The above tag lines from the advertising campaign for Sean Connery's first breakaway venture into the world of outright comedy were supplemented with the notation, "We should all be so crazy." Indeed. *A Fine Madness* was a 1960s version of what would traditionally have been termed a screwball comedy—save for the fact that there is nothing traditional whatsoever about this offbeat film. Sean eagerly accepted his role as beat poet Samson Shillitoe because it was light-years away from the character of 007. Filming began in New York City in October 1965, and the shoot helped to distract Connery from the mammoth campaign that would greet the release of *Thunderball* in December. Roles such as this helped keep Connery sane and allowed him to stretch his acting skills while the press continued to blur his real-life persona with that of James Bond. Through his non-Bondian efforts, Sean was quenching his soul's thirst for exhibiting the fierce independence he had known since childhood.

In *A Fine Madness*, Connery displayed a wide range of emotions and made it quite clear that this difficult starring role could only successfully be brought to life by an actor of considerable skill. Sean's Samson Shillitoe of Elliot Baker's well-received 1964 novel is an arrogant, rebellious, and frustrated poet. When not abusing his wife, cheating creditors, or seducing lovely ladies with his animal magnetism, he spends most of his time battling a case of writer's block while trying to complete a collection of poems he feels will be judged his masterpiece. As his creativity suffers, he

A FINE MADNESS   On the set with Joanne Woodward (left), Jean Seberg, and director Irvin Kershner.

becomes violently antisocial. Wife Joanne Woodward pleads with snooty psychiatrist Patrick O'Neal to examine Connery and save him from self-destruction. The incorrigible Connery is sent to an institution where a panel of doctors are fascinated by this sometimes despicable yet undeniably brilliant man. However, when charismatic Sean seduces O'Neal's sexually frustrated wife (Jean Seberg), the psychiatrist arranges for a lobotomy for his patient. This fails to tame Connery's behavior, and he resumes his love/hate relationship with Woodward, while leaving a trail of shocked and destroyed lives among those who seek to "save" him.

A Fine Madness is like a Three Stooges version of *A Clockwork Orange,* mixing outright slapstick with rather insightful commentaries about society's obsession to make people conform. Connery's participation in the film resulted from the cancellation of plans to star with his wife, Diane Cilento, in a project entitled *Call Me When the Cross Turns Over,* which was to be filmed in Cilento's native Australia. The constant separation inevitable in any marriage between two working actors was causing a strain, and the Connerys felt that a joint film project might help relieve tensions. However, when such plans kept falling through, Diane signed to star opposite Paul Newman in *Hombre,* which was being shot in Arizona. (In a platonic case of mate swapping, Mrs. Newman—Joanne Woodward—would star opposite

93

FEATURE THE NAME OF
SEAN CONNERY
—one of todays biggest box office stars—

IN EVERY ONE OF YOUR

PUBLICITY ANGLES !

Still No. 609   Price 1/6 each

Use these four stills of Sean Connery in every available medium of advertising the film programme by . . . .

Sending the set of 4 illustrations to film editors of local newspapers, together with a synopsis of the picture.

Ordering 18″ x 24″ enlargements for displaying in the theatre 'star' frames. (15/- each)

Printing up a set of 4 fan portraits and distributing them to the public in busy shopping areas, and sports functions, and in public houses etc.

Designing a throwaway leaflet incorporating all four stills and stressing the star value of Sean Connery by refer ing to his past successes, notably as James Bond.

Arranging shop window tie-ups on gents. outfitting and mounting a still on each showcard.

Using the portraits as a lead in to a film quiz in which you ask for longest list of Sean Connery film titles.

Still No. 636   Price 1/6 each

Still No. 600   Price 1/6 each

Still No. 635   Price 1/6 each

A FINE MADNESS   The British pressbook advised theater owners on how to capitalize on Sean's popularity.

Sean in *A Fine Madness*.) Connery's location work allowed him to commute on his days off between New York and Phoenix, where Sean and Diane made the most of their time together.

Sean accepted his role as Samson for a salary considerably less than Bondian standards. However, he did manage to get Warners to concede a cut of the film's grosses. He explained his willingness to take less for this special project: "When I decide to do something—a part now in any film—it is because I think it will work out well. Take *A Fine Madness*. Samson is a man whose unorthodoxies society tries to suffocate. I thought it was worthwhile doing." Nevertheless, when shooting ran overschedule, Connery slapped the studio with a lawsuit for extra compensation. This caused industry tongues to wag as *no one* would have considered incurring the wrath of mogul Jack Warner. Despite a war of words, Warner paid Sean an additional $50,000—a fact that the star delighted in referring to over the years. This incident also contributed to Connery's career-long distrust of movie studios.

While on location, Sean made the most of his time in the Big Apple, enjoying the counterculture scene in Greenwich Village and immersing himself in pastimes far removed from those expected of 007. Onscreen, he also made the most of his opportunity to distance himself from "the Frankenstein monster" he felt Bond had become. With a no-holds-barred characterization to revel in, Sean gives a larger-than-life performance—tweaking society's nose at every opportunity. He displayed a wonderful screen chemistry with Woodward, who also excels as Samson's long-suffering wife. Their constant battles remind one of a more perverse Ralph and Alice Kramden, and Connery is probably the only actor in the world whose charisma could remain intact after belting his on-screen spouse after she informs him she is pregnant. Shillitoe's attempts to "behave himself" are all the more amusing because we know this man is a time bomb waiting to go off. In one sequence he reluctantly agrees to earn a few dollars by reading poetry before a group of pretentious, well-to-do women. The results are predictable, but hilarious. Complementing Connery is a sterling supporting cast headed by Colleen Dewhurst, John Fielder, and the ever-amusing Jackie Coogan, as well as Jean Seberg and Patrick O'Neal.

94

The film was director Irvin Kershner's second motion picture, and he just let the cameras roll while his actors had a field day. (Kershner would later direct Sean's 1983 Bond film *Never Say Never Again*.) By not restraining Connery in any way or attempting to glamorize his character, he afforded Sean one of his most successful performances. Critics agreed, and the film opened to largely favorable reviews. Howard Thompson, in the *New York Times*, claimed, "At times, it's as funny as all get-out. . . . Give it an A for effort and a B for impudence and originality. It flounders but it gleams. . . . Unfortunately, our hero is an oaf. Mr. Connery plays him well, too, with his shoulders slumped and that bonded dimple narrowed into a cynical crevasse." *Variety* praised the film as a "far-out sex comedy-drama . . . a sort of *Tom Jones* and *A Thousand Clowns* combo." The paper's critic felt that "[Kershner] demonstrates a remarkable pictorial sense [and has] drawn [an] effective performance from Connery, who makes a good comic kook in a switch from the somnambulism of his James Bond roles."

Unfortunately, *A Fine Madness* continued the pattern of Sean's non-Bondian efforts failing at the box office, it being difficult to market and tough to describe through word of mouth. The antihero's actions were rather controversial at the time and alienated many people who wanted to see Sean portraying a hero in a white hat. If ever a film was ahead of its time, this was it. Sean recalled years later, "[The movie] didn't make a penny, of course. It was a highly unsuccessful film, as quite a few of the others I've done, too. I think it was Garson Kanin who wrote to me saying, 'You mustn't be surprised that the public aren't interested in writers or poets.' And I think that's probably true because I don't know of any film that's ever been made that's been a success about a writer or poet. Also, I think that [Samson's] behavior in that picture would be totally acceptable today, and they would think it was funny and they might cheer him, and what have you."

Ironically, by the time the movie was released in May of 1966, the world was still caught up in the mania of *Thunderball*, which had become the largest-grossing 007 film to date. To add to Connery's frustrations, he had to prepare for Bond #5—*You Only Live Twice*, which would turn out to be the most grueling of the series. Tensions with Broccoli and Saltzman were becoming more pronounced than ever, while cinematically the trio were experiencing financial rewards that would have seemed inconceivable only a few years before. Perhaps if any of the fine films Connery had made outside of the Bond series had attained any level of popular success, he would have been more tolerant of 007.

A FINE MADNESS   Colleen Dewhurst finds Connery's wild behavior irresistible.

YOU ONLY
LIVE TWICE

1967

Released by United Artists

CAST:

James Bond: Sean Connery; *Aki:* Akiko Wakabayashi; *Tiger Tanaka:* Tetsuro Tamba; *Kissy Suzuki:* Mie Hama; *Osato:* Teru Shimada; *Helga Brandt:* Karin Dor; *Miss Moneypenny:* Lois Maxwell; *"Q":* Desmond Llewelyn; *Henderson:* Charles Gray; *"M":* Bernard Lee; and Donald Pleasence as *Ernst Stavro Blofeld.*

CREDITS:

Director: Lewis Gilbert; *Producers:* Albert R. Broccoli and Harry Saltzman; *Screenplay:* Roald Dahl, based on the novel by Ian Fleming; *Director of Photography:* Freddie Young; *Editor:* Thelma Connell; *Production Designer:* Ken Adam; *Music:* John Barry. *Running Time:* 116 minutes.

"I am *not* James Bond!" This was an increasingly frustrated Sean Connery's stern reminder to the world press as he boarded an aircraft for the Far East for *You Only Live Twice,* his fifth and presumably final cinematic mission as Agent 007. As vociferous as his remarks may have been, they were all but drowned out in the huge publicity campaign that ironically stressed the tag line "Sean Connery IS James Bond!" Exploitation materials attempted to blend the man and his on-screen alter ego into one identity at the very time Sean was trying to make a distinction between the two. Like many actors before him, Connery was so adept at portraying a specific role that the danger of typecasting was becoming increasingly possible. He reiterated his frustration by stating, "I am an actor who is fortunate to play James Bond. I have existed before Bond and I will exist after him. Do I have to put a sign around my neck saying what other parts I've played?" The question may not have been as rhetorical as it seemed. Although he had made some impressive films outside the Bond series, even those that were critically acclaimed (e.g., *The Hill*) were virtually ignored by audiences.

Connery's formal announcement that *Twice* would mark his swan song as Bond was not made on a whim. Rather, it was the result of a growing accumu-

lation of mental and physical strains brought on by five years in "Bondage." As each succeeding 007 epic became more exotic and spectacular, the time needed for filming kept increasing. Connery routinely complained that he could do several films in the time devoted to bringing 007 back to the screen, and he had to reject many offers because he was contractually committed to the series. The producers were not totally unsympathetic. Their initial contract with Sean stipulated that his non-Bond films would be made for Broccoli and Saltzman. When he balked that this would make him their indentured servant, the two voided that part of the contract, and Sean was free to find vehicles outside the Eon universe. Recalled Harry Saltzman, "What so few people realized was that Sean was a far, far better actor than he was given credit for. The trouble was that his friends kept telling him he was under the rock of Bond and ought to get out."

Connery had been at odds with the producers since they refused to make him a full partner in the series. Sean would get a considerable salary and a percentage of the profits, but would not benefit as a member of the Eon partnership. By the time *Twice* was being filmed, the relationship between actor and producers had deteriorated. Cubby Broccoli said, "Sean got mad at us early on. By *Goldfinger* he knew he was indispensable to us." Adding to the tension were the well-publicized differences between the producers.

For Sean, the worst part of Bondmania was the intrusion on his private life. While he conceded "it goes with the territory" when you become a superstar, he was increasingly intolerant of the press, which often acted as though no question was too personal or insensitive. After putting in a twelve-to-eighteen-hour day, attending a press conference was not on Connery's list of favored activities. "I get angry when [the press] ask me if I'm like James Bond, or if they should call me Connery or Bond; when they plague me with idiocies of that kind." Connery later complained that he was "bored to tears" with 007 and could find little new to add to the characterization. Although he was contractually obligated to do two more Bond films—*You Only Live Twice* and *On Her Majesty's Secret Service*—Broccoli and Saltzman attempted to ease the tension by dropping the requirement for the second film. They were supposedly confident Sean could be wooed back after he had cooled off awhile. The decision would be one they would later regret, as *On Her Majesty's Secret Service* could have provided Sean with his strongest performance as 007 in the only downbeat film of the series. (As is well known, newcomer George Lazenby

YOU ONLY LIVE TWICE   Sean's identification with the Bond role was so strong that
this teaser poster did not even have to identify his name.

played Bond in the film—only to have Connery return to the series two years later in his weakest 007 movie, *Diamonds Are Forever*.)

Connery found that his trip to Japan for location filming on *Twice* was the first step in a long journey toward completion of principal photography. Shooting took place over twenty-eight arduous weeks, a necessity as this epic would dwarf all the others in terms of sheer spectacle. Filming key scenes in nine major locations from the tip of Kyūshū to Tokyo required more than three thousand miles of travel by air and rail. The entire way, Sean was menaced by a foe far more formidable than SPECTRE—the Japanese press corps. Initially, Sean was the ultimate professional and displayed admirable patience. However, this intensely private man soon became the center of a never-ending obsession on the part of the press. Hundreds of journalists followed him everywhere, asking rude or inane questions. A tour of Tokyo by Sean and Diane had to take place in the dead of night, but even this could not prevent the legions of reporters and paparazzi from tailing them everywhere. He became infuriated when photographers attempted to get shots of him inside a rest room. By the time filming entered its final stages, Connery was counting the days till his retirement from Her Majesty's Secret Service.

Given all the ill will on the set, *Twice* holds its own alongside the classic Bonds. The film boasts lightning-fast editing by Thelma Connell and stunning photography by Freddie Young. A new director—Lewis Gilbert—brought vitality to the proceedings, even if Roald Dahl's screenplay seemed rather uninspired. (For the first time, virtually every aspect of a Fleming

YOU ONLY LIVE TWICE Blasting the bad guys at the Kobe docks.

YOU ONLY LIVE TWICE 007 enjoys a brief fling prior to his "murder."

novel would be discarded.) The plot was reminiscent of *Dr. No* with SPECTRE's interference with the U.S. and Soviet space programs bringing the world to the verge of World War III. Where the film succeeds most is in its production design, with Ken Adam's volcano headquarters of SPECTRE a masterpiece of design and construction. (A full $1 million of the hefty $9.5-million budget was allocated to this one set—and this was in 1966 dollars!) This, combined with rarely photographed areas of Japan, helped make *Twice* the most visually impressive of the series to date.

Twice also boasted some of the most spectacular action sequences ever committed to film. An aerial battle between 007's heavily armed "Little Nellie" autogyro and a squadron of helicopters was shot over the Costa del Sol in Spain. Despite the use of some obvious miniatures, it's a thrilling set piece. Likewise, Thelma Connell's cutting together of the many fist-fights is up to the standards set by former editor Peter Hunt—and Bond's tangle with a sumo wrestler is

YOU ONLY LIVE TWICE   Aboard "M's" command sub, Bond begins his "second life."

YOU ONLY LIVE TWICE   Getting some advice on Ninja fighting in Japan.

YOU ONLY LIVE TWICE   This shot of Sean joking on the set belies his feelings of frustration with the role of Bond.

YOU ONLY LIVE TWICE   Original artist sketch for the poster design . . .

YOU ONLY LIVE TWICE ... and the finished product.

YOU ONLY LIVE TWICE As Bond requests a cigarette, Blofeld (Donald Pleasance) advises that it won't be the nicotine that kills him.

YOU ONLY LIVE TWICE Bond shoots it out while escaping Osato's headquarters.

particularly exciting. Most impressive is the climactic battle within the hollowed-out volcano, where Bond and an army of ninjas lead an all-out assault against SPECTRE. Looking at this sequence even by contemporary standards, one has to wonder how it was brought off so successfully. The movie also benefits from some above-average casting. Bond at various times beds two oriental beauties—Akiko Wakabayashi (as Secret Service agent Aki) and Mie Hama (as his "bride," Kissy). Both are quite lovely and competent, but alas, they are living proof that not every Bond girl becomes a star. Tetsuro Tamba makes an able ally as Tanaka, even if he is a bit young to be "M" 's counterpart in the Japanese Secret Service. Bond's archenemy Blofeld is finally seen in this one, and he is played in a properly bizarre fashion by Donald Pleasence (who replaced ailing actor Jan Werich). Adding their usual support are the stalwart trio from "the office": Bernard Lee, Desmond Llewelyn, and Lois Maxwell.

Yet, *Twice* is not a film without flaws. In addition to its rather uninspired screenplay, the movie sacrifices logic and characterization for the sake of spectacle and gadgetry. As with *Thunderball,* there is little suspense as Bond is so laden with devices from Q branch that he merely presses a few buttons to get out of the most dangerous situations. Additionally, the very end of the film is a direct takeoff of *Goldfinger* with Bond feverishly attempting to avoid a holocaust by stopping a bomb from exploding. As for Connery himself, he gamely goes through the motions, but seems somewhat distracted and bored. Yet, on the whole, *Twice* is smashing entertainment.

The movie received a Royal Premiere in June 1967, and Connery surprisingly was in attendance. He did, however, use the occasion to reiterate—in a response to a question from the Queen—that this was, indeed, his final appearance as 007. *Twice* debuted to a predictable frenzy at the box office, making it one of the smash hits of 1967. This was despite the fact that Columbia had simultaneously released an all-star megabudget 007 satire, *Casino Royale*, which ended up a money loser for the studio. Reviewers had long ago conceded that the Eon-produced Bonds were "critic proof," but they went through the motions of evaluating the film anyway. The movie received respectable notices from a technical standpoint, but more and more critics complained that 007 was losing his personality amid all the girls and gadgets. Sean eagerly said adieu to the role he had turned into a worldwide cinematic legend and announced he would go full circle and star in a western, reminding the press, "You only live *once,* and I do not want to live my entire life as James Bond."

SHALAKO

1968

Released by Cinerama Releasing Corp.

CAST:

Shalako: Sean Connery; *Irina:* Brigitte Bardot; *Fulton:* Stephen Boyd; *Daggett:* Jack Hawkins; *Von Hallstatt:* Peter Van Eyck; *Lady Daggett:* Honor Blackman; *Chato:* Woody Strode; *Mako:* Eric Sykes; *Clarke:* Alexander Knox.

CREDITS:

Director: Edward Dmytryk; *Producer:* Euan Lloyd; *Screenplay:* J. J. Griffith, Hal Hopper, and Scot Finch, based on the novel by Louis L'Amour; *Director of Photography:* Ted Moore; *Editor:* Bill Blunden; *Music:* Robert Farnon. *Running Time:* 113 minutes.

Sean Connery's first post-Bond vehicle proved to be as far removed from the world of 007 as anyone could imagine. The film *Shalako* transported him into the wild West, where he portrayed the reluctant title hero of this expensive adaptation of Louis L'Amour's novel. Connery chose this project neither quickly nor out of desperation to leave behind the image of Bond. In fact, he had always enjoyed westerns and had made no secret over the years of his desire to star in one. Obviously, opportunities were not plentiful for the debut of the screen's first Scottish cowboy. However, because of Sean's box-office clout, producer Euan Lloyd gambled that audiences would accept Connery, accent and all, in a completely new heroic image. Connery made no attempt to disguise his heritage, arguing sensibly, "It would have been a bad mistake to try a completely American accent. There were plenty of Scots immigrants in the West, so I had no fear of being out of character."

In fact, Connery looks "home on the range" when contrasted with the other principal players from Europe: Brigitte Bardot, Jack Hawkins, Peter Van Eyck, Stephen Boyd, and Sean's *Goldfinger* flame, Honor Blackman. If the casting sounds bizarre, it should be mentioned that the script made such choices an inevitability. The plot centers on a party of hopelessly snobby European aristocrats who visit the West in the hopes of hunting dangerous game, thereby enlivening their boring lives. Among the participants is the group's sponsor, Count Von Hallstatt (Van Eyck), the glamorous countess (Bardot), an elderly aristocrat (Hawkins) whose fortunes have recently fallen, and his sexually frustrated wife (Blackman). The group is guided by Fulton (Boyd), a man of such obvious criminality, it is a wonder anyone would walk across the street with him, let alone entrust their lives to him and his gang.

When Fulton knowingly violates a treaty by taking the group into Indian territory, he is warned by Shalako (Connery), a cynical frontiersman, to evacuate immediately or face extermination. The group laughs off the warning, but soon finds itself on the losing end of a battle, rescued only by Shalako's ingenuity. When Fulton deceives the group and robs them of their jewels, it is up to Shalako to save them. The script is basically a formula horse opera, made somewhat more watchable by the unusual European presence. Every effort is made to demean the bourgeois lifestyle of these noblemen, but refreshingly, a few are allowed to show they have "true grit" in the face of battle.

Unfortunately, for all the advance speculation about the sparks that would ignite on-screen between Connery and Bardot, the chemistry is as flat as week-old champagne. Bardot wears so much Pan-Cake makeup and eye shadow that she looks like a frontier version of Tammy Faye Bakker. She also appears rather bored, although in fairness, the script gives her little to do except fire weapons unconvinc-

SHALAKO Pressbook advertisement.

ingly and walk around in the desert mouthing such pronouncements as "Deenir ees served!" Things perk up a bit when Connery stumbles upon Bardot conveniently bathing herself sans top, but—dammit all—good taste wins out, and the scene discreetly fades. (Something that would never have occurred in the 007 films!)

Bardot was cast at about the same time Cubby Broccoli and director Peter Hunt had approached her to star opposite Connery's replacement as 007, newcomer George Lazenby. The film *On Her Majesty's Secret Service* required a strong female presence for the role of Tracy, the ill-fated wife of James Bond. Broccoli and Hunt met with Bardot, but she informed them that, ironically, she was contracted to star with none other than Sean Connery in *Shalako*. If the Eon team was disappointed, it could later take pride in the fact that Diana Rigg's casting helped insure the next 007 adventure as one of the best of Bond series. On the *Shalako* set, Bardot reportedly sometimes acted like a prima donna, and her entourage added to a circus atmosphere. The set was already rather tense due to the severe heat of the location in Almería, Spain. (Mexico was the original choice, but a pending labor strike resulted in a last-minute change of plans.)

SHALAKO German lobby card.

SHALAKO   A duel to the death with Woody Strode.

SHALAKO

SHALAKO   With Brigitte Bardot.

SHALAKO   Japanese souvenir program.

105

create a little heat between Connery and Bardot. Ted Moore, the 007 cinematographer, captures some sweeping landscapes, and even Connery's Bondian stunt director, the legendary Bob Simmons, is back doubling as Sean. The film has two major flaws—an absurdly abrupt ending that does not even allow Connery and Bardot to shake hands in parting, and probably one of the most laughable title songs ever.

Shalako was a major release internationally and even benefited from a Royal Premiere in London. Critics were lukewarm to Connery's efforts to redefine his image, and many felt he should have chosen a more prestigious effort. The public likewise was unenthused about the film, which did not lure many of Sean's fans to theaters. However, contrary to what many believe, the film was a moneymaker, due to producer Euan Lloyd's shrewd concept of "preselling" the film to thirty-six countries before the cameras began rolling. This practice, common today, was innovative at the time and allowed the principals and the production company to insure there would be profits. *Shalako* is rarely discussed in analyses of Connery's career. Though not a ground-breaking film artistically, it was the first step in the long road out of Bondage.

Additionally, there was friction between Bardot and Boyd, with whom she was once reportedly romantically involved. Some speculated she also resented the fact that Connery was paid far more handsomely than she. Bardot later somewhat acknowledged her rather lackluster performance by stating, "*Shalako* is Sean Connery's film. He carried the whole weight of it on his shoulders."

As entertainment, the movie is quite watchable. Connery handles both the dramatic and action sequences with considerable skill, although the script frustratingly fails to give any depth to his character. This was intentional, as Connery explained at the time: "For this film, a cardboard character is all you want. [The screenwriters] were going to try and give him a lot of depth and background, but in a western like this we decided to keep him a mystery figure." More successful is the story's evolution of the aristocrats from "above it all" idealists to participants in a deadly game of survival. Some rise to the challenge, while others—including Blackman—die horribly. Veteran director Edward Dmytryk keeps the pace moving well, except for the obligatory attempt to

THE MOLLY MAGUIRES

1970

Released by Paramount Pictures

CAST:

James McParlan: Richard Harris; *Jack Kehoe:* Sean Connery; *Mary Raines:* Samantha Eggar; *Davies:* Frank Finlay; *Dougherty:* Anthony Zerbe; *Mrs. Kehoe:* Bethel Leslie; *Frazier:* Art Lund.

CREDITS:

Director: Martin Ritt; *Producers:* Martin Ritt and Walter Bernstein; *Written by:* Walter Bernstein, suggested by a book by Arthur H. Lewis; *Director of Photography:* James Wong Howe; *Editor:* Frank Bracht; *Music:* Henry Mancini. *Running Time:* 125 minutes.

Sean Connery was noticeably disappointed when *Shalako* failed at the box office as he looked upon it as

THE MOLLY MAGUIRES Australian daybill poster.

a sort of litmus test to prove his popularity extended beyond the Bond films. Recognizing Sean's frustration, his agent encouraged him to aggressively seek new roles, warning that the stigma of box-office poison could engulf him if he waited for masterpieces to come his way. For this reason, Connery signed with director Martin Ritt to star in a big-budget social drama, *The Molly Maguires*. Ritt had spoken to him about the project as early as 1967 when the actor visited the set of Ritt's *Hombre*, costarring Sean's (then) wife, Diane Cilento. Connery commented, "I wanted to do this film very much; it excited me because it offered me a meaty portrayal, and the story itself has a contemporary quality about it since it holds much in common with the activities of minority groups and the growing violence in the world today."

Ritt had an impressive track record—hits such as *The Long, Hot Summer, Hud, The Spy Who Came In*

From the Cold, and *Hombre.* Only recently had he stumbled, as his 1968 Mafia film, *The Brotherhood,* undeservedly flopped. Like Connery, he, too, was anxious to prove he could again make films that pleased both audiences and studio accounting offices. Ritt, who had been blacklisted during the McCarthy era, felt *The Molly Maguires* would be a noble venue for protesting political inequities in American society. Consequently, he had invested two full years preparing to bring this epic to the screen. Paramount gambled the enormous sum of $11 million, feeling that, although the events in the film took place a century earlier, the parallels to today's society would make the story controversial and timely. It's not difficult to see where most of the money went. Connery was teamed with fellow "heavyweight" actor Richard Harris, and both men commanded hefty salaries. Asked why he allowed Harris to receive top billing, Sean scoffed, "They're paying me a million dollars for this picture. For that, they can put a mule ahead of me." (No offense was obviously intended toward Harris!)

Filming took place primarily in the tiny hamlet of Eckley, Pennsylvania, a coal town that was suitable for many of the mining sequences. However, the location meant virtually every necessity had to be flown to the set at great expense. Indeed, some of the locations were inaccessible by foot, and all the equipment had to be airlifted by helicopters. Through it all, Ritt kept shooting regardless of the weather or other

THE MOLLY MAGUIRES Tangling during the riotous Rugby game.

THE MOLLY MAGUIRES   Giving an impromptu autograph session for some young fans.

THE MOLLY MAGUIRES   A light moment on the set with Samantha Eggar and Richard Harris.

obstacles, once keeping the cast and crew filming for sixteen consecutive days.

The story of *The Molly Maguires* was inspired by the plight of nineteenth-century Irish coal miners in Pennsylvania who were forced to endure subhuman conditions by the owners. After a week of backbreaking work in the claustrophobic shafts, a miner was likely to be told on payday that his efforts barely compensated for what he owed the company for tools, equipment, and groceries purchased at the "company store." According to legend, Molly Maguire was an Irish widow—"a giant of a woman with a pistol strapped to each thigh"—who led a band of rebels disguised as women on daring sabotage raids against the mine owners. While there is no evidence such a person existed, her name was taken by a secret society who engaged in murderous acts against their employers. The movement was eventually crushed, but it planted the seeds that ultimately led to the formation of the powerful United Mine Workers union.

Richard Harris is cast as a detective hired to infiltrate the group, identify its leaders, and insure they are brought to trial. He finds the assignment easier said than done, as the Molly's ringleader, played by Sean Connery, is a dour and suspicious man not easily given to trusting strangers. Harris informs the police it will be necessary for him to participate in criminal acts in order to win Connery's trust, and the plan succeeds. Working side by side with the miners, Harris develops close ties with the group and experiences firsthand the inequities of the system. Despite his newfound sympathies, Harris sees the job through and ultimately betrays the gang and insures that all will be hanged.

The Molly Maguires was faulted as almost entirely lacking in humor. Connery agreed and felt the somber script alienated audiences. "It had a good script and a good cast. It was well-intentioned, and a good film, really. But it never caught fire. One reason was the fear that humor might intrude, whereas in actual fact, it can enhance a situation." The film was also criticized for its failure to provide a feel-good ending in which Harris, presumably seeing the nobility of the Mollys' cause, saves his confederates. Admittedly, it is rather shocking when this likable man blindly follows orders and seals the doom of those he has begun to sympathize with. Yet, this unpredictability is what makes the film so engrossing. As for the complete absence of joviality, it does not stretch the imagination to believe that these were people with little to be jovial about.

This moody, brooding film was destined from the

108

start not to find its audience. Its title was confusing and meant nothing to cinemagoers. Additionally, the U.S. ad campaign downplayed the stars and concentrated on an image of a grimy fist. At least the movie was recognized for its depiction of the unrelenting conditions inside the minds that turned young men into cripples. At Oscar time, *The Molly Maguires* received a nomination for Art Direction/Set Decoration.

The performances are flawless, with Connery and Harris displaying the kind of chemistry one would anticipate. The Harris character is actually central as the story is seen through his eyes. Yet, Connery generates the most sympathy. He is the tragic figure, his onetime allowance of trust in another human being bringing him the disaster he has always feared. The final sequence in which Connery confronts Harris following his conviction for murder is what powerful acting is all about.

The film has many other attributes: James Wong Howe's atmospheric camerawork, Ritt's beautifully paced direction, and Henry Mancini's memorable score. For all that, however, *The Molly Maguires* was a major box-office disaster. Connery had to endure yet another fine film failing to find its niche among critics and audiences.

THE MOLLY MAGUIRES   Leading off in the no-holds-barred Rugby match.

THE MOLLY MAGUIRES   With Richard Harris, Anthony Costello, and Anthony Zerbe in the mines.

THE RED TENT

1971

Released by Paramount Pictures

CAST:

General Nobile: Peter Finch; *Amundsen:* Sean Connery; *Valeria:* Claudia Cardinale; *Lundborg:* Hardy Kruger; *Biagi:* Mario Adorf; *Romagna:* Massimo Girotti.

CREDITS:

Director: Mikhail K. Kalatozov; *Producer:* Franco Cristaldi; *Screenplay:* Ennio de Concini and Richard Adams; *Director of Photography:* Leonid Kalashnikov; *Editor:* John Shirley; *Music:* Ennio Morricone. *Running Time:* 121 minutes.

Sean Connery experienced a rather auspicious start to 1969, with the Scottish National Party inviting him to run for Parliament—an honor he humbly declined. He also made an uncharacteristic appearance on television, his first in six years, in *Male of the Species,* for which he reaped enthusiastic reviews for his role of a cad. Following this project, Connery agreed to appear in *The Red Tent,* an ambitious Italian/Soviet joint venture that could be described as a microcosm of the détente that East and West embraced during the Nixon era. Filming had begun almost one year earlier, while Sean had been completing *Shalako.* Preproduction on *The Red Tent* extended back to 1966, with the logistical problems of coordinating the Italo-Soviet crew no easy obstacle to overcome.

No expense was spared in Russian director Mikhail Kalatozov's attempt to accurately re-create the tragic 1928 arctic expedition of explorer Umberto Nobile, whose dirigible *Italia* crashed in the frozen tundra, thus condemning its crew to certain death in the icy wastelands. Filming began in Estonia, the site of the original airship's takeoff and then the center of the rescue attempts. The filmmakers would even enlist the services of the real General Nobile (then eighty-four years old) to insure historical accuracy. When Connery finally joined the location filming, it marked the first time that the principals in the cast had met. His initial scenes had been filmed in a studio in Rome, wherein Nobile (Peter Finch) is subjected to mind tricks as the defendant in a mock trial where the witnesses are his doomed crew and would-be rescu-

ers. These ghostly apparitions are summoned by Nobile himself in hopes of clearing his conscience of charges of cowardice in allowing himself to be rescued before his crew. Nobile continually rationalizes this action by claiming it was necessary for him to coordinate vital rescue measures for the other men. Subconsciously, however, even Nobile comes to doubt the legitimacy of his actions. Connery appears as famed Norwegian explorer Roald Amundsen, who died in an ill-fated rescue attempt of the *Italia's* crew. With his hair distractingly white, Connery does cut a noble figure as he convinces Nobile his course of action was indeed justified.

Following this sequence in Rome, Sean flew to the Soviet Union for location filming in Moscow. Here, he shot a haunting scene wherein he discovers the frozen bodies of stragglers from the main group of crash survivors. Connery was intrigued by the Soviet Union, but also felt its apparent failures in virtually every aspect of providing a decent life for its citizens should have been taken as a lesson for left-wingers. He later recalled, "I was very aware of the fear element. . . . We'd drive to Mosfilm—it was bigger than all the American film studios put together—and they made you go through this ritual of checking who you were . . . and the interpreters were invariably KGB." Connery was also irked by the disorganization of the Soviet film industry: "There was no sense of time or program. No urgency about anything in filming the production. Took forever to light and shoot. They just had a whole different concept of time, in fact, and it was reflected in the movie, which ran four hours something in Russia and two hours in America. . . . Yet, it was a big internal success. Never a success anywhere else."

Sean was basically an unknown face in the Soviet Union, as the James Bond films had long been a thorn in the side of Kremlin leaders. Agent 007 was the epitome of everything Communists were supposed to detest, and there was little recognition among the populace of Connery's internationally famous face. In fact, on one occasion, he was barred from entering the British Embassy Club by an overly protective security guard.

Connery received second billing on the film, despite the fact he had worked for a total of only three weeks. His actual screen time amounts to less than Brando's appearance in *Superman.* In contrast, costar Peter Finch spent nine arduous months of filming before the project wrapped. The movie premiered domestically at Radio City Music Hall in 1971 and immediately laid a dirigible-sized egg at the box office despite some favorable reviews. Burdened by a bor-

THE RED TENT   Original poster.

THE RED TENT   Amundsen participates in General Nobile's imaginary trial.

THE RED TENT   As Roald Amundsen.

ing and largely confusing title, *The Red Tent* (which refers to a shelter holding the stranded crew's supplies) became one of the great failures of the cinema, grossing less than $900,000 in rentals on a budget that exceeded $10 million. A muddled and subdued ad campaign insured audience disinterest.

Artistically, the movie is rather intriguing, especially when it concentrates on the adventure aspects. The film is aided immeasurably by some first-rate cinematography that helps capture the stark terror of the frozen tundra. The performances are all literate and intelligent, although some reviewers felt they were *too* restrained. *Variety* touted Sean as "very convincing," but the lion's share of praise went to the always reliable Finch, who had the challenge of aging decades throughout the story. The film is somewhat sabotaged by the pretentious and unnecessary device of the imaginary trial, which only slows the action. Had the film concentrated on being a straight adventure story, the results would have been more impressive.

THE RED TENT With Claudia Cardinale.

THE ANDERSON TAPES

1971

Released by Columbia Pictures

CAST:

Duke Anderson: Sean Connery; *Ingrid:* Dyan Cannon; *Tommy:* Martin Balsam; *Pat Angelo:* Alan King; *Captain Delaney:* Ralph Meeker; *The Kid:* Christopher Walken; *Socks:* Val Avery; *Mrs. Kaler:* Margaret Hamilton; *Mrs. Hathaway:* Judith Lowry: *Spencer:* Dick Williams; *Pop:* Stan Gottlieb.

CREDITS:

Director: Sidney Lumet; *Producer:* Robert M. Weitman; *Screenplay:* Frank R. Pierson, based on the novel by Lawrence Sanders; *Director of Photography:* Arthur J. Ornitz; *Editor:* Joanne Burke; *Music:* Quincy Jones. *Running Time:* 99 minutes.

THE ANDERSON TAPES Pressbook advertisement.

It is difficult to overstate the significance of *The Anderson Tapes* on Sean Connery's career. Generally remembered as a popular, exciting escapist film—not necessarily Oscar caliber stuff—it is a solid thriller. However, its success went a long way in proving to

Sean—and the industry—that the actor had box-office clout away from the world of Bond. Connery had endured the frustration of seeing every one of his non-Bondian efforts rejected by the public. The failure of *The Molly Maguires* and *The Red Tent*—two expensive films that came nowhere near recouping their negative costs—had started tongues wagging in the film trade that Sean without Bond was like a fish out of water.

Another industry person feeling frustrated was Robert M. Weitman, a former stage producer and broadcast executive (he helped launch Frank Sinatra into the big leagues) who had also served as a production bigwig at MGM and Columbia Pictures. Weitman had long felt the urge to produce his own films and took a gamble by resigning from his post at Columbia. The same studio, however, agreed to release his first motion picture—an adaptation of Lawrence Sanders's best-selling novel *The Anderson*

THE ANDERSON TAPES   As Duke Anderson.

THE ANDERSON TAPES Japanese souvenir program.

ショーン・コネリー
盗聴作戦

Tapes. Per Weitman: "I chose *The Anderson Tapes* for my production debut after reading many books and plays. I read the Sanders novel before it came out in bookstores and bid for it. So did others, but I wanted it so much, I outbid the rest. It's about the planning and execution of a million-dollar robbery by a character named Duke Anderson after his release from a ten-year prison stretch for safecracking. There is an intriguing subplot involving the ubiquity of wiretapping, taping, bugging, and other means of photographic surveillance in our daily lives."

Weitman's first insightful move was to hire Sidney Lumet to direct the New York–based story. He recalled, "Because the film was set in Manhattan, I could see nobody but Sidney Lumet directing. Sidney is a New Yorker by birth and spirit. . . . [He's] an expert at putting action and characterization against the proper New York backgrounds." Indeed. Lumet, who at that point shot virtually all of his films in the Big Apple, proved to be the man for the job, with his intrinsic understanding of the New York atmosphere and its characters. New York is America's melting pot, and this is reflected in the wide range of types who appear within the film. Weitman went against the grain by casting Sean Connery as the tough, charismatic career criminal Duke Anderson. Ignoring those who envisioned Sean's Scottish burr throwing the character out of synch, Weitman maintained the role

THE ANDERSON TAPES Enjoying a laugh on the New York location with director Sidney Lumet.

THE ANDERSON TAPES Connery released from jail, with cohorts Stan Gottlieb (left) and Christopher Walken.

of Anderson was "perfect for Connery." He then enlisted a sterling supporting cast that included Dyan Cannon, Alan King, Ralph Meeker, a young Christopher Walken, and Martin Balsam as an aging homosexual queen. (And they said *Connery* was miscast!)

The plot is relatively simple. As soon as Connery emerges from Riker's Island jail, he makes his way to

girlfriend Cannon's plush apartment on the upper East Side (actually, the old Convent of the Sacred Heart on Fifth Avenue). Cannon's now a kept woman, but this is resolved in true Bondian style when one glimpse of Sean causes her to brush off her benefactor in a two-second phone conversation. After a few heated sexual encounters, Connery looks at the elegant surroundings and begins to mastermind an elaborate plot to "rob the guts" out of the other apartments over Labor Day weekend. This is to be accomplished by getting financing from mob boss Alan King, and by recruiting a team of oddball confederates including black militants, a racist mafioso, a somnambulistic young safecracker, an out-of-the-closet homosexual, and a half-crippled senior citizen.

This motley crew enters the well-secured apartment complex with a full-size moving van, disarming the security guard, rounding up as hostage all the tenants, and systematically robbing them of selected priceless possessions. The plan almost comes off, but an invalid boy reports the crime on a ham radio. In a superbly directed and prolonged climax, the police cordon off the surrounding blocks and scale the skyscraper with ropes and pulleys in hopes of surprising the crooks. Connery catches on, but it's too late. Despite a daring and elaborate escape attempt, most

THE ANDERSON TAPES Helping Dyan Cannon remove those cumbersome articles of clothing.

of his cohorts are killed, and Connery is seriously—and probably mortally—wounded.

The tapes in the title are those obtained by various law enforcement agencies who are seen illegally eavesdropping and recording from listening devices planted in the apartments of several tenants for unconnected reasons. Although each of these agencies overhears snippets of the crime being planned and executed, they are unable or unwilling to piece it all together to stop Connery. As police swarm into the apartment, the irony is that these "snoopers" are themselves committing crimes, and they rush to destroy the tapes. It is here that the film transcends being a popular entertainment and makes a valid social commentary. It warns us that the ease of electronic surveillance makes it an inevitability that it will be abused by those who seek to undermine our right to privacy. Keep in mind this was a full year before Watergate. Duke Anderson, a man who was an expert at pulling off crimes, emerges from prison to find a new world he no longer understands. He is haunted every step of the way by devices he is unaware of, and he is unable to grasp the very possibility of their existence. Ironically, it is not this technology that destroys him, but that of a child's radio transmitter.

The Anderson Tapes provided Connery with one of the most charismatic roles of his career. While his character is clearly a scoundrel—and not a very lovable one at that—it is a tribute to his acting skill that the audience can't help but side with this man and hope he can pull off his caper. Balsam is particularly hilarious as the prissy art dealer whose blatant attempts to seduce Connery generate some of the film's biggest laughs. Dyan Cannon has little to do, but seeing her in a bra and panties more than justifies her costarring status. Alan King, Stan Gottlieb, and Christopher Walken excel in their roles as well. Even the smallest parts are meticulously cast, and this makes the movie enjoyable even after repeated viewings. Contributing to the success are Joanne Burke's crisp editing and Quincy Jones's memorable score.

Lumet guides the film at a fast pace, and the climax is so gripping that one critic reported, "Audiences at the packed house got so involved . . . they were rooting, loudly, for the thieves to make a getaway." The general consensus from the critical establishment was that this was first-rate entertainment. New York *Daily News* critic Wanda Hale gave the movie four stars and touted the "almost unbearable suspense." Her review went on to say that "Duke Anderson is Connery's best role since *Goldfinger* . . . with one characteristic held over from Operator 007: he's loaded with sex ap-

peal." *Variety* called *The Anderson Tapes* "slick, engrossing entertainment . . . the climactic getaway and resulting seven-car crash is breathtaking stuff."

The movie proved to be a good-size hit, though not of Bondian stature. Yet, its success was enough to break the bond of Agent 007. Sean Connery had his *own* successful film, far away from the shadow of Mr. Bond. Ironically, following the completion of *The Anderson Tapes*, but prior to its release, an announcement stunned the entertainment world: Sean Connery's next film would be *Diamonds Are Forever*, in which he would play a slightly familiar character called James Bond.

DIAMONDS ARE FOREVER

1971

Released by United Artists

CAST:

James Bond: Sean Connery; *Tiffany Case:* Jill St. John; *Blofeld:* Charles Gray; *Plenty O'Toole:* Lana Wood; *Willard Whyte:* Jimmy Dean; *Saxby:* Bruce Cabot; *Mr. Wint:* Bruce Glover; *Mr. Kidd:* Putter Smith; *Felix Leiter:* Norman Burton; *Dr. Metz:* Joseph Furst; *"M":* Bernard Lee; *"Q":* Desmond Llewelyn; *Shady Tree:* Leonard Barr; *Moneypenny:* Lois Maxwell.

CREDITS:

Director: Guy Hamilton; *Producers:* Albert R. Broccoli and Harry Saltzman; *Screenplay:* Richard Maibaum and Tom Mankiewicz, based on the novel by Ian Fleming; *Director of Photography:* Ted Moore; *Editors:* Bert Bates and John W. Holmes; *Production Designer:* Ken Adam; *Music:* John Barry. *Running Time:* 120 minutes.

Sean Connery's departure from the James Bond series after *You Only Live Twice* did not prove to be the end of the franchise, as some had predicted. Producers Cubby Broccoli and Harry Saltzman commenced preproduction for *On Her Majesty's Secret Service*, sixth in the 007 lineup. Their seemingly insurmountable challenge was finding an actor to replace the "irreplaceable" Sean Connery, who had stated at the end of *Twice*, "I have no intention of getting back into

DIAMONDS ARE FOREVER   With director Guy Hamilton

Bond gear unless they offered me . . . $1 million tax free or if they bought me an island that would be absolutely mine." Yet, the fickle Connery refused an eleventh-hour appeal and the lure of a $1-million salary to return to "Bondage" for the sixth film. The actor commented, "I thought I could put up with the hardships of working in yet another Bond film for one million dollars—but money isn't everything!" Convinced Connery was unbendable in his convictions, the producers signed Australian model George Lazenby for the coveted role of Agent 007. Lazenby, however, proved to be temperamental, despite having had no previous acting experience. Before filming had been completed, he informed the world this would be his debut and swan song as Bond. Annoyed at the arrogance of the newcomer, the international press lambasted his performance, and the film was a box-office disappointment by Bondian standards. In recent years, however, the movie has been reassessed and justifiably ranked as one of the best of the series. Even Lazenby is now regarded as having made a significant contribution to the Bond legend, political battles aside.

For the next Bond epic, *Diamonds are Forever*, Broccoli, Saltzman, and United Artists had little doubt there was only one way to insure the continued

118

DIAMONDS ARE FOREVER Receiving the usual chastisement from "M" (Bernard Lee).

years . . . but I'm not such an idiot to forget the money and fame Bond brought me. Fortunately, the character is larger than life and there is fun in the role."

The announcement that Sean Connery would return in the role "he was born to play" brought hosannas from Bond fans and the media alike. Sean seemed to take it all in stride this time, enjoying the Las Vegas setting where he bypassed the gaming tables to play golf with fellow *Goldfinger* alumni director Guy Hamilton and set designer Ken Adam, both returning to the 007 fold with *Diamonds*. Skeptics wondered whether even Connery could maintain the public's interest in James Bond, as cultural values and attitudes had changed so dramatically since the series had been introduced a decade earlier. That question was answered when United Artists took out a double-page ad in *Variety* the week after *Diamonds* premiered, bragging, "Proudly Announcing the Greatest 3-Day Gross in the History of Motion Pic-

DIAMONDS ARE FOREVER Using one of "Q's" gadgets to gain entry to the White House.

success of the series: get Sean Connery back. Although American actor John Gavin had been signed for the role, clandestine negotiations began to see if Connery would reinstate his license to kill. Sean spurned several offers, but to the amazement of the industry, finally relented. "I took a week to make the decision whether to play Bond again," he declared. What finally won him over was the single most lucrative film contract in the history of motion pictures. "Why did I come back?" Sean asked rhetorically. "Well, the money offered me [$1.25 million] was tremendous, and by doing the film, I could give a lot of money to my charity, the Scottish International Education Trust [a foundation he helped establish to assist aspiring actors in Scotland]. Along with a healthy percentage of *Diamond*'s grosses [12.5 percent], I also extracted a promise from United Artists that I could make two non-Bond films on my own. . . . [Also] the film schedule was tightened up so that I wouldn't have to give up almost a year of my life to do it." A clause was also written mandating huge payments to Connery for every week the production ran over schedule. (It didn't.) Despite all that's been said, Connery never detested the character James Bond, but rather, the international hoopla that accompanied each film. He had stated earlier, "It is disturbing for an actor to play the same role for ten

tures!!" The film catapulted Connery into a top box-office attraction for the first time in years. His one Bond film absence hardly diminished his instant audience recognition as the one and only 007 and, in fact, seemed to reignite his fondness for the role. Critics generally agreed that this was Sean's most inspired Bond performance since *Goldfinger*. This, despite the actor's undeniable paunch and occasionally unflattering hairpiece. In a way, the more mature 007 only increased audience sentiment.

DIAMONDS ARE FOREVER Moneypenny (Lois Maxwell) requests that 007 bring her back a diamond engagement ring from Holland. Bond's reply: "Would you settle for a tulip?"

Connery's costars included leading lady Jill St. John as Tiffany Case, a character the actress described as "a survivor who gets along quite well, thank you very much." Originally, Faye Dunaway, Jane Fonda, and Raquel Welch were considered for the role. However, attorney Sidney Korshak, who assisted in finding suitable locales for filming, suggested his friend St. John for the supporting role of Vegas bimbette Plenty O'Toole. Guy Hamilton was inspired enough by her abilities to cast her as the female lead, explaining, "I always felt [Bond] needed a strong co-lead, a woman who could answer up to him." As Tiffany, St. John puts up a brash, moody, tough front, at times rivaling Connery's machismo. While her performance deteriorates into that of a bubble-headed Lucy clone, Jill's striking looks did make rumors of an off-set romance with Connery inevitable.

Eventually, the role originally slated for St. John—007's ill-fated groupie Plenty O'Toole—was "filled" by the ultrabuxom Lana Wood (Natalie's sister) after the producers were impressed by a *Playboy* photo spread. While Wood was perfect for her role, *Diamonds* does suffer from some crucial casting errors. In addition to the less-than-inspired choice of St. John, the pivotal role of archnemesis Blofeld is limply played by Charles Gray, a witty and competent actor who is far too charming to instill any sense of menace. Like other characters in the film, he's playing everything for laughs. (Gray was also handicapped in not

even resembling his two predecessors in the role—Donald Pleasence and Telly Savalas.) It can be argued that the lighthearted approach that characterized the Bond films throughout Roger Moore's "reign" actually began with *Diamonds Are Forever*. Completing a trio of miscast actors is Norman Burton as a buffoonish Felix Leiter.

Better cast was country singer cum sausage magnate Jimmy Dean as Willard Whyte, the Howard Hughes–like billionaire who figures prominently in the script when Blofeld kidnaps him and uses his empire to attempt global domination. The real Howard Hughes played an important part behind the scenes, allowing the filmmakers to use his casinos and other properties as locations. (His fee? One 16mm print of the final film.) Hughes's shadow hovered over the screenplay as well. The kidnapping and impersonation of the Whyte character by Blofeld was inspired by a dream of Cubby Broccoli's. Screenwriter Tom Mankiewicz quickly amended Richard Maibaum's original screenplay to reflect these elements. (The initial concept was to have the world menaced by Goldfinger's brother, and Gert Frobe was being contemplated to return as the twin of his cinematic alter ego.)

The end result of all this rewriting was a screenplay that was often confusing, if not downright incomprehensible. At its most basic, the film harkens back to the glory days of the series with Connery still dashing as legendary 007. There are also the standard witty one-liners and double entendres, a pinch of suspense, and some well-choreographed action sequences such as Bond's battle with a smuggler in a glass-enclosed elevator. The movie eventually runs out of steam in the last reel, with the climactic helicopter assault on Blofeld's oil rig not up to Bondian standards in either pacing or spectacle. Part of the reason was a last-minute rewrite of the script, coupled with minimal use of John Barry's classic action themes. The hurried look to the climax was also caused by Guy Hamilton's illness. Like other 007 epics, however, there is an effective, sting-in-the-tail climax after the climax, with Bond neatly dispatching two gay thugs. (The insensitivity of the homosexuals' portrayal would make a similar sequence all but impossible to film today.)

Without question, *Diamonds Are Forever* is still first-rate entertainment, even if it ranks among the weaker 007 epics. The film's highlight is undoubtedly the presence of Sean Connery, who reclaimed his ownership of the role without missing a beat. For Bond fans, this was manna from heaven. Critics universally praised Sean's return to Bondage with *Time* magazine noting, "Connery turns his contempt

120

DIAMONDS ARE FOREVER   A rare shot of Sean enjoying a bit of 007 merchandise (a 1965 beach towel). Maybe his assistant has something to do with his mood.

DIAMONDS ARE FOREVER   Despite his aversion to publicity, Connery attended a press conference for *Diamonds Are Forever.*

JAMES BOND 007
FILM FESTIVAL – LICENSED TO KILL
MAN WITH THE GOLDEN GUN GOLDFINGER FROM RUSSIA WITH LOVE

DIAMONDS ARE FOREVER   Film festival poster stressing the double excitement of Connery and Moore.

for the Bond character into some wry moments of self-parody." Roger Ebert called Connery "born for the role," and *Variety* felt that Connery "still packs a wallop" as 007. Premiering as United Artists' major Christmas release for 1971, the movie quickly soared to the top of the box-office rankings where it remained for many weeks. Yet, while diamonds may have been forever, Sean Connery's enlistment as Bond was not. He told the press, "With this picture, I'm finishing a part of my life. I will have accomplished quite a few things . . . and bought a bit of breathing space to look at my life and decide what I'm going to withdraw from, reach for, and what I really need." He later rejected $5 million to star in the next Bond film, *Live and Let Die,* and allowed his old friend Roger Moore to assume the 007 mantle—which he would do quite successfully in his own inimitable style. As for Sean's vow to permanently resign from Her Majesty's Secret Service, time would prove that he should have learned to never say never.

THE OFFENCE

1973

Released by United Artists

CAST:

Detective Sergeant Johnson: Sean Connery; *Cartwright:* Trevor Howard; *Maureen:* Vivien Merchant; *Baxter:* Ian Bannen; *Jessard:* Derek Newark; *Panton:* John Hallam.

CREDITS:

Director: Sidney Lumet; *Producer:* Denis O'Dell; *Screenplay:* John Hopkins, based on his stage play *This Story of Yours; Director of Photography:* Gerry Fisher; *Editor:* John Victor Smith; *Music:* Harrison Birtwhistle. *Running Time:* 112 minutes.

> *The Offense* was *the* reason for going back to the Bond films.
>
> —*Sean Connery*

The authors of this book have debated for years which of Sean Connery's screen portrayals can be considered his finest acting achievement. Each of his performances has been top-notch, even when the film is less than impressive, so selecting is not easy.

"SEE IT YOU MUST...
the sort of film that grips from the first title shots and holds you so fiercely that you daren't spend a penny...
SEAN CONNERY is terrific... *THE SUN*

Powerful
Potent Stuff
SUNDAY MIRROR

A gripping performance by SEAN CONNERY
DAILY EXPRESS

A RIVETING EXPERIENCE
SUNDAY TELEGRAPH

SEAN CONNERY
as Detective-Sergeant Johnson

TREVOR HOWARD

IN **"THE OFFENCE"** X

WITH **VIVIEN MERCHANT · IAN BANNEN**

WRITTEN BY JOHN HOPKINS / PRODUCED BY DENIS O'DELL / DIRECTED BY SIDNEY LUMET
A TANTALLON FILM / COLOUR

United Artists

THE OFFENCE British pressbook advertisement capitalized on the film's strong reviews.

We have concluded that the two leading contenders are Connery's work in *The Hill* and *The Offence*—curiously, two of his least-seen films. Not coincidentally, Sidney Lumet was director on both occasions. At a time when many felt Sean's abilities did not extend far beyond James Bond's bedroom antics, he continued to challenge himself by accepting roles far from the commercial mainstream. This practice eventually paid off handsomely, with Sean not only receiving the respect of critics but also being able to diversify beyond the inevitable man-of-action roles that were inevitably offered to him.

The Offence is one of the least commercial films Connery has done to date. He delivers a brilliant performance as a world-weary British detective whose many years of investigating horrendous crimes have brought him to the verge of a mental breakdown. Some police officers are able to insulate themselves from the horrors of their work by establishing a separate inner self that shuts out their work

THE OFFENCE As Det. Sgt. Johnson.

123

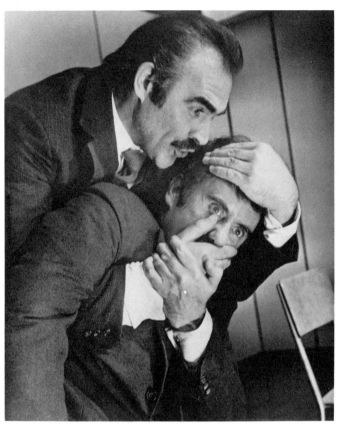

THE OFFENCE   Connery's interrogation of Ian Bannen quickly gets out of hand.

THE OFFENCE   As Det. Sgt. Johnson.

THE OFFENCE   Connery's discovery of the abused child (Maxine Gordon) causes his emotional breakdown.

at the end of the day. As Detective Sergeant Johnson, a twenty-year veteran of the force, Connery can no longer do so. His downfall is the arrest of a seemingly mild-mannered man who is the key suspect in the molestation of a little girl. This case adds to the cumulative burden of his previous cases, many of which repeat themselves in a bloody orgy of sadistic images in his subconscious.

The film would never have been made had it not been for Sean's deal with United Artists to do *Diamonds Are Forever*. The studio had to pledge to finance any two films of Connery's choice, providing they were limited to budgets of $1 million or less. Connery had wanted to bring *The Offence* to the screen ever since he saw it as a play, *This Story of Yours,* in London in 1968. At one point, he had even considered playing the lead onstage. He set up his own production company—Tantallon Films—to get the creative process working, and then United Artists had to put up the money. The deal also required that Tantallon receive 50 percent of any profits, although both Connery and the studio were somewhat dubious about the box-office viability of this dark and brooding work. Nevertheless, Sean was more enthused about the project than any other film in recent memory. He told a reporter, "This is the perfect vehicle for what I want to do from now on. The Bond films took forever to make and made any kind of artistic rhythm or mood impossible. This film is being done so cheaply, there's no chance we'll be taken to the laundry on it—even though, because of the subject, there's not much chance of an American TV sale." (Connery was wrong on both counts. The film took eight years to show a small profit, and it was seen on television in the United States many years later.)

Connery surrounded himself with a talented group of professionals. He reteamed with Sidney Lumet largely because he was impressed by the director's no-nonsense approach to filming. Connery stated, "We worked so well together on *The Hill* and *The Anderson Tapes*. Sidney has a fine sense of tempo and pace. He knows how to develop ensemble playing as you can tell by films like *Twelve Angry Men,* and he gets into the spirit of a story with uncanny immediacy. . . . Best of all, there's none of the eight or nine takes nonsense for him. You do that and everything becomes very leisurely, the days start to slip away, and before long you start to wonder why you're being paid to get a suntan." Connery insisted that British playwright John Hopkins adapt his own story for the screen. Connery reflected, "For me, it's very revealing—what Hopkins wrote remains word for word with not one thing changing from the original script. . . . It's the most difficult role I've ever taken on."

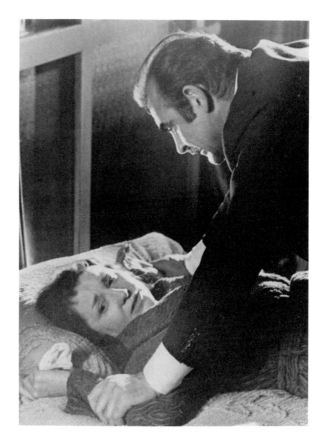

THE OFFENCE Making a frustrated attempt to convey the horrors he has seen to his long-suffering wife (Vivian Merchant).

First-rate acting support was provided by Trevor Howard as the chief inspector and Ian Bannen (Connery's nemesis in *The Hill*) as the suspect who precipitates a tragic fate for himself and Connery. Noted actress Vivien Merchant was cast as Sean's long-suffering spouse in a largely loveless marriage. *The Offence* was originally titled *Something Like the Truth,* which was probably a bit more intriguing than the end result. (The vagueness of *The Offence* title was probably intentional. Does it refer to the crime committed against the young girl? Does it relate to Connery's beating of the suspect? Is it a reference to the offense against Connery's inner mind?) To insure the film lived up to his hopes, Connery was active behind the scenes as well as in front of the camera, often devoting up to twenty hours a day on the grueling and economical shoot, which was completed in just twenty-eight days. (The film came in under schedule and under budget.)

Filming commenced in April 1972 at Twickenham Studios following a rigorous ten-day rehearsal schedule designed to let the cast get "in synch" with their roles and each other. "We couldn't possibly shoot the

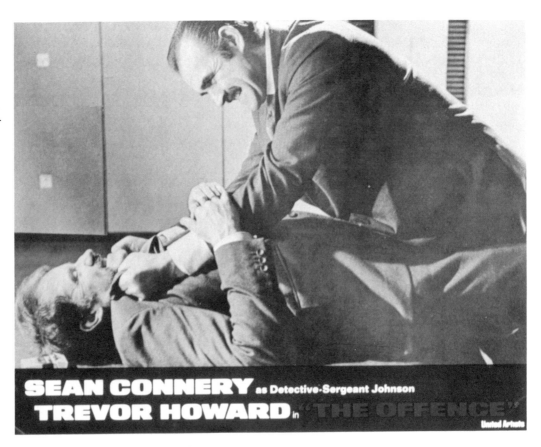

THE OFFENCE Lobby card depicting Connery's assault on Baxter (Ian Bannen).

film without heavy rehearsals," Connery admitted. "Every movement had a special meaning for each of the performers." Location work found the cast and crew in Bracknell NewTown in Berkshire, where Sean found time to sign autographs for the locals, especially children who recognized him as James Bond, despite a receding hairline, bushy mustache, and bulky sheepskin coat. Other locations in and around London were used, primarily for a sequence depicting a large-scale police manhunt.

The film is structured much like the play, with three central "acts," each providing a key confrontation. The first is somewhat surrealistic with intermittent images of Sean brutally beating an unknown man, played by Ian Bannen. We later see Connery in a tense interrogation of the man in a sequence so powerful that John Huston referred to it as some of the best filmmaking he had ever experienced. It is revealed that Bannen is the suspected molester, although the evidence is never more than circumstantial. The scene shows that Connery's hatred of the suspect is only partly motivated by the crime that has been committed. Connery also hates Bannen because he represents Connery's own dark side, which the detective has suppressed for years. This revelation causes Connery to beat the man to death in a fit of rage—a sequence shown later in the film.

THE OFFENCE Australian cable television showed *The Offence* with warning stressing the strong subject matter.

The second confrontation occurs between the detective and his wife. Connery has long been detached from anything other than the peripheral elements of his marriage. Although Merchant begs her husband to allow her to help exorcise his demons, she is subjected to a tirade in which Connery tries to illustrate the numerous horrors haunting his mind. When she becomes ill at the description, he flies into more of a rage. The third and final confrontation occurs as a result of the prisoner's death. Connery must justify his actions to a board of inquiry, headed by Trevor Howard, a sympathetic man who, Connery reasons, has nonetheless been insulated from the problems of the average cop. Ultimately, Howard fails to delve deep enough into Connery's psyche to be able to rationalize the man's actions.

The Offence premiered in London in January 1973 to some of the best critical notices of Sean's career. British critic Marjorie Bilbow expressed the popular consensus best, noting, "When any two characters are locked in spoken combat, the film is both moving and intellectually stimulating." Box-office figures, however, were as grim as the story line. The film fared even worse in the United States, opening in one art house without the benefit of a major ad campaign. However, critics were impressed. Vincent Canby of the *New York Times* wrote, "Connery and Bannen are so fine, and the feelings prompted so intense, that I wouldn't be at all surprised if the [interrogation] sequence could stand on its own as if it were a one-act play. Everything that has gone on before seems to have been so much vamping for time. . . . *The Offence* has one big, carefully worked out, dramatic moment, which is more than most movies have these days." New York's *Daily News* concurred and referred to Connery's performance as "superb." Longtime *Playboy* film critic Bruce Williamson recently commented that, had the film been given proper promotion, it would certainly have resulted in an Oscar nomination for Connery. Again, Sean had to suffer the indignity of having a superb performance appear in a film that went largely unseen. This remarkable example of ensemble acting could well be shown as a textbook example of acting perfection.

Trivia Note: The second film agreed to by United Artists under Sean's *Diamonds Are Forever* contract was never made. There was talk of a movie depicting the life of British explorer Sir Richard Burton, and John Hopkins even delivered a screenplay. However, the $1-million budget was far too little to do justice to this ambitious project, and the idea was shelved.

ZARDOZ

1974

Released by 20th Century-Fox

CAST:
Zed: Sean Connery; *Consuella:* Charlotte Rampling; *May:* Sara Kestelman; *Friend:* John Alderton; *Avalow:* Sally Ann Newton; *Zardoz (Arthur Frayn):* Niall Buggy.

CREDITS:
Written, Produced and Directed by: John Boorman; *Director of Photography:* Geoffrey Unsworth; *Editor:* John Merritt; *Production Designer:* Anthony Pratt; *Music:* David Munrow. *Running Time:* 106 minutes.

Sean Connery has never starred in another film remotely like *Zardoz,* and it is doubtful that either he or anyone else ever will again. If originality inevitably led to success, director John Boorman would have been hailed as the Orson Welles of his day. Unfortunately for Boorman, who also wrote and produced this bizarre trip into the year 2393, the financial failure of his film would lead to its being dismissed from any enduring critical discussions. If Boorman deserves the credit for originating a bold and new concept for the science fiction genre, he must also take the blame for failing to see that the concepts that were so ingrained in his mind could not be easily transplanted into the psyches of moviegoers. Watching *Zardoz* is like spending an evening with a woman with the body of Madonna and the brain of William F. Buckley, Jr.—it's great to look at, but one ultimately grows weary of its pretentious intellectualism. Like every noble failure, however, it could have been worse. (Imagine spending the evening with a woman with the brain of Madonna and the body of William F. Buckley, Jr.!)

Connery's involvement with the production had unusual origins. Directing his first film since receiving an Oscar nomination the previous year for the brilliant *Deliverance,* Boorman had hoped to cast Burt Reynolds (who rocketed to stardom in that film) as the lead in *Zardoz.* Before production could begin, however, Reynolds was hospitalized for a ruptured ulcer and underwent an extended convalescence. Boorman sent the script to Connery, who, as luck would have it, was impatient to make a film with a different slant. Sean later recalled, "After about twenty pages [of the script], I was absolutely caught

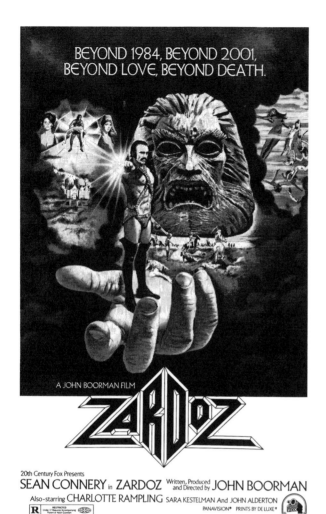

BEYOND 1984, BEYOND 2001,
BEYOND LOVE, BEYOND DEATH.

A JOHN BOORMAN FILM

ZARDOZ

20th Century Fox Presents
SEAN CONNERY in ZARDOZ Written, Produced and Directed by JOHN BOORMAN
Also-starring CHARLOTTE RAMPLING SARA KESTELMAN And JOHN ALDERTON
R RESTRICTED   PANAVISION® PRINTS BY DE LUXE®

ZARDOZ   Pressbook advertisement.

by its originality. It was one of the best ideas I'd come across in ages. . . . What gripped me especially was the direction the people in it were taking in their future existence, as opposed to spaceships and rockets and all that. . . . I'm not a science fiction buff. What does interest me is the possible development of society in centuries to come. The way different levels and types evolve in the script is intriguing and refreshing and could well be true."

The normally cautious actor responded spontaneously to Boorman's desperate need to find a leading man immediately. Connery wasn't used to getting scripts with other actors' fingerprints on them, but ego has never been one of his drawbacks. Boorman was grateful and impressed by Sean's enthusiastic agreement to star in the film and later recalled, "Sean said yes. In the movie business, yes is hedged round with buts and maybes. Not so Connery. He stayed at

my side. When the going got tough, he got stronger. He is loyal and true. His masculine power is so evident that it gives him the confidence to expose his poetic, feminine side. He is a complete man, standing alone, making his own judgments, realized and balanced."

Studios recognized Boorman's film as an avant-garde piece with a limited audience. Warner Bros. and Columbia showed some interest in financing the production, but Boorman turned them down, refusing to relinquish total artistic control. He feared, probably correctly, that studio brass would attempt to remove the very elements that made the story so unique and blend it into another standard futuristic B movie. Eventually, 20th Century-Fox agreed to back the movie, but only if the budget were kept almost impossibly low. To insure this was so, both Boorman and Connery relinquished their normally sizable salaries, opting instead to take a percentage of the profits. Boorman shot the film in County Wicklow in Ireland. Incredibly, despite numerous special effects and extensive action sequences, principal photography wrapped a scant ten weeks later. If only Boorman

ZARDOZ   As Zed, the exterminator.

128

Rare poster art for *Thunderball* (1965)

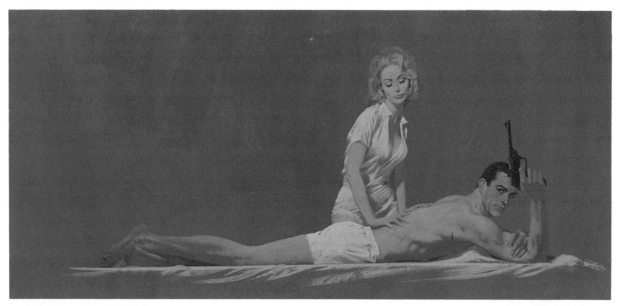

Italian Poster for *Thunderball* (1965)

With Gina Lollobrigida in *Woman of Straw* (1964)

As Robin Hood in *Robin and Marian* (1976)

Sean's only U.S. product endorsement to date.
Circa 1966.

Publicity shot for *Goldfinger* (1964)

With Michael Caine in *The Man Who Would Be King*
(1975)

Belgian poster for *Shalako* (1968)

With Lois Maxwell in *Dr. No* (1962)

As Zed in *Zardoz* (1974)

From the trailer for *Diamonds Are Forever* (1971)

On location for *The Russia House* with Michelle Pfeiffer

Enduring a Japanese press interview for
You Only Live Twice (1967)

With Alec Baldwin in
The Hunt for Red October (1990)

On Ken Adams's fantastic volcano set for *You Only Live Twice*
(1967) with (from left) Lois Maxwell, Akiki Wakabyashi, Karin
Dor, and Mie Hama

As Ramirez in *Highlander* (1986)

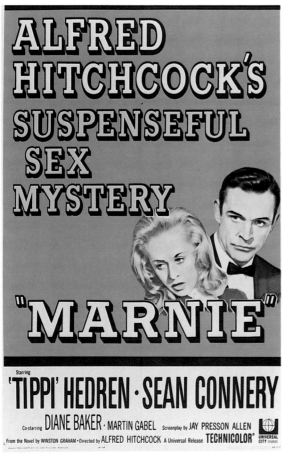

Poster for Hitchcock's *Marnie* (1964)

With Barbara Carrera (left) and Kim Basinger on the set of
Never Say Never Again (1983)

Publicity shot, circa 1964.

As Marshall O'Neill in *Outland* (1981)

Immortalized on the billboard of the Astor Theater in New York's Times Square, 1967

International ad campaigns for *Wrong Is Right* (1982) spoofed Sean's 007 image

With Micheline, 1983

On the set of *Woman of Straw* (1964)

さらば
キューバ

Japanese souvenir program for *Cuba*
(1979)

French lobby card depicting Connery in *The Name of the Rose* (1986)

LE NOM DE LA ROSE

Japanese poster for *Never Say Never
Again* (1983)

With Harrison Ford in *Indiana Jones and the Last Crusade* (1989)

ジョーン・コネリー主演007最新作

SEAN CONNERY is 007 in
ネバーセイ・ネバーアゲイン
NEVER SAY NEVER AGAIN

French reissue poster for *Goldfinger*

British pressbook promotion for *On the Fiddle,* released in the U.S. as *Operation SNAFU*

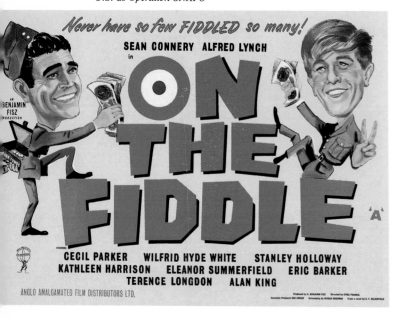

Original Mexican lobby card introducing 007 to fans south of the border

JUST CAUSE   Connery indulging in his greatest passion—golf.

コネリー　　　　　スナイプス

東洋と西洋が
衝突するとき、
誘惑と殺人の
陰謀がめぐらされ、
伝統と権力が
闘いを繰り広げる。
ビジネスは戦争だ。

フィリップ・カウフマン監督作品
ライジング・サン
全世界驚異のベストセラー衝撃の映画化！

RISING SUN

A GOOD MAN IN AFRICA   As Dr. Alex Murray—the last good
man in Africa

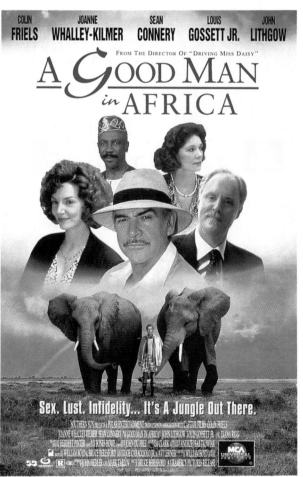

COLIN   JOANNE   SEAN   LOUIS   JOHN
FRIELS   WHALLEY-KILMER   CONNERY   GOSSETT JR.   LITHGOW

FROM THE DIRECTOR OF "DRIVING MISS DAISY"

A GOOD MAN
in AFRICA

Sex. Lust. Infidelity... It's A Jungle Out There.

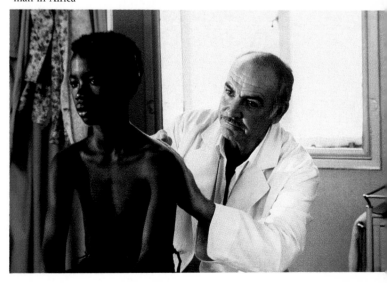

A GOOD MAN IN AFRICA   The poster for the film played up its first-rate
cast.

JUST CAUSE   Connery tries to remain cool in the face of Lawrence Fishburne's threats.

RISING SUN   Connery and Wesley Snipes in the controversial film version of the novel *Rising Sun* (1993)

JUST CAUSE   Armstrong's investigation leads to the Everglades—and the uncovering of a terrifying secret.

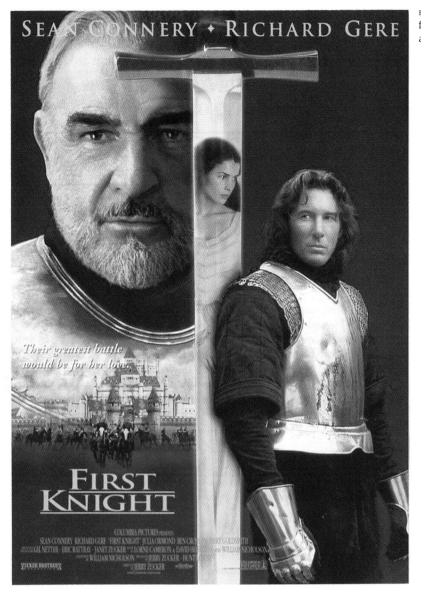

SEAN CONNERY ◆ RICHARD GERE

*Their greatest battle
would be for her love.*

FIRST
KNIGHT

COLUMBIA PICTURES PRESENTS

SEAN CONNERY · RICHARD GERE · FIRST KNIGHT · JULIA ORMOND · BEN CROSS · JERRY GOLDSMITH

GIL NETTER · ERIC RATTRAY · JANEY ZUCKER · LORNE CAMERON & DAVID HOSELTON and WILLIAM NICHOLSON

WILLIAM NICHOLSON · JERRY ZUCKER · HUNT LOWRY

ZUCKER BROTHERS · JERRY ZUCKER

FIRST KNIGHT   The largest-budgeted film in which Connery had yet appeared

FIRST KNIGHT   Imploring Guinevere (Julia Ormond) to ''marry the king, but love the man''

FIRST KNIGHT   As Arthur of Camelot

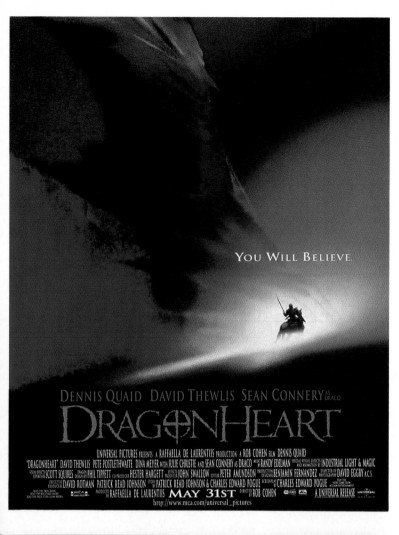

DRAGONHEART   Poster art.

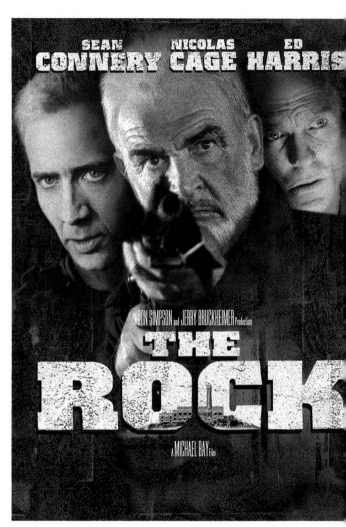

THE ROCK   Poster art

JUST CAUSE   Sean Connery today—the icon

ZARDOZ   Zed infiltrates the sanctum of the god Zardoz.

ZARDOZ With Charlotte Rampling.

ZARDOZ Connery and Charlotte Rampling give the ultimate "gift" to the Immortals: death.

could have brought such conciseness to the rambling screenplay.

Zardoz is complex enough to make *2001: A Space Odyssey* seem as simplistic as *Plan 9 From Outer Space*. John Boorman had to encourage critics to attend *two* press screenings, as a single viewing might only serve to confuse rather than enlighten members of the audience. Extensive press guides were given to critics, each containing a mini-dictionary of "Zardozian" language to help sort out the different characters and terms. The tactic only baffled reviewers and audiences alike. People do not want to feel as if they are taking a final exam when they go to the movies, and *Zardoz* required a detailed study of the handout material if one were to grasp its message.

The story opens three hundred years in the future. The world as we know it is gone, presumably depleted from years of pollution, greed, crime, and chaos. The intellectuals—known as Eternals—have long since shielded themselves in an area called the Vortex, which is impenetrable due to a transparent force field. The Eternals are intent on controlling the Brutals—those outside the Vortex. These desperate people struggle to survive among the ruins of the earth. To keep the Brutals' population in check, they are hunted, killed, or made to harvest food for the inhabitants of the Vortex by a band of savage warriors, Exterminators, who pray to a giant flying head of stone known as Zardoz, little realizing that the being is a trick created by the Eternals. Among the nuggets of wisdom this granite savior spews forth are such memorable lines as "The penis is bad, the gun is good." (One occasionally suspects the script was ghostwritten by that pathetic antiporn feminist, Andrea Dworkin.)

Within the Vortex, however, life is not a bowl of cherries. Having found the secret to eternal life, the inhabitants have grown tired of the paradise to which they are confined. The men have all lost their will, and the society is dominated by females who, if they are not actually identified as lesbians, can best be described as women in "comfortable shoes." Overt sexuality has become obsolete, and people display affection through a spiritual meeting of the minds, as thought control is also prevalent within the Vortex. Death is not permitted or possible, although most of the Eternals now crave it. Crimes are punishable by a fate worse than death—no, not an endless series of Scientology or Amway seminars, but an existence in perennial senility (Eternals also do not age unless sentenced to do so as punishment.)

Into this bizarre scenario comes Sean Connery's Zed, an Exterminator who has managed to pierce the force shield protecting the Vortex. The Eternals' initial reaction is to kill him, but they are fascinated by this barbarian, and he soon revives their long-dormant feelings of sexuality and revolution. The hopelessly convoluted plot ends with Connery bringing about the destruction of the Vortex, which in essence enables nature to correct the imbalances the Eternals had created. Zed then hides from the Exterminators with his lover (the sensuous Charlotte Rampling), who bears him a son. The film ends with a haunting image of Connery and Rampling aging decades in seconds and ultimately reverting to dust. The abominations of the future have at last been replaced by a return to normality.

Zardoz is a difficult film to watch, much less comprehend. However, what was incomprehensible in theaters can be studied at leisure on video, and this does allow for a great deal more insight. It's not easy to recommend the film, yet it has too many merits to dismiss. For one, Boorman did succeed in creating an original story populated by offbeat characters, some of whom bore you to tears, while others generate substantial interest. The film has ingredients linked to everything from *2001* to *The Wizard of Oz* (which provides the explanation for the movie's title). It also recalls elements of *The Prisoner,* Patrick McGoohan's classic 1968 TV series. Boorman works wonders with the $1.1-million budget, which probably couldn't pay for the catering on a film today. *Zardoz*'s expensive look is reinforced by the special effects and production designer Anthony Pratt's memorable sets. There is also a highly intriguing musical score by David Munrow, who used medieval instruments to reinforce the movie's sense of timelessness. Equally memorable is Geoffrey Unsworth's magnificent cinematography.

The performances are incidental to the plot, and Connery's character is not particularly interesting, being merely the catalyst for the events that unfold. Clothed in what can only be described as a distracting red adult diaper, Connery initially appears to be suffering from incontinence. With his drooping mustache and bandolier of ammunition strung across his chest, he resembles a combination of Pancho Villa and Baby Huey. To his credit, however, Sean's physical prowess overcomes these drawbacks, and he is the very essence of masculinity. The supporting cast is adequate, and the primary fault lies in the screenplay, which is often disjointed and boring. After preview screenings left many critics confused, a brief prologue was added showing the character of Zardoz (poorly played by Niall Buggy) "clarifying" what is to follow. This did not impress critic Rex Reed, who bellowed

that "wild horses" couldn't drag him back to the theater "kicking and bleeding" to experience the reworked film.

Most critics were somewhat kinder, proclaiming the project an impressive failure. *Variety* compared the movie to the comet Kohoutek, in that it promised more than it delivered, and stated that *Zardoz* "remains a very unique if terminally fumbled foray into abstract melodrama." The *New York Times* found that the "major attributes are technical . . . more confusing than exciting," and in a rare pan, called Connery "moodily energetic but unimpressive." The New York *Daily News* was more enthused and called *Zardoz* "a rich, exciting film. . . . There aren't many productions that are this consistently good from top to bottom."

Nevertheless, audiences were alienated and Boorman's film disappeared from movie houses quickly, adding another frustrating failure to Connery's checkered box-office record. In fairness, the movie was unfortunately released too late for the psychedelic sixties craze that made *2001* a cult classic, and it preceded the sci-fi rage initiated several years later by *Star Wars.* Yet, *Zardoz* remains impressive on many levels, and Connery and Boorman deserve praise for at least attempting to revitalize the science fiction genre. However, the teaser ad for the publicity campaign read, "Zardoz says, 'I have seen the future, and it doesn't work,' " and in the end, neither did the movie.

THE TERRORISTS

U.K. TITLE: *RANSOM*

1974

Released by 20th Century-Fox

CAST:

Nils Tahlvik: Sean Connery; *Petrie:* Ian McShane; *Captain Denver:* Norman Bristow; *Bert:* John Cording; *Mrs. Palmer:* Isabel Dean; *Ferris:* William Fox.

CREDITS:

Director: Casper Wrede; *Producer:* Peter Rawley; *Screenplay:* Paul Wheeler; *Director of Photography:* Sven Nykvist; *Editor:* Thelma Connell; *Music:* Jerry Goldsmith. *Running Time:* 94 minutes.

THE TERRORISTS   German theater poster.

The post-007 box-office slump of Sean Connery continued with this minor entry whose subject matter exploited a contemporary fear: air piracy coupled with international terrorism. Distressed by the tendency of many governments to surrender to the demands of extremist groups, producer Peter Rawley sought to make a cinematic statement about one man's desire to take a stand and protect international law and order. Connery met Rawley at a cocktail party for the new president of Columbia Pictures, and weeks later, when Rawley was pondering who should play the lead in his film, the recent encounter with Connery brought the actor to mind. His suggestion was seconded by John Boorman, the director of *Zardoz,* who had read the script to Rawley's film and had been planning to suggest Connery for the lead. Rawley conferred with Casper Wrede, who was signed to direct *The Terrorists,* and he, too, agreed.

Filming commenced in January 1974 amid sub-zero temperatures, heavy fog, and snowfalls at Fornebu International Airport in Oslo, Norway. Seventy percent of principal photography would take place here, with interiors shot at Shepperton Studios

THE TERRORISTS   *The Terrorists* was released as *Ransom* in England.

THE TERRORISTS   As Nils Tahlvik.

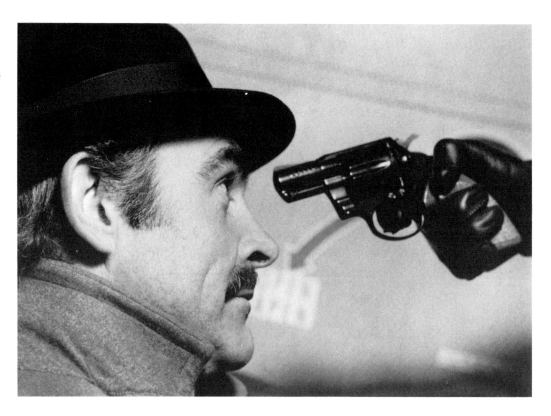

THE TERRORISTS Sean gets
a lesson in terrorist
negotiation tactics.

in Britain. Connery flew directly from the set of *Zardoz* in Ireland to Oslo for a ten-week shoot. During a warming trend, the filmmakers faced a crisis of rapidly melting snow, which necessitated the importation of megatons of a salt mixture as a substitute. When this was insufficient, chemicals were used to turn the fog into snow. Additionally, the Norwegian pilots union threatened to strike in protest of what they felt might be a film glamorizing hijacking. The union was assured by the filmmakers and the government that this was not the case. Connery also tried to appease the protestors by stating, "The film deals with how to prevent a hijack, not perform one. It does not accuse Norway—rather we are using Norway as a location so that the snow and subzero temperatures add to the dramatic effect of the story."

While on location in Oslo, Connery could neither golf nor ski (the latter due to insurance regulations). He spent a good deal of time playing tennis indoors with costar Ian McShane. Once, a dinner companion of Sean's was approached by a middle-aged woman who asked if he were dining with James Bond. "No," was the reply, "I am dining with *Sean Connery!*" "Oh," remarked the lady with obvious disappointment, "he *looks* like James Bond!" Connery took it all in stride and commented later, "There was a time I had to prostitute myself to pay the bills. I am grateful to the Bond films for ending that."

During filming, Sean met famed Soviet novelist Alexander Solzhenitsyn, who was then in the public eye due to his banishment from the U.S.S.R. and the publication of *The Gulag Archipelago*. Solzhenitsyn was attending a screening of *One Day in the Life of Ivan Denisovich*, a film directed by Casper Wrede and based on the novelist's haunting story.

The screenplay for *The Terrorists* is only mildly engaging, and Connery's presence and performance are the most distinguishing aspects of a not overly distinguished thriller. Norwegian police chief Connery is attempting to thwart a group of anarchists who have kidnapped the British ambassador to Norway and two of his staff. The ransom demanded is the freeing of several prisoners from a British jail, as well as safe passage out of Norway for the kidnappers. Several subplots involve hijackings, double crosses, and Connery's insistence that one cannot negotiate with terrorists. The film culminates in a rather abrupt, unremarkable climax.

Connery gets to display all too little of his trademark wit. (He breaks off heated negotiations with the villains by calmly stating, "I'm going to lunch.") As with many of his films from this era, Sean's ability to turn a wisecrack is downplayed in favor of his serious side. Positive elements include a good rapport between Connery and villainous Ian McShane, conveyed primarily through their cat-and-mouse negotiations over a two-way radio, impressive cinematography that captures the icy beauty of Norway, and competent direction by Casper Wrede.

The Terrorists debuted in London in February 1975 following an initial run in Rome. Reviewers—those who did not ignore the film altogether—unanimously panned it as pedestrian and falling below the usual Connery standard. Sean received the usual compensatory notices—i.e., his performance was the only noteworthy element. When the picture had its delayed opening in the United States, it was the bottom half of double bills—certainly a first, and hopefully a last, for any film in which Sean Connery has received star billing.

THE TERRORISTS   Connery assumes command of the operation.

MURDER ON THE ORIENT EXPRESS

1974

Released by Paramount Pictures

CAST:

Hercule Poirot: Albert Finney; *Mrs. Hubbard:* Lauren Bacall; *Bianchi:* Martin Balsam; *Greta:* Ingrid Bergman; *Countess Andrenyi:* Jacqueline Bisset; *Pierre:* Jean-Pierre Cassel; *Colonel Arbuthnot:* Sean Connery; *Beddoes:* John Gielgud; *Princess Dragomiroff:* Wendy Hiller; *McQueen:* Anthony Perkins; *Mary Debenham:* Vanessa Redgrave; *Hildegarde:* Rachel Roberts; *Ratchett:* Richard Widmark; *Count Andrenyi:* Michael York; *Hardman:* Colin Blakely; *Doctor:* George Coulouris; *Foscarelli:* Denis Quilley.

CREDITS:

Director: Sidney Lumet; *Producers:* John Brabourne and Richard Goodwin; *Screenplay:* Paul Dehn, based on the novel by Agatha Christie; *Director of Photography:* Geoffrey Unsworth; *Editor:* Anne V. Coates; *Production Design and Costumes:* Tony Walton; *Music:* Richard Rodney Bennett. *Running Time:* 128 minutes.

Having experienced the disappointment of three consecutive box-office bombs—*The Offence, Zardoz,* and *The Terrorists*—Sean Connery reteamed with the prolific Sidney Lumet for a high-profile, surefire hit: an elaborate adaptation of Agatha Christie's classic mystery *Murder on the Orient Express.* The famed novelist had inexplicably rejected any attempts to film this popular work since it was initially published in 1934. If she had held out to insure the screen version would be given a first-class production, the strategy worked. *Murder on the Orient Express* was referred to in its advertisements as "The Who's Who of the Whodunnit." For once, this was not a publicist's exaggeration. If any film could rightfully boast an all-star cast, this was it.

Lumet was a curious choice for director. He generally specialized in gritty, slice-of-life dramas that were light-years away from the world of Agatha Christie. However, he professed to be delighted at the opportunity to put aside social relevance and simply have

some fun. He explained that he wanted to embellish the film with a spirit of "gaiety, humor, and the very best fakery. . . . There is truth in Agatha Christie, but never reality. We are dealing with a kind of myth, straight out of the thirties, and I have even used the filmmaking style of that period." Indeed, Tony Walton's opulent production design meticulously re-created the actual Orient Express, which by 1974 had fallen from grace and had been reduced to a glorified cattle car. (The train has since been restored to its former elegance.) Walton, in addition to creating the elaborate costumes from the 1930s, actually brought in various sections of the original train and put them together like a gigantic jigsaw puzzle at Elstree Studios in England. Both exterior and interior production designs were superbly done and transfixed the viewer in the atmosphere of the period.

Though the film is filled with stars, only one actor is central at all times: Albert Finney, playing Christie's famed detective Hercule Poirot. If Sidney Lumet was an odd but inspired choice for director, certainly this was no less the case for Finney as Poirot. Only thirty-eight at the time, to portray the much older sleuth, Finney underwent a two-hour makeup session each day to fit him with a putty nose, creamed and dyed hair, and thirty pounds of body padding to simulate Poirot's comfortable girth. Finney emerged virtually unrecognizable thanks to the efforts of Charles Parker, one of the world's leading makeup artists.

The alphabetical roster supporting Finney's robust performance reads like a casting director's dream: Lauren Bacall, Martin Balsam, Ingrid Bergman, Jacqueline Bisset, John Gielgud, Anthony Perkins, Vanessa Redgrave, Richard Widmark, Michael York and other notables; all were murder suspects on this ill-fated journey of the Orient Express. For Bergman, this was the vehicle that lured her back before the cameras after she had retired from films. She recalled, "A year ago I vowed I would not make another film. There were no good parts coming along anymore. But when I read the script and discussed the concept, I changed my mind. A lady is allowed to, isn't she? . . . I felt absolutely awed when we first gathered together for a cast and crew party." Likewise, Richard Widmark had retired to his ranch the previous year—presumably for good. However, no one could refuse the honor of participating in the all-star film event of the year. Connery confessed, "It was the chance to join an incredible cast. . . . It's all very stylish, very much in the vein of the Bond films." (Perhaps his triumph over Robert Shaw in the fight aboard the Orient Express in *From Russia With Love* had made

Sean wax sentimental for a return trip aboard the legendary train.)

The plot is loosely based on the famed Lindbergh baby kidnapping, for which Bruno Hauptmann was convicted and sentenced to death for the abduction and killing. As Lumet's film opens, the crime is re-created through use of murky images, fleeting glimpses of those involved, and newspaper headlines. The fictional crime of the story finds the perpetrators escaping after the child is found murdered. The victim's family and acquaintances all fall to tragic fates as a direct result of the crime. The scene then switches to eccentric Belgian detective Hercule Poirot, who is returning to France following his "cracking" of another case of international importance. He is invited to travel in the first-class Calais Coach aboard the Orient Express—a luxurious car that is segregated from the rest of the train. The sophisticated but seemingly unrelated individuals aboard each arouse Poirot's natural curiosity. The most controversial is a gangster named Ratchett (Widmark), who unsuccessfully appeals to Poirot for protection following the receipt of a dozen different death threats.

As the train lies immobile in a snowstorm in the Balkan Mountains, Ratchett is murdered in the night. Poirot investigates and discovers that the man was the brains behind the infamous kidnapping in the beginning of the film. Poirot slowly, meticulously interrogates everyone aboard the train. Each seems strange in his or her own way, but all seem to have a valid

MURDER ON THE ORIENT EXPRESS   With (from left) Wendy Hiller, Rachel Roberts, Lauren Bacall, Anthony Perkins, and Martin Balsam.

MURDER ON THE ORIENT EXPRESS   Acting suspicious with Vanessa Redgrave.

alibi. Poirot finally discovers that each had a link to the family of the kidnapped child, and each had a reason for revenge. The surprising conclusion finds that Ratchett was murdered by *all* of the passengers, who had conspired to pull off this elaborate scenario. Poirot, however, agrees to lead the police on a wild-goose chase as he sympathizes with these wretched souls and the way they have suffered because of the child's murder.

Murder on the Orient Express is a good, solid old-fashioned mystery that succeeds in holding the viewer's interest despite the stuffy atmosphere. The film could easily be transformed into a play, and Lumet directs it as though it were. Aside from a few brief exposition sequences that take place outdoors, the viewer is confined within the train compartments along with the murder suspects. Paul (*Goldfinger*) Dehn's screenplay is occasionally too talky and meandering, and this is not helped by Finney's mumbling (the only valid complaint in an otherwise virtuoso performance), allowing vital clues to be lost to the

audience. However, the slow pace is actually refreshing in an age in which the main objective is to cut through the talk and get to the action. Lumet proves he handles a "fun" assignment as well as he does heavy dramas.

Not surprisingly, the cast is marvelous to behold. A great deal of work went into assuring that no egos were bruised by having one actor outshine another. Bergman, however, is particularly fascinating as an old maid religious fanatic, for which she won her third Oscar. (At the Academy Award ceremony, Ingrid sauntered to the podium and said in a ho-hum voice, "It's always nice to win an Oscar.") Richard Widmark is impressive in the briefest of the roles as the murder victim (has anyone ever noticed how much he sounds like Frank Sinatra?) and John Gielgud is excellent as—what else?—a gentleman's gentleman. Connery more than holds his own as a

temperamental retired army colonel who is having an affair with Vanessa Redgrave. The part allows him the joy of hamming it up along with his peers, but the role is no more significant than any of the others. For the first time in years, however, he looks as if he's enjoying a part. He later related that his appearance in the film—toupéed with an elegant mustache—was inspired by a real-life acquaintance: "I remembered a character I'd met in the navy, an officer who had iron kind of gray hair and parted on what we used to call 'the woman's side.' The men always used to part their hair on the right. And I remember he got quite upset when that was pointed out. And that was the reason I fancied putting that kind of hairpiece on."

Murder on the Orient Express was an international hit and spawned a number of Agatha Christie film adaptations, none of which were as successful. The movie had stiff competition from the other all-star blockbusters of 1974—*Earthquake* and *The Towering Inferno*—but held its own against these special-effects-laden spectaculars. In addition to Ingrid Bergman's Oscar, nominations also went to Albert Finney for Best Actor, Paul Dehn's screenplay adaptation, Geoffrey Unsworth's glorious photography, Tony Walton's costume design, and the lush musical score of Richard Rodney Bennett. Curiously, Walton's superb art direction did not get a nomination.

MURDER ON THE ORIENT EXPRESS   Poirot (Albert Finney, center) confronts the suspects: (from left) Jean-Pierre Cassel, Anthony Perkins. Vanessa Redgrave, Connery, Ingrid Bergman, George Coulouris, Rachel Roberts, Wendy Hiller, Denis Quilley, Michael York, Jacqueline Bisset, Lauren Bacall, and Martin Balsam.

THE WIND AND THE LION

1975

Released by United Artists

CAST:

Raisuli: Sean Connery; *Eden:* Candice Bergen; *Theodore Roosevelt:* Brian Keith; *Secretary Hay:* John Huston; *Gummere:* Geoffrey Lewis; *Jerome:* Steve Kanaly; *Chadwick:* Roy Jenson; *Bashaw:* Vladek Sheybal.

CREDITS:

Director and Writer: John Milius; *Producer:* Herb Jaffe; *Director of Photography:* Billy Williams; *Editor:* Bob Wolfe; *Production Designer:* Gil Parrondo; *Music:* Jerry Goldsmith. *Running Time:* 119 minutes.

HISTORY HAS WRITTEN MANY GREAT ADVENTURES . . .

AND MANY GREAT LOVES . . .

"GONE WITH THE WIND"

"LAWRENCE OF ARABIA"

"DR. ZHIVAGO"

BUT NOW, SWEEPING ALL BEFORE IT—

"THE WIND AND THE LION"

Thus read the immodest ad campaign for Sean Connery's epic adventure that was to provide him with one of the favorite roles of his career. The film is a liberal interpretation of an actual historical incident. According to the movie, on October 15, 1904 (contrary to the date the film's own trailer refers to), half the world nearly went to war, incited by the unprovoked kidnapping of an American woman—Eden Pedicaris—and her family in Tangier. This outrageous act was perpetrated by a renegade Muslim chieftain, Mulay Achmed el Raisuli, commonly referred to as The Lion. Raisuli wanted hostages as pawns to win control over his own tiny kingdom from Arab dignitaries as well as European and American imperialists. In a tense situation similar to the 1979 taking of U.S. hostages in Iran, Americans seethed with anger. Pres. Teddy Roosevelt, known to Arabs as The Wind, kept nationalist tempers burning back home, in part to help his election campaign. Finally, he ordered a detachment of marines to "invade" Morocco and free the captives.

The Wind and the Lion documents this turn-of-the-century action/adventure/love story, leaving out a few minor details, such as that most of the events depicted on-screen never occurred. Though studio press kits promised the film was "well grounded in authenticity . . . reflecting a respect for history," director-screenwriter John Milius was taken to task for the dramatic license he took in re-creating events of the day. (Perhaps Milius used Oliver Stone as a researcher!) Milius defended his script, explaining that his main goal was to provide a sweeping entertainment: "I approached *The Wind and the Lion* as a David Lean film, to do that style, on a grand scale."

Foremost among the inaccuracies is the fact that the kidnapping victim was actually a *Mr. Ion Pedicaris,* a bald, overweight semi-invalid in his seventies. In an inspired bit of casting, Milius decided there was only one logical person suitable to portray this victim: Candice Bergen. In another minor bit of fact-tampering, the real-life Mr. Pedicaris's fellow hostage—his stepson—is replaced with two young children, both the on-screen offspring of Bergen. Likewise, the invasion of Morocco by U.S. Marines never happened, and the actual crisis was resolved rather unspectacularly (and uncinematically) by the Raisuli's order to free the two men. Roosevelt, ever the opportunist, saw to it that the Raisuli received a stern telegram— "Pedicaris alive or Raisuli dead"—*after* being informed the hostages were quite safe.

The Wind and the Lion is prime example of the debate that goes on to this day regarding filmmakers' abilities to take creative license with facts. No one denies their right to do so, but films such as *Born on the Fourth of July* and *JFK* came under fire for not admitting the extent to which historical information has been altered. Regardless of one's stand on the issue, the fact remains that *The Wind and the Lion* is an exceptionally entertaining film, one that helped Sean Connery retain his status as one of the screen's most dynamic and charismatic leading men. Disguised behind a flowing gray beard and Arabic wardrobe, the turban-clad Connery presented an image as far removed from that of 007 as could be imagined. "It would be rather silly for a fifty-year-old Arab to have a James Bond look, wouldn't it?" asked Connery rhetorically. "I didn't know a great deal about Islam before the picture. In fact, I was quite ignorant about it—but I've been learning. Raisuli is a very interesting role . . . very different. Whether he was a moral man or not is difficult to judge. However, he's been written into the picture as a well-rounded, full-fledged man who lived by the Islamic code—and I find that stimulating."

THE WIND AND THE LION   Japanese souvenir program.

141

THE WIND AND THE
LION   The barbarian
Raisuli (Connery) tries
to entice Candice
Bergen to a civilized
game of chess.

THE WIND AND THE LION   With Candice Bergen.

One must admire director Milius for having the foresight and confidence to cast Connery against type in the role of Raisuli, an old-fashioned warrior out of step with a new age—a hero to his people in an age when heroes were in short supply. The natural inclination would have been to cast an Omar Sharif type. However, the role is enacted magnificently—making Raisuli one of those larger-than-life characters in the Connery repertoire. Critics agreed enthusiastically that Sean was a delight to watch, even if one did amusingly note, "Allah must have been puzzled to hear a sheik talking with a Scottish accent!" Sean embellishes his character with a wide range of emotions: he can be terrifyingly brutal and unpredictable—a man who feels at ease at decapitation, but is humbled at the embarrassment of falling from his steed. At other times, he displays childlike innocence and sensitivity, as well as a dry wit. Connery enjoyed working with Milius, and this enriched his interpretation of the role. He commented at the time, "I think John is very clever, very talented, and find him refreshing."

Milius had tried to bring *The Wind and the Lion* to fruition for over a decade. Eventually, he secured a budget of $4 million, but his skillful filmmaking gives the impression the movie cost many times that sum. Shooting began in August 1974 on Spanish soil, doubling for the Moroccan locales. The locations included Gabo de Gata, where Sean had made *The Hill* almost ten years earlier. The film wrapped a mere

THE WIND AND THE LION As Raisuli.

THE WIND AND THE LION   Matching wits with Candice Bergen.

thirteen weeks later—an astounding accomplishment considering the epic quality of the finished product. *Wind* has so many magnificent images that linger in the mind, it is impossible to discuss them all. Among the highlights is the terrifying opening sequence in which Bergen and her children enjoy a peaceful afternoon tea only to be attacked by the Raisuli's savage hordes. Also memorable are the large-scale battle scenes that rival any in *Lawrence of Arabia,* the storming of the bashaw's palace by U.S. Marines, and some engaging cinematography by Billy Williams.

Aside from its technical merits, the film offers an abundance of terrific performances besides Sean's. In a role originally set for Faye Dunaway, Candice Bergen began with this movie a cycle of quality films that finally led to her quieting the many jokes that she had less animation than her father Edgar Bergen's dummy, Charlie McCarthy. Her revulsion to Connery's character in *Wind* ultimately turns to admiration and passion. To Bergen's credit, she makes this

unlikely occurrence ring true. Perhaps her motivation can be found in a rather surprising statement she made to the press: "I think somewhere all women want to get kidnapped and taken away by a handsome but benevolent kidnapper and taken care of all their lives." (Unfortunately, Candy, most women who are kidnapped do not find themselves at the mercy of a Sean Connery clone, but more likely a sexually frustrated, fat, balding hulk with name of Murray.) Another gem of a performance is Brian Keith's interpretation of Teddy Roosevelt. Keith looks every bit like his historical counterpart, with many of his lines derived from actual Roosevelt speeches. Critics moaned that Connery and Keith share no scenes together, but Milius viewed it as being more effective if these two remarkably similar "old-order chivalrous men yelled at each other across the vastness of the ocean." Keith steals all of his scenes and makes it all the more curious that Hollywood has ignored him in big-screen films.

The Wind and the Lion was only a modest hit, given

the upbeat reviews. It's difficult to say why audiences did not respond more favorably, except perhaps that they were preoccupied with the *Jaws* phenomenon, which occurred shortly on the wings of *Wind.* Nevertheless, the movie helped Connery reaffirm his heroic image in a role far removed from Bond. He soon began making plans to act under the direction of one of his costars from *The Wind and the Lion,* John Huston, in the legendary director's long-awaited "dream project," *The Man Who Would Be King.*

Trivia Note: The bashaw in *The Wind and the Lion* is played by Vladek Sheybal, Kronsteen in *From Russia With Love.* Sheybal always found it amusing that he was cast in Milius's film as Connery's brother, since the two men could not resemble each other less.

THE WIND AND THE LION   Lobby card depicting Connery's preparations for decapitating criminals.

THE MAN WHO WOULD BE KING

1975

Released by Allied Artists

CAST:

Daniel Dravot: Sean Connery; *Peachy Carnehan:* Michael Caine; *Rudyard Kipling:* Christopher Plummer; *Billy Fish:* Saeed Jaffrey; *Kafu-Selim:* Karroum Ben Bouih; *Commissioner:* Jack May; *Ottah:* Doghmi Larbi; *Roxanne:* Shakira Caine.

CREDITS:

Director: John Huston; *Producer:* John Foreman; *Screenplay:* John Huston and Gladys Hill; *Director of Photography:* Oswald Morris; *Editor:* Russell Lloyd; *Production Designer:* Alexander Trauner; *Music:* Maurice Jarre. *Running Time:* 129 minutes.

"I think it's one of the greatest adventure stories ever written. It has excitement, color, spectacle, and humor. It also has some spiritual meaning, which becomes clear toward the end of the story. Besides that, it's a wonderful story of the warm friendship between two men—two tough and likable rogues whose loyalty is to each other and their own view of integrity." Thus spoke John Huston as he prepared to realize his long-standing dream of bringing an adaptation of Rudyard Kipling's *The Man Who Would Be King* to the screen in an epic, $8-million production. Huston had read the novella a quarter of a century before and had hoped to film it in the 1950s with Clark Gable and Humphrey Bogart. When Bogart died, Huston shelved the project until 1964, when he briefly entertained the idea of teaming Richard Burton and Peter O'Toole in the starring roles. This, too, failed to materialize. While filming *The Mackintosh Man* with Paul Newman in 1972, Huston discussed the project as a possible vehicle for another Newman-Redford teaming. Newman wisely turned down the offer, plausibly stating that audiences would never accept him and Redford as British rogues. It was Newman, however, who encouraged Huston to approach Sean Connery and Michael Caine for the leads.

With producer John Foreman, who discovered a great amount of research Huston had completed years before, the veteran director was finally able to obtain financing and sign his stars. The logistics for the filming were considerable. Huston originally intended to shoot the movie in Afghanistan because little had changed there in the last century, but he discovered "that's just the trouble. When we found out what it would cost to haul crews and equipment over nonroads into those mountains, we knew we were out of luck." Eventually Huston settled on Morocco because it had an antiquated atmosphere along with modern facilities and conveniences. Additionally, as Foreman described it, the country has a "timeless quality" that allowed the countryside to duplicate India, Afghanistan, and the long-vanished nation of Kafiristan. A crew of two hundred technicians created the ancient city of Sikandergul, where the heroes establish themselves as semigods. Conditions were rugged in the sweltering heat, and Connery would occasionally retire to his "dressing room"—in reality a minibus that he had personally driven to the set. At night, there was little to do, and at one point Connery found himself watching reruns of *The Untouchables* dubbed into Arabic! Yet, morale on the set remained high—it was as if all knew they were working on a winner.

To this day, Sean Connery professes that filming *The Man Who Would Be King* was the happiest professional experience of his career. The opportunity to star with old friend Michael Caine instilled an enthusiasm in Connery that had been missing for many years. He recalled, "The cast got on famously. We prepared a week in advance of shooting and then came on set and showed Huston what we had worked out. Then he would move it around. It was a collective operation—most enjoyable." In fact, Huston so liked the improvisations Connery and Caine made that he rarely offered any directorial advice. (Caine would later joke that Huston felt that with the salaries the duo had commanded, they should *know* how to act!) After a while, Huston ceased referring to his actors as Sean and Michael, calling them instead by their characters' names: Danny and Peachy.

On location, Connery and Caine would try to entertain themselves and their "better halves." (Connery formally announced on the set that he and Micheline had married months before, and Caine's wife, Shakira, was making her film debut as an Indian beauty whose marriage to Danny leads to the heroes' downfall.) Caine recalled an evening when the two men tried to have a boys night out: "We were in this little town at the edge of the Sahara, and there was nothing to do at night except go to this disco. But it was men dancing with men because women aren't allowed out at night. So we're standing at the bar watching all these guys dancing, when Sean leans

LONG LIVE ADVENTURE!
Rudyard Kipling's epic of splendor, spectacle and high adventure at the top of a legendary world.

Emanuel L. Wolf presents

Sean Connery and Michael Caine
Christopher Plummer

In the John Huston-John Foreman film **The Man Who Would Be King**

Also starring **Saeed Jaffrey** and introducing **Shakira Caine**

Screenplay by **John Huston** and **Gladys Hill** based on a story by **Rudyard Kipling**   Music composed and conducted by Maurice Jarre

Produced by **John Foreman** Directed by **John Huston**   Production Services by Royal Service Company Technicolor® Panavision®   A Persky-Bright/Devon Picture

An Allied Artists-Columbia Pictures Production ⊂ID An Allied Artists Release   ORIGINAL SOUNDTRACK ALBUM AVAILABLE ON CAPITOL RECORDS.

PG PARENTAL GUIDANCE SUGGESTED
SOME MATERIAL MAY NOT BE
SUITABLE FOR PRE-TEENAGERS

THE MAN WHO WOULD BE KING   Pressbook advertisment.

over and says to me, 'Do you mind if I dance with your driver? Mine's too ugly!' " Sean later reflected, "The great pleasure in making movies is when one has a subject that one is totally buoyant about and everyone is enthusiastic and you have a very good crew, and in this case one had a marvelous cast with Michael, Christopher Plummer, and John Huston. . . . Making the film was very arduous and difficult under normal circumstances, but . . . I enjoyed very much working with professionals. I'd be on the floor laughing with Michael because he's one of the best joke tellers I know. It was a great kind of pleasure—it was a thrill it succeeded."

The plot of *The Man Who Would Be King* is deceivingly simple at first glance. Danny (Connery) and Peachy (Caine) are two rough but charming rogues who, subsequent to their military careers, play elaborate con games among the well-to-dos in India. In an inspired bit, the Huston–Gladys Hill screenplay writes Rudyard Kipling into the story as a confidant of the men. As played by Christopher Plummer, he's a

warm and endearing man. Danny and Peachy announce their grand scheme: to travel through the treacherous Khyber Pass and locate the faraway kingdom of Kafiristan. Here, they will impress the natives with their military skills and the power of their rifles. They will then depose the resident chieftain and unite the various tribes, establishing themselves as kings. After looting the people of their treasures, they will return to civilization as rich men. The plan works magnificently, and Danny is looked upon as a god when the tribesmen believe that a miracle saves him from death in a fierce battle. The rogues uncover a collection of priceless jewels, and Peachy advises that they should take the money and run, but Danny has now come to believe his destiny is in ruling these naive people. With an increasingly pompous attitude, he insists on marrying a local beauty and in doing so arouses the suspicions of the populace, who feel a true god would never cohabitate with a mere mortal. When a bite from his bride draws blood, Danny is uncovered as mortal. The tribesmen revolt and, after

exploit the people, covet their women, steal their treasures, and destroy a culture—all in the name of money. It is to Connery's and Caine's credit and charm that audiences empathize with these charlatans when justice finally catches up to them. Connery and Caine are obviously having the time of their lives, and the resulting chemistry on-screen is what great acting is all about. Both give performances that are among the best of their careers. As for Huston, one can only say that he successfully accomplished the dream he had envisioned for so many years. Huston, so often called a "man's director" due to the classic adventures he has brought to the screen, is in his element, and the movie provides many unforgettable moments.

The Man Who Would Be King was a renaissance project for both Huston and Connery. Both men had drifted through largely indifferent films that many felt were below their talents. (Connery's well-received *The Wind and the Lion* had not yet been released). Sean was but a bit player in *Murder on the Orient Express* and had had three straight box-office bombs prior to that. Huston, too, was floundering; he had not had a critical hit since *The Night of the Iguana* (1964) and had not made a popular success since *Heaven Knows, Mr. Allison* (1957). There was considerable buzz that this film was a worthy comeback attempt, and the movie was shown in competition at the Teheran Film Festival. Surprisingly, the reaction was mixed, with critics divided into two distinct

a brief battle, force Danny onto a bridge, where he is made to plummet to his doom—all the while singing victoriously. Peachy is forced to watch, then tortured and sent back to India a disfigured cripple. He meets up with Kipling and relates this tale of woe, leaving the writer with a rather haunting "souvenir"—the severed head of Danny, still wearing his golden crown.

Had Huston made the film in the fifties, the prevailing wisdom would undoubtedly have been to cast Gable and Bogart as white-hatted heroes whose noble deeds are misunderstood by the tribesmen (who would inevitably be portrayed in "the white man's burden" school of thought). By 1975, however, a more thought-provoking script was called for. While Danny and Peachy are charismatic and likable, there is no attempt to sugarcoat their actions. Aside from a fierce loyalty to each other, they have few redeeming qualities. In what was meant to be a microcosm of British colonialism, their intrusion on the native kingdom is motivated out of pure greed. They will

THE MAN WHO WOULD BE KING Danny (Connery) and Peachy (Caine) are astonished at the riches they uncover within their kingdom.

THE MAN WHO WOULD BE KING   Leading the assault on a rival tribe.

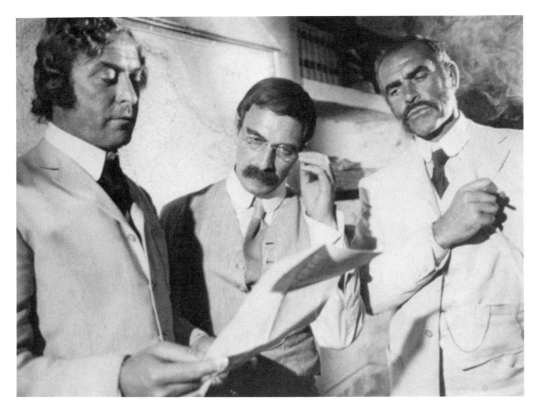

THE MAN WHO WOULD BE KING Danny and Peachy boldly outlining their scheme to Kipling (Christopher Plummer).

categories: those who saw it as a feeble and pretentious mess, and others who proclaimed it an instant classic. *Variety* termed the film one of the festival's "biggest disappointments," citing the overemphasis on comedy, and for some bizarre reason termed Michael Caine's superb performance "poor." Yet, many other critics praised the film upon its general release. *Time* hailed it as "one of the year's ten best! A mellow, brassy, vigorous movie, rich in adventure." Gene Shalit on NBC-TV declared the film "a prince among pictures. It is flat-out entertainment—a headlong story, head-crunching action, good acting, intelligent and witty dialogue, and mind-wiping, exotic setting, and it has been craftily directed by John Huston." Jeffrey Lyons echoed the sentiment, calling *King* "a huge entertainment epic. Great fun, one of the year's most entertaining films."

Audiences responded favorably to the movie, whose inspired ad campaign harkened back to *Gunga Din* and promised "Adventure in All Its Glory!" The film was a sizable hit and garnered four Oscar nominations (Screenplay Adaptation, Editing, Costume Design, and Art/Set Decoration), but disappointingly, none in the "big" categories. The movie has fared better in recent years, now that Connery and Huston are seen as icons, with this being representative of their finest work. Alas, there proved to be trouble in paradise, however. In early 1978, Connery and Caine

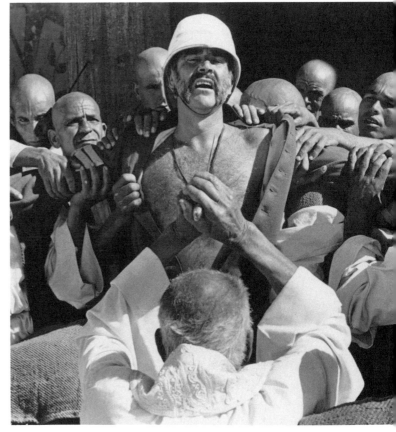

THE MAN WHO WOULD BE KING The tribe rebels when Danny is unmasked as a fraud.

151

filed a lawsuit against distributor Allied Artists, contending they had been cheated out of their fair percentages of the gross. Connery says in retrospect, "These percentage deals are a farce. A picture can outperform *Star Wars*, but if you don't get your money up front, you'll never see a penny of profit." He later claimed his trust in studios led him to be "screwed more times than a hooker." The two actors won the highly publicized lawsuit and were awarded extensive damages. They also won a countersuit filed by the studio based on allegedly libelous remarks the duo had made. Allied Artists filed for Chapter 11 sometime thereafter. Whether this was due entirely to Connery and Caine's suit remains to be seen, but Sean has enjoyed telling the press, "I bankrupted them, I'm thrilled to say."

Long after the movie had been released, Connery and Caine visited Huston at Cedars-Sinai Medical Center in Los Angeles. The director was suffering from his umpteenth "fatal illness" and the actors longed to cheer him. They strode into Huston's room re-creating an amusing and exaggerated military walk they had devised for the film. Upon seeing them, Huston shouted, "Danny and Peachy have come to see me!" (As usual, Huston recovered and went on to make some successful films.) Connery and Caine would both appear in *A Bridge Too Far* (1977), but frustratingly did not share any sequences together. In interviewing Roger Moore for our book *The Incredible World of 007—A Celebration of James Bond,* the authors were informed that he, Sean, and Michael Caine were actively searching for a joint film project. One can only hope it materializes.

With the release of *The Man Who Would Be King,* the ghost of James Bond began to fade, and Sean enjoyed being judged on his own merits. The film has a sentimental spot in his heart, and although he keeps virtually no mementos from his films ("Not a single photo!" he told Larry King), his home in Marbella does sport an otherwise inconspicuous pillow embroidered with "The Man Who Would Be King—1975"—a subtle testimony to his love for this film.

THE MAN WHO WOULD BE KING   Walking to his doom after his short-lived reign as the Man Who Would Be King.

ROBIN AND MARIAN

1976

Released by Columbia Pictures

CAST:

Robin Hood: Sean Connery; *Marian:* Audrey Hepburn; *Sheriff of Nottingham:* Robert Shaw; *King Richard:* Richard Harris; *Little John:* Nicol Williamson; *Will Scarlett:* Denholm Elliott; *Sir Ranulf:* Kenneth Haigh; *Friar Tuck:* Ronnie Barker; *King John:* Ian Holm.

CREDITS:

Director: Richard Lester; *Producer:* Denis O'Dell; *Screenplay:* James Goldman; *Director of Photography:* David Watkin; *Editor:* John Victor Smith; *Production Designer:* Michael Stringer; *Music:* John Barry. *Running Time:* 106 minutes.

Following the critical praise he received for *The Man Who Would Be King* and *The Wind and the Lion*, Connery scored again with his sentimental portrayal of the aging Robin Hood in *Robin and Marian*. This was one of the most sensitive films to be directed by the generally madcap Richard Lester, who gained fame as the ringmaster to the Beatles with *A Hard Day's Night* and *Help!* As with his two previous films, Sean enjoyed sharing top billing with a strong costar. In this case, you couldn't ask for a classier or more respected name, Audrey Hepburn, who was returning to the screen following a nine-year hiatus.

Robin and Marian is a low-key and economically filmed look at the Robin Hood legend from a different perspective. Screenwriter James Goldman wisely refused to compete with the lingering vision of Errol Flynn's immortal portrayal of the famed hero. Instead, he concentrated on a mature Robin, one who is disillusioned, lost, and depressed—until his long-dormant romance with Marian is rekindled and gives meaning and drive to his life once again. Goldman had envisioned bringing this new slant to the celebrated tale to the stage as early as the mid-1960s. However, the project never jelled until someone suggested the premise would be more suited to a film. Despite having no formal script, Goldman got a go-ahead from Columbia Pictures in 1971. Financial woes affecting the studio, though, caused the project's shelving for a couple of years.

ROBIN AND MARIAN   Assisting a disguised Marian (Audrey Hepburn).

The concept was revised at a later date, and Goldman tried to interest David Lean to direct. Through a miscommunication, Goldman was led to believe Lean had rejected the proposal, when in fact the director had not even seen the script. Later, John Frankenheimer agreed to direct, but he eventually bailed out, but not before suggesting the script be passed on to Audrey Hepburn. Goldman wanted Hepburn for the role of the now mature Marian, but felt approaching her would be an exercise in futility as the actress had retired years before and had refused all film offers. Ironically, when she received the script, Hepburn wanted the role badly but felt she would not be formally asked. Many months were wasted with both the actress and screenwriter presuming the other wasn't interested. Hepburn later recalled, "I thought I was a little too old to play Marian . . . but when I started to read the script, I couldn't put it down. Not only was it beautifully written, but I discovered that it contained a role for me that was so appealing because it was a rare opportunity to play a

For
Robin and Marian

Love is the greatest adventure of all.

COLUMBIA PICTURES and RASTAR PICTURES present

SEAN CONNERY   **AUDREY HEPBURN**   IN   **ROBERT SHAW**

"ROBIN AND MARIAN"

A **RICHARD LESTER** FILM

NICOL WILLIAMSON

DENHOLM ELLIOTT   **RONNIE BARKER**
KENNETH HAIGH   **IAN HOLM**

and **RICHARD HARRIS** as Richard the Lionheart

ROBERT SHAW   NICOL WILLIAMSON   DENHOLM ELLIOTT   RONNIE BARKER   KENNETH HAIGH   IAN HOLM   and RICHARD HARRIS
as The Sheriff of Nottingham   as Little John   as Will Scarlet   as Friar Tuck   as Sir Ranulf   as King John   as King Richard The Lionheart

A **RAY STARK-RICHARD SHEPHERD** Production · Music by **JOHN BARRY**
Executive Producer **RICHARD SHEPHERD** · Written by **JAMES GOLDMAN**
Produced by **DENIS O'DELL** · Directed by **RICHARD LESTER**

PG PARENTAL GUIDANCE SUGGESTED
SOME MATERIAL MAY NOT BE SUITABLE FOR PRE-TEENAGERS

Columbia
Pictures

THEATRE

ROBIN AND MARIAN   Advertisement from screening program.

154

ROBIN AND MARIAN   Premiere program from Radio City Music Hall.

woman my own age." Once Hepburn signed, Goldman set about finding his Robin of Locksley. In a project laden with ironies, Goldman proposed Sean Connery for the role of Little John, only to have the actor convince the filmmakers he would be more appropriate for the character of Robin. Goldman then suggested Richard Harris for Little John, and Nicol Williamson as the evil King Richard. Neither had any interest, but coincidentally both made separate requests on the same day to play each other's role. In a casting coup, Connery's *From Russia With Love* nemesis, Robert Shaw—by now a successful leading man—signed to play the sheriff of Nottingham.

To keep the budget in check, the movie was shot in Spain, where the likelihood of bad weather was remote and there were no expensive labor unions. Locations varied from the historic town of Burgos to the principal site at Pamplona, where Sherwood Forest was re-created on the Urbassa Plain. This location allowed convenient access to nearby Madrid, where the daily rushes were developed and viewed. By all accounts, the filming was an upbeat affair. Connery told the press, "Our film is a realistic story, but it has a sense of humor, which all good stories must have. . . . [The film] appealed to me not because it is an interesting legend, but because it is an *examination* of that legend." Sean was also effusive in his praise of his costar: "I've worked with many actresses in my time, but Audrey Hepburn is one of the few *ladies* I've had the privilege of working with. And she's a bloody fine actress; a joy, a professional." Hepburn responded with similar praise, making the on-screen chemistry all the more convincing.

The plot finds Robin and Little John returning from

ROBIN AND MARIAN
Thirteen years after *From Russia With Love,* Connery and Robert Shaw do battle once again.

the disastrous Crusades after discovering their exalted King Richard (wonderfully played by Richard Harris) is, in fact, a genocidal madman. Fleeing back to Sherwood Forest, they find their once "merry men" to be middle-aged derelicts not terribly unlike those who presently reside in New York's Port Authority Bus Terminal. Robin and the men are reinvigorated when long-absent Marian reluctantly decides to give up being a nun to resume her romance with a hopefully more mature Robin. However, her aging Romeo still acts as though he were twenty years younger, and along with his now rather portly band of followers, he once again sets out to right injustices. Chief on his list of enemies is his old nemesis the sheriff of Nottingham (Robert Shaw's villainy is so subtle you can't help but like the cad). The two enemies duel to the death, weighed down not only by their armor but also by their advancing years also. Although Robin slays his foe, he is badly wounded. Despite promises of future triumphs, Marian realizes "he'll never have a better day than this." She slips poison into their wine, and in a bittersweet finale, both lovers slip gently into "that good night."

Robin and Marian remains one of Sean Connery's

favorites among his films. He reflected years later, "I liked the film and have marvelous souvenirs about it, apart from the fact that I liked the casting of the picture. But the film was originally called *The Death of Robin Hood,* and I think that's where they started to go a bit wrong by trying to make it something else by calling it *Robin and Marian.* It was an examination of a legend and a hero who was over the top, as it were, and showing and revealing he was not really that intelligent. The really intelligent one was the sheriff and not him. It showed so many flaws, as it were, that perhaps the public doesn't want to see that side of somebody who is considered a hero."

Connery may have been correct. Although director Lester urged the studio to retain the original title and to market the film as a straight drama, the ad campaign focused on the love story. Audiences expecting to see the usual lighthearted approach to the Robin Hood legend felt frustrated by the somber mood of the movie. Yet, *Robin and Marian* is witty and abounds with precious little sequences of gentle humor that linger in the mind (e.g., Robin's embarrassment at almost relieving himself in the presence of Marian; the good-natured rivalry between Robin and the

ROBIN AND MARIAN   Marian and Little John (Nicol Williamson)
come to the aid of the mortally wounded Robin Hood.

157

sheriff—reflected on their field of battle when the two aging warriors must help each other up from their prayer positions before trying to annihilate one another; etc.). The marvelous performances are the most noteworthy element. Connery's Robin Hood is one of his great screen roles and he performs magnificently—making the world-weary Robin a sometimes pathetic but always noble figure. Hepburn is the personification of class and dignity. As for Shaw, his screen time is far too brief to do justice to this wonderful actor. His duel with Connery brings back sentimental memories of the superb pairing of these men in *From Russia With Love*. A wonderful cast of supporting actors—highlighted by Nicol Williamson's Little John—insures the movie is first-rate entertainment.

On the technical side, the production designer and special-effects team work wonders with the limited budget, making *Robin and Marian* both look and feel like an expensive film. Director Richard Lester tones down his usual penchant for slapstick, and this film rivals his best work. David Watkin's gorgeous cinematography and John Barry's lushly sentimental score additionally contribute to the overall artistic success of the film. Sadly, that success did not carry over to the box office. Connery tried hard to promote the film—going so far as to appear onstage with Hepburn at the Radio City Music Hall premiere. Yet, the movie was routinely dismissed by critics and public alike. In an astonishingly inappropriate review, *Variety* actually called the film "an embarrassment," and another critic jabbed that with an aging Robin and Marian the movie was a film about "fallen archers." Some reviewers were considerably kinder. *The New Yorker*'s notoriously snooty Pauline Kael gushed about Connery: "He is animal-man at his best . . . naked and unrestrained . . . in all his pictorial beauty. Apart from Olivier and Brando, there's no other actor I would rather watch."

Today, the film is regarded as a highlight in Sean's career by critics who appreciate—at least in retrospect—its many delights. Years later, when Kevin Costner's *Robin Hood—Prince of Thieves* was generally panned, more than one reviewer suggested that film buffs rent a video of Connery's version instead. In what is undoubtedly the most perceptive analysis of *Robin and Marian*, Frank Rich—then film critic for the *New York Post* (now the scourge of Broadway)—wrote: "You know that Robin and his merry band will always be with us, and after seeing this movie, you can't help but feel that Connery, Hepburn, and Lester will be, too. . . . All three return to the forefront of our movies, and they do so by embracing their pasts, even as they temper those pasts with the mellowness, and wisdom, age has given them. . . . Connery and Hepburn seem more fascinating than they ever were before because the youthful, larger-than-life fires that burn within them contrast so mightily with the aging flesh of their bodies and the growing weariness of the worlds they inhabit. The process of growing older adds layers of mystery and splendor to their beauty."

THE NEXT MAN

1976

Released by Allied Artists

CAST:

Khalil Abdul-Muhsen: Sean Connery; *Nicole Scott:* Cornelia Sharpe; *Hamid:* Albert Paulsen; *Al Sharif:* Adolfo Celi; *Justin:* Marco St. John; *Dedario:* Ted Beniades; *Fouad:* Charles Cioffi.

CREDITS:

Director: Richard C. Sarafian; *Producer:* Martin Bregman; *Screenplay:* Mort Fine, Alan R. Trustman, David M. Wolf, and Richard C. Sarafian, based on a story by Trustman and Wolf; *Director of Photography:* Michael Chapman; *Editors:* Aram Avakian and Robert Q. Lovett; *Music:* Michael Kamen. *Running Time:* 107 minutes.

Following his well-received portrayal of the aging Robin Hood, Sean Connery returned to the contemporary world, starring in *The Next Man*, a political thriller centering on tensions in the Middle East. The story was the brainchild of producer Martin Bregman, who had recently enjoyed the success of two of the most popular films of the 1970s, *Serpico* and *Dog Day Afternoon*. Bregman's track record was good, and there was every reason to believe his Midas touch would extend into the world of international intrigue. Bregman approached Richard C. Sarafian, the primary director of the classic *I Spy* television series, to both direct the film and help finalize a screenplay. Sarafian agreed, but soon came to regret his decision. Bregman had ever-changing ideas about the direction of the story, and rewrites were constant. Recalled Sarafian, "After six months of rewrites, I was ready to pack it in. You have to realize, I hadn't been at a

THE NEXT MAN   With Cornelia Sharpe.

THE NEXT MAN   Striking a Bondian pose as Khalil.

bring peace to the Mideast by some startling proposals. He runs up against various factions who for their own selfish interests want to thwart his quest for peace. It's an intelligent film about what's happening now, and it has plenty of excitement."

At first glance, the script must have seemed promising. Connery's character stuns the world by an-

typewriter for a long time. It was nerve-racking. Mort Fine, who was with me on *I Spy,* came into the project and really pulled the script together. Ten months from the start of the project, we finally had a script that was satisfactory." In fact, two other writers also contributed to the script, and the result is a choppy screenplay that displays the fingerprints of too many cooks.

A sizable budget was granted, with $4 million spent on location shooting in such exotic locales as France, Austria, Germany, the Bahamas, England, Ireland, and Morocco. Primary filming took place in New York City, where sequences took advantage of such local landmarks as the Wollman ice-skating rink, Central Park, Greenwich Village, and Park Avenue. A large-scale re-creation of the U.N. General Assembly was built on the recently reopened stages of the famed Astoria Studios, where many of the earliest films were shot. Connery was enthused about the project and explained his rationale for accepting the role of Khalil Abdul-Muhsen, a Saudi Arabian minister: "I decided to take this role because it's an unusual one. I play an Arab statesman who tries to

160

nouncing Saudi Arabia plans to make peace with Israel, then join its former enemy in production of petroleum, which will be distributed free to Third World nations. While these liberal political daydreams might have caused Ted Kennedy to be aroused, their occurrence in real life is about as likely as a Dukakis-Mondale landslide in the next election. Nevertheless, the pie-in-the-sky optimism of the scriptwriters does make it possible for Connery to be placed in constant jeopardy as he tries to evade numerous assassination plots masterminded by Arab terrorists.

Connery sidesteps many attempts on his life with the aid of bodyguards and his right-hand man and close friend, Hamid (Albert Paulsen). However, like his Bondian alter ego, Sean has a weakness for the ladies, and this allows him to fall for Nicole, a gorgeous blonde who also happens to be a professional assassin. As played by model Cornelia Sharpe, this ravishing femme fatale has a personality that can cure insomnia. Critics sneered when this modest talent was given star billing along with Connery, and one lady journalist suggested Sharpe was given this honor because she happened to be Bregman's girlfriend. To her defense came Connery, who, enraged, phoned the journalist and informed her rather indelicately what he thought of her opinion. Small wonder Sharpe described Sean as "a true professional and a wonderful person. He has helped me to feel confident every step of the way. When he walks into a room, he

THE NEXT MAN   Struggling with a would-be assassin.

THE NEXT MAN   Addressing the United Nations General Assembly with a plan for Mideastern peace.

commands attention. He would even if he weren't a movie star."

The script jumps haphazardly from location to location with little attempt to fill in the plot holes. Although it is Sharpe's mission to kill Connery, she inexplicably helps him to fend off numerous other assassins. Likewise, when the "shock ending" reveals Hamid to be in alliance with Sharpe, the question is once again posed as to why he would have aided Connery so many times in escaping attempts on his life. Ultimately, Connery is killed by Sharpe, although the script has led us to believe she would renounce her wicked ways to live with him in splendor in Arabia. This twist to the plot is never quite as startling as it should be, largely because Sharpe gives an emotionless, one note performance that makes it difficult to believe there was ever any real chemistry between the lovers. As for Connery, he is as watchable as ever, even though the screenplay makes him a virtual saint. A few warts would have made Khalil far more intriguing. Additionally, Connery makes no attempt to disguise his Scottish brogue, which detracts from our accepting him as a Saudi minister. Still, he delivers his usual solid performance and has a memorable fight scene.

The Next Man is filled with missed opportunities. Location shots are well photographed, but, like many films from the seventies, have a garish tint to the colors. The editing is straight out of the "movie of the week" film school, and one expects commercials to appear at any moment. In addition, the chance to reteam Connery with Adolfo (*Thunderball*) Celi never materializes because no one had the foresight to write a single scene for the two men to share. Despite Celi's prominent billing, he is in fact killed off in first few minutes of the film, having suffered the indignity of a largely wordless role. Except for Connery's, *The Next Man* lacks a single memorable performance. Richard C. Sarafian's direction is serviceable, but little more. He keeps the pace moving quickly, but fails to evoke much interest in the characters. Sean later stated, "Basically, it was a good idea that went off half-cocked because we didn't have a good script. We tried to salvage it through editing, but that can never be done."

The film was released in the United States by Allied Artists, the same studio Connery would later help bankrupt when he successfully sued for missing royalties from *The Man Who Would Be King*. Public and critical reaction to *The Next Man* only added to the company's woes. *Variety* dubbed it "a slick travesty" and predicted a "fast play-off." The review did have kind words for Sean, who never seems to have gotten a bad personal notice: "Connery is such a command-ing screen figure that his presence in almost any scene subordinates the posturing imposed on the character he plays." Nevertheless, the movie proved to be such a major box-office disappointment that it became the only Connery film to date not to be released theatrically in the United Kingdom. It eventually premiered there on television. Time has dealt the movie several other blows as well: it is available on video under the titles *The Arab Conspiracy* and *Double Hit*. Both versions are severely edited, thus rendering a mediocre film almost unwatchable.

A BRIDGE TOO FAR

1977

Released by United Artists

CAST:

Lt. Gen. Frederick Browning: Dirk Bogarde; *Staff Sgt. Eddie Dohun:* James Caan; *Lt. Col. "J.O.E." Vandeleur:* Michael Caine; *Maj. Gen. Robert Urquhart:* Sean Connery; *Lt. Gen. Brian Horrocks:* Edward Fox; *Col. Bobby Stout:* Elliott Gould; *Maj. Gen. Sosabowski:* Gene Hackman; *Lt. Col. John Frost:* Anthony Hopkins; *Gen. Karl Ludwig:* Hardy Kruger; *Dr. Spaander:* Laurence Olivier; *Brig. Gen. James Gavin:* Ryan O'Neal; *Maj. Julian Cook:* Robert Redford; *Lieutenant General Bittrich:* Maximilian Schell; *Kate ter Horst:* Liv Ullmann.

CREDITS:

Director: Richard Attenborough; *Producers:* Joseph E. Levine and Richard P. Levine; *Screenplay:* William Goldman, based on the book by Cornelius Ryan; *Director of Photography:* Geoffrey Unsworth; *Editor:* Anthony Gibbs; *Production Designer:* Terry Marsh; *Music:* John Addison. *Running Time:* 176 minutes.

Sean Connery's string of successes had suffered a detour with *The Next Man*, but his follow-up film to that disappointment had all the makings of a blockbuster: the epic adaptation of Cornelius Ryan's mammoth book *A Bridge Too Far*. Ryan, the superb writer whose *The Longest Day* stands for many as the definitive book about war, had spent years researching *Bridge*, which chronicled one of the most massive and controversial engagements in the history of modern warfare. To get a perspective on the magnitude of

Joseph E. Levine presents

A BRIDGE TOO FAR

starring (in alphabetical order)

Dirk Bogarde
James Caan
Michael Caine
Sean Connery
Edward Fox
Elliott Gould
Gene Hackman
Anthony Hopkins
Hardy Kruger
Laurence Olivier
Ryan O'Neal
Robert Redford
Maximilian Schell
Liv Ullmann

From the book by
Cornelius Ryan
Music by
John Addison
Screenplay by
William Goldman
Produced by
Joseph E. Levine
and
Richard P. Levine
Directed by
Richard Attenborough

Panavision®

United Artists
A Transamerica Company

ORIGINAL MOTION PICTURE SOUNDTRACK ALBUM AND
TAPE AVAILABLE ON UNITED ARTISTS UA RECORDS

Lieutenant-General 'Boy' Browning

Staff Sergeant Eddie Dohun

Lieutenant-Colonel 'Joe' Vandeleur

Major-General Robert Urquhart

Lieutenant-General Brian Horrocks

Colonel Bobby Stout

Major-General Stanislaw Sosabowski

Lieutenant-Colonel John Frost

General Karl Ludwig

Dr. Spaander

Brigadier-General James M. Gavin

Major Julian Cook

Lieutenant-General Wilhelm Bittrich

Kate ter Horst

THEATRE

A BRIDGE TOO FAR   Pressbook advertisment.

163

Ryan's project and the resulting film, it is necessary to review the events in question.

By September 1944 the stunning Allied success at the beaches of Normandy had left the Nazis in a massive retreat across France and Belgium, into Holland. However, Allied progress had stalled somewhat, making many generals impatient for a knockout blow against the Reich. Generals Montgomery and Patton, long bitter enemies, each vied for Eisenhower's favor in hopes of being the one to deliver that blow. Montgomery convinced Ike to endorse, however reluctantly, a daring plan, code-named Operation Market Garden, to end the war in Europe by December. The theory was to parachute more than thirty-five thousand troops sixty-five miles behind enemy lines to secure six key bridges. Simultaneously, massive numbers of ground soldiers and tanks would cut through Holland to reinforce the paratroopers, secure the key bridge at Arnhem, and then cross the Rhine and destroy Germany's industrial capacity. Unfortunately, the plan was a rushed affair created by impatient men hungry for results and glory. Despite initial success, bad strategy, worse weather, miscommunications, and supply foul-ups left the paratroopers alone to defend the bridges against overwhelming enemy forces. Ultimately, the Allies retreated, having suffered over seventeen thousand casualties to the German's estimated three thousand. More men were killed or wounded in this battle than at the beaches of Normandy. Although Montgomery declared the operation 90 percent successful, most historians feel it was the last major Allied defeat of the war.

Legendary producer Joseph E. Levine became intrigued by Ryan's book while it was still in the research stage, and he bought the rights from the author, who was terminally ill while completing the manuscript. (He did live to see the book become an international best-seller.) When Levine tried to interest studios in financing a screen version, he was roundly rejected as the scope of the project cried out for a megabudget at a time when Hollywood was still somewhat conservative. Levine stated, "It's the best damned story I've ever read," then broke his cardinal rule by financing much of the movie himself. The ultimate budget would reach $25 million—a phenomenal amount for the late seventies.

Actor cum director Richard Attenborough was hired to helm the massive production, and he spent close to a year in preparation before the cameras would turn. Meanwhile, master negotiator Levine was keen on recouping his money before the film was even released. To get international distributors to pay sums that would get the film in the black, he had to

A BRIDGE TOO FAR   Defending a wounded officer while seeking refuge in a cottage.

A BRIDGE TOO FAR   On the set with his on-screen alter ego, Maj. Gen. Robert "Roy" Urquhart—one of the heroes of the Arnhem invasion.

165

lure a cast of superstars. One of the first to sign was Sean Connery, although the actor was initially reluctant. "I turned the film down twice, first of all because . . . it was a very disturbing book and I really felt that I didn't want to go back and be involved with re-creating all that," Connery explained. "Then I got the script and read it, and the script was a very good reproduction of the events—very much highlighted and explained—and I felt even more that I didn't really want to do it. Then I spoke to Richard [Attenborough], and in the interim I read *A Man Called Intrepid*—about what happened with Hitler and the Nazis—and I had the realization that this whole generation . . . have forgotten what happened, and regardless of what errors were made, if it had gone entirely the other way and we had been left with what the Nazis were advocating, it would have been dreadful, really." (Connery was also reportedly reluctant to participate because a relative had been killed at Arnhem and the film might prove to be too close to home.)

Sean's patriotic mood, alas, was about to be shattered. He had signed for the film early in the planning stages and had agreed to a salary of $450,000—adequate he felt for his limited role, even if he was to be on-screen more than any of the other actors. Meanwhile, as successive superstars enlisted, word got out that their salaries were in the $750,000 range. The coup de grace, however, was the much-publicized signing of Robert Redford for a short role in return for the then-astronomical salary of $2 million. (Steve McQueen had initially been approached for the role, but his demands were excessive even for the free-spending Levine.) Connery, feeling exploited, hit the roof. He later recalled Levine answering his complaints with the statement, "It's not my fault you've got a lousy agent!" Sean's response: "You're absolutely right, so we'll change that." Levine later felt bad for Connery and in an amazing act of goodwill, brought the actor's salary up to $750,000. Connery didn't pay his agent a commission on the difference and, in fact, fired the man shortly thereafter. Sean recently reflected on the developments, saying, "I showed the people back in Hollywood I don't play second string. Redford, I learned, was getting X amount, so I wanted X amount! I wasn't going to be shortchanged because he signed on the dotted line after I did. I raised a ruckus and my price went way up." Connery did earlier concede, however, that Levine did not have to grant him the increase. He returned the favor by adjusting his filming schedule and helping Levine avoid over a million dollars in losses due to a production snafu. As thanks, Levine offered Sean a new Rolls-Royce—which Connery graciously refused. Levine then sent *Mrs. Connery* a check for $50,000. "That was Joe," reflected Sean. Levine later said of Connery, "He's a straightforward guy. He could have made millions staying with James

A BRIDGE TOO FAR   As General Urquhart.

Bond, but he didn't want to be typed. Now he's one of the few actors it doesn't matter how their films do, they'll get their million and a half dollars tomorrow. In two seconds, I'd let him play in anything I've got." (Amazingly, this analysis still holds true for Sean, although $1.5 million would barely pay for his coffee by his current salary demands.)

This largest-scale war film since *The Longest Day* was shot in England and Holland. To insure accuracy, many participants from the battle served as technical advisers on the film. Whenever possible, shooting took place at actual locations or close by. The famed Arnhem Bridge could not be used because the surrounding area had become too industrialized. The town of Deventer, forty kilometers away, was an amazingly similar site, and the populace allowed the bridge there to be closed periodically for filming. In return, fifteen hundred local residents were employed as extras. Eventually, the crew numbered three hundred and more than one hundred acting roles were cast. Trying to find a suitable number of period costumes and relics, the crew solicited museums and private collectors for use of their "treasures." The gliders used in the actual raid no longer existed, not even the blueprints. They were eventually re-created through photos and memory. Many of the scores of tanks and vehicles depicted on-screen were built from fiberglass, only to be destroyed in the numerous action sequences.

Connery, in the key role of Maj. Gen. Robert Urquhart, had the good fortune to have his real-life counterpart on the set as an adviser. Urquhart was a genuine hero. His paratroopers were forced to land eight miles from the bridge, and their ground transportation did not arrive. Then his radio equipment failed, rendering him incommunicado. To make matters worse, Urquhart himself was almost captured behind enemy lines and was missing and presumed dead for thirty-nine hours. When he returned to his men, he was informed that their much needed supplies were being routinely captured by the Germans, who had overrun the drop zones. Urquhart eventually lost a large number of his men before getting the order to retreat. He led his troops through a blinding rainstorm in the dead of night after having heroically held the Arnhem Bridge for over nine days. Urquhart was characteristically unfazed by being portrayed on-screen by one of the cinema's great sex symbols. He stated, "I'm not a great cinemagoer so I'm afraid these names don't mean quite the same things to me as to other people. But when my wife and daughters were told that Sean Connery was to play my part, they were thrilled!"

A Bridge Too Far is inevitably compared to *The Longest Day* for obvious reasons: both were go-for-broke, all-star vehicles that meticulously re-created important battles of World War II. *Bridge*, though, never received the recognition it deserved. Perhaps, as John Wayne discovered with his megabudget and underrated production of *The Alamo*, audiences simply don't respond favorably to films about the good guys being defeated. This in no way undermines the quality of this film, however. Director Attenborough actually brought the movie in under budget and under schedule—a feat all but impossible today. Viewing the film, one must be impressed by the scope of the production and the magnificent action sequences. To the credit of Attenborough and screenwriter William Goldman, much effort is made to insure that the fireworks don't overpower the human elements.

Yet, it cannot be denied that *A Bridge Too Far* fails to move us in the same way as *The Longest Day*. It is difficult to establish why. However, the former film did meticulously re-create the agony of the wait to go into battle—the constant false starts and the increasing edginess of the troops. *Bridge* jumps through most of the talk and rushes into the action sequences. As impressive as these are, the audience is left somewhat confused as to the objectives of the various combatants depicted. The scenes switch almost too frequently, and despite the film's length, a longer running time might have insured better audience identification with the characters and their goals. (Attenborough shot five hundred thousand feet of film. The final cut contains thirty thousand.) The director succeeds in his goal of establishing the horror of war, but we are curiously indifferent to the fate of many key players.

For the most part, Attenborough uses his stellar cast intelligently and does not try to overwhelm the viewer with pointless interminglings of these big names. Some of the performers are excellent: Connery, Dirk Bogarde, Edward Fox, Anthony Hopkins, James Caan. Others are competent, but their roles are too vague for them to display much skill: Laurence Olivier, Liv Ullmann, Michael Caine. Still others are rather unsatisfactory: Gene Hackman trying unsuccessfully to master a Polish accent; Ryan O'Neal enunciating every greeting through gritted teeth as though suffering chronic constipation; and Elliott Gould's cigar-chomping cornball cameo that is straight out of a *Sgt. Fury and His Howling Commandos* comic book. As for the much-vaunted Redford role, it lasts all of ten minutes and the actor is not required to strain. However, the sequence in which he leads his brave men on a river crossing under merciless enemy fire is harrowing and memorable.

Technically, the film is superb on all counts. Geoffrey Unsworth's masterful cinematography captures both the splendor and horror of battle, production designer Terry Marsh's attention to detail is meticulous in every way, and John Addison's thundering march music is suitably stirring. In a monument to injustice, the film did not receive a single Oscar nomination.

Through Levine's preselling of the film, the producer had insured he would make a profit before the film even wrapped. Movie houses were not so fortunate, however, and the restrictive terms they had to agree to in order to play this prestigious film led to disappointing results and ill will toward distributor United Artists. The film opened soft—by no means disastrously, but well short of the kind of momentum that would have insured a blockbuster. The summer of 1977 belonged to *Star Wars, The Spy Who Loved Me,* and other escapist fare. Audiences were distancing themselves from a depressing historical epic. Critical notices were mixed with some reviewers labeling the film the definitive war movie, while others, such as Rex Reed, dismissed it with ridiculously simplistic critiques stating the whole affair was simply about "a lot of exploding tanks."

Long after the film version of *A Bridge Too Far* fades from memory, however, history will honor the gallant participants of a battle that, if successful, would have shortened the war by many months and probably have prevented the infamous German offensive in late 1944 known as the Battle of the Bulge. Perhaps General Montgomery said it best when he stated, "So long as we have officers and men who will do as you have done, then we can indeed look forward with complete confidence to the future. In years to come, it will be a great thing for a man to say, 'I fought at Arnhem.' "

THE GREAT TRAIN ROBBERY

U.K. TITLE: *THE FIRST GREAT TRAIN ROBBERY*

1979

Released by United Artists

CAST:

Edward Pierce: Sean Connery; *Agar:* Donald Sutherland; *Miriam:* Lesley-Anne Down; *Trent:* Alan Webb; *Fowler:*

Malcolm Terris; *Sharp:* Robert Lang; *Clean Willy:* Wayne Sleep; *Burgess:* Michael Elphick; *Emily:* Pamela Salem.

CREDITS:

Director and writer: Michael Crichton, screenplay based on his novel; *Producer:* John Foreman; *Director of Photography:* Geoffrey Unsworth; *Editor:* David Bretherton; *Production Designer:* Maurice Carter; *Music:* Jerry Goldsmith. *Running Time:* 111 minutes.

Connery followed up his powerful role in *A Bridge Too Far* with *The Great Train Robbery,* a stylish caper movie with absolutely no pretense about making a social message. Connery was approached by novelist-filmmaker Michael Crichton, who planned an ambitious screen adaptation of his best-selling novel, a semifactual, largely romanticized retelling of the exploits of Edward Pierce, a gentleman rogue with a unique niche in history. Seems he was the mastermind behind the first robbery of a moving train, swiping a large gold shipment intended for payment of troops fighting the Crimean War in 1855. At the time, Pierce became a sort of legend and inspired widespread support, as charismatic crooks have shown a knack for doing throughout history. Presumably, Pierce was a Victorian G. Gordon Liddy—a man who turned a criminal act into a cottage industry.

Crichton wanted Connery for the role of Pierce, but the actor refused. Sean explained, "The first script I read was pretty awful. . . . It was very heavy and obvious. One was aware of the fact that it was a period piece, in the worst sense. . . . [However] I was coaxed a bit by John Foreman, who had produced *The Man Who Would Be King,* to read the novel in its original state, and I liked it quite a bit." With Connery's tentative support, Crichton rewrote the screenplay and satisfied one of Sean's other concerns: how to handle the Victorian dialogue without alienating modern audiences. Connery expressed a fondness for working with directors who were also screenwriters: "It's easier to get answers and resolve any of the apparent problems at the early stage of preproduction, rather than attempting to resolve them when you're shooting."

Unfortunately, more problems arose that forced Sean to withdraw from the project temporarily. The studio had planned to do most of the filming at Pinewood Studios in England, home of the James Bond movies. If Sean had worked more than a token number of days in England, he would be subject to such tax penalties that he would have ended up doing the film for basically nothing. As it turned out, Con-

THE GREAT TRAIN ROBBERY   The British release title: *The* First *Great Train Robbery.*

nery rejoined the project when Crichton and the technicians discovered that modern England was too industrialized to allow for re-creation of the Victorian era. The movie was relocated to Ireland, where in the countryside it was possible to shoot the extensive locomotive footage without the interference of present-day landscapes. Authentic period trains were donated by the Railway Preservation Society and manned by volunteers. Production designer Maurice Carter worked wonders in creating an atmosphere that seems to capture the feel and flavor of the era. In all, an eight-week shoot took place on Irish soil, with limited interiors shot on the soundstages of Pinewood.

Donald Sutherland was cast in the key role of Connery's henchman—a somewhat oafish but clearly capable safecracker with a talent for duplicating keys. Connery plans on stealing and duplicating four keys that are needed to open the safe on the train. However, all the keys are closely guarded by various members of a banking concern with whom Connery socializes. Through their loose tongues he ascertains the location of the keys, but has to employ some ingenious methods for securing the duplicates. For this he gets the assistance of Miriam, a gorgeous lady of questionable morality who is not above using her body to help the plan succeed. In her first major role, Lesley-Anne Down is one of the sexiest ladies ever to share the screen with Connery. Her role was origi-

nally intended for Jacqueline Bisset, but it's doubtful even that talented lady could have made a better screen impression. The sight of Down in a Victorian bustier and garter belt is a vision to behold. The scenes in which this trio of Connery, Sutherland, and Down bluff their way into the confidence of the bank officials are both amusing and suspenseful.

The highlight of the film is the actual robbery—a scene so elaborate that it required ten full days to shoot. As with *The Anderson Tapes,* we are spared footage of the crooks going through the finer points of their scheme. This makes the enacting of the actual crime all the more suspenseful, since we don't know precisely how all the potential problems will be overcome. A good deal of publicity focused on the amazing stunt work performed by Sean Connery, and it's quite possible that *The Great Train Robbery* was his most physically demanding film. Connery is required to run atop the speeding train and jump from car to car, while ducking the low-lying bridges that appear with little warning. He considered using a stuntman, but ended up doing the dangerous work himself, reasoning: "They get the camera as close as possible before they cut away, and it starts to really work, and then if they pull back far enough to disguise the fact that you're not doing it, the scene loses reality. . . . For example, there was a sequence coming out of the train, over the top, and down inside and back again, and we did it with a helicopter, and if you had

THE GREAT TRAIN ROBBERY Connery performed many of his own stunts at great personal risk.

tried to cut it in any way, it would have spoiled the whole rhythm of the scene."

Connery acknowledged that he underestimated the risks he would be taking: "There were some dangerous routines . . . like going through tunnels. But we had worked it out in advance, although in jumping between the trains, it got a little risky when I was supposed to almost fall—the almost became for real." Indeed, there is a heart-stopping moment when Connery does almost plunge over the side of the train, and one wonders how he was protected. The answer, as we now know, is that he wasn't. In the midst of the action, Connery had to keep watch for the upcoming tunnels, as they barely allowed him enough room to hug the roof of the train.

At another point, cinders from the engine set fire to Sean's hair—but what caused him to be a hothead was an entirely different matter: he discovered that assurances from the engineer that the train would not go over thirty miles per hour were inaccurate. The helicopter crew that filmed the scene informed Sean that the train was speeding at almost *twice* that rate. The engineer remained steadfast, even though his method of calculating speed was rather shaky: he counted the telephone poles! Risks of this type on the part of superstars are rather rare because of insurance regulations. Had Sean been severely injured, the entire film would have been jeopardized. One cannot deny, however, that the sequence is one of the most exciting and memorable of the actor's career. Con-

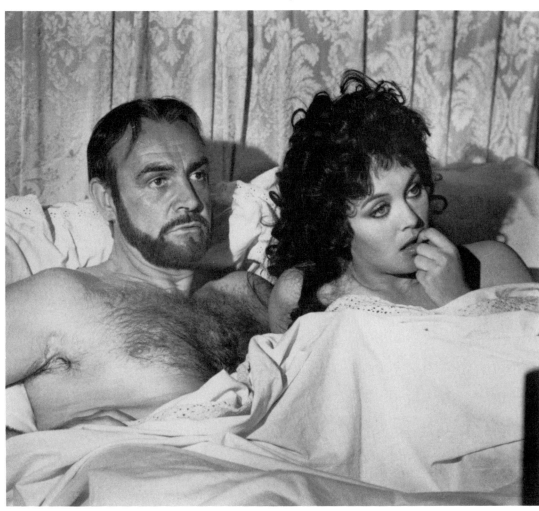

nery admitted that his wife, Micheline, became quite upset when she saw the film for the first time, and the danger Sean had placed himself in. "She hadn't known I was doing all that," he later admitted. "If she'd known beforehand, there would've been a bit of a fight."

The Great Train Robbery is filled with humor, impressive sets, snappy dialogue, and impeccable acting, with the three stars genuinely seeming to enjoy the entire affair. The supporting roles, filled by actors largely unknown to American audiences, are equally wonderful with Malcolm Terris particularly amusing as a sexually frustrated aristocrat who's obsessed with Down. Crichton shows he is multitalented by insuring that the dialogue is never too long or heavy, and

he keeps the action scenes flowing at a breakneck clip. Jerry Goldsmith provides a lively and melodious score, and the beautiful cinematography is by the late Geoffrey Unsworth. (The end credits carry a touching dedication to this talented craftsman.)

For all its merits, *The Great Train Robbery* was a box-office disappointment, especially in the United States. This, despite largely favorable reviews, such as the one in *Variety*, which praised Connery's "splendid wickedness" and the "ingenious theft." The New York *Daily News* cited it as a "charmingly lighthearted movie" and singled out Connery's "amazing agility." *Playboy*'s Bruce Williamson, however, was less kind, comparing the film's leisurely pace to "wandering through a Victorian bric-a-brac. It's overstuffed, fussy

THE GREAT TRAIN ROBBERY Outlining the caper to Lesley-Anne Down.

THE GREAT TRAIN ROBBERY As Edward Pierce.

174

in detail, extravagant. But nothing really leaps out of the cobwebbed past to grab you." Williamson did, however, praise Sean's "suave, tongue-in-cheek" performance. Expectations for the film were high, and early returns at the box office looked to insure a hit, but attendance fell off dramatically and the film went down as a flop. Connery tried to find out why and approached the top brass at United Artists. He later stated, "After the good reviews—better than any U.A. picture in a long time—and strong openings, I was told the picture had 'no legs.' I never got an entirely satisfactory answer." He later theorized that the studio abandoned aggressive advertising campaigns the minute the film waned, and this insured failure. Connery was disappointed and pondered openly whether the studio owed him something for all the hits he had produced for it over the years, but did confess he owed United Artists as well, not having ever brought to fruition the second film he was to make as part of his contract for *Diamonds Are Forever.*

METEOR

1979

Released by American International Pictures

CAST:

Bradley: Sean Connery; *Tatiana:* Natalie Wood; *Sherwood:* Karl Malden; *Adlon:* Martin Landau; *Dubov:* Brian Keith; *Easton:* Joe Campanella; *Hughes:* Trevor Howard; *The President:* Henry Fonda.

CREDITS:

Director: Ronald Neame; *Producers:* Arnold Orgolini and Theodore Parvin; *Screenplay:* Stanley Mann and Edmund H. North; *Story:* Edmund H. North; *Director of Photography:* Paul Lohmann; *Editor:* Carl Kress; *Special Effects:* Carl Kress and Glen Robinson; *Music:* Laurence Rosenthal. *Running Time:* 107 minutes.

Into each actor's life a little rain must fall—only in Connery's case, it proved to be a shower of meteors! Sean's presence in this largely forgotten debacle left him unscathed, but continued the disappointing box-office trends of his post-007 work. To call this film "rock bottom" entertainment would be an unpardonable but accurate pun. It is somehow fitting that *Meteor* ushered out the decade of the seventies—an

METEOR Connery in "Q" branch? Sean demonstrates a model of a scientific marvel.

era generally devoid of any lasting cultural phenomenons. In fact, the movie has much in common with that other notorious flop of the 1970s—the leisure suit. Both looked cheesy and were hopelessly outdated by the time they were thrust upon an unresponsive public. What is amazing is that the indications of *Meteor*'s inevitable failure were as apparent in 1979 as those for a sequel to *Hudson Hawk* would be in the 1990s. In spite of this, many talented people who should have known better eagerly signed to join Connery in this last-ditch attempt to milk the "disaster film" genre.

Few involved with *Meteor* could have been naive enough to think the film would be a critical success. Yet, there was a precedent for believing the project would succeed at the box office. Although the disaster-film concept could be traced back to Hollywood's origins, it gained new life in 1970 with the corny but entertaining hit *Airport.* That film spawned several sequels and ignited a short-lived but lucrative trend

METEOR   The tag line "There's no place to hide" could have also referred to the critical response to *Meteor*.

METEOR   As Dr. Paul Bradley.

that continued with the release of *The Poseidon Adventure* and *Earthquake*. The genre peaked—financially and artistically—with *The Towering Inferno* in late 1974. The general concept never varied: place as many highly paid superstars as possible into a big-budget extravaganza, then come up with entertaining methods to fry or drown them. Several attempts to continue these epics fell flat by the late 1970s, with "disaster master" Irwin Allen's flops *The Swarm* and *When Time Ran Out*. Curiously, the producers of *Meteor* blissfully continued preproduction and secured the then-sizable budget of $16 million, of which $5 million was to be spent on miniatures and $3 million on special effects.

One of the most obnoxious and unintentionally hilarious publicity campaigns in history was perpetrated upon a completely disinterested moviegoing public. "The most monumental film project to be launched in Hollywood in twenty years!" boasted the press kit. (This must have come as news to the folks who made such "intimate epics" as *Cleopatra, The Longest Day,* and *Apocalypse Now!*) For a while it seemed as though everyone in show business was jumping on the prospectively lucrative *Meteor* band-wagon, with even Isaac Asimov (whose article inspired the concept) trying to stir up a fear of meteors among the public the way *Jaws* succeeded with sharks. The problem is, meteors just aren't very scary, as witnessed by the following rather benign "warning" from the sci-fi novelist: "The chance of such a strike is very small, but it is not zero. . . . The chance of [a meteor] hitting a populated center, even in the case of a strike, is very small—but not zero—and it might even be Manhattan tomorrow. Don't bet on it, but . . ." Not exactly the type of statement that caused audiences to run home and don their pith helmets. Besides, most New Yorkers would probably welcome a meteor strike as the only real urban renewal to take place in Manhattan in decades.

The plot centers on a giant meteor that is hurtling to earth at incredible speed—its impact destined to threaten the very existence of the planet. Connery plays a grumpy professor who is placed in charge of deploying secret U.S. nuclear weapons positioned in

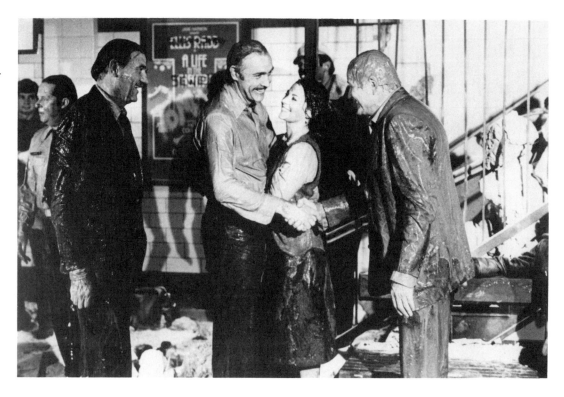

METEOR Survivors of the catastrophe: Karl Malden (left), Sean, Natalie Wood, and Brian Keith.

space to destroy the meteor. When it is discovered that U.S. firepower alone can't do the trick, the Soviets sheepishly admit to having their own space weapons system in place. They agree to divert the course of their missiles in a last-ditch attempt to hit the hellish rock with everything the earth can muster. The movie's wit is demonstrated in the naming of the once rival nuclear missile systems: "Hercules" versus "Peter the Great." Sounds like the title of an old Steve Reeves movie.

To keep the audience from snoring while enduring the interminable wait for the climax, several advance meteor particles arrive like clockwork every twenty minutes, as we witness the destruction of minor population centers such as Hong Kong and Austria. The implication throughout, however, is that as long as New York survives, nothing terribly bad has really occurred. Every time we see another country destroyed, we are introduced to minor characters who pop up out of nowhere, so the audience will identify with them prior to their demise. B movie sexpot Sybil Danning inexplicably shows up at a ski resort, prompting the more lecherous members of the audience to await her inevitable disrobing. But the producers are so out of touch with the audience that Danning is allowed to perish while covered head to toe in a ski suit. (Couldn't she at least have been buried by the avalanche while leaving the shower?)

The script is full of knee-slapping dialogue. When

the president, Henry Fonda, asks if the nuclear firepower will succeed in demolishing the meteor, NASA chief Karl Malden replies with a straight face, "Well, you know, Mr. President, we've never done this before." No kidding, folks! A temperamental outburst by the requisite Pentagon mad general (Martin Landau) is exceeded in unintentional hilarity only by his "heart-warming" apology later. A great deal was made about the fact that this would not be a film that concentrated on hardware at the expense of characterization. Yet, Natalie Wood parades about in a dour business suit, while the most complimentary camera angles are reserved for the nuclear missiles, which the camera glides across endlessly, as though they were Madonna!

A great deal of work went into this misguided epic. Ronald Neame, the director of *The Poseidon Adventure*, oversaw numerous production challenges. The original script, written by Edmund North (*The Day the Earth Stood Still*), was deemed unsatisfactory by all involved. According to Connery, "initially, the idea of a meteor striking the earth—which is a definite possibility—was, I thought, a very good idea for a film . . . the basic idea was good, but the script had to be rewritten entirely. So Ronnie Neame and Stanley Mann rewrote it from scratch." (One can only wonder how bad the original effort must have been if the revised script was deemed acceptable!) Over $100,000 was spent on re-creating the U.N. Security

178

Council for a scene lasting less than one minute. For a sequence set in Siberia, four tons of ice and hundreds of Noble pine trees were transported to the set.

The set for the climax, which takes place in a New York subway, took four months, eight thousand man hours, and enough supplies to construct a ten-story office building. Additionally, the script required over 1 million tons of mud for the scene in which the principals are pounded when the river breaks through the subway tunnel. Connery called the sequence "the most frightening set I've ever worked on." Medics and oxygen were always at the ready, and an actor who slipped in the mud might be hopelessly buried before anyone could find him. To make matters worse, when the mud was warmed, it caused steam, and thus the actors had to go about their paces in chilling temperatures.

Despite all of this effort, *Meteor* looks curiously cheap. The meteor is photographed from every possible angle and is inevitably accompanied by bombastic music. Nevertheless, it never looks more menacing than a pet rock, and with its cavernous potholes and jagged edges, it often resembles a teenager with a bad case of acne, topped off by a Don King hairdo. For some reason, it is also photographed moving at a geriatric speed, so that one suspects all the earthlings will have to do is merely step aside as it plunks harmlessly to the ground. None of this is surprising, since the producers actually publicized the fact that the "meteor" was a piece of lava rock unearthed in Ronald Neame's backyard! Connery himself later referred to the meteors as resembling "little balls of shit."

The best that can be said for the performances is that, with the exception of Landau, none of the actors embarrass themselves. Connery goes gamely through the motions of taking this nonsense seriously, but seems a bit apologetic. As expected, there is no opportunity for sparks to fly between him and Natalie Wood, although both flirt around the coffee urn while preparing for Armageddon. The always watchable Brian Keith is amusing as a Soviet scientist who speaks only in Russian, which Keith does convincingly. Henry Fonda lends some brief credibility as the president, although he probably had to pretend he was reviving his role from *Fail Safe* in order to keep a straight face. All other aspects of the film are laughably bad, despite the talent involved. In fairness, the film's release was delayed when a lack of money compromised the special effects. Despite a "meteoric" publicity campaign, *Meteor* was greeted not as a disaster film, but as a disastrous film. The cycle had long ago run its course, and poor reviews hurt. The

film was a costly failure for American International Pictures, which had hoped to graduate into the big leagues and shed its reputation for beach movies and B horror flicks. *Meteor* did manage to resemble one actual solar phenomenon—Halley's comet—in that we probably won't see this type of film again for another seventy-five years.

METEOR Bracing for the worst, with Brian Keith, and Natalie Wood.

CUBA

1979

Released by United Artists

CAST:

Robert Dapes: Sean Connery; *Alexandra Pulido:* Brooke Adams; *Gutman:* Jack Weston; *Ramirez:* Hector Elizondo; *Skinner:* Denholm Elliott; *General Bello:* Martin Balsam; *Juan Pulido:* Chris Sarandon; *Faustino:* Alejandro Rey; *Therese:* Lonette McKee; *Julio:* Danny de la Paz; *Miss Wonderly:* Louisa Moritz; *Press Agent:* Dave King; *Don Pulido:* Walter Gotell.

CREDITS:

Director: Richard Lester; *Producers:* Arlene Sellers and Alex Winitsky; *Executive Producer:* Dennis O'Dell; *Screenplay:* Charles Wood; *Director of Photography:* David Watkin; *Editor:* John Victor Smith; *Production Designers:* Gil Parrando and Philip Harrison; *Music:* Patrick Williams. *Running Time:* 122 minutes.

Sean Connery did not have to attend a screening of the final cut for *Meteor* to know the project was a career misstep. He was anxious to find a prestigious project to compensate for the sagging box-office revenues generated by his recent films. He could at least console himself with the critical praise he had received for such financial failures as *The Wind and the Lion, Robin and Marian,* and *The Great Train Robbery.* However, his flops led critics to wonder if Connery were losing his generally enviable intuition for selecting worthwhile projects.

Sean signed for director Richard Lester's curious epic *Cuba* despite the fact a script had not yet been finalized. Connery and Lester had worked well together on *Robin and Marian,* and both men hoped this film would reignite the chemistry. Lester had long envisioned a romantic thriller set in the chaotic final days of Batista's Cuba. He stated, "Within my lifetime, it was the most extraordinary, successful revolution. I wanted to portray an impression of the moment that one regime was replaced by the next. I thought it would be fascinating as a piece of film. . . . I wanted to make a political film within which no one spoke about politics and a love story in which no one spoke about love." To bring this dream to reality, Lester hired longtime collaborator Charles Wood to pen the original screenplay, while simulta-

neously coordinating the massive logistics inevitable in filming this expensive period piece.

Connery—always reluctant to become associated with "works in progress"—was sufficiently impressed by a first-draft script to sign for the lead. Originally, he anticipated that filming would commence shortly, and continue for an abbreviated time, on location in Spain, as shooting in Castro's Cuba was obviously not a possibility. This suited Sean fine, especially when several of the locations allowed him to drive to his home in Marbella after a day's work. Alas, this dream project quickly turned into a nightmare for all concerned. Connery, whose intolerance for production delays was a large factor in his resigning from the Bond films, was frustrated when a finalized script could not be agreed upon by all parties. While rewrites were being done, filming was delayed three times over a period of months. Eventually, with the weather threatening to close production entirely, the cast and crew commenced filming while work on the script continued. Lester told the press this would provide a spontaneity that would result in more exciting performances. However, no one was fooled. The set of *Cuba* was as ripe for revolution as Havana was in 1959.

Further hindering progress was the withdrawal of Diana Ross as the leading lady. Lester replaced her with Brooke Adams, who had recently made a splash as the most curvaceous of alien bean pods in the well-received remake of *Invasion of the Body Snatchers.* A powerful lineup of supporting actors was also enlisted, including such durable names as Denholm Elliott, Jack Weston, Martin Balsam, and Walter Gotell, Roger Moore's KGB nemesis from the 007 films. Nevertheless, the director was very nervous as seventy-eight shooting sites were required as well as a huge number of cars and props from the period. Additionally, authentic costumes for more than three thousand actors and extras had to be imported from London.

For all the effort, Lester received scant compensation from either critics or the public. Reviewers felt the story was rambling and disjointed. The plot has Connery's Robert Dapes arriving in Havana in the days immediately preceding the collapse of Batista's corrupt government. A professional soldier of fortune, Connery has been hired in the vain hope he can prevent the rebels from advancing. He recognizes the cause is hopeless but is enticed to stay in Cuba when he happens upon Alex, a former lover, portrayed by Brooke Adams. Through some sketchy reminiscences, we learn all too little about this May/ December romance or the reasons for its on-again,

CUBA   Love among the ruins—with Brooke Adams.

CUBA Promotional brochure cover.

CUBA As Robert Dapes.

CUBA Connery as Dapes, a mercenary with a hopeless mission: Saving the failing Batista regime.

off-again nature. Adams is now the wife of a playboy aristocrat (weli played by charismatic Chris Sarandon) who doesn't see that the end of his world is imminent.

Interwoven with these central characters are a number of supporting players each interested in exploiting what he can out of Cuba before the iron curtain falls around it. Jack Weston is particularly good as an opportunistic "ugly American" businessman who barely succeeds in escaping with his life. Denholm Elliott is on-screen all too briefly in a role that appears to have had a disastrous encounter with the editor's shears, while Martin Balsam gives a good turn as a corrupt Cuban general.

Connery appears confused throughout, but whether this is actually due to his character's situation or to the lack of a finalized script may never be known. He *looks* great, sporting a Bondian hairpiece and distinguished-looking mustache. To his credit, it's another winning performance in spite of the well-known fact that he was most unhappy on the set. Adams is gorgeous to watch and a capable actress as well. The vagueness of her love affair with Connery extends to the final frames and the film's ambiguous ending. (Several finales were filmed, and then the one selected was probably the least satisfying to audiences and critics.)

Connery was disgruntled with *Cuba* from shortly

after he arrived on the set. His negative reaction to the finished film caused a strain with director Lester, who felt Sean had unfairly painted him as the main culprit for the movie's failure. Connery would later state, "It was the least satisfying [film] in the end, considering the original idea, which was Dick Lester's, was very promising. We had no script to begin with and there were other problems. I had to postpone the picture three times—the result in the end sort of shows. . . . *Cuba* is the only film I have reservations about, apart from the very early B films, of course, but that's something else." *Variety* echoed these sentiments, dismissing the movie as a "hollow, pointless nondrama. . . . There's no reward to be found . . . either for filmmaker or audience."

Both Connery and the press have been overly harsh about *Cuba*. Though hardly a riveting drama, it is often fascinating, with a marvelous sense of atmosphere. At times it is impossible to believe the story wasn't actually shot on location during the dark days of the revolution. The characters are interesting and the performances are universally admirable. Sadly, due to the bad press, *Cuba* had the feel of a loser long before it opened. Released during Christmas 1979, it fell victim to an avalanche of hits, and it is rarely discussed in retrospectives of Sean's career. Despite this, it remains another buried treasure in the Connery archive—well worth a perusal to savor its many memorable moments.

TIME BANDITS

1981

Released by Avco Embassy Pictures (A Handmade Films Release)

CAST:

Robin Hood: John Cleese: *King Agamemnon:* Sean Connery; *Pansy:* Shelley Duvall; *Mrs. Ogre:* Katherine Helmond; *Napoleon:* Ian Holm; *Vincent:* Michael Palin; *Evil Genius:* David Warner; *Supreme Being:* Ralph Richardson; *Ogre:* Peter Vaughan; *Randall:* David Rappaport; *Fidgit:* Kenny Baker; *Wally:* Jack Purvis; *Og:* Mike Edmonds; *Strutter:* Malcolm Dixon; *Vermin:* Tiny Ross; *Kevin:* Craig Warnock.

CREDITS:

Director and Producer: Terry Gilliam; *Executive Producers:* George Harrison and Denis O'Brien; *Screenplay:* Michael Palin and Terry Gilliam; *Director of Photography:* Peter Biz-

iou; *Editor:* Julian Doyle; *Production Designer:* Millie Burns; *Music:* Mike Moran; *Songs and Additional Material:* George Harrison. *Running Time:* 116 minutes.

A lengthy sixteen-month absence from the screen for Sean Connery followed the release of the trouble-plagued *Cuba*. During this time, he simply didn't receive a screenplay that enthused him. He had rushed into the *Cuba* fiasco and was still licking his wounds, vowing not to commit to another project unless he felt relatively sure of its artistic integrity. There were persistent rumors that he was considering starring in the epic television miniseries *Shogun,* but these were silenced when Richard Chamberlain signed for the lead. Ultimately, Sean would return to the screen to star in Peter Hyams's sci-fi thriller *Outland.* However, there was to be a brief detour in a most unlikely screen vehicle—the madcap comedy *Time Bandits.*

Sean's participation in the film came about when writer/producer/director Terry Gilliam encountered Connery on a Los Angeles golf course. Gilliam was well-known as a key member of the immortal Monty Python group. He explained to Sean that he was preparing a movie for Handmade Films, a new production company owned in part by ex-Beatle George Harrison. Connery later recalled, "George Harrison and his associate, Denis O'Brien, telephoned me to say, 'We have a script with a role for you—the trouble is we only have two and half million dollars with which to make the film [implying that Connery's usual megabuck salary would be out of the question]. Would you like to see it anyway?' I said yes; the script arrived and it was one of the best scripts I had ever read." The story so intrigued Connery that he agreed to appear in the film for no salary, accepting a percentage of the gross instead.

Terry Gilliam dreamed up the incredible premise of the film over an otherwise ordinary weekend. He quickly drafted a seven-page outline of the plot and met with Harrison and O'Brien, who were known to be looking for low-budget, experimental film properties. The ever-animated Gilliam performed an entire miniversion of the movie for the producers, enacting all the important roles. Receiving a green light, Gilliam then enlisted his Monty Python cohort Michael Palin to coauthor the screenplay.

The plot concentrates on a band of mischievous dwarfs who steal a map from the Supreme Being (amusingly played by the great Ralph Richardson). The map leads to the greatest treasure in the universe, and possessing the document allows the group to travel back and forth in time. Eventually they pop up

TIME BANDITS   Pressbook advertisement [courtesy, Handmade Films].

in the bedroom of an imaginative and precocious young boy named Kevin (Craig Warnock), a lad who is all but ignored by his materialistic parents, who are obsessed with keeping up with the Joneses. Kevin reluctantly joins the party and encounters many historical figures along the way, including Robin Hood (another ex-Pythoner, John Cleese), Napoleon (Ian Holm), and King Agamemnon (Sean Connery). Defying death at every turn, they are lured into a trap by the Evil Genius (David Warner) and a dizzying climactic fight to the death. The film ends on a down note, which was quite a jolt to some viewers who had enjoyed the levity of the preceding sequences. In the controversial scene in question, Kevin awakens to find his adventure was apparently a dream and he is in the midst of being rescued from his burning house. He soon finds proof, however, that the events he recalled were indeed real, but he cannot prevent his parents from being destroyed. *Time Bandits* ends with the haunting image of the boy trying to grasp his parents' destruction. It's yet another unusual scene in a most unusual film.

When Gilliam received Connery's consent to appear in a small but pivotal supporting role as the heroic Agamemnon, he was quite surprised. Sean informed him that he had but a brief time in which to shoot his scenes, as production on *Outland* would begin soon. Gilliam, still in the embryonic stages of preparing his film, was not about to lose the opportunity to have Connery. He quickly cast the remaining roles and found a location in Morocco to double for Agamemnon's kingdom. The temperature approached 130 degrees, and the locale could only be reached by mule, but the cast and crew persevered. According to Gilliam, "Sean was great. He suggested ways of shooting around scenes to get his sequences done. He simplified it for me, and I think he'd make a damn good director. We wanted a hero and Connery *is* a hero!" Sean was also helpful in advising eleven-year-old Craig Warnock, who in his film debut not only had to contend with the miserable location but also hold his own against one of the screen's superstars. When Sean's work was completed, the pace relaxed a bit and the rest of the filming could be done in England.

To say *Time Bandits* is a unique film would be an understatement. It does not wholly succeed as entertainment, largely because the script is so unstructured it often resembles a Monty Python sketch gone amok. (If that isn't a redundancy!) However, it has its moments, and the production design is superb. The film works wonders with a limited budget, and the special effects are state-of-the-art. The obsession with imagery, though, comes at the expense of the human element. How much more involving the screenplay would have been had it concentrated on the characters portrayed by the highly engaging cast. Craig Warnock is wonderfully endearing as the wide-eyed juvenile swept up in a deadly but exciting adventure of a lifetime. Likewise the actors portraying the "little people" are alternately funny and touching, and the film refreshingly does not mock their physical appearance. David Warner, Katherine Helmond, Peter Vaughan, Michael Palin, John Cleese, and Ian Holm all contribute yeomanly cameos, but the scenes between Connery and Warnock are the most moving

TIME BANDITS As King Agamemnon [courtesy, Handmade Films].

187

and memorable. Indeed, Connery's Agamemnon is one of the few genuinely heroic figures who lives up to his historic reputation. It's a witty and delightful portrayal, and keep an eye out for Sean's short but important reappearance as a fireman at the film's climax. Ironically, Gilliam had envisioned Sean's appearance as being perceived as a one-note joke. He explained, "We had written in this screenplay that this Greek warrior after this battle removes his helmet revealing himself to be none other than Sean Connery. So it was a joke. It was great because I couldn't think of anybody else who had the qualities Connery has. He had to be a hero, a king, and he also had to be a father figure, be able to do magic and twinkle." To no one's surprise, Connery did not disappoint.

British comedy has generally been a hard sell in the United States, but thanks to an impressive $6-million ad campaign the film became a surprise hit in July 1981. Critics were also generally kind, with *Us* magazine calling it *"The Wizard of Oz of the eighties!"* and David Ansen of *Newsweek* referring to it as "flat-out hilarious." Sheila Benson in the *Los Angeles Times* labeled *Time Bandits* "one of the great fantasy fulfillment films . . . what emerges is marvelous!" while Peter Rainier in the *Los Angeles Herald Examiner* gushed that the movie "deserves to be called a classic." *Variety* was a bit more sober, noting that "when you can count the laughs in a comedy on one hand, it isn't so funny." Nevertheless, worldwide box-office results were impressive, and Sean's five-minute appearance played no small part in its ultimate success. His gamble on sacrificing his salary also proved to be a wise choice as *Time Bandits* offered him lucrative rewards for a very abbreviated shooting schedule—something the actor has always described as his ideal situation.

OUTLAND

1981

Released by Warner Bros.

CAST:

O'Neil: Sean Connery; *Sheppard:* Peter Boyle; *Lazarus:* Frances Sternhagen; *Montone:* James B. Sikking; *Carol:* Kika Markham; *Ballard:* Clarke Peters; *Sagan:* Steven Berkoff; *Tarlow:* John Ratzenberger.

CREDITS:

Director and Writer: Peter Hyams; *Producer:* Richard A. Roth; *Director of Photography:* Stephen Goldblatt; *Editor:* Stuart Baird; *Production Manager:* Denis Johnson; *Art Director:* Malcolm Middleton; *Special Effects:* John Stears. *Music:* Jerry Goldsmith. *Running Time:* 109 minutes.

The *Star Wars* phenomenon made possible Connery's return to the sci-fi genre for the first time since the ill-fated *Zardoz* in 1973. Sean was enthused about this cinematic sojourn into the future, largely because he felt the script successfully combined stunning technology with a suspenseful story that emphasized characterization over hardware. He commented, "It's one of the first space films I've seen where I could understand what it was all about without getting into those jet packs and ray guns. *Star Wars* and *The Empire Strike Back* were a complete mystery to me. I was drawn to *Outland* because it was about a man on his own particular odyssey—alone against the system." Not that *Outland* lacks state-of-the-art special effects. The film boasts some of the most impressive set designs to be seen to that time, and while the budget of $14 million was not inconsequential, this appears to be a much more expensive cinematic experience.

The story finds Connery as a federal marshal assigned the dubious honor of policing a sulfur-mining camp on the planet Io—a miserable, sun-baked desert on which the inhabitants cannot leave their massive prisonlike dormitories without the aid of cumbersome space suits. The lure of Io is obvious—workers are paid abnormally high wages for backbreaking work in the most depressing of environments. Connery, however, does not even have wages as incentive. His one-year tour of duty is so unappealing that his wife spirits away their son to a nearby space station to await a shuttle to Earth, where Connery will join them when completing his duties.

No sooner does Connery get acquainted with the way of life on Io then he becomes aware that a series of workers have suddenly gone insane and ended their lives through grotesque methods. The general manager of the mining camp, played by Peter Boyle in a slimy yet somehow likable way, assures Connery the deaths are due to burnout. However, Sean's investigation leads him to the discovery that Boyle is encouraging the use of a dangerous drug that increases worker productivity, often at the cost of their lives. Boyle has a hand in every pie, and even Connery's deputies betray him. When it becomes clear the marshal cannot be bribed or frightened, Boyle marks him for death.

OUTLAND

OUTLAND   Screening program.

OUTLAND   Hunting his foes outside the space station.

Much was made about the similarities between *Outland* and *High Noon*. Indeed, the parallels were so obvious that *Outland* was denounced by *High Noon* director Fred Zinnemann. Yet, Hyams has woven the most memorable elements of the western classic into a futuristic atmosphere with often stunning results. He described the planet Io as "a combination of the Dodge Citys of the past and the oil rigs of the present." Connery persuaded Hyams to film the entire movie at Pinewood Studios in England. Here, a 1:200 scale model of the planet was built by Martin Bower, Bill Pearson, and John Steers, who earlier won an Oscar for his visual effects for *Thunderball.* (Stears also provides the special effects here.) The model measured eighteen feet long, yet contained over four miles of fiber optics to provide the extravagant lighting required. Thanks in no small part to Stephen Goldblatt's photographic methods, the audience has no trouble convincing themselves they are observing a full-size city. The interior designs are equally as impressive, and one is almost overwhelmed by the dark, smoky, thoroughly depressing atmosphere.

Major set pieces include the exterior of the mine camp, a cocoon-like structure that towers above the sands, and a gigantic greenhouse where the planet inhabitants supplement their diets with homegrown vegetables. Within these settings, the film's exciting climax takes place. As with *High Noon*'s hero, Connery cannot convince either his fellow lawmen or the citizens to help him stave off three professional killers who are stalking him. His only ally is a woman. Here, instead of steadfast Grace Kelly, we have Frances Sternhagen as a cantankerous doctor who rallies to the cause. (Connery had initially hoped to have Colleen Dewhurst, who was unavailable.)

Hyams directs the climax with enough suspense to keep viewers riveted, although Connery seems to dispose of his adversaries a bit too effortlessly. The *real* climax occurs earlier in the story when there is a thrilling chase between the marshal and a drug dealer that spans the entire length of the complex and culminates in as exciting a fight scene as has ever been seen in a 007 epic. Even Connery agreed that the action set pieces were somewhat reversed. He later judged, "The fight at the end took place in space and therefore was very slow . . . and the real villain of the

190

piece was resolved with one punch. That was bad because the film had a marvelous climax in the very middle of it that should have been topped at the end." Nevertheless, there are plenty of other positive aspects to *Outland* including a memorable supporting performance by James B. Sikking as Connery's Judas-like deputy; a sleazy bar featuring live sex acts and prostitutes that makes the Milk Bar from *A Clockwork Orange* look like Mr. Rogers's neighborhood; and an impressively filmed battle to the death outside the mine camp between Connery and a killer that is marred only by the necessity of filming in slow motion to simulate the gravity-free atmosphere. Surprisingly, the human element never gets lost, and *Outland* provides Connery the opportunity to emote the anguish of a man who is torn between his duty and his family.

If the film has a shortcoming, it is that the villains aren't memorable. Most of the bad guys are one-dimensional extras with little or no characterization. Boyle is seen periodically in some verbal duels with Connery, but these are more amusing than chilling. Boyle is too avuncular a presence here to provide much in the way of terror—we never *really* believe he'd do anything to hurt good ol' Sean. There are also a few brief sequences in which the use of miniatures is apparent. However, the film deserves credit for its utilization of a process called Introvision, which combines live action and rear-screen projections with

OUTLAND   Arguing with his only friend: the gutsy Frances Sternhagen.

seemless results. Jerry Goldsmith's score is properly haunting and appropriate.

Outland was a somewhat frustrating project for Connery. Although he admired Hyams as a no-nonsense director, Sean was distracted by what he felt were injustices in the British tax laws. As a resident of Spain, Connery was only allowed to work ninety days a year in Great Britain. To comply with the requirement, Connery had to fly out of the country every weekend to insure he maintained enough days to complete filming. This aggravated him enormously, and he complained of government officials, "They seem to be more flexible with villains who break the law!" The irony of the situation is that the U.K. was biting the hand that fed it. Many major British stars had moved out to escape the outrageous taxes on their incomes. Yet, Connery's influence helped bring about employment for a large group of actors and technicians. He proposed revisions in the tax laws which he felt would help create more jobs for people in the film business but his pleas fell on deaf ears. The tax issue was a sore point throughout production, especially near the completion of the film, when it occasionally looked doubtful that Sean would have adequate time to shoot his scenes.

Outland opened to generally good to excellent reviews in the United States. Hard-to-please Rex Reed exalted, "Io provides the most terrifyingly ominous setting to unfold since *Alien*," and he went on to praise Connery as "a perfect screen hero—brick hard, vulnerable, ready to die for the cause of justice." Ernest Leogrande of the New York *Daily News* gave the film three and a half stars and praised it as

OUTLAND   Battling Steven Berkoff in the commissary.

"big-scale pop art that gives the opportunity to cheer justice being done, virtue being rewarded, and respect being won." *Variety* noted, "Connery delivers a stellar performance . . . [he] fleshes out all of the tender and hardened edges of this man's personality without ever seeming maudlin or overbearing." Bruce Williamson of *Playboy* favored the film by stating, "*Outland* goes like gangbusters, with Connery as a sheriff whose presence assures us The Force is in his trigger finger."

Given the positive word of mouth, Connery had every reason to believe *Outland* would be a smash. For the first time in years, he extensively promoted a film and even held a gala premiere in Scotland to benefit the Scottish International Education Trust. He willingly stepped into the spotlight on this occasion and was led to the stage by bagpipers. (In addition to a star-studded guest list, attendees included Sean's brother, Neil, who now bears an amazing resemblance to his famed sibling.) Surprisingly, *Outland* was a box-office disappointment. Why may never be clear, but it is possible that sci-fi audiences weaned on laser beams and speeding spacecraft could not identify with the low-key mystery elements of Connery's film. The movie brought in respectable grosses, but did little to return Sean to the top of the box-office heap. Reportedly frustrated and saddened by *Outland*'s lukewarm reception, he could nevertheless take comfort in Peter Hyams's praise of him: "His emotions seem so very close to the surface of the skin that when you see him on-screen, you can truly sense what he is feeling. Certainly an enormous asset for a film actor. Sean is an extraordinary actor and tremendous craftsman." The film may not have found the audience it deserved, but Connery could take pride in having made an excellent contribution to the sci-fi genre.

WRONG IS RIGHT

U.K. TITLE: *THE MAN WITH THE DEADLY LENS*

1982

Released by Columbia Pictures

CAST:

Patrick Hale: Sean Connery; *President Lockwood:* George Grizzard; *General Wombat:* Robert Conrad; *Sally Blake:* Katharine Ross; *Philindros:* G. D. Spradlin; *Homer Hubbard:* John Saxon; *Rafeeq:* Henry Silva; *Mallory:* Leslie Nielsen; *Harvey:* Robert Webber; *Mrs. Ford:* Rosalind Cash; *Helmut Unger:* Hardy Kruger; *Hacker:* Dean Stockwell; *King Awad:* Ron Moody.

CREDITS:

Director and Producer: Richard Brooks; *Executive Producer:* Andrew Fogelson; *Screenplay:* Richard Brooks, based on the novel *The Better Angels* by Charles McCarry; *Director of Photography:* Fred J. Koenekamp; *Editor:* George Grenville; *Production Designer:* Edward Carfagno; *Music:* Artie Kane. *Running Time:* 117 minutes.

> It was a time when outer space was filled with incredible machines whose telescopic eyes and ears witnessed our most sensitive secrets; information that could (and did) change the fate of nations;
> It was a time when no one on earth could hide from technology—no one was safe;
> It was a time between Now and Later, when Dark is Light, Down is Up, Foul is Fair, and WRONG IS RIGHT!

The apocalypse as brought to you courtesy of the evening news is the theme of this offbeat, cynical Sean Connery vehicle—one of the few films to exploit his comedic talents. The movie was viewed as a personal statement by director Richard Brooks, who delivered a scathing critique of contemporary international politics. With its preoccupation with spy satellites, atomic bombs, political double-talk, arms deals, terrorism, corruption, and plain insanity, it could be argued that this was to be Brooks's own *Dr. Strangelove*. "It's about the craziness of 'today' . . . enabling one to laugh at the insanity that is about to explode on the world," noted the director.

Wrong Is Right presents us with a politically unstable world that fiddles while the countdown to Armageddon ticks away. The unfolding madness is entertainingly reported to the masses by the World Television News Network's superstar anchorman Patrick Hale (Sean Connery). Hale is wined, dined, and placed on a pedestal by the international political community, which both courts and fears the power of his enormous impact on global audiences. Hale earns his money, resorting to daredevil tactics to get his stories on the air. His viewers love this cross between James Bond and Walter Cronkite, and the network reaps incredible profits from him. When we first meet Hale, he is hosting a show that can best be described as a gruesome combination of *Westworld* and *Fantasy Island*. Here, ordinary citizens playact their fantasies, including robbing banks and murdering their spouses. Hale presides over the proceedings like a perverse Ed McMahon, introducing each new act with relish.

He becomes embroiled in the story of his career, however, and such "lighthearted" TV fare is soon dispensed with as he travels to the Middle East. Here, he hopes to interview an Arab king to see why he has suddenly aligned his nation with a terrorist move-

WRONG IS RIGHT   Covering Armageddon for the *Evening News*.

WRONG IS RIGHT   In the center of action as Patrick Hale.

ment. Hale is accompanied by colleague Sally Blake (Katharine Ross), who is actually a CIA agent investigating separate reports that the king has purchased two nuclear bombs to be used in an attack against Israel. When Sally is murdered, Hale takes up the investigation and unravels a complex scenario in which an unpopular American president, the terrorists, the king, and Hale himself embark on separate crusades to obtain the weapons. (Hale foresees an Emmy if he does!) The screenplay varies between witty observations about present-day political hypocrisies and enough violence and shock value to remind audiences that Brooks excels at making action movies. (Merely watch his western classic *The Professionals*, for example.)

WRONG IS RIGHT   As Patrick Hale.

193

For the larger-than-life role of Patrick Hale, Connery was Brooks's first choice, not only because they were old friends. "I needed an international star, someone known all over the world. Someone who is by his very appearance a superstar. Sean Connery came to mind!" recalled Brooks. Connery insisted upon seeing the script first, a practice that Brooks was generally opposed to. Such was Sean's clout, however, that Brooks, who usually presented scripts to his actors only after filming had begun, relented. Connery felt the screenplay, which Brooks had adapted from Charles McCarry's novel *The Better Angels,* had potential, but was too long and rambling. He and Brooks settled in to streamline it and tighten up the characterizations. When shooting began, no actor other than Sean had seen the script, and the cast was given pages only for the next day's filming.

"Patrick Hale is more than just a journalist, he's sort of a superstar TV anchorman who works in the field. It's not so much what he says, but how he looks and what he does that make him a TV superstar. He's a globe-trotting combination of Ernest Hemingway and Barbara Walters," stated Connery. The production schedule was hectic and, combined with recently completed projects, insured that Sean Connery had a mere three weeks of rest at his home over twelve months. The location filming alone required him to do as much globe-hopping as his on-screen alter ego. Shooting took place in New York, England, Rome, Zagreb, Texas, Marseilles, and other widely diverse terrains. When the last shots were completed, it ended over three years of constant work by Richard Brooks on the project.

Despite the painstaking work and ambitious goals, *Wrong Is Right* failed to click with audiences, perhaps because, as *Variety* put it, "the film is impossible to pigeonhole." Too violent to be called a comedy, yet too humorous to appeal to hard-core action fans, the movie was difficult to market. In overseas showing, it was titled *The Man With the Deadly Lens* and featured Connery in the ads in a not-so-subtle Bond-type pose with a camera aimed in the fashion of a gun. The ploy did not work, and international audiences were as indifferent as Americans. Critical assessment was mixed. Some reviewers felt the movie's overload of cynicism detracted from providing a coherent plot. The *New York Times,* in a rare shot at Connery, claimed the actor gave the only uncertain performance of his career. Other critics were kinder, if not ecstatic, at Brooks's attempt to make a "different" kind of entertainment. Rex Reed felt the film had "enormous brilliance, humor, imagination, originality, and style. Richard Brooks is a great director who makes great movies, and this is perhaps his finest film." The *Daily News* cited Sean's "instant charisma" in a rave review, and *Playboy*'s Bruce Williamson wrote, "The [ideas] don't all work, yet Brooks forces laughter while skirting the abyss, ultimately gaining the pace, momentum, and class of a James Bond adventure, with Connery in rare form as your genial host on the yellow-brick road to Armageddon."

Not the least of the film's many attributes is a diverse and interesting cast, featuring everyone from Robert Conrad and John Saxon to Leslie Nielsen and Dean Stockwell. Some of the criticisms may have been valid, but many poignant moments linger in the mind, and Connery is superb throughout. "Remember," he tells a gung ho army officer leaping into battlefield action, "nothing has happened until it happens on TV!" In another hilarious swipe at the hypocrisy of image-conscious celebrities, Connery whips off his toupee in the free-for-all climax as though finally to allow his audience to see the real Patrick Hale as he plunges to his death. This caused Connery biographer Michael Feeney Callan to observe: "It's a moment of black comedy that properly evokes a laugh and a sigh, almost subliminally reminding us of the gap between the man and the image, a gap that existed with *Dr. No* and before, but that now lies too exposed and demands a different kind of bridging."

FIVE DAYS
ONE SUMMER

1982

Released by Warner Bros.

CAST:

Douglas: Sean Connery; *Kate:* Betsy Brantley; *Johann:* Lambert Wilson; *Sarah:* Jennifer Hilary; *Brendel:* Gerard Buhr; *Kate's Mother:* Isabel Dean.

CREDITS:

Director and Producer: Fred Zinnemann; *Screenplay:* Michael Austin, based on the short story "Maiden, Maiden" by Kay Boyle; *Director of Photography:* Giuseppe Rotunno; *Editor:* Stuart Baird; *Production Designer:* Willy Holt; *Music:* Elmer Bernstein. *Running Time:* 108 minutes.

Five Days One Summer is yet another in the long list of underappreciated films in which Sean Connery has starred. This project was harshly panned by most critics, who thought that any joint effort between Connery and director Fred Zinnemann should have yielded something far more consequential than this

somber love story, which is virtually devoid of any action. Ironically, many of these same critics were generally quick to decry the absence of old-fashioned "people-oriented pictures" in the post–*Star Wars* era. To be sure, *Five Days* is not only old-fashioned, but also positively archaic. Not an alien or a car chase is in sight, and it is bewildering how anyone could have felt the film would have a life outside of art houses. Yet, the filmmakers and studio deserve praise for funding such an effort, as the very factors that limit its popular appeal make it refreshing.

FIVE DAYS ONE SUMMER   As Douglas

FRED ZINNEMANN'S
FIVE DAYS
ONE SUMMER

FIVE DAYS ONE SUMMER   Screening program.

Expectations were perhaps unnaturally high when seventy-four-year-old Zinnemann announced his intention to bring this film to reality. The director of *High Noon, From Here to Eternity, A Man for All Seasons*, and *Julia* had a track record of making message movies that not only won awards but generally drew big box office, also. The idea for the film was "slowly percolating on the back burners of my mind" for forty years, Zinnemann later said. He had grown up in the mountain region of Austria and had a lifelong obsession with the Alps and those who climb the snow-topped peaks for pleasure. In 1950, Zinnemann had been inspired by a short story called "Maiden, Maiden" by Kay Boyle and had wanted to re-create the tale on the big screen. When filming finally began in June 1981, Zinnemann secured a then-sizable budget of $17 million from the Ladd Company, and Warner Bros. agreed to distribute.

The story can be termed "interminably slow" by its detractors or "leisurely paced" by its defenders. Either way, the tale relies almost entirely on the audience's interest in the main characters. The film provides Connery with another role as a tragic figure. In fact, the three main characters are all tragic, indeed, and their sense of helplessness is exactly what Zinnemann had hoped to convey. Connery plays a fiftyish married doctor in 1930s England who is having a torrid affair with a young woman (Betsy Brantley) half his age. As with most lovers in such illicit circumstances, despite the thrill of eroticism they are caught in a tangled web that can never be totally satisfying. When Connery and Brantley arrive for a holiday in the Swiss Alps, they are deeply troubled people trying desperately to hold on to a relationship that they know is ultimately doomed. Brantley is Connery's niece, and the young girl's lifelong obsession with her uncle can never be legitimized, even if Connery were to divorce his wife.

The two lovers alternate between blissful romantic encounters and depression. As they prepare for their mountain-climbing expedition, they are joined by a young guide (Lambert Wilson), whom Brantley quickly befriends (and, it is hinted, becomes sexually involved with). This causes more emotional distress for all. Connery selfishly hopes to hang on to his lover, despite the inevitable deprivation of a normal life for her that would result. Brantley is torn between her obsession for her aging uncle and the arousal of a man her own age. Lambert is agonized by Connery's "use" of a woman he feels he could make happy. As the tension mounts, Connery and Wilson embark on a dangerous climbing expedition, during which one of them dies in a rock slide. In the rather contrived shock ending, Connery is the survivor. Brantley, however, ends the relationship and leaves the stunned Connery emotionally devastated.

Connery, asked what drew him to the role, replied, "One reason was Zinnemann himself—after all, the man is a living legend. I saw *High Noon* when I was struggling to get into the business. Also the role itself is fascinating." For his part, Zinnemann confessed that Sean was always his only choice for the role "because no one else could undertake the hazardous exercises required and yet was mature and yet again could *act!*" Connery delivers an outstanding performance, conveying both the selfishness and charm of a man who is destined to be haunted by guilt for the rest of his days. Betsy Brantley, who was performing in a musical at London's Drury Lane when discovered by Zinnemann, holds her own in the company of her famous costar. Brantley exudes a natural innocence that makes her manipulation at Connery's hands quite believable. *Five Days* was her first film, but it did not launch her on a successful career in movies. Lambert Wilson, a bit player in *Julia*, has little to do other than look hunky, but handles himself adequately.

The film boasts some of the most impressive scenery imaginable, all lushly photographed by Giuseppe Rotunno. Yet, the serenity shown on film belies the extensive challenges in bringing this tale to the screen. Zinnemann spent many years finding a suitably remote location that had remained untouched over the decades. In 1979, he stumbled upon the Swiss village of Pontresina, a remote hamlet in the shadow of the Alps. Getting permission to film there was another matter, as the Swiss are notoriously protective of their natural resources. Every piece of garbage had to be removed daily—often by helicopter. Vehicles were forbidden on many of the locations, and equipment had to be transported by horse and buggy. Much of the filming took place at over ten thousand feet. Consequently, the cast and crew had to endure temperatures that ranged from below zero in the morning to scalding in the midafternoon. Sudden storms were always a threat, and the instability of the snow base could be deadly. Several climbers had died in the weeks before the filmmakers arrived, and the crew actually stumbled upon the preserved body of a climber who had been missing for decades. (This mirrored a segment in the film in which the three principals find the body of a climber missing for forty years. In a haunting sequence, the man's fiancée—now an elderly woman—is given the opportunity to step back in time by viewing the perfectly preserved body of her lover.)

As a reminder of the danger, a rock slide once slammed into a camera, ruining an entire day's takes.

elevator shaft." Reed did, however, acknowledge "a wonderful performance by Connery." *Variety* called the film a "glacially slow drama with dim box-office appeal. Feels more like 'Five Summers One Day.'"

The film played in a few houses before vanishing without the benefit of a wide release, becoming another money loser to which Connery had lent his name. Box-office figures aside, anyone with the slightest interest in Sean's career should experience this fine film on video, where its leisurely pleasures can best be enjoyed. (Do *not* watch the television version of the film, which director Zinnemann himself has supposedly edited by almost twenty minutes.)

SWORD OF THE VALIANT

1983

Released by Cannon Releasing

CAST:

Gawain: Miles O'Keeffe; *Linet:* Cyrielle Claire; *Humphrey:* Leigh Lawson; *The Green Knight:* Sean Connery; *King Arthur:* Trevor Howard; *Seneschal:* Peter Cushing; *Oswald:* Ronald Lacey; *Lady of Lyonesse:* Lila Kedrova; *Fortinbras:* John Rhys-Davies.

CREDITS:

Director: Stephen Weeks; *Producers:* Menahem Golan and Yoram Globus. *Executive Producers:* Michael Kagan and Philip M. Breen. *Screenplay:* Stephen Weeks, Philip M. Breen, and Howard C. Pen; *Directors of Photography:* Freddie A. Young and Peter Hurst; *Editors:* Richard Marden and Barry Peters; *Production Designers:* Maurice Fowler and Derek Nice; *Action Sequences Director:* Anthony Squire; *Music:* Ron Geesin. *Running Time:* 142 minutes.

For no logical reason other than to collect a quick paycheck, Sean Connery agreed to lend his talents to this minor sword-and-sorcery effort that sought to capitalize on the success of the Conan genre. Connery didn't even have to trouble himself to fly to exotic locations. All of his scenes were shot in France while he was in the midst of filming *Never Say Never Again*. *Sword of the Valiant* probably looked a lot more promising on paper than the end result would indi-

FIVE DAYS ONE SUMMER   The ménage à trois—Lambert Wilson, Betsy Brantley, and Sean.

Zinnemann also had to be patient as sands blowing all the way from the Sahara would often coat the mountains, leaving them with a temporary orange glow. To lend authenticity to the climbing sequences, the three leads did most of their own stunts. This proved to be far more dangerous than anyone had anticipated. Connery later reflected, "I try to go as far as I can doing my own stunt work, even if over the years it becomes harder. A double in a scene often dilutes the screen quality, especially if, as in this instance, the cameras are lined up for close shots. Some of the location filming of *Five Days* was the most audacious I've ever been involved in. It was all very hairy." To make matters more difficult, the cast had to utilize 1930s climbing equipment to insure accuracy.

For all the effort, appreciative audiences were sparse. Rex Reed labeled *Five Days* "a lazy, gorgeous meaningless film . . . a worthy failure . . . lushly mounted, impeccably directed, elegantly photographed, sensitively acted—but it is ultimately as empty, airless, and inconsequential as an abandoned

cate. Just as *Meteor* arrived far too late to exploit the disaster-film genre, so did *Sword* miss the short-lived sword-and-sorcery craze by a couple of years.

The film was the brainchild of director-writer Stephen Weeks, who had made a little-seen variation of the Sir Gawain/Green Knight fable in 1972. For this new effort, he managed to entice an interesting cast. In addition to Connery, there are Peter Cushing, Trevor Howard, John Rhys-Davies, Lila Kedrova, the always watchable Ronald Lacey, and even a cameo from Wilfred Brambell (Paul's "clean old grandfa-

ther" in *A Hard Day's Night.*) However, Weeks does not know what to do with this talented lineup, and most of the actors' scenes are superfluous and forgettable, save Connery's appearances, which bookend the film nicely.

The story finds the bold Sir Gawain of King Arthur's court (Miles O'Keeffe) the only one with the courage to accept the challenge of the evil Green Knight (Connery) to participate in a game of life and death. Although Gawain succeeds in decapitating the Green Knight, the latter reconstructs his body. Re-

SWORD OF THE VALIANT
As the Green Knight.

SWORD OF THE VALIANT   Video
advertisement.

specting Gawain's courage, the Green Knight gives him one year to solve a riddle that is only slightly less complicated than the script to *Zardoz*. When they next meet, Gawain must either satisfactorily answer the riddle or sacrifice his life to the Green Knight. These opening scenes are quite entertaining thanks to Connery's scenery-chewing performance. Dressed in

SWORD OF THE VALIANT

A CANNON FILMS RELEASE

SEAN CONNERY   MILES O'KEEFFE   CYRIELLE CLAIRE   LEIGH LAWSON

201

a bizarre costume and covered head to toe in green dye, he looks like the result of an affair between the Little Mermaid and the Jolly Green Giant. (The makeup required over an hour to apply, and upon seeing her husband for the first time on the set, Micheline admitted, "He scared me to death!")

The script takes Gawain through several grand adventures in his quest to learn the meaning of life. Naturally, there is a maiden who never seems to be out of distress (the lovely Cyrielle Claire) and many friends and foes straight out of the British equivalent of Central Casting as stock supporting characters. The script is also full of such timeworn clinkers as "It's quiet, isn't it?"—to which someone actually replies, "Too quiet." (Somehow the phrase "I don't like it" escaped the screenplay.) The locations in France, England, and Wales distract from the corniness, but director Weeks suffocates the actors in tiresome close-ups. He had apparently only recently discovered the existence of the zoom lens and uses it more frequently than tourists at Disney World with their first camcorder. Also, the cheesy musical score resembles the theme for a professional wrestling program.

One feels sorry for leading man Miles O'Keeffe, who has made a career out of playing the lead in pseudo-Schwarzenegger quickies such as this. He is Arnold's equal in the physique department, but seems uncertain of his lines. He is also forced to contend with a laughably distracting Prince Valiant hairdo that makes him look like a medieval incarnation of Dana Carvey in *Wayne's World*. Yet, there is something natural and likable about him, and at times he both resembles and sounds like the young George Lazenby. He also holds his own in the intimidating presence of Connery, who appears for about five minutes at the beginning of the story, then even more briefly at the climax, in which he withers away like the Wicked Witch of the West. In keeping with several *Wizard of Oz*–inspired scenarios, he also pops up midway through the story taunting Gawain through a crystal ball like a satanic version of Auntie Em.

Sword of the Valiant belongs to another era. Despite some obligatory bloodshed and the prerequisite (albeit shoddy) special effects, this is actually an innocent and tender fable that would have played better in the 1950s. In fact, it's probably the only film in memory wherein the virginal maiden remains virginal throughout! The movie was yet another in the long line of action-adventure films churned out by Cannon Releasing in the 1980s. Done on limited budgets, yet often boasting major talents, the studio's films were the envy of the industry before fickle audiences deserted this type of product. This rather

dim-witted yet entertaining mini-epic was given a very limited theatrical release in the United States. It can be found on video, however, where one can savor the charm of the least-seen Connery vehicle since *The Offence*. As for Connery, the lack of theatrical showings spared him the critical barbs about trashing his talent in such an undemanding project. He knew the inevitable success of *Never Say Never Again* would overshadow this minor effort. As icing on the cake, in one of the few formal reviews of the film, *Variety* praised Sean's "robust" performance. (By the way, Sean's appearance did allow for one of the most unusual credits to appear in any film, as it is unlikely we will again see a blurb for "Green Knight Head Effects" in the average moviegoer's lifetime!)

SWORD OF THE VALIANT   Bond, he's not. Sean rendered unrecognizable as the Green Knight.

NEVER SAY NEVER AGAIN

1983

Released by Warner Bros.

CAST:

James Bond: Sean Connery; *Largo:* Klaus Maria Brandauer; *Blofeld:* Max von Sydow; *Fatima Blush:* Barbara Carrera; *Domino:* Kim Basinger; *Felix Leiter:* Bernie Casey; *"Q" Algy:* Alec McCowen; *"M":* Edward Fox; *Miss Moneypenny:* Pamela Salem; *Small-Fawcett:* Rowan Atkinson; *Lady in Bahamas:* Valerie Leon.

CREDITS:

Director: Irvin Kershner; *Producer:* Jack Schwartzman; *Screenplay:* Lorenzo Semple, Jr., based on an original story by Kevin McClory, Jack Whittingham, and Ian Fleming; *Director of Photography:* Douglas Slocombe; *Editor:* Ian Crafford; *Production Designers:* Philip Harrison and Stephen Grimes; *Music:* Michel Legrand. *Running Time:* 134 minutes.

"James Bond isn't back—He's *here!* He has never left!" Thus spoke producer Jack Schwartzman upon witnessing the first filmed footage of a cinematic event that many felt the world would never see—Sean Connery's return as 007 in *Never Say Never Again.* As critic Roger Ebert proclaimed, the encore by Sean was "one of those small show-business miracles that never happen. There never was a Beatles reunion. But here, by God, is Sean Connery as Sir James Bond!" Yet, for all the hoopla attached to this project, the road back to Bondage would prove to be far more arduous than anything Sean could have imagined.

Its origins made *Never* the most logistically challenging film of Connery's career. To understand the pitfalls, one must return to the late 1950s when Ian Fleming collaborated with Kevin McClory and Jack Whittingham on an original screenplay titled *James Bond of the Secret Service.* The plan was to develop a pilot for a television series, but for various reasons the story was shelved. Fleming, however, incorporated much of the screenplay into his 1961 Bond novel *Thunderball,* which prompted a plagiarism suit by McClory, who later won the court battle and was

NEVER SAY NEVER AGAIN   Swedish advertisement.

awarded screen rights to the novel. In 1965, as discussed, he produced *Thunderball* with Broccoli and Saltzman.

McClory's deal with Eon Productions allowed him to make another Bond film anytime after 1975, as long as it was based on the *Thunderball* novel or the aborted screenplay with Fleming. McClory miraculously enlisted noted espionage writer Len Deighton and Sean Connery to write an updated screenplay of *James Bond of the Secret Service,* although Connery insisted he had no interest in playing 007 again. According to Sean, the original script "had all sorts of exotic events. You know those airplanes that were disappearing over the Bermuda Triangle? We had SPECTRE doing that. There was a fantastic fleet of planes under the sea—a whole world of stuff had been brought down. They were going to attack the financial nerve center of the United States by going through the sewers of New York, which you can do, right into Wall Street. They'd have mechanical sharks

in the bay and take over the Statue of Liberty, which is quite easy, and have the main line of troops on Ellis Island. That sort of thing." One winces at the thought of Bond tangling with SPECTRE in the sewers like a sort of Double-O Ed Norton, but the screenplay did elicit a full-page ad in *Variety* from mega-agent Irving "Swifty" Lazar proclaiming it one of the most exciting scripts he's ever read.

Despite McClory's own bold two-page ads announcing various start dates, Cubby Broccoli jumped into action with some trade-paper warnings threatening legal action against anyone who tried to make a Bond film outside the Eon empire. For some time, these "dueling headlines" became increasingly adversarial as the producers went eyeball-to-eyeball to see who would blink first. Ultimately, the legal obstacles posed by Eon made investors in McClory's project nervous and financing did not materialize. Over the next several years, McClory made various announcements that he had an agreement in principal to have Connery return to *star* in his Bond film, now retitled to an equally uninspired *Warhead*. This perked up interest, and McClory announced he had secured a $22-million budget and had cast Orson Welles as Blofeld and Trevor Howard as "M." This, too, proved to be just so much bluster as Eon's renewed legal obstacles resulted in the project's being shelved once again. By this time, Connery bowed out, presumably for good, blaming the armies of lawyers.

Warhead lay dormant until 1982 when independent producer and show business attorney Jack

NEVER SAY NEVER AGAIN   Discussing a shot with director Irvin Kershner.

204

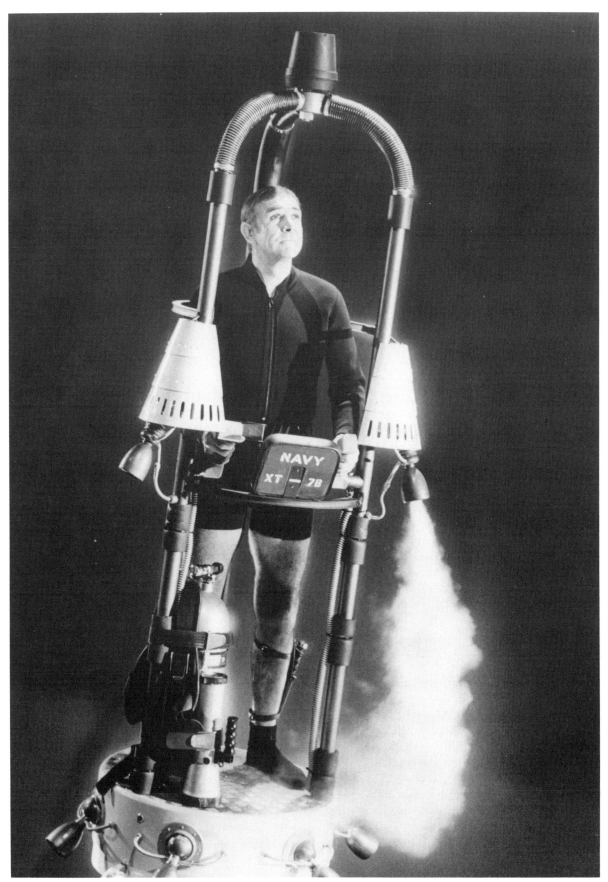

NEVER SAY NEVER AGAIN   Utilizing some CIA gadgetry to aid in the search for Largo.

Schwartzman convinced McClory that only he could weave through the legal problems. He struck a deal to make a James Bond film on the basis that future rights to the work revert back to McClory. Schwartzman cut through enough red tape in four months to assure investors and secured financing for the $34-million epic, largely by convincing Sean Connery to star. Connery was to receive an extraordinary deal: $5 million in salary, a percentage of the profits, and approval of the script, director, and major casting choices. Left out in the cold was McClory, who agreed to give up creative control of the project in return for screen credit. Additionally, the *Warhead* screenplay would be scrapped in favor of an original one that, to thwart Eon's legal challenges, had to closely resemble *Thunderball*.

When the project became reality, the worldwide media blitz was incredible. Asked why he was tempted to slip back into Bondage, Connery replied, "Micheline encouraged me to think about it carefully: 'Why not play the role? What do you risk? After all these years, it might be interesting.' The more I thought about it, the more I thought she was right. There was also a certain amount of curiosity in me about the role, having been away from it so long." (Micheline also created the film's title and receives screen credit for it.) Cynics said that Sean was merely trying to regain his footing at the box office after appearing in quite a few flops. Certainly the money and his popularity had to play some part in his

decision, but keep in mind Sean *did* collaborate on the first version of the screenplay in the mid-1970s, with no intention of starring in the film, so his interest in the character was legitimate. Again, Connery has never been critical of his James Bond films—only the logistics and financial aspects of making them.

Shooting began in September 1982 in southern France, with later filming done in Monte Carlo and Nassau/Paradise Island in the Bahamas. Interiors were done at EMI Elstree studios in London. At any given time, three separate units were shooting simultaneously: the main unit, an underwater unit, and a crew to film the elaborate action sequences. Connery used his creative control to enlist an impressive cast. Klaus Maria Brandauer was signed as the villainous Largo—a much more youthful presence than his predecessor Adolfo Celi in *Thunderball*. The most impressive Bond girl in years proved to be Kim Basinger's Domino. Basinger was largely unknown at the time, but *Playboy* film critic Bruce Williamson perceived star potential and arranged for an elaborate photo spread, which helped convince the producers to sign the extraordinarily glamorous actress for the role. This film's "black widow" character is Barbara Carrera's Fatima Blush, a woman of unspeakable beauty and deadly allure. (Her wonderful, over-the-top performance resulted in a Golden Globe nomination.) Supporting players include Edward Fox as an amusingly obnoxious "M"—a youngish technocrat with no use for over-the-hill double-O agents; Bernie

Casey, impressive as the first black Felix Leiter; the inimitable Alec McCowen as a whining and frustrated "Q" (whose underfunded workshop is the antithesis of Desmond Llewelyn's state-of-the-art lab); and Pamela Salem (from *The Great Train Robbery*) as Moneypenny.

Irvin Kershner signed on to direct *Never,* having been chosen by Connery and Schwartzman after they were impressed with his recent *The Empire Strikes Back.* (Sean's first choice, Richard Donner, passed on the project.) Kershner decided to disregard all previous Bond films and pretend this was the first one. He was delighted to see the fifty-two-year-old Sean in extraordinarily fit condition, a fact noticed by Schwartzman, who said, "Sean looks sensational. He spent months getting into shape. . . . The first time Sean came on the set was a great moment. He even received an instantaneous round of applause from the crew. I sat there and thought, 'Even with all the travail, it's been worth it.' And when I finally saw him on film, I knew it had been justified." Just the same, the Eon legal machine continued to pound heavily on Schwartzman during production, reminding him that his film better bear a close resemblance to *Thunderball* or an injunction would be sought to prevent distribution.

Cubby Broccoli was trying not only to protect his carefully cultivated image of Bond, but also to insure that his upcoming Roger Moore Bond *Octopussy* would not suffer from an overabundance of 007s during the summer of 1983, when both films were aiming for release. The press had a field day playing up "The Battle of the Bonds" and left Connery and Moore, both old friends, in the awkward position of defending their own film but not insulting the other. Sean dismissed the entire "battle" by saying, "This silly rivalry between Roger and me is being carried to daft extremes." Sean has always acknowledged that while he respected Moore's interpretation of 007, he felt his friend had overemphasized the humor. He stated, "I play him for the reality of the situations. Everything I do is physically possible, if not probable. I find that provides a more lasting form of humor. What Roger does is more comedy-parody, as opposed to humor. *From Russia With Love,* my all-time favorite Bond picture, had the most interesting chemistry, I think. It was more a detective story than some of the later Bonds, and that detective element, which we tried for in *Never,* makes the part more humanized." In essence, Connery promised to downplay the technology and emphasize the human element.

Despite all the posturing and promises, *Never Say Never Again* proved to be an arduous task in comparison to that of Broccoli's well-oiled team working on

the equally epic *Octopussy* in India. (Schwartzman originally offered to team with Broccoli on *Never,* but the latter declined.) What exactly went wrong? Many different theories were offered, but Connery insists it was incompetence on the part of many associated with the production, and he criticized Schwartzman. "He may be a good lawyer," he told the *Wall Street Journal,* "but as a producer, he never knew where all the moving parts were. . . . It seemed as long as all other six [Bond films] I'd made put together." He later added, "There was so much incompetence, ineptitude, and dissension . . . that the film could have disintegrated. It was a toilet. What I could have done is just let it bury itself. I could have walked away with an enormous amount of money and the film would never have been finished. But once I was in there, I ended up getting in the middle of every decision. The assistant director and myself really produced that picture."

Not helping matters were the "creative differences" between director Kershner and Kim Basinger. The script had to be rewritten on several occasions as well, and Connery was called back to the Bahamas to shoot additional footage after the film had wrapped, prompting rumors the movie was in trouble. Schwartzman acknowledged the problems, but downplayed the differences, stating, "There were simply things we couldn't control. We had weather problems, car crashes that didn't work, boat scenes that didn't go smoothly. We also had three units shooting at one time: two in the south of France, one in the Bahamas. We were using two directors, a very large crew. I wish it wasn't costing as much, but I think we're ending up with a very fine picture." He later pleaded in response to increasing cost overruns, "I think people should judge the film, not the process."

And just how does the film fare, given its rocky road to completion? Contrary to popular expectations, this was not "007 Visits *Heaven's Gate.*" The movie turned out amazingly well, and many critics cited it as a successful attempt to return Bond to his basics. The central strong point is obviously Sean's return as Bond. This is no sleepwalking performer going through the motions while waiting for a paycheck. Despite his frustrations on the set, Connery delivers one of his best Bondian performances. He wisely plays 007 as a man in his fifties—world-weary, with all the body aches that a middle-ager would suffer, given a lifetime of hairbreadth escapes, endless womanizing, and enough vodka martinis to refloat the *Titanic.* Refreshingly, when we first meet Bond, he is all but regarded as a relic by the bureaucratic "M." Then, SPECTRE hijacks two atomic weapons and blackmails the world. In a marvelously satisfying moment, a reluctant "M" is ordered to "reactivate the double-O's." Before you know it, Bond is back in action, also proving he hasn't lost his sex appeal. Connery is one of the few actors who doesn't appear foolish when girls half his age melt in his arms.

Never makes the most of many opportunities, but misses on so many others. There's great rapport with "M" and "Q," but no development at all of the relationship with Moneypenny. Max Von Sydow seems wonderful as Blofeld, but the character appears only in a few brief scenes. (A sequence depicting his death via a scratch from his cat's poison-coated claws was mysteriously cut from the film.) Brandauer is magnificent as Largo—a hip, nouveau riche maniac with a sarcastic wit. His deadly computer-game duel to the death with Bond is a highlight. Equally impressive is Carrera's Fatima Blush (a loosely reworked version of Luciana Paluzzi's Fiona from *Thunderball*), a character that is truly a classic in the Bond gallery of villains. As Domino, Kim Basinger makes her character both beautiful and tragic. Unlike so many other Bond women, her lines never elicit unintentional laughs, and the part put her on the path to stardom. Bernie Casey is an inspired choice as Leiter and is allowed a major role in the action.

The script is rather messy and uninvolving, and the direction and editing occasionally allow the film to drag. Therefore, the sum of the film is less than its parts. Fortunately, many individual sequences work quite well. Bond's battle with a hulking assassin in the health club is a prolonged but highly entertaining affair reminiscent of the earlier films (although the humor is a bit overemphasized). And all of Sean's scenes with the ladies work marvelously. Especially amusing is a bedroom scene in which he escapes death while barely interrupting his lovemaking with knockout Valerie Leon. The lengthy motorcycle chase has outstanding stunt work, and Connery's destruction of Fatima Blush is imaginatively handled. An exciting escape on horseback from Largo's headquarters culminates in a thirty-foot plunge from a cliff into the ocean. (British censors trimmed a few seconds on the basis that it depicted cruelty to animals.) Another highlight is Bond's brush with killer sharks inside an ocean wreck. (Connery fears these creatures with good reason, but, trooper that he is, performed many of his own stunts.)

Some negative elements could easily have been corrected. For one, the music is almost nonexistent, allowing key action sequences such as the motorcycle chase to go largely unscored. Michel Legrand's title song is adequate, but his background music does not rise above that of any episode of television's *Mannix*.

The editing is also questionable, with key scenes cut short and inconsequential ones dragging on. The climactic battle between Largo's forces and the navy is but a pale shadow of *Thunderball*'s underwater battle. The pace is much slower here—and *this* was shot on dry land! (Production photos indicate that quite a bit of impressive footage may have been cut from this scene.) Also, the all-important fight to the death between Bond and Largo is shot underwater and so murkily photographed that the action is almost impossible to discern. This robs a key scene of any tension. The film additionally has a greasy look to it, and the color processing and cinematography appear somewhat wanting.

Despite all this, the return of Connery is still cause for rejoicing, and *Never Say Never Again* remains a worthy addition to the Bond lineup, despite not having the polish of the Eon Bonds. When the film opened (having survived an eleventh-hour appeal for an injunction from Eon), most critics hailed Connery's encore appearance, with Rex Reed speaking for most when he wrote: "Sean Connery is back—older, hairier, grittier, and greater than ever. . . . He is the real thing because he seems to take Bond seriously instead of laughing him off as a comic-strip buffoon. When it comes to 007, I hope he says, 'Never say never again.' " Other critics compared the movie to the gilt-edged Bonds of the sixties, most notably *From Russia With Love*. The production delays did have one beneficial effect—they postponed the movie's release, thus avoiding a showdown with *Octopussy* at the box office. Despite all the speculation as to whose Bond would bury whose, there was a wide audience for both films. Roger Moore's epic outgrossed Sean's by several million dollars in the U.S., proving Roger had his own loyal army of fans and was no pushover. Connery's film, however, did well despite having to open in October and set attendance records for the greatest fall movie opening in U.S. history to that time. Internationally, both movies were sizable hits.

Connery dutifully attended the premieres and plugged the film on the talk show circuit, with nary a bad word to say. However, sometime later, he filed suit against Schwartzman for not paying his agreed-upon share of the profits. By the time the dust settled, both men agreed that, when it came to making another film about James Bond, neither would "never say *ever* again."

Note: As of this book's publication, it is rumored that Jack Schwartzman is planning a laser disc reissue of the film that will include extensive footage cut from the initial release. The film may also be rescored.

THERE'S NO STOPPING THE NEWSPAPER HEADLINES

SEAN CONNERY
IS JAMES BOND IN
NEVER SAY NEVER AGAIN

STOP PRESS...STOP PRESS...STOP PRESS...STOP PRESS...

FEED THIS EXCITING INFORMATION TO YOUR LOCAL MEDIA,
PRESS KITS — B & W STILLS — COLOUR — AVAILABLE NOW FREE
FOR PLACEMENT WITH YOUR LOCAL MEDIA

NEVER SAY NEVER AGAIN   The British media made the most of Sean's return as Bond.

HIGHLANDER

1986

Released by 20th Century-Fox

CAST:

Connor MacLeod: Christopher Lambert; *Brenda Wyatt:* Roxanne Hart; *Kurgan:* Clancy Brown; *Ramirez:* Sean Connery; *Heather:* Beatie Edney; *Moran:* Alan North.

CREDITS:

Director: Russell Mulcahy; *Producers:* Peter S. Davis and William N. Panzer; *Screenplay:* Gregory Widen, Peter Bellwood, and Larry Ferguson, from a story by Widen; *Director of Photography:* Gerry Fisher; *Editor:* Peter Honess; *Production Designer:* Allan Cameron; *Music:* Michael Kamen, songs and additional music by Queen. *Running Time:* 111 minutes (128 outside of the United States).

Treading on ground that was somewhat reminiscent of *Zardoz,* Sean Connery returned to the science fiction genre with *Highlander,* a $16-million epic shot on location in Scotland and New York, with studio scenes filmed in England. *Variety* dismissed the film as a "mishmash," but it has a durable worldwide audience. Like *Zardoz,* the plot concentrates on the agonies faced if one could achieve immortality, and the inevitable obsession with living a normal life. The two films are also similar in that, despite their faults, their themes are explored in highly visual ways that are often so impressive they distract from the weakness of their scripts. Calling *Highlander* the more comprehensible of the flicks may be akin to referring to Uncle Fester as the most handsome member of the Addams family, but the movie is infinitely more interesting than the earlier *Zardoz.*

Director Russell Mulcahy's pace is lightning fast, and *Highlander* begins with a stunning action set piece under Madison Square Garden. Here, MacLeod (Christopher Lambert) is engaged in a spectacular but initially inexplicable swordfight with a seemingly dauntless assailant. MacLeod finally destroys his foe by beheading him, and puzzled, we are suddenly transported back to sixteenth-century Scotland where we find MacLeod as the leader of a fierce tribe of warriors known as Highlanders. The film shifts back and forth between centuries in an often frustrating manner, but it is later explained that following his death at the hands of an evil and immortal adversary named Kurgan (Clancy Brown), MacLeod is chosen to become an Immortal by Ramirez (Sean Connery), a mystical mentor who has lived for over two thousand years. Ramirez informs his reluctant protégé that he is being entrusted with the pursuit of Kurgan through the centuries, as the latter attempts to kill his peers and become the only remaining Immortal in the universe. The downside of immortality is that one cannot reproduce and should not enter romantic relationships, as you will inevitably watch your lover grow old and die while you remain young. Also, one should watch those swords as an Immortal can indeed bite the dust if decapitated. Got it so far?

MacLeod ignores his mentor's advice and marries Heather (Beatie Edney), only to have to bury his beloved when she dies of old age. (Critics accurately complained about the substandard makeup job on the "elder" Edney, as, aside from a white mane, she still looks mighty fetching for a septuagenarian.) The film follows MacLeod through time to present-day New York, where Kurgan has reappeared and beheaded several adversaries in his search for the ultimate duel with MacLeod. Even in Manhattan, serial beheadings still get some attention in the press, and MacLeod is shadowed by police forensic expert Brenda Wyatt (Roxanne Hart), who, in addition to being beautiful, also authored *The Metallurgical History of Ancient Sword Making* in her spare time(!). Naturally, a romance begins with Brenda later taken as a hostage to lure MacLeod to a spectacular duel to the death atop a factory.

While Connery is not on-screen much, he lights up the film with a witty and vigorous performance. Interestingly, *Highlander* makes more physical demands on the actor than most of his starring roles. As the wise swordman of the centuries, Connery is given some engaging and occasionally moving dialogue, as he reminisces about lovers lost over the seemingly endless passage of time. His character is basically a combination Obi-Wan Kenobi and Jor-El, and Connery convinces you he has indeed seen the wisdom and mistakes of the ages through his weary eyes. Connery looks marvelous here in a graying wig with ponytail, mustache, and goatee. In some splendid sequences he trains MacLeod in swordplay and physical fitness, framed by the magnificent Scottish highlands. While the scenes often resemble *Rocky* in kilts, the camerawork by Gerry Fisher more than compensates for the clichés.

Connery's character meets his fate in a spectacular

HIGHLANDER   As Ramirez.

swordfight with Kurgan, leaving MacLeod to face the brute in the aforementioned battle in New York. Why present-day Manhattan? It appears destiny has mandated the Immortals meet there for the Gathering, a sort of Elks Club convention for higher beings from which only one will survive. (And to think the city gets excited by hosting the Democratic convention!) Naturally, the fate of the world depends upon whether good or evil emerges victorious. By this time, Kurgan has transformed into a vile, leather-clad, church-desecrating fiend who annoys and offends all those around him—sort of like a heavy metal band. His final confrontation with MacLeod is truly a stunner, with the combatants destroying an entire building in a blinding shower of neon glass, explosions, and fires. (Strangely, no one in the neighborhood seems to notice any of this. While New Yorkers are known for their casual acceptance of mayhem, this is sort of like napping on Normandy Beach on D day.) When the smoke clears, Kurgan has been beheaded

212

and MacLeod earns the "gift" of mortality, allowing him to live a long and happy life with Brenda (at least until summoned for the film's sequel in 1991).

Highlander was yet another Connery vehicle that suffered from a poor advertising campaign, although it admittedly was not an easy film to market. The title gave no indication of the sci-fi nature of the story, and the print ads only confused audiences. The movie was dismissed by critics as incomprehensible (though it is not) and directed in the fashion of an MTV video (which it is). The casting is generally inspired, although lead actor Christopher Lambert's strength is clearly in the action scenes. While possessing a forehead only slightly smaller than that of a face on Mount Rushmore, he needs to be more charismatic in the dramatic scenes. More impressive is the technical work, with outstanding special effects and art direction. Director Mulcahy is in no danger of winning an Oscar, but he knows how to keep a confusing story moving. The addition of music from the rock band Queen fits appropriately, although it is doubtful anyone left the theater humming any memorable songs.

The film was a financial flop domestically and was quickly withdrawn from movie houses. However, it was a hit on video and in the international cinemas, where the film had a longer running time. Connery could find consolation for a weak U.S. box office by savoring his constantly growing appreciation in other parts of the world. By no means is Sean responsible for the entire success of this underrated film, but it is safe to say he more than earned his (considerable) salary.

THE NAME OF THE ROSE

1986

Released by 20th Century-Fox

CAST:

William of Baskerville: Sean Connery; *Bernardo Gui:* F. Murray Abraham; *Adso:* Christian Slater; *Severinus:* Elya Baskin; *Jorge de Burgos:* Feodor Chaliapin, Jr.; *Umbertino de Casale:* William Hickey; *The Abbot:* Michael Lonsdale.

CREDITS:

Director: Jean-Jacques Annaud; *Producer:* Bernd Eichinger; *Executive Producers:* Thomas Schuehly and Jake Eberts.

Screenplay: Andrew Birkin, Gerard Brach, Howard Franklin, and Alain Godard, based on the novel by Umberto Eco; *Director of Photography:* Tonino Delli Colli; *Editor:* Jane Seitz; *Production Designer:* Dante Ferretti; *Music:* James Horner. *Running Time:* 130 minutes.

Following his commitment to *Highlander,* Sean Connery was rumored to be set for the oft-delayed screen adaptation of James Clavell's *Tai-Pan,* but this was inaccurate. (*Tai-Pan* would be an expensive dud for eventual leading man Bryan Brown.) Instead, Connery signed on for one of the most unusual roles of his career: a sleuthing Middle Ages Franciscan monk in the $20-million adaptation of Umberto Eco's international best-seller *The Name of the Rose.* The six-hundred-page novel told a Conan Doyle–type mystery described by its director as an "unholy murder [investigated] by a man of reason in a fourteenth-century world of blind faith."

One man who was seized by this extraordinary tale of intrigue and death set within a gloomy ancient cloister was French director Jean-Jacques Annaud, who had previously made an international splash with the highly unusual *Quest for Fire.* A self-confessed addict for medieval lore, Annaud was obsessed with securing film rights to the novel before he had even finished reading it. Aside from the attraction of

THE NAME OF THE ROSE   As William of Baskerville.

213

LE NOM DE LA ROSE

the time period, he found the unusual plot fascinating: "In most murder mysteries, the motive is banal—money, an inheritance. . . . Here, [friars are murdered after stumbling upon] a book in Greek dealing with comedy! It's about suppression of knowledge, the danger of communication . . . the danger of laughter!"

While the central character is Connery's Brother William of Baskerville (an obvious homage to Sherlock Holmes), the audience sees the mystery unravel through the eyes of his young apprentice, Adso (Christian Slater). The two holy men arrive in a remote and eerie Italian abbey where a papal conference has been convened to decide whether the Church's riches should be abandoned as a violation of Christ's teachings. Before the debate can be settled, a series of gruesome murders terrorizes the inhabitants of the abbey. Are the deaths a foretelling of the events of the Apocalypse, or are they the work of a twisted human mind? The task of solving this mystery is placed upon William and Adso. Their task is further impeded by the arrival of the inquisitor, Bernardo Gui (F. Murray Abraham), a medieval Joseph McCarthy who sees a heretic under every bed and justifies torture as a means of "confession." He warns William

that further investigation might lead to his own death, but the amateur sleuth is determined to unveil the truth—regardless of the risks.

Casting for the roles was predicated on a simple premise—the actors had to be right for the part, regardless of whether they were established stars. Annaud's first choice for the role of William was Roy Scheider. However, the idea was dismissed after a few initial meetings as Annaud feared the actor was "too American" to be accepted by the audience. Annaud had also briefly considered Michael Caine, but he decided to send the fifteenth draft of the script to Connery, who was immediately captivated: "I found my character so attractive to identify with because it's such a pleasure to play somebody who's reasonably intelligent, witty, and humorous. Most movies are bereft of that. . . . It got me excited, which rarely happens." Connery's enthusiasm carried over onto the set, where he entertained the cast and crew by joking and playing magic tricks over dinner. Said Annaud, "Sean protects himself. He's afraid of emotions, so when he opens the gate, it's really something to see."

The actual filming was a challenge for all. Locations in Italy were cold and uncomfortable. Commented

Connery, "I wore a monk's outfit, thermal underwear, and space boots—and my arse was still freezing." Annaud did little to add to the comforts, being convinced that the inconveniences would only add to the realism of the performances. As for Connery, he agreed that the atmosphere was disturbingly true to medieval times, and he later regretted not shooting the film in sequence to further heighten his emotional involvement with the story. Production designer Dante Ferretti's magnificent re-creation of the monastery was to be set afire for the film's exciting climax. Rain, however, prevented anything more than a few matchlike fires from igniting, causing numerous retakes and endless frustrations for the crew.

Christian Slater, then in the early stages of evolving into a teenage heartthrob, reported that he and Connery rarely spoke at first. Gradually, though, the relationship warmed and the two would play practical jokes on each other. The rapport translates effectively in the finished film. F. Murray Abraham, fresh from his triumphant Oscar win in *Amadeus,* was also impressed by working with Connery. Abraham appears late in the film, but his fiery performance nearly steals the show from Connery, who was consciously taking a low-key approach to properly emulate the actions of a monk.

The supporting cast is a fascinating lineup of actors made up to resemble *The Good, the Bad, and the Ugly.* Chilean beauty Valentina Vargas deflowers Slater in one of the most erotic sex scenes to make it into a mainstream film. With few exceptions, the other actors appear so grotesque that they make the zombies in *Night of the Living Dead* look like Chippendale dancers. Although *Variety* pondered why everyone was made up to look "like Klaus Kinski in *Nosferatu,* Annaud responded that the look was necessary because "in order to recreate the world at 1326 A.D., I had to consider the health of that period. . . . Medieval Europe had Gothic faces."

To achieve historical accuracy, three years of research and preparation preceded filming. The fourteenth century was an age of despair and questioning of one's faith. The filmmakers have succeeded in capturing this atmosphere of crisis and upheaval caused by the many social and cultural changes sweeping the world. Every prop, right down to the last book in the abbey's massive library, was painstakingly re-created in authentic period style. Many of the interiors were actually filmed in the eight-hundred-year-old Kloster Eberach near Frankfurt, Germany. All this meticulous attention helps to convey another time, and one begins to feel one is *inside* that dreary monastery, where danger and death lurk in every shadowy corner.

THE NAME OF THE ROSE   A tense meeting with Inquisitor F. Murray Abraham.

THE NAME OF THE ROSE Discussing the murders with Christian Slater.

THE NAME OF THE
ROSE French lobby card.
Sean with Christian Slater.

LE NOM DE LA ROSE

As a basic whodunit, *The Name of the Rose* is as engrossing as any mystery involving Sherlock Holmes, Columbo, or other twentieth-century favorites. As a character study, Connery's William is a fascinating figure: quiet, humble, and occasionally doddering, he can also snap quickly to life and become a true man of action. It's a joy to watch charismatic Sean patiently work out clues that are virtually indecipherable to anyone else, while treating the audience to witticisms James Bond would envy. The real star of the film, however, is production designer Ferretti, whose work here should have received an Oscar.

The Name of the Rose was a flop in the United States. Connery blamed the ad campaign and specifically cited Fox bigwig Barry Diller for not insuring a more creative launch for the film. The first mistake was to open this intimate, atmospheric mystery in hundreds of theaters, instead of letting audiences build gradually in a handful of playdates. The uninspired ad campaign featured cartoon likenesses of the cast that implied this was to be a lighthearted romp. In fairness, however, the film's confusing title did not help, as it conveyed nothing about the subject matter. Critics were also divided, with *Variety,* astonishingly, dismissing the movie as "sorrowfully mediocre." (The paper did cite Connery's performance, noting that "[he] lends dignity, intelligence, and his lovely voice to the proceedings [and is] about the only blessing to be found in this plodding misfire.") *The Wall Street Journal* was more attuned to the film's intentions, claiming it was a "quite enjoyable movie. . . . Sean Connery [is] one of the few actors imaginable who can seem to be all things. . . . His expressive restraint lets you know his character is a man who's learned long ago to hold back. . . . So when William lets loose a rare whoop of excitement . . . you get a chill."

The movie's failure in the United States remains a bitter point for Sean, and the mention of *Rose* inevitably leads to his expressing sadness that the audience was deprived of perhaps his finest work. Ironically, *Rose* was a smash throughout the rest of the world, following its gala premiere in Florence. While American critics were baffled by the movie, their European peers were ecstatic in their praise for both the film and Sean's performance. Indeed, the British Academy of Film and Theatre Arts bestowed upon him its award for Best Actor—the U.K. equivalent of the Oscar. Connery could have ended up doing the film for no compensation, as he was to receive a percentage of the U.S. profits—which were nonexistent. But in a rare act of generosity within the film community, producer Bernd Eichinger cut Sean in for 2 percent of the $100-million international gross. This was a fitting reward for an actor whose superb performance played the major role in insuring the success of a most unusual film.

THE UNTOUCHABLES

1987

Released by Paramount Pictures

CAST:

Eliot Ness: Kevin Costner; *Jim Malone:* Sean Connery; *Oscar Wallace:* Charles Martin Smith; *George Stone:* Andy Garcia; *Al Capone:* Robert De Niro; *Mike:* Richard Bradford; *Payne:*

THE UNTOUCHABLES   This Czech poster illustrates the international success of *The Untouchables.*

THE UNTOUCHABLES   Restraining Eliot Ness (Kevin Costner) from attacking Al Capone. (Photo credit: Zade Rosenthal).

Jack Kehoe; *George:* Brad Sullivan; *Frank Nitti:* Billy Drago; *Catherine Ness:* Patricia Clarkson.

CREDITS:

Director: Brian De Palma; *Producer:* Art Linson; *Screenplay:* David Mamet; *Director of Photography:* Stephen H. Burum; *Editors:* Jerry Greenberg and Bill Pankow; *Visual Consultant:* Patrizia Von Brandenstein; *Music:* Ennio Morricone. *Running Time:* 119 minutes.

The Untouchables elevated Sean Connery to a popularity unmatched since his Bondian heydays of the 1960s, not that one had to hold any charity benefits for the middle-age actor, who had by this time become a millionaire many times over. Despite his enduring popularity, though, the common thought was that Sean was too outspoken and too removed from the political games in Hollywood to ever receive formal recognition by his peers. The critics of course were generally kind to him, even when the films didn't measure up, and no one was about to question his talent. However, at the time Sean began filming *The Untouchables* in August 1986, not only had he failed to be nominated for an Oscar, but he had yet to even attend one of the ceremonies. In fact, Sean had never even bothered to join the Academy of Motion Picture Arts and Sciences. His admirers had long ago reconciled themselves that Connery would never be Oscar-nominated. If the Academy had overlooked his superb work in such films as *The Hill, The Offence, The Wind and the Lion, The Man Who Would Be King,* and *Robin and Marian,* the odds were against this aging star continuing to get the kind of roles that make nominations a sure thing.

Connery's involvement with *The Untouchables* seemed unlikely even to producer Art Linson and director Brian De Palma. It had long been Linson's dream to fabricate a big-screen version of the classic television show. His goal, however, was to have the film rooted in aspects of the TV series while creating a unique perspective to tell the story. The main characters were to remain intact: crime-busting federal agent Eliot Ness, legendary mob boss Al Capone, and his henchman Frank Nitti. The script would also copy the series by exaggerating Ness's exploits, when, in fact, his role in Capone's downfall was far less significant than the television series or film would indicate. De Palma himself was an unlikely candidate to helm this big-budget epic. While undeniably a commercial director, De Palma had generally found his success with thrillers that emulated Alfred Hitchcock far too closely for most critics. De Palma was eager to prove

he could extend his talent to a mainstream box-office hit that dealt with real people in real situations instead of *Psycho*-inspired chillers.

If Linson went against popular opinion in choosing De Palma, industry eyebrows were really raised when he convinced noted playwright David Mamet to concoct the original screenplay. Mamet was hot from winning the Pulitzer Prize for his play *Glengarry Glen Ross.* Linson met Mamet over lunch and told him sarcastically that, having just won a Pulitzer, the obvious career move was to write a script based upon a somewhat ancient TV series. Remarkably, Mamet thought the idea was a good one and became immediately enthused.

With Mamet on board, casting was the next priority. Linson decided to go with instinct instead of blockbuster box-office appeal for most of the main characters. Kevin Costner, who had only recently experienced some minor success in *Silverado,* was to play Ness. Charles Martin Smith, heretofore known primarily as a nerd from *American Graffiti* many years before, and fast-rising Andy Garcia were cast as two of Ness's team. The key remaining role was that of Jimmy Malone, the aging Irish beat cop who reluctantly joins the Untouchables in their seemingly Quixotic quest to bring down Al Capone, who is unofficially known as the *real* mayor of Chicago. Linson wanted Sean Connery for the role, but how does one engage the services of a genuine superstar for a supporting role and then tell him he will be billed below Costner? "It's real simple," explained Linson. "You develop a wonderful script with a great writer and it makes the producers look like they know what they are doing! The part of Jimmy Malone is brilliantly written, and I believe that Sean Connery will be nominated for an Oscar." Sean, enthused about working with De Palma and Mamet, signed for the role, accepting a low salary in favor of a percentage of the gross. The next casting coup was signing Robert De Niro for the small but pivotal role of Al Capone. True to form, method actor De Niro gained weight and had clothes custom-tailored to Capone's specifications so that he might get the feel of the actual person.

Connery prepared for the role by first reading only those pages of the script in which he appeared. He then went back and read only those in which he did not appear. He explained, "That way, I get to know what the character is aware of and, more importantly, what he is not aware of. The trap that bad actors fall into is playing information they don't have or playing scenes before they get to them." He patterned the character of Malone on an actual policeman from his

THE UNTOUCHABLES   Enlisting Andy Garcia (left) onto the team, while Kevin Costner observes. (Photo credit: Zade Rosenthal)

THE UNTOUCHABLES   As Jimmy Malone, Sean's Oscar-winning role. (Photo credit: Zade Rosenthal)

old neighborhood in Edinburgh: "We would watch him coming down the street. If he was walking at his usual, measured pace, all was well. But if not, if he was really moving, then someone was in for it." Sean has long been critical of actors who soften their characters on-screen to appeal for more sympathy from the audience. Not so with his interpretation of Malone. Connery intentionally overstated the character's harsh side, but this made his moments of softness all the more moving. To ensure the team of "Untouchables" had developed genuine rapport, the cast rehearsed for a full week before the cameras rolled. During this time Sean enacted his role of arrogant, stubborn Jimmy Malone off the set as well. "I began playing the old cop, the old teacher, giving these fledglings a bit of a rough time, saying slightly

THE UNTOUCHABLES   On the set with Kevin Costner and director Brian De Palma (seated left), Robert De Niro, and producer Art Linson.

THE UNTOUCHABLES   The untouchables (from left: Charles Martin Smith, Kevin Costner, Connery, and Andy Garcia) celebrating their success prior to tragedy. (Photo credit: Zade Rosenthal)

anti-American things to annoy them while they tried to top me." The strategy worked beautifully, and the cast began to act like their on-screen personas. The benefits of this are obvious on the screen, as the audience loses sight of the fact these are actors, having related to them as real people.

Mamet's script is more impressive when viewed as a series of individual scenes, as opposed to a consistent story line. The basic premise is old hat: Eliot Ness, the incorruptible lawman, is sent into Capone's Chicago to enforce the unpopular Prohibition laws, which Big Al has made a fortune violating. He finds most of the police and city officials are in the gangster's pocket, and no one can be trusted. Ness forms a ragtag team consisting of Connery's honest, streetwise, but weary Malone; Charles Martin Smith's accountant, who is forced to become a man of action; and Andy Garcia as a dedicated but cocky police recruit. At first their efforts are sabotaged and the team becomes an object of mockery. They eventually succeed, though, in thwarting many of Capone's schemes, which results in a contract being put out on their lives. Ultimately, what brings about Capone's downfall is not guns but accounting ledgers, as he is eventually forced to plead guilty to income tax evasion.

Though unstartling, the story is beautifully told and enacted. This is a rare case of ensemble acting with no weak links. The film is violent and bloody, but not unnecessarily so, and De Palma shows he can handle the emotional and sensitive sequences with surpris-

ing skill. Connery is in most of the film's many memorable sequences. From his first appearance, strikingly handsome in his police uniform as he berates Ness for littering without knowing this is his future boss, to his sensational death sequence wherein he is machine-gunned by the mob, this is acting of such brilliance that for once an Oscar nomination seemed assured. Connery's Malone is a lonely, displaced man who uses his suicidal involvement in Capone's destruction as a way to give value to an unsatisfying life. When this heroic man's life is taken so horribly, audiences could be heard crying aloud.

It would be unfair, however, to give all of the attention to Connery's triumphant performance. After all, this is the film that elevated Kevin Costner to superstar status and made Andy Garcia a very visible presence in movies. Equally wonderful is Charles Martin Smith, who is so watchable in all his roles that one wonders why the industry does not utilize his talents more often. Smith, too, falls victim to the mob, and his death has an equally tragic effect on audiences—which is testimony to his skill as an actor. As for Robert De Niro, his robust performance as Capone manages to dominate the screen even though he appears only sporadically throughout (and shares but one brief scene with Connery). De Niro replaced Bob Hoskins, who was previously signed for the role. Fat, greasy, and obnoxious, De Niro brilliantly plays up Capone's humorous side when speaking to the press or gangland cronies. Yet, he shows us this is a man to be taken seriously, especially when he interrupts a formal dinner to use a baseball bat to crush the skull of an underling. Like Connery, De Niro does not allow his ego to stand in the way of taking a good supporting role, and his contribution to *The Untouchables* is enormous.

Patrizia Von Brandenstein, the Oscar-winning set designer for *Amadeus,* perfectly re-creates the Chicago of 1930. The sets included replicas of lush hotel lobbies, speakeasies, old warehouses, and common street shots that required over sixty cars from the era. The climactic shoot-out at Union Station took twenty crews two weeks to prepare. Costume designer Marilyn Vance gets credit for the large number of outstanding period costumes. Ennio Morricone, the composer for Sergio Leone's "spaghetti western" trilogy of Clint Eastwood films, delivered one of his best scores for *The Untouchables*—sparse but hard-driving and suspenseful. All of this works wonderfully in conjunction with Mamet's script, which was so good that Connery related even the writer was surprised when the filmmakers left the dialogue virtually intact.

Word of mouth on *The Untouchables* was not particularly good before the picture premiered. Many in the industry felt it would lay an egg at the box office, as its cast were either largely unknown or, like Connery and De Niro, had not experienced a big hit domestically in quite some time. This feeling was reinforced when Paramount strictly limited advance critics screenings, a frequent practice when a film appears to be a loser. To the surprise of many, the film opened as a critical and box-office blockbuster and shortly made the cover of *Newsweek.* Connery was immediately singled out for the most lavish praise, with *Variety* echoing most of the critical sentiments by stating, "[He] delivers one of his finest performances ever. It is filled with nuance, humor, and abundant self-confidence." Roger Ebert called Connery's work the best performance in the picture, and Rex Reed labeled the film "an American classic."

In February 1988 the Oscar nominations were announced. For once, justice prevailed and Sean Connery's name was among those listed for Best Supporting Actor. Although *The Untouchables* received three other nominations—set design, costumes, and music score—it was locked out of all other categories, an incredible oversight that infuriated producer Art Linson. Nevertheless, on the evening of the awards, one of the loudest and most heartfelt ovations in recent years was heard when the name of Sean Connery was announced as a winner. Nearing the age of sixty, Sean was to find that with the Oscar win behind, some of the best roles of his career were right around the corner.

THE PRESIDIO

1988

Released by Paramount Pictures

CAST:

Caldwell: Sean Connery; *Austin:* Mark Harmon; *Donna:* Meg Ryan; *Maclure:* Jack Warden; *Peale:* Mark Blum; *Colonel Lawrence:* Dana Gladstone.

CREDITS:

Director: Peter Hyams; *Producer:* D. Constantine Conte; *Screenplay:* Larry Ferguson; *Director of Photography:* Peter Hyams; *Editor:* James Mitchell; *Production Designer:* Albert Brenner; *Music:* Bruce Broughton. *Running Time:* 97 minutes.

Sean Connery's follow-up film to his Oscar triumph in *The Untouchables* proved to be a punt rather than another touchdown. *The Presidio* had one strike against it already, a title that might be meaningful to military historians and residents of San Francisco, but one that left most people puzzled. For the record, the Presidio is the nation's oldest active military base, dating back over two hundred years. Its primary duty is still to protect the bay area of Frisco. Expectations were high for this film, as it reunited Connery with *Outland* director Peter Hyams, replacing *Top Gun* director Tony Scott, who had withdrawn at the last minute. It was also rumored that Marlon Brando was being wooed to costar. This was not to be, and Mark Harmon's above-the-title billing alongside Connery seemed rather anticlimactic. Sean accepted the role because "I was very interested in making a human side of the American soldier, that in a funny way got lost since the Vietnam War. That fellowship was what we really wanted to examine."

Connery is cast as Lieutenant Colonel Caldwell, a hardheaded career military man on duty at the Presidio. The murder of a female M.P. reunites him with a former subordinate, played by Harmon. Seems the two had bumped heads during the latter's tenure at the fort, causing the younger man to resign and become a San Francisco detective. Soon the two adversaries are forced to team up to solve the case. The idea of antagonistic investigators compelled to work together was already stale when Mel Gibson

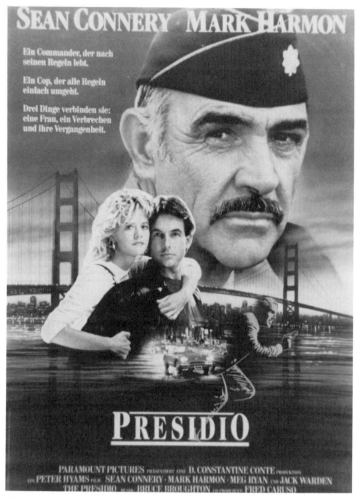

THE PRESIDIO   German theater poster.

The Presidio is undoubtedly a slickly made thriller. Hyams, who is also credited as cinematographer, succeeds in creating an authentic military atmosphere. The crew worked extensively with army advisers to insure that all procedures depicted were accurate. Location filming at the Presidio helped, too, but the institution is never dwelt upon and simply provides atmosphere. Where the film truly succeeds is in the action sequences, disjointed though they may be. Hyams has a knack for creating prolonged chase scenes. The opening one took two weeks to film, but provides a good number of thrills. (Besides, it takes guts even to consider staging a car chase in San Francisco after *Bullitt*.) There's also a dandy pursuit on foot through Chinatown between Harmon and a villain, aided substantially by the former performing all of his own stunts. Connery gets his licks in as well in the film's most amusing sequence, demolishing a hulking barroom bully by using only his thumb! However, Sean's most challenging sequence to film had nothing to do with brawls: "[It] was marching in formation at the opening. It was very difficult not to march like a British sailor. I was sixteen when I went in and was quite conditioned by it."

The film's weakest aspect is the script by Larry Ferguson, who cowrote the screenplay for *Highlander*. For starters, the mystery is never very interest-

and Danny Glover were in diapers. (Aren't investigators ever forced to work with *friendly* partners?)

As one critic noted, "the plod thickens" when Harmon falls madly in love with Sean's gorgeous and frustrated sexpot daughter, played by Meg Ryan. Despite her joyriding at high speed through the city streets and making torrid love shortly after meeting Harmon, the script asks us to accept that this woman is a daddy's girl who lives in paranoid fear that Poppa Sean will order her not to date her new beau. This is the most unlikely plot contrivance since forty-year-old Neil Diamond was "forced" to become a cantor instead of a rock star in *The Jazz Singer*. The scenes between Harmon and Ryan are pretentious and boring, as are many of those between the two leads. This is another contemporary thriller that feels compelled to insert as many expletives as possible. That may be the way a lot of guys talk, but the effect is wearying. Also, Harmon is reduced to speaking the prerequisite tag lines that all action stars must now verbalize since Clint Eastwood immortalized "Make my day!"

THE PRESIDIO   With Mark Harmon. (Photo credit: Bruce Talamon)

ing and there's no major nemesis. When the loose ends are tied together, they amount to little more than a standard smuggling plot. Somehow, deliveries of bottled water fit into the scheme, though after several viewings we confess we are still ignorant as to why. This plot contrivance does allow the climax to take place within a large set doubling for a bottled-water plant. The effect of blazing Uzi machine guns on all that H_2O and glass was obviously irresistible to Hyams, and to his credit the scene is quite exciting. (Can someone explain, though, why legions of machine-gun-toting villains are always incapable of hitting the broad side of a barn?) Gun enthusiasts might also be interested to note that weapons can apparently be relied upon to fire despite being submerged in water. There are other lapses of logic, such as Connery constantly parading about in uniform while working undercover. He and Harmon also shadow a delivery truck so obviously that they may as well have attached a tow bar between the two vehicles.

Connery received praise from otherwise unimpressed critics. Although he is seemingly miscast as a career U.S. Army officer, the Scottish brogue is explained by the fact that he immigrated to America at age ten. Unconvincing as this may seem, the filmmakers did base Connery's character on an actual lieutenant colonel who left the USSR at age twelve. In any event, Connery dominates the entire film and looks smashing in his dress blues. *USA Today* noted, "Sean Connery negotiates the line between testy and tender with a gymnast's grace. . . . He never lets up—teasing, cajoling, and forcing viewers to follow wherever he chooses to take them. . . . [He] and the chases will keep your pulse pounding." *Variety* praised "the vivid chase scenes and worthy performances," but dismissed the affair as "an elaborate distraction built around a slight crime story. . . . Connery is the most compelling of the stars as the topflight old officer with the lingering Scottish burr, his contradictions glimmering just beneath the surface of a tough hide." Critic Roger Ebert complained, "The whole movie has the feeling of a clone, of a film assembled out of spare parts from other movies out at the cinematic junkyard." Of Sean, however, he stated, "Connery has a few good moments, largely created by his own energy and effort, as when he uses his perfect timing to give ordinary dialogue the feeling of humorous understatement."

Connery is the glue that holds most of the elements together, and he is at his best when sharing scenes with stalwart pro Jack Warden (although a drunken heart-to-heart baring of the souls between the men is poorly written). Sean's eulogy of his old friend in the film's closing minutes is quite moving, largely be-cause it is one of the few occasions in his career where Connery is allowed to break down in tears. His relationship with Mark Harmon, however, seems forced and contrived. Harmon does not embarrass himself opposite Connery's intimidating presence, but he underplays his role to the point of inducing boredom. Connery himself later admitted, "I suppose Harmon could have been stronger, like Costner or that chap [Don] Johnson." Harmon does excel in the action scenes, though, and that is really what *The Presidio* is all about. Meg Ryan is lovely and sexy but has little to do other than slink about the house in designer dresses, as though she might be momentarily summoned to the Oscar awards.

The Presidio failed to click with audiences, and the box-office tallies were disappointing. Had Connery foreseen his Academy Award win, he might have been a bit more selective about his next project.

THE PRESIDIO Reluctant partners: Sean Connery and Mark Harmon. (Photo credit: Ralph Nelson, Jr.)

THE PRESIDIO Shooting it out in the violent climax. (Photo credit: Ralph Nelson, Jr.)

THE PRESIDIO Arguing strategy with Mark Harmon. (Photo credit: Ralph Nelson, Jr.)

MEMORIES
OF ME

1989

Released by Metro-Goldwyn-Mayer

CAST:

Dr. Abbie Polin: Billy Crystal; *Abe Polin:* Alan King; *Lisa:* JoBeth Williams; *Dorothy Davis:* Janet Carroll; *First Assistant Director:* David Ackroyd.

CREDITS:

Director: Henry Winkler; *Producers:* Billy Crystal, Alan King, and Michael Hertzberg; *Screenplay:* Eric Roth and Billy Crystal; *Director of Photography:* Andrew Dintenfass; *Editor:* Peter E. Berger; *Production Designer:* William J. Cassidy; *Music:* Georges Delerue. *Running Time:* 103 minutes.

Sean Connery's presence in this little-seen comedy may come as news to even those very familiar with his career. To put it in perspective, Sean is on-screen for all of thirty seconds, but after all, that isn't substantially less than his much-vaunted cameo in *Robin Hood: Prince of Thieves.* An underrated comedy, *Memories of Me* centers on the strained relationship between Billy Crystal, a stressed-out New York surgeon, and his usually obnoxious estranged screen father, Alan King. Seems Poppa went Hollywood decades ago in hopes of finding stardom as a comic in films. Things didn't work out quite that way, but he has made a modest living as "King of the Extras"—a status he takes great pride in. ("I was the fifth guy to yell out, *'I am Spartacus!'* ")

When Crystal suffers a heart attack, he becomes aware of the value of life. He visits his father in Hollywood to attempt a reconciliation, but finds him to be as crazy and self-centered as always. However, the man is idolized by his fellow extras, who are depicted as the most lovable group of losers since Woody Allen's buddies in *Broadway Danny Rose.* The father-son reunion is a disaster, with both men sniping at each other mercilessly. King, however, develops a convenient incurable disease that immediately reinforces family values between him and his son. Crystal arranges for King to audition for a speaking role—the old man's lifelong dream. Naturally, he dies

MEMORIES OF ME   Sean's cameo while on the set for *The Presidio.*

on the eve of getting the job. The film's final moments are rather touching as King's lonely funeral is disrupted by a parade of extras in costume—a tribute to their fallen friend's many roles.

Sean Connery appears while King (wearing a full-length lobster costume) is showing Crystal and his girlfriend (JoBeth Williams) around the movie lot where he is shooting a commercial. After he brags to the unbelieving duo about the many stars he calls friends, Connery walks by in full military regalia (he was shooting *The Presidio* at the time) and briefly greets King, to the astonishment of Crystal and Williams. The scene is short, but does merit a "Special thanks to Sean Connery" in the credits. The overall film, as directed by Henry Winkler, may be overly sentimental, but is worth a look. Crystal is always engaging—even in this pre–*City Slickers* box-office flop—and King is properly charismatic, although his wisecracks could have been sharper. What is distracting, however, are the numerous mysterious plugs for Paramount Pictures. (The film was released by MGM!) For example, the movie set Crystal tours happens to have the Paramount logo emblazoned on a conveniently located water tower. Connery's presence in his *Presidio* uniform is a blatant advertisement for that Paramount film, and a later sequence takes place in front of the famed Chinese Theatre with Paramount's *Fatal Attraction* prominently displayed on the marquee. No wonder MGM has suffered so in recent years—it is handling the marketing duties for rival studios! Still, one could do worse than spending a couple of hours with *Memories of Me*. Memories of the film may not linger, but it's a neat little time killer.

Trivia Note: If Connery's presence alongside Alan King seems odd, keep in mind this represents Sean's third appearance with the actor-comedian. They previously costarred in *Operation Snafu* (1961) and *The Anderson Tapes* (1971).

INDIANA JONES AND THE LAST CRUSADE

1989

Released by Paramount Pictures

CAST:

Indiana Jones: Harrison Ford; *Dr. Henry Jones:* Sean Connery; *Marcus Brody:* Denholm Elliott; *Elsa:* Alison Doody; *Sallah:* John Rhys-Davies; *Walter Donovan:* Julian Glover; *Young Indy:* River Phoenix; *Vogel:* Michael Byrne.

CREDITS:

Director: Steven Spielberg; *Executive Producers:* George Lucas and Frank Marshall; *Producer:* Robert Watts; *Screenplay:* Jeffrey Boam, from a story by George Lucas and Menno Meyjes, based on characters created by Lucas and George Kaufman; *Director of Photography:* Douglas Slocombe; *Editor:* Michael Kahn; *Production Designer:* Elliot Scott; *Music:* John Williams. *Running Time:* 127 minutes.

If one needs to define the term *blockbuster entertainment,* one need only look as far as *Indiana Jones and the Last Crusade,* the third—and presumably final—chapter in the thrilling adventures of the most exciting screen hero since James Bond. The 007 link to these films is more than coincidental. Director Steven Spielberg has freely admitted that the inspiration leading to the creation of Indiana Jones came from the fascination he and George Lucas held for the Bond movies. Spielberg had always toyed with the idea of directing a Bond epic, but decided to go one better and help create a new enduring hero who was every bit as daring as Agent 007. Indiana Jones was born from ideas suggested by any number of talented people, but it was Lucas and Spielberg who secured from Paramount Pictures the sizable budget required to do the film justice. Not that there was much doubt about the investment: Spielberg and Lucas struck gold whenever they turned their talents to mass-audience pleasers such as *Jaws* and the *Star Wars* films.

The first Indy adventure, *Raiders of the Lost Ark* (released in 1981), exceeded even the most optimistic hopes. It not only garnered massive revenues, but also earned critical acclaim as well as a slew of Oscar nominations. The film also catapulted Harrison Ford—already a popular actor through the *Star Wars* films—into an international superstar. Three years later, the film's sequel, *Indiana Jones and the Temple of Doom,* was released to enthusiastic audiences who paid over $100 million to follow Indy's further adventures. Yet, this time around there were complaints that the film was far more brutal than its predecessor, and Spielberg was accused of concentrating on gore rather than humor. The director later acknowledged, "I wasn't happy with the film at all. It was too dark, too subterranean, and much too horrific. . . . There is not an ounce of my personal feeling in *Temple of Doom.*" Spielberg wanted to do the third Indy not only to keep his promise to George Lucas to direct all three films, but also to bring the concept back to a lighthearted approach. However, the production schedule precluded him from directing *Rain Man,* a troubled project he had worked on for years. Spielberg eventually sat by and watched Barry Levinson win an Oscar for directing a film he had helped bring to reality.

Lucas and Spielberg embarked upon their own crusade to find an angle that would keep Indy's last cinematic adventure in the same spirit as the first. The result: a decision to introduce Indy's father, Prof. Henry Jones, who has mysteriously disappeared on his lifelong quest to locate the Holy Grail, the chalice

228

**Der Mann mit dem Hut ist zurück.
Und dieses Mal bringt er seinen Vater mit.**

HARRISON FORD   SEAN CONNERY

Indiana Jones

und der

Letzte Kreuzzug

PARAMOUNT PICTURES PRÄSENTIERT EINE LUCASFILM LTD. PRODUKTION
EIN STEVEN SPIELBERG FILM
HARRISON FORD
INDIANA JONES AND THE LAST CRUSADE DENHOLM ELLIOTT ALISON DOODY JOHN RHYS-DAVIES JULIAN GLOVER
und in der Hauptrolle mit SEAN CONNERY als PROFESSOR JONES
Musik von JOHN WILLIAMS Kamera DOUGLAS SLOCOMBE Schnitt MICHAEL KAHN, A.C.E. Kostüme ANTHONY POWELL Ausstattung ELLIOT SCOTT Ausführende Produzenten GEORGE LUCAS und
FRANK MARSHALL Geschichte von GEORGE LUCAS und MENNO MEYJES Drehbuch von JEFFREY BOAM Produzent ROBERT WATTS Regie STEVEN SPIELBERG
EIN PARAMOUNT FILM IM VERLEIH DER ᴵᴾ

INDIANA JONES AND THE LAST CRUSADE German pressbook advertisement.

229

INDIANA JONES AND THE LAST CRUSADE   Alison Doody prepares to elimate the Joneses: Harrison Ford and Sean Connery. (Photo credit: Murray Close)

from which Christ drank at the Last Supper. Initially, the elder Jones was not to have been introduced until late in the script. Spielberg, however, felt this would change if he succeeded in convincing Sean Connery to take the part. Spielberg has counted himself a Connery fan since age seventeen when he saw Sean in *The Hill.* Per Spielberg: "He's done so many incredible parts that you can pretty much cast him in any nationality, from the Raisuli to the Irish cop in *The Untouchables,* and people accept Sean."

Spielberg felt the odds were slim that Connery would accept the role: "I didn't think Sean would want to play Indy's father. Obviously, Sean had his trademark on the James Bond movies, and we are a kind of James Bond movie ourselves." To Spielberg's amazement, Connery signed for the role, with the condition that he had creative input. Connery confessed he was not happy with the part as originally written. He described the initial concept of Professor Jones as being that of "an elderly, gnomish, Yoda-like figure. . . . It didn't add up in my book. I was after something a bit more Victorian and flamboyant, like one of the old explorers—Sir Richard Burton and Mungo Park, who went off to the hinterlands and were missing for months . . . that's what we got." Spielberg was all too happy to listen to Sean's theories

and generally ended up agreeing with him about his concepts for filming certain scenes. Spielberg stated, "He was instrumental in all the rewrites, and when he gets a good idea—which is about twenty times a day—he is such a child; his face lights up." The director was delighted with the chemistry generated by Harrison Ford and his screen "poppa," Connery. Said Spielberg, "I couldn't imagine anyone with less screen power than Sean Connery to be the famous Indiana Jones's father. . . . Ford takes up a lot of screen, and I didn't want Harrison diminishing any father in screen presence." He later queried, "Who better than the original James Bond to have given birth to this archaeologist and adventurer?"

For Indy's swan song, most of the behind-the-scenes talent from the first film reunited with several actors from the original *Raiders,* including Denholm Elliott as the bumbling accomplice to Indy and John Rhys-Davies as the rascally but good-hearted Arab swindler who comes to the hero's aid. A tidy sum of $36 million was allocated, and the preproduction work was enormous. Cameras began to turn in May of 1988, with the film scheduled for a Memorial Day release in the following year. Locations included Spain, Venice, and Jordan. Studio work was completed with a ten-week shoot at Elstree outside of

INDIANA JONES AND THE LAST CRUSADE   As Dr. Henry Jones. (Photo credit: Murray Close)

INDIANA JONES AND THE LAST CRUSADE   Enjoying a laugh with Steven Spielberg (left) and Harrison Ford. (Photo credit: Murray Close)

London. The film boasts a terrifically exciting pro-logue with River Phoenix as a young Indy, trying to prevent looters from stealing ancient treasures. He loses this round, but the device helps explain several key elements from the previous films (e.g., the origin of Indy's hat, his aversion to snakes, etc.). These spectacular scenes were shot in Colorado, New Mex-ico, and Utah.

As anticipated, the logistics of bringing this epic to the screen could not be overstated. For an eerie sequence in the sewers of Venice, Ford and female lead Alison Doody must walk in the midst of seven thousand rats. To make matters worse, one thousand mechanical rodents were added to the fray to insure the real critters weren't harmed during a spectacular fire. Plywood boats were created for the exciting speedboat chase and fistfight on the Venetian canals, which climaxes with the villain's boat being churned to pieces by the propeller of a ship. More challenging was recreating 1938 period costumes, cars, and fur-nishings. Spielberg even throws in a spectacular Nazi book-burning rally in Berlin where Indy—disguised as a German soldier—finds himself face-to-face with Der Führer. (Hitler merely thinks Indy wants an autograph and willingly complies.) During filming in

Spain and Jordan, the desert heat took its toll on the cast and crew, and many became quite ill. Connery coped with the intense heat by simply removing his woolen trousers when not on-camera and parading about in only his shirt and vest. (James Bond would cringe at this fashion blunder!)

By all accounts, Spielberg had the time of his life directing this installment. The enthusiasm was conta-gious, and many of the technicians reported this to be one of the happiest film sets in memory. The director was delighted with the rapport between Ford and Connery. The two stars had few rehearsals and im-provised much of the small talk and badgering they engage in. Spielberg recalled, "The biggest thrill was putting Harrison and Sean in a two-shot and calling 'Action!' and trying not to ruin the take by laughing." The filmmakers wisely decided not to concentrate on spectacle at the expense of characterization. The script has more than its share of special effects and magnificent action set pieces, however. One climax follows another until the viewer is almost exhausted. An elaborate and innovative sequence wherein Indy squares off on horseback against a Nazi tank to save his father expertly mixes humor with suspense.

The plot is not particularly riveting. Indy simply

232

travels the continents to find his estranged father, whose quest for the Grail has led him into Nazi hands. Indy befriends a gorgeous German scientist (Alison Doody) who turns out to be a Nazi agent who, it is revealed in a hilarious scene, has slept with both Joneses to get information leading to the Grail. The main villain is Julian Glover as an evil millionaire who believes that possession of the Grail will insure immortality. He's a slick villain, but one wishes he had more screen time to flesh out his character. The climax is where the film goes awry a bit. While it is filled with tension, it crosses over into science fiction with medieval knights and magical formulas. Indy should keep his feet in reality, no matter how much logic might be strained in the interest of suspense. The James Bond films never cheated by bringing in metaphysical solutions to problems, and once that occurs, anything can happen. The series owes a debt to 007, and the filmmakers don't hide the similarities. (In fact, Julian Glover, Alison Doody, John Rhys-Davies, and of course, Sean Connery are all Bond veterans.)

Criticisms aside, *Indiana Jones and the Last Crusade* is a marvelous adventure and remains a worthy climax to this astounding trilogy. Critics generally agreed, with all but a few spoilsports enthusiastic. *People* magazine instructed audiences to "take a good look at this movie. In fact, go back four or five times and take four or five good looks. In this imperfect world, you're not likely to see many man-made objects come this close to perfection." *Variety* praised

INDIANA JONES AND THE LAST CRUSADE   Connery and Ford as the bickering Joneses. (Photo credit: Murray Close)

the teaming of Ford and Connery as "one of the most pleasant screen pairings since Newman and Red-ford," and noted, "Connery confidently plays his aging character as slightly daft and fuzzy-minded, without blunting his forcefulness and without sacrificing his sexual charisma." Mike Clark in *USA Today* raved, "Connery has never been better. . . . *Crusade*

INDIANA JONES AND THE LAST CRUSADE   On the quest for the grail with John-Rhys Davies (left) and Harrison Ford. (Photo credit: Murray Close)

rivals the early and superior James Bonds with its smooth mix of action and comedy."

Predictably, the film was a blockbuster, tying the rental dollars earned by the original *Raiders* (a neat $115 million in the United States and Canada alone). The movie also earned Connery a Golden Globe Award nomination and, more importantly, kept this senior statesman of the action-film genre a relevant and popular presence with contemporary audiences. At an age when most leading men's careers are in decline, Connery's star keeps rising. Was *Last Crusade* really the end of Indy and his dad's screen exploits? According to the filmmakers, it was indeed. But as Sean Connery learned, when a series is surefire at the box office, "never say never again."

FAMILY BUSINESS

1989

Released by Tri-Star Pictures

CAST:

Jesse: Sean Connery; *Vito:* Dustin Hoffman; *Adam:* Matthew Broderick; *Elaine:* Rosana DeSoto; *Margie:* Janet Carroll; *Christine:* Victoria Jackson; *Doheny:* Bill McCutcheon.

CREDITS:

Director: Sidney Lumet; *Producer:* Lawrence Gordon; *Screenplay:* Vincent Patrick, based on his novel; *Director of Photography:* Andrzej Bartkowiak; *Editor:* Andrew Mondshein; *Production Designer:* Philip Rosenberg; *Music:* Cy Coleman. *Running Time:* 113 minutes.

Sean Connery reteamed with director Sidney Lumet for the first time since *Murder on the Orient Express* for this offbeat seriocomedy revolving around three generations of the McMullen family, wherein the only hereditary factor is an addiction to crime. The high-profile production boasted a cast that seemed to insure big box office: Connery, Dustin Hoffman, and Matthew Broderick. As with most Lumet films, shooting took place primarily in New York City, with a week of filming on Long Island and in Jersey City, New Jersey. Lumet, a strong believer in preproduction preparation, had his three leads rehearse for several weeks in a large hall on New York's lower East Side before principal photography began in Novem-

ber 1988. Lumet stated, "One of the reasons for my vaunted speed [in filming] is because of the rehearsals. It's an irreplaceable process of getting to know the actors. When we get on a set, an awful lot has already been locked into place for us."

Lumet had been intrigued by the screenplay by Vincent Patrick, based upon the latter's novel. He approached Broderick first, recalling, "I asked him to come along with the film even though his part hadn't been fleshed out. He was somebody I wanted to work with, and thank God, he went on my word and we did flesh out the role." The next link in the chain was Hoffman, cast as Broderick's father, Vito. Lumet and producer Lawrence Gordon agreed that there was only one man for the role of the irascible Jesse, the charming but hopelessly corrupt family patriarch: Sean Connery. Said Lumet, "As far as I knew, the only one who could play Jesse would be Sean. And if I couldn't get Sean, I wouldn't have done the picture. . . . There's no vanity about him. He has no worry about playing a hero or a villain, a good guy or bad, looking ugly or pretty. He's so sure of himself, he goes for the best parts. He's close to being a legend. But there's no change in him. He's the most level-headed person I know."

Initially, Connery was dissatisfied with the script's interpretation of Jesse McMullen, feeling the character had too many redeeming qualities for a man who was supposed to be addicted to ripping off even those few souls who still loved him. Connery insisted on making his screen persona less lovable. According to Vincent Patrick, "Connery's the only person in the Western Hemisphere who would say that. This guy [Jesse] was about as hard as they came—until I met Sean."

Industry gossips speculated that there might be tension between Hoffman and Connery. The former was known to have a penchant for numerous delays while he concentrated on his character's motivations. Sean, of course, is a no-nonsense actor who wants to expedite filming and avoid retakes if possible. To the surprise of many, the two superstars developed an immediate rapport and chemistry that translates onto the screen. Lumet remembered, "Sean is extremely disciplined and Dustin is very improvisational, all over the place with his lines. I didn't know where it would end up, but Sean met Dustin improvisation for improvisation, and a great deal of richness and humor came out of it." Hoffman later recalled his experience at the 1989 Academy Awards, where he brought home the Best Actor Oscar for *Rain Man:* "I'm there holding the Oscar and there's this amazing standing ovation. And I'm looking out into this sea of people, and the only person I saw was Sean Connery.

FAMILY BUSINESS As Jesse.

I'm not kidding. He's in the fifth row, looking like a leprechaun on steroids, with those pointed ears and that sweet smile of his, and I could read his lips: 'I told you.' " Matthew Broderick recalled doing imitations of Sean as 007 behind the actor's back. When tipped off on the joke, Connery queried, "Why doesn't Matthew do it for me?" Told the younger man was too intimidated, Connery quipped with mock seriousness, "Good. He should be afraid!"

Family Business emerged a very underrated film and was all but buried in the rush of Christmas releases in 1989. It was difficult to sell as it varied wildly between outright comedy, tragedy, and a standard caper story. The ambiguous title only added to the confusion, and the ad campaign stressed the three superstars but said little about the subject matter. The film's financial failure is truly a shame, as this is a very watchable and worthwhile achievement. The story centers on the estrangement between Vito (Hoffman), a middle-age man trying to succeed in a legitimate business, and his hopelessly corrupt but charming father, Jesse (Connery). The two cross paths again when Vito's son, Adam (Broderick), a brilliant but bored yuppie, falls under the influence of his grandfather and begins to plan a "foolproof" million-dollar heist of a scientific discovery. Vito begs his son to stay away from Jesse's hypnotic influence, but ends up reluctantly falling under the old man's spell himself and actually participating in the crime. Ironically, only through the planning of the robbery do the three men feel a bond of love. This eventually reverts to hatred when the robbery goes awry and Jesse refuses to turn himself in with Vito to get Adam freed.

The screenplay is short on action and long on characterization, which is pretty much a rarity in this age of special-effects-laden epics. Some critics scoffed at the notion of these three actors, who bear no physical similarities, playing relatives. This glaring distraction is explained rather awkwardly within the film, but it comes across as a pretentious plea to the audience to shut up with the logic and just sit back and enjoy the performances. Assuming one does just that, one is in for quite a treat. Connery is superb as the aging patriarch of a rather shameful family. You feel guilty liking him, as he shows virtually no redeeming qualities, but to Sean's credit you are immediately taken by his charisma. It's not hard to imagine him wielding an unholy influence over his son and grandson. Hoffman is also excellent, showing a wide range of frustration and pathos at his inability to resist being led down the path to self-destruction. As for Broderick, he remains one of the most natural of the younger actors, exuding a totally sympathetic aura, even when being cruel to his well-intentioned father.

The film has a relatively upbeat ending, with Vito and Adam reunited at Jesse's funeral. While this might tie up loose ends a bit too neatly, it is infinitely more satisfying than letting these likable characters remain distanced.

Lumet's direction is as admirable as ever, and aside from Woody Allen and Martin Scorsese, no one can do cinematic justice to New York the way he can. Lumet has a wonderful ability to translate the very essence of life in Manhattan onto the screen. Admittedly, *Family Business* could have been made decades ago with little change to the script. Perhaps because of the power of Lumet's previous ventures with Connery, expectations could only be disappointed by this lightweight comedy from them. The film has its flaws. Some of the supporting characters (such as Hoffman's all-too-Jewish mother-in-law) are straight out of Central Casting. Also, it suffers from a woefully inappropriate score by Cy Coleman that is reminiscent of a 1960s sitcom. The music remains jazzy and upbeat even during scenes of tension and tragedy.

Critics were generally unimpressed, although the individual performances received praise. The *Newark Star Ledger* wrote perceptively, "Sean Connery simply

knocks your socks off with his combination of urbanity, hair-trigger temperament, sly humor, and genuine machismo. For an actor whose disappearance from the profession was widely predicted when he gave up being James Bond, this treasure has gone from strength to strength. And he's never been better than as sly rogue Jesse McMullen in this emotionally and morally complex charmer." The *New York Times* was less charitable, noting, "It's not really funny or believably eccentric, and except for Mr. Connery, it is short on charm. . . . The three stars are good actors, but they have nothing much to work with. Their biggest challenge is to make the audience believe they are blood relatives." Roger Ebert complained, "What happens to Connery [in the climax] is sudden, unprepared, and dramatically unsatisfactory. And then what happens between Hoffman and Broderick seems to belong in a different movie." In a more enthusiastic review, *Variety* stated, "Sean Connery steals scenes as well as merchandise in an immensely charismatic turn to make *Family Business* one of the year's better films. . . . [Connery] dives headfirst into his part with a character to rival his Oscar-winning role in *The Untouchables*."

FAMILY BUSINESS   As Jesse McMullen, ever charming, ever crooked.

There's nothing like a good robbery to bring a family together.

DUSTIN HOFFMAN   SEAN CONNERY   MATTHEW BRODERICK

FAMIL BUSINESS

FAMIL BUSINESS

FAMILY BUSINESS   Japanese souvenir program.

FAMILY BUSINESS   Exerting a bad influence over grandson Matthew Broderick.

Despite the film's mixed reviews, no one was prepared for its total failure at the box office. Audiences ignored the cast and stayed away in droves, and within a couple of weeks, *Family Business* was all but gone from theaters. The movie's crash landing mystified even Connery, who claimed, "I'll tell you, it's amazing to me. I would have assumed people would have gone to it just out of the curiosity value," adding with characteristic honesty, "But it was a real flop. I don't know why."

Once again, Connery emerged from the ashes of a film that deserved a much better fate, his reputation well intact, courtesy of having stolen the lion's share of praise from critics. Had the film been a success, it would probably have resulted in another Oscar nomination for Sean. Reflecting on his latest cinematic caper with Connery, Sidney Lumet stated, "Most people think of him as a legendary star. I don't, but only because we go to the toilet together. . . . Most actors, if they are lucky, stay as good as they are. Sean is one of the rare ones who got better."

THE HUNT FOR RED OCTOBER

1990

Released by Paramount Pictures

CAST:

Capt. Marko Ramius: Sean Connery; *Jack Ryan:* Alec Baldwin; *Capt. Bart Mancuso:* Scott Glenn; *Captain Borodin:* Sam Neill; *Admiral Greer:* James Earl Jones; *Lysenko:* Joss Ackland; *Jeffrey Pelt:* Richard Jordan; *Putin:* Peter Firth; *Dr. Petrov:* Tim Curry; *Jones:* Courtney B. Vance; *Tupelov:* Stellan Skarsgard; *Tyler:* Jeffrey Jones.

CREDITS:

Director: John McTiernan; *Executive Producer:* Larry De Waay and Jerry Sherlock; *Producer:* Mace Neufeld; *Screenplay:* Larry Ferguson and Donald Stewart, based on the novel by Tom Clancy; *Director of Photography:* Jan De Bont; *Editors:* Dennis Virkler and John Wright; *Production Designer:* Terence Marsh; *Music:* Basil Poledouris. *Running Time:* 137 minutes.

Sean Connery was genuinely puzzled by the failure of *Family Business* following its 1989 Christmas re-

lease. He lamented that "the picture hasn't had anything like even a curiosity success—you know, a measure of, 'Well, let's go see it because . . .' " Sean also had reason to be nervous about the March 1990 release of one of his highest-profiled projects: a $30-million adaptation of Tom Clancy's Cold War techno-thriller *The Hunt for Red October*. In a town where actors are valued not on the basis of their skills but their drawing power, two costly failures in a row could have damaged Connery's bankability in Hollywood. Paramount, which financed *Red October*, was becoming increasingly jittery. The film was originally to have starred Klaus Maria Brandauer as the maverick skipper of a new Soviet nuclear sub who daringly defects to the West. When Brandauer was unavailable, the studio decided to boost the budget significantly and succeeded in signing Connery. Offsetting this coup was the fact that Sean's reputed $4-million salary made the film's break-even point even higher.

Why were there so many nervous executives when the film was based on a wildly popular novel and starred an actor who had recaptured his mantle as one of the top leading men in the action-adventure genre? The answer was politics. By the time the cameras began to roll for the sixteen-week shoot commencing in April 1989, a lot of cold water was being thrown on the Cold War. Gorbachev's policy of glasnost had virtually eliminated the omnipresent tension in Soviet/U.S. relations that had prevailed since the end of World War II. Every day, the international press recorded stories of the new openness and freedom inside the Soviet Union—tales that would have been unthinkable only a few years before. Could anyone really get excited about an espionage story that was now almost an impossibility? The Soviets were not only ceasing to be villified in the West, but also Gorbachev had recently been named *Time* magazine's Man of the Decade and was being greeted in the States by cheering crowds.

The producers took the only logical course they could, inserting a message at the beginning of the film informing the audience that this tale took place in the era immediately preceding the period of glasnost. The filming of *Red October* itself got off to a rocky start. Director John McTiernan had recently become a hot name in Hollywood, thanks to *Predator* and *Die Hard*. However, the logistics of bringing Tom Clancy's complicated tale to the screen went beyond McTiernan's ability to keep the schedule moving smoothly. Tensions mounted as Connery became increasingly temperamental, as he admits to doing when he sees inefficiency. He lost no time in exerting his star power to organize matters. He recalled, "We were all crowded on this little platform that moved at a

THE HUNT FOR RED OCTOBER Promo featuring Sean Connery and Alec Baldwin.

forty-five-degree angle—eighty percent real Russians, half of whom couldn't speak English, film crew, wardrobe, fighting, people operating smoke guns, extractor fans. Everybody was talking at the same time, so I had to get that sorted out. I said everybody must be absolutely silent during the actors' run-through, and everybody should also remain absolutely silent when the director says 'Cut!' because nobody could do anything until he decided if he would print the take." In essence, Sean declared that no one should expect his participation unless things were well structured.

Sean was held in awe by most of the cast and crew—even the seasoned professionals who filled out the illustrious supporting cast. Per producer Mace Neufeld: "He's the quintessential professional. Perfect on dialogue every time. Nobody wants to screw up around Sean. He walks around inside a kind of envelope that says, 'I know what I'm doing, let's hope you know what you're doing.' " According to costar Sam Neill, "Sean walked onto the set and it was like the grand old man had arrived. People treated him with a tremendous amount of respect." This may

THE HUNT FOR RED OCTOBER Avoiding the pursuers. (Photo credit: Bruce McBroom)

239

have been reinforced by Sean's "wolfish" physical appearance in the film—sporting a mane of shocking gray hair, a gray beard, and mustache. He looks like a man who means business. The crew deferred to Connery's sensitivity about James Bond, and a running joke started when McTiernan informed Connery that he looked far too comfortable handling a pistol for a man who'd spent his life inside a submarine. He reminded Sean he was no longer playing "you know who." Early frustrations aside, by all accounts Connery came to enjoy his experience on the film. He was delighted to be working at all, having recently endured a potentially life-threatening medical problem that resulted in some benign tumors being removed from his throat.

The logistics of bringing *Red October* to the screen were considerable. The largest replica of a submarine ever built (five hundred feet long) was also engineered to actually dive and surface. The central set, used as the interior of the various subs, was built twenty-two feet in the air on movable platforms that would sway precariously to simulate the movement inside a real submarine. The effect was realistic enough to cause some members of the cast to experience genuine seasickness. Realism extended to the script, which the screenwriters had to adapt from Tom Clancy's highly technical four-hundred-page novel. To keep as much accuracy as possible, costars Alec Baldwin and Scott Glenn and the technicians spent extensive time aboard actual U.S. subs during their routine missions. One skipper actually helped Glenn, who was portraying a submarine captain, to get a true feel for being in command by instructing the crew to report to the actor as well as himself. The production design for the film is quite a triumph, although designer Terence Marsh admitted this was one area where liberties were taken, as the real sub interiors were so confined and dark, they would not translate well onto theater screens.

The plot of *Red October* centers on a well-respected Soviet naval captain named Ramius (Connery), who, along with his sympathetic officers, decides to defect to the West. Each man has his own reasons, but Ramius is disenchanted with Communism and terrified that his new ship—the *Red October*—will shift the balance of military power to the Soviets. The sub carries nuclear armaments and is undetectable by sonar. Ramius fears it will be used as a first-strike weapon against the United States. When the Soviet brass learn of the plot, the entire fleet is in hot pursuit to destroy the ship rather than let it fall into U.S. hands. Simultaneously, the U.S. Navy is ordered to launch a search-and-destroy mission, having been

erroneously told that Ramius is a lunatic intending to launch nuclear missiles. However, CIA technocrat Jack Ryan (Alec Baldwin) suspects the truth and convinces the navy to gamble on welcoming Ramius while duping the Soviets into believing they have destroyed the *Red October*. The film then becomes a cat-and-mouse game with the vessel narrowly escaping the pursuing Soviet fleet as well as attempts of a hidden saboteur on board to destroy the sub.

The Hunt for Red October is a slow-paced thriller that eventually builds to a riveting climax. The abundance of confusing latitude readings are meaningless to the audience, and the actors spend too much time studying sonar screens, but while the film may be overlong, amazingly it is never dull. This is partly because the script does not lose the human element among all the technicalities. Director McTiernan does not overload the production with explosions and gimmicks to compensate for its measured pace. Connery's Ramius is one of his more memorable, larger-than-life characters, although he plays the role with a quiet and dignified tone. Once again, his commanding presence gives the film a spark that seems to bring out the best

THE HUNT FOR RED OCTOBER   Connery defects to Alec Baldwin (center) and Scott Glenn. (Photo credit: Bruce McBroom)

THE HUNT FOR RED OCTOBER   Discussing the few options with chief officer Sam Neill (left). (Photo credit: Bruce McBroom)

in his costars. Alec Baldwin is marvelous in a star-making turn as Ryan, the hero of several other Clancy novels. His reluctance to participate in any dangerous actions is refreshing and realistic, but of course, he turns into a man of true grit when the chips are down. The marvelous supporting cast includes Scott Glenn's low-key but charming American skipper, Sam Neill as Connery's second-in-command (whose death is foreshadowed once he starts making a particularly corny speech about being a cowboy in Montana), James Earl Jones, Richard Jordan, and Tim Curry.

Critics generally responded favorably to the film, with all praising its technical qualities. Several reviewers, however, expressed disappointment that the distance shots of the subs made them undistinguishable whalelike blobs. On video they look worse, but on the Letterbox laser disc they fare better. The critics split when it came to the actual story. Rex Reed found the plot totally incomprehensible, while Roger Ebert praised the film for being so easy to understand. (Clearly, Reed should start accompanying his fellow writer to screenings as we side with Ebert.) David Brooks in the *Wall Street Journal* called the film the

THE HUNT FOR RED OCTOBER   As Marko Ramius. (Photo credit: Bruce McBroom)

241

finest thriller since *The Manchurian Candidate,* and *Variety* found it a "terrific adventure yarn . . . that looks like a box-office smash." Of Sean, the paper said, "Looking magnificent in his captain's uniform and white beard, Connery scores another career highlight." Ian Johnstone in London's *Sunday Times* noted, "Connery dominates the movie like a Lithuanian colossus."

Audiences agreed, and to the surprise of many (and the delight of Paramount), the movie became a smash throughout the world. This despite its release in March—generally considered to be a Death Valley period for a major film to premiere. To date, it is one of the highest-grossing movies of Connery's career, and one that insured his popularity with a new generation of fans. With all due respect to Klaus Maria Brandauer—who would undoubtedly have given a terrific performance as Ramius—no small part of *Red October*'s success was due to the presence of Sean Connery.

Trivia Note: Alec Baldwin's role of Jack Ryan was originally offered to Harrison Ford, who rejected it, thinking, "Who the hell wants to see a submarine movie?" Ford later confessed, "Not doing that film was one of the biggest mistakes of my career." Ironically, when Baldwin was asked to sign a multipicture deal for a series of films based on the Ryan character, he played hard to get and demanded more money than the studio was willing to pay. Baldwin lost his bluff, and the role was assumed by Ford, who wasn't going to make the same mistake twice. Ford introduced his version of the Ryan hero in 1992's *Patriot Games,* which was also a hit at the box office.

THE RUSSIA HOUSE

1990

Released by United Artists

CAST:

Barley Blair: Sean Connery; *Katya:* Michelle Pfeiffer; *Russell:* Roy Scheider; *Ned:* James Fox; *Dante:* Klaus Maria Brandauer; *Brady:* John Mahoney; *Clive:* Michael Kitchen; *Quinn:* J. T. Walsh; *Walter:* Ken Russell.

CREDITS:

Director: Fred Schepisi; *Producers:* Paul Maslansky and Fred Schepisi; *Screenplay:* Tom Stoppard, based on the novel by John le Carré; *Director of Photography:* Ian Baker; *Editor:*

Peter Honess; *Production Designer:* Richard MacDonald; *Music:* Jerry Goldsmith, featuring Branford Marsalis. *Running Time:* 123 minutes.

The Russia House accomplishes what one would think was impossible: turning a big-budget espionage thriller toplining Sean Connery into an unspeakably dull film. Eagerly awaited as the studio's prestige picture for Christmas, 1990, the movie boasted a topflight cast, superb production values, exotic and rarely seen locations inside the Soviet Union, a screenplay by noted playwright Tom Stoppard, and a source novel by master spy writer John le Carré. For all that, *The Russia House* proved to be as exciting as a tour of a babushka factory, and the story behind the making of the film is far more interesting.

The Russia House is undeniably a landmark production, being the first Western-Soviet joint film venture given unlimited access to the Soviet Union's facilities. Director Fred Schepisi was determined to bring the novel to the screen, having read the book in galley form in February 1989. Losing no time, he contacted a Russian-German company that gave essential advice on how to overcome the seemingly endless red tape inside the Soviet Union. The Gorbachev regime was allowing an opening up of self-criticism, and although *The Russia House* is generally more critical of the West, it doesn't paint a very favorable picture of the Soviet government. Prior to Gorbachev, making a film such as this in the Soviet Union would have been an impossibility.

Somehow, Schepisi managed to swiftly bring all the essential elements together, and shooting began at Leningrad's Palace Square (where the Russian Revolution began) in October 1989. Per Schepisi: "When I went on my first location scout, it was incredible because I was there when they were making historic changes in the country. You could feel the excitement; there was uncertainty and worry. I thought John le Carré's book was a real look at glasnost and the end of the Cold War and a look at the people who should know better. The spymasters of East and West are the people who should appreciate that the Cold War is over, but they seem to want to perpetuate it to keep their jobs going." Equally enthused about the project was Sean Connery, Schepisi's first choice for the lead role. According to the director, "When you think of someone who is considered box office, someone who will attract attention and possibly be surprising in the role, it all comes down to Sean Connery." Sean, too, had been intrigued by the story line prior to the book's actual publication. He recalled, "I had the galley proofs

SEAN CONNERY   MICHELLE PFEIFFER

FRED SCHEPISI film

THE RUSSIA HOUSE

ROY   JAMES   JOHN   KLAUS MARIA
SCHEIDER   FOX   MAHONEY   BRANDAUER

PATHE ENTERTAINMENT Presents SEAN CONNERY MICHELLE PFEIFFER in FRED SCHEPISI film JOHN le CARRÉ'S THE RUSSIA HOUSE
also starring ROY SCHEIDER JAMES FOX JOHN MAHONEY and KLAUS MARIA BRANDAUER Music by JERRY GOLDSMITH Edited by PETER HONESS
Production Designer RICHARD MACDONALD Screenplay by TOM STOPPARD Based on the novel by JOHN le CARRÉ Produced by PAUL MASLANSKY and FRED SCHEPISI Directed by FRED SCHEPISI

THE RUSSIA HOUSE   Teaser poster.

THE RUSSIA HOUSE   Taking possession of the secret manuscript from Klaus Maria Brandauer.

THE RUSSIA HOUSE   Comforting Michelle Pfeiffer in a moment of crisis.

. . . which I thought were terrific. My character, Barley Blair, starts out as this boozy, saxophone-playing publisher whose whole life and situation is in chaos. The people he meets in Russia and the experience of this moral dilemma with which he is faced help connect him back, finally, to the world."

A strong leading lady was required for the role of Katya, the beautiful Soviet editor who risks her life to smuggle a top-secret manuscript to Connery's publishing firm. Although the filmmakers first considered casting a Russian actress, they went full circle, hiring Michelle Pfeiffer, who's quite convincing in the role, underplaying her good looks. One might still be skeptical that such a stunning woman would be found in a squalid administrative office, but after all, this is a movie (and of course, she did play a hash-slinger in the subsequent *Frankie and Johnny*). Would anyone want to see Connery become smitten by Miss Tractor Factory Employee? An equally impressive supporting cast was headed by Roy Scheider and James Fox as the manipulative CIA and British Intel-

ligence heads, and Klaus Maria Brandauer reteamed with Sean in the small but pivotal role of a Soviet scientist who becomes a martyr in his attempt to blow the lid off the USSR's defense capabilities. According to Connery, "Klaus and I have a very strange relationship. I wanted him for *The Russia House;* I got him for

243

my Bond (*Never Say Never Again*) and I replaced him in *The Hunt for Red October*."

For Sean, filming inside the Soviet Union rekindled memories of his prior trip there to shoot *The Red Tent* two decades earlier. He found that "a lot is exactly the same and a lot has just changed so much you can't believe it. . . . The difference this time was, one knows something about what's behind it [the system] and how incompetent it is and how the whole infrastructure is really geared to the military and to state police rituals and bureaucracy—that artisans don't even know how to hang a door. There's no sense of apprenticeship. And they are totally indifferent to standards. Nobody knows, because nobody cares. You can see that it's rotten. The general level of health is pretty pathetic. . . . It's like wartime Britain. Long queues." He did find a shocking change in people's ability to express politically incorrect opinions without fear. "They are outspoken to an extreme in criticizing Gorbachev; they don't seem to be conscious of how big a leap they've taken compared to when I was there before." He was also surprised at how many citizens recognized him: "When I went there before, nobody knew me except people who were associated with the embassy—they had sixteen-millimeter prints of the Bond films, whereas out on the streets, they wouldn't know you from a bag of beans."

Locations on *The Russia House* included Leningrad and Moscow, where the filmmakers were able to get some eye-popping shots of many historic locations. Additional shooting took place in Lisbon and Vancouver, with studio work done in London. The Soviets did everything possible to cooperate with the crew and insured the movie was kept on schedule and within the budget. This was a far cry from previous Western films shot within the USSR (the most notorious being the megabomb musical *The Blue Bird,* which was plagued by so many Soviet foul-ups that a war almost broke out on the set).

Amazingly, aside from Ian Baker's stunning cinematography that capitalizes on the rarely filmed locations for all they are worth, a lush romantic score by Jerry Goldsmith, and competent if unremarkable performances, *The Russia House* has absolutely nothing else to recommend it. Le Carré specializes in talky, complicated espionage plots, which if adapted to the screen properly can be quite gripping, as evidenced by the superb film version of *The Spy Who Came In From the Cold.* The mistake was assigning playwright Tom Stoppard to pen the screenplay. Stoppard fails to open up the story and writes as though he were creating a stage play as opposed to a megabudget movie. The "action" moves from stuffy drawing rooms to stuffy administrative offices, with the only breath of fresh air coming from the frequent, but all too fleeting, glimpses of Soviet street life. After a while, one has little to do but admire the furniture because the talk is so boring. At times, *The Russia House* is like a cinematic tour through the Ikea furniture catalog.

The script had two strikes against it before the cameras rolled. While no one could foresee the rapid disintegration of the USSR, there had certainly been a significant lessening of East-West tension since Gorbachev had come to power. Trying to resurrect Cold War paranoia at this stage was an exercise in futility. (At least the makers of *Red October* had the sense to set the film in the preglasnost era.) With the eventual collapse of Communism virtually a foregone conclusion, the film has less tension than a wait in a Soviet bread line. Not helping matters is an almost incomprehensible plot. If a film doesn't grab an audience immediately, they are probably lost for good. *The Russia House* both begins and ends on a whimper, with nary a bang in sight. In a vulgar connotation, this also includes the love scenes, which fail to elicit any sparks, although Connery is so convincing an actor he makes the May-December romance look perfectly plausible. The script also lacks a central antagonist. Instead of a larger-than-life bad guy, the enemies here are colorless bureaucrats who can only torture by boring their victims to death. You know the movie is dull when you look forward to Connery's occasional lip-sync playing of a saxophone in a band. What most good spy movies need is sex and violence. What this one provides (in Gilda Radner's words) is sax and violins.

Connery and the cast try hard to make things work. Sean is a seedy-looking, washed-up alcoholic publisher who gets one last chance to do something heroic by agreeing to publish a smuggled manuscript that we are told is of staggering significance. Turns out, the document in question simply reiterates that Soviet military power has been greatly overstated in the interest of prolonging the Cold War. British and U.S. intelligence force Connery into spying for them, but he deceives them in return for their securing safety for his lover (Pfeiffer), who is in danger for having smuggled the documents to the West. Connery is watchable as always, but his character is dull and Sean can do only so much to salvage the script. Pfeiffer is also credible, but realism could have taken a backseat if it allowed her to be a little sensual. Roy Scheider is totally wasted as a foulmouthed CIA man who for some reason sports an unintentionally goofy-

THE RUSSIA HOUSE   On location with Michelle Pfeiffer

looking bow tie that makes him resemble a cross between Jimmy Olsen and Pee-wee Herman. Like the other cast members, he has little to do other than shuffle papers and fill coffee cups.

The Russia House met with respectable reviews, as though critics were afraid to come out totally against a film that at least tried to present an intelligent story line instead of megabudget special effects. Most, however, complained of the lack of action and called the film noble but boring. Despite an aggressive marketing campaign the financially strapped studio suffered the disappointment of not having the film garner a single Oscar nomination. The movie was far from a disaster at the box office, but was still a financial failure. Sean emerged with the usual glowing notices and his reputation intact. For his fans who had been awaiting his return to the world of espionage, however, the movie was a distinct letdown, one of the few Connery vehicles that is too dull to justify repeated viewings. The studio, though, should look into one way to gain revenue from the film, perhaps packaging the script, shipping it to pharmacies, and marketing it as a cure for insomnia. Perhaps it could be called *Thunderbore* or *From Russia With Lethargy*.

THE RUSSIA HOUSE   Japanese souvenir program.

ROBIN HOOD: PRINCE OF THIEVES

1991

Released by Warner Bros.

CAST:

Robin Hood: Kevin Costner; *Azeem:* Morgan Freeman; *Will Scarlett:* Christian Slater; *The Sheriff of Nottingham:* Alan Rickman; *Marian:* Mary Elizabeth Mastrantonio.

CREDITS:

Director: Kevin Reynolds; *Producers:* John Watson, Pen Densham, and Richard B. Lewis; *Executive Producers:* James G. Robinson, with David Nicksay and Gary Barber. *Screenplay:* Pen Densham and John Watson from a story by Densham; *Director of Photography:* Doug Milsome; *Editor:* Peter Boyle; *Production Designer:* John Graysmark; *Music:* Michael Kamen. *Running Time:* 144 minutes.

Although Sean Connery's contribution to this film was minimal, his brief appearance was the subject of a great deal of press attention, much to the chagrin of the studio, which had hoped to downplay his end-of-the-film cameo in order to surprise audiences. One newspaper referred to the Connery walk-on as "Hollywood's worst-kept secret of the year." In actuality, advance press material from the studio never mentioned Sean's involvement. The beans were spilled officially in a rather fascinating article in *Premiere* magazine that preceded the film's release and detailed its production troubles.

Robin Hood: Prince of Thieves was an exasperating experience for all involved. Writers Pen Densham and John Watson had long envisioned filming an updated version of the Robin Hood legend, feeling the project could appeal to modern audiences. The script was sold to Morgan Creek Productions for $1 million, with the stipulation that the writers also serve as producers. Ultimately, a $50-million budget was assigned to the film, with Warners contributing $14 million in return for distribution rights. Trouble began almost immediately. Director Kevin Reynolds had only ten weeks to prepare and later found that

virtually all rehearsal time had to be sacrificed when the shooting schedule was cut from fifteen to thirteen weeks.

The presence of Reynolds was instrumental in the signing of his old friend Kevin Costner for the title role. Costner knew he was not the most appropriate person to play the larger-than-life Robin of Locksley, but was eventually coaxed into the project by Reynolds, with whom he was eager to work again. (The two had collaborated on *Fandango* years earlier.) Once on the set, Costner complained the production was too loosely planned and the actors were being deprived of vital rehearsal time necessitated by daily changes in the script. Frustrations were also heightened by the presence of no less than six producers, which caused strategies to be debated endlessly.

Adding to the dilemma was the switch from leading lady Robin Wright, cast in the role of Marian. Wright announced her pregnancy shortly before filming commenced, and she was replaced at the last minute by Mary Elizabeth Mastrantonio. Even the weather would not cooperate, and a gray, cold mist hung over the entire production, which was filmed in England and France. Time was the biggest enemy. The shoot was so rushed that Costner felt the quality of the performances was being sacrificed to keep on schedule, while Reynolds favored proceeding at a fast clip. Frustrated at having gone directly from making *Dances With Wolves* into another massive project, with virtually no time to prepare, Costner began to contemplate using his clout to close down production until common strategies could be agreed upon. Additionally, his concern about mastering an English accent began to affect the naturalness of his performance, and he tried to correct his speech patterns with dubbing during editing. Ultimately, the film wrapped three weeks over schedule with hard feelings all around, although Costner and Reynolds have since patched up their differences.

Given these circumstances, it is amazing how well the film turned out. *Robin Hood: Prince of Thieves* is one of the most impressive action adventures in recent years. In certain areas it is no less than a triumph, specifically in terms of costume design, art and set decoration, and cinematography. This is a gritty, more realistic Robin than has previously been seen, although Connery and company did a fine job with their 1976 production. Here, however, the brutality of the era is not glossed over, with many harrowing and disturbing sequences. Costner was quick to praise the immortal vision of Errol Flynn's Robin Hood, but correctly pointed out that Flynn's version was more lighthearted and almost totally devoid of suspense. This version has audiences on the edge of

ROBIN HOOD: PRINCE OF THIEVES   Sean's cameo as King Richard

man exhorts the peasants to revolt in the name of freedom, you want to run up and join him as well.

Sean Connery contributed one day's work to the film, which resulted in a scant thirty seconds of screen time. He appears in the final frames as King Richard, turning up at Robin and Marian's wedding. His arrival was kept a secret even from the cast and crew, despite rumors that a "very expensive Scot" was due on the set. Expensive indeed, as Sean was paid $500,000 for the day (all of which was donated to charity). His presence on the set provided a much-needed break in the tension, and he mesmerized everyone by recalling his experience with *Robin and Marian*. "We filmed [it] for five million dollars in five weeks," he told an incredulous Kevin Reynolds. "And we did three days of reshoots. . . . It was a good film." One would have hoped that Connery's appearance would have been more substantive, and indeed Reynolds had envisioned a sequence in which Connery and Morgan Freeman's character scrutinize one another in anticipation of a fight. Unfortunately, lack of time caused the sequence to be dropped.

Critics shot more arrows at *Robin Hood: Prince of Thieves* than were launched during the film's climactic battle. Most barbs centered on the film's brutality and dark mood and the miscasting of Costner. Audiences disagreed and the film was a phenomenal hit, grossing over $150 million in theaters alone. It has also become a smash on video and laser disc, indicating that like the legend itself, no one cared for Robin Hood except the common folk—in this case audiences who *pay* to see their films.

their seats with nerve-racking narrow escapes and epic battles.

The performances are also mostly on the mark. Critics were almost universal in their belief that Costner was miscast and never came close to mastering anything resembling a British accent. These criticisms are true, but they miss the larger point: this film is not about heavy acting. Rather, it dwells on thrills, action, and adventure and needs a leading man who is skilled in these areas. Costner fits the bill magnificently. His extensive training in archery and swordsmanship pays off handsomely, as does his willingness to perform most of his own stunt work. If he looks a bit uncomfortable when not engaged in daring deeds, at least he never embarrasses himself. The supporting cast is equally enjoyable, especially Alan Rickman's over-the-top performance as the evil sheriff. Mastrantonio is properly gorgeous as Marian, and the wonderful Morgan Freeman capitalizes on his considerable charisma with a delightful performance as a Moor who becomes Robin's best friend. When Free-

HIGHLANDER 2:
THE QUICKENING

1991

Released by Interstar Releasing

CAST:

Connor MacLeod: Christopher Lambert; *Ramirez:* Sean Connery; *Louise Marcus:* Virginia Madsen; *General Katana:* Michael Ironside; *Alan Neyman:* Allan Rich; *Blake:* John C. McGinley; *Cabbie:* Phil Brock; *Drunk:* Rusty Schwimmer; *Jimmy:* Ed Trucco; *Hamlet:* Stephen Grives; *Horatio:* Jimmy Murray; *Zeist Chief Justice:* Bruno Curichelli.

CREDITS:

Director: Russell Mulcahy; *Executive Producers:* Guy Collins and Mario Sotela; *Producers:* Peter S. Davis and William Panzer; *Coproducers:* Alejandro Sessa and Robin Clark; *Screenplay:* Peter Bellwood; *Story:* Brian Clemens and William Panzer, *based on characters created by* Gregory Widen; *Director of Photography:* Phil Meheux; *Additional Photography:* Jamie Thompson; *Editors:* Hubert C. de la Bouillerie and Anthony Redman; *Production Designer:* Roger Hall; *Music:* Stewart Copeland; *Music performed by* the Seattle Symphony and Symphony Chorale. *Running Time:* 88 minutes.

It is rare indeed for the United States to be considered an incidental market for the financial success of a film. Yet this was precisely the case with Sean Connery's 1991 sequel to the 1986 science fiction sleeper *Highlander.* That epic was all but ignored in the United States by critics and audiences alike, but was a major hit elsewhere. Unsurprisingly, U.S. distributors were not lining up to bid for the honor of releasing the sequel. Connery was once again appearing only in a supporting role, and the film was eventually released in the United States by an independent company called Interstar.

Originally titled *Highlander 2020: The Quickening,* the film began shooting in early 1990. The primary location was Argentina, but the film immediately ran into problems that caused the $17-million budget to soar to over $30 million. This was partly caused by Argentina's runaway inflation, which sparked a devaluation of the currency. Additionally, director Russell Mulcahy widened the scope of the film at the last minute and began insisting upon more elaborate sets and special effects. For *Highlander 2,* $14 million was raised from international distributors before the cameras even rolled. Distribution deals for Japan, France, and Australia were set as early as 1987! One of the single biggest expenses was Sean Connery's salary. The actor balked at reappearing in the series (indeed he was killed off in the first film), but a Brandoesque $3-million paycheck convinced him to put in the requested ten days of filming.

Those who found the original *Highlander* confusing will not be enlightened by the continuing adventures of "Immortal" Connor MacLeod. As there is little continuity between the films, however, even those who understood the prior tale might be puzzled. The film opens with MacLeod (again played by stone-faced Christopher Lambert) as an elderly man surviving in the garish world of the not-too-distant future. We are now told he somehow originated on the planet Zeist (sounds like a laundry detergent). This is totally at odds with the first tale, in which MacLeod was a sixteenth-century Scottish tribesman who was granted immortality in order to fight the evil Kurgan. The virtually incomprehensible plot now finds MacLeod banished to Earth for leading a revolt on Zeist against Kurgan. (How did all these earthbound folks suddenly find themselves cavorting about in outer space, when such an existence was never mentioned previously?)

On Earth, MacLeod's mortality is deemed a punishment by the Immortals for all the trouble he caused up on Zeist. MacLeod has become a noted scientist who developed a shield to cover the earth and protect its inhabitants from the effects of the deteriorating ozone layer. (This leads to such dialogue as "They'll remember this for a thousand years—the day we saved the planet from the sun!") A side effect from this is a constant heat wave, but why wouldn't an ice age be the logical consequence of not having a sun? The plot zips quickly between centuries and planets as evil Zeistians, in conjunction with evil U.S. corporate executives (are there any other kind?), try to thwart a rejuvenated MacLeod's plans to destroy the shield after he finds the ozone layer has repaired itself. The villains will benefit from continued use of the now obsolete shield, despite the fact that existence under the once lifesaving device has thrown Earth into total despair.

As played by Lambert (yes, his forehead is still the size of the Eiffel Tower), MacLeod is a somnambulistic hero devoid of personality. He does, however, look good in a torn shirt, and in this age of Schwarzenegger types, that qualifies for top billing in a movie. The main villain, played by Michael Ironside, obviously learned acting from overdosing on old Jack Nicholson films. His resemblance to and impersonation of Nicholson is remarkable, but would be more suited to a *Star Search* appearance than to the big screen, where the rip-off becomes distracting. The movie is redeemed by the appearances of Sean Connery, who seems to be having fun and is obviously counting the minutes until he can cash his paycheck. Yes, his character of Ramirez, the mystical swordsman from centuries ago, did indeed die in part one. Ten minutes after this film ended, we could not recall if his reappearance here was even explained, but we all know the real reason is that box-office clout can make the cinematic dead rise like Lazarus. (Remember Spock's "death" in *Star Trek II: The Wrath of Khan*?) The fun is watching Connery providing much-needed wit, but the material is clearly beneath his talents—like watching De Niro in a *Gilligan's Island* reunion movie. It's doubtful Connery started to

HIGHLANDER 2: THE QUICKENING   Poster art.

dust off the mantlepiece making room for a second Oscar on the basis of his appearance here.

The special effects are only sporadically effective. The futuristic sets are appropriately depressing and make those in *Blade Runner* look like Club Med. Yet, unlike the first film, which capitalized on magnificent scenery, the sequel has a confined feel to it, as though virtually everything was filmed on a tiny set with the props moved around for each scene à la the infamous *Plan 9 From Outer Space*. You have to wonder where the extensive budget actually went.

Despite its faults, *Highlander 2: The Quickening* is a painless time killer. Director Mulcahy's obsession with swordfights is almost pornographic, his cameras lingering on the rapiers, yet he knows how to stage an exciting action sequence. The film also displays occasional wit and suspense.

HIGHLANDER 2: THE QUICKENING   Ramirez, the immortal.

249

The critical reception to this movie made it appear as though the original film was received as *Citizen Kane*. Gene Siskel and Roger Ebert immediately called *Highlander 2* one of the year's worst films, and their sentiments were generally echoed by their peers. It did, however, open surprisingly well in the United States despite its modest advertising campaign and actually stayed around for a few weeks before vanishing to the video stores. Predictably, the reception was even better overseas where the film ran 12 minutes longer than U.S. prints. Connery emerged unscathed, as usual, with dignity in place, reaping the only positive notices for the movie. *Highlander 2* now fulfills its intended destiny as a popular cult video. In 1992, it even spawned a TV series—sans Sean. For those wondering just what "The Quickening" is, it's a ceremony in which Zeistian citizens enact an intergalactic version of "Slap me five!"

MEDICINE MAN

1992

Released by Hollywood Pictures

CAST:

Dr. Robert Campbell: Sean Connery; *Dr. Rae Crane:* Lorraine Bracco; *Dr. Miguel Ornega:* José Wilker; *Tanaki:* Rodolfo de Alexandre; *Jahausa:* Francisco Tsirene Tsere Rereme.

CREDITS:

Director: John McTiernan; *Producers:* Andrew G. Vajna and Donna Dubrow; *Screenplay:* Tom Schulman and Sally Robinson; *Director of Photography:* Donald McAlpine; *Editor:* Michael R. Miller; *Production Designer:* John Krenz Reinhart, Jr.; *Music:* Jerry Goldsmith. *Running Time:* 104 minutes.

In 1991, Sean Connery—at age sixty-one—was approaching the period in his life in which he would legally be considered a senior citizen. Admittedly, one cannot envision Sean taking advantage of senior's discounts on bus tickets or at the local supermarket. Yet, history has shown that with few exceptions, action stars who continue to pursue dynamic leading-man roles into their sixties are regarded as looking ridiculous. Not so with Sean Connery. He has joined an elite group of thespians who are seemingly

immune from the ravages of time. As they did with John Wayne, critics seem to relish Sean's "golden years" and savor each performance, even if they do not respond to the film itself. Such was the case with *Medicine Man.*

The script was written by Tom Schulman and Sally Robinson on spec, meaning it was not commissioned by a studio. Writers who have faith in a particular story line author a screenplay then submit it to the studios for bids. Schulman was hot, having recently won an Oscar for his screenplay for *Dead Poets Society,* and in a bidding war the script sold for $3 million—an extravagant price even by today's standards. Originally titled *The Stand,* then *The Last Days of Eden,* the script was partially rewritten by Sally Robinson and an uncredited Tom Stoppard. The film would be released by Hollywood Pictures, a subsidiary of the Walt Disney organization. The director would be John McTiernan, with whom Connery had worked on *The Hunt for Red October.* It was widely reported that McTiernan was paid $6 million and Connery $10 million, causing the budget to soar to $40 million despite the absence of large-scale special effects. (McTiernan has claimed these salary estimates were overstated.)

The script centers on a brilliant but reclusive biochemist (Connery) who has been slaving away for years in the Amazon doing research for a major corporation. When he breaks off communication with the outside world, a Nobel Prize–winning female biochemist is sent to South America to investigate the status of his work. Connery resents the intrusion, takes an immediate dislike to his younger colleague, but finds she is as stubborn and ill-tempered as he is, and just as fearless. Connery later attributes his frustration to having found the cure for cancer, only to have misplaced the formula. The battling scientists put aside their differences and make a concentrated effort to rediscover the cure. Although they succeed, their research center and the surrounding area are destroyed by overly aggressive developers.

The story mandated the casting of a strong female lead for what is essentially a two-character film. Lorraine Bracco, an Oscar nominee as Ray Liotta's bubble-headed wife in Scorsese's *Goodfellas,* was signed to star opposite Sean, who incidentally is credited as executive producer. Recalled Connery, "She came into my office to see me and I liked her immediately. She's not obvious casting for this film at all, but she has a marvelous sense of humor and an amazing direct quality. She's a very physical actress, and when you get out there in the middle of the

250

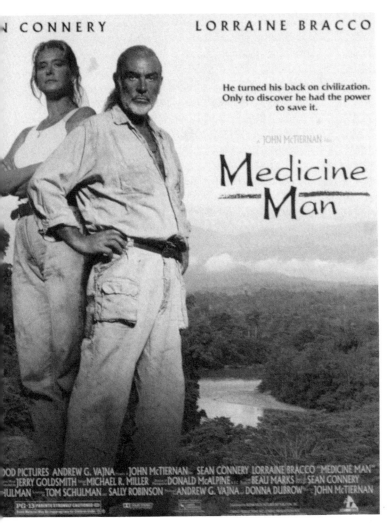

MEDICINE MAN   (Top left) A confrontation with Lorraine Bracco. (Bottom left) Connery and Bracco on the verge of success in finding the cure for cancer. (Right) The stars did their own stuntwork at treetop level. (Photo credits: Phil Bray, C. Cinergi Productions, Inc., and Cinergi Productions, N.V. All rights reserved.)

MEDICINE MAN   (Left) As Dr. Campbell. (Top right) With Lorraine Bracco. (Bottom right) With Francisco Tsirene Tsere Rereme. (Photo credits: Phil Bray, C. Cinergi Productions, Inc. and Cinergi Productions, N.V. All rights reserved.)

jungle with the insects and the humidity, you don't need an actress who is going to be too concerned about her hair and makeup." Ironically, it was reported that Bracco was pretty much the antithesis of this type of actress once she arrived on location. In a devastating on-location article printed in *Premiere* magazine, Bracco was depicted as temperamental and pampered. She traveled with an entourage consisting of an acting coach, makeup person, cook, nanny, kids, and—sorry, Sean—personal hairstylist. It was also reported that Bracco would forget lines, giggle at the prospect of retakes, and become quite moody. (One person on the set observed the film should be retitled either *Days of Vines and Boas* or *Who'll Stop Lorraine*.) While Connery has always been chivalrous and not criticized his leading ladies, those on this production knew that he was intolerant of anyone not prepared with their lines. Sean hates to waste time on any set, and *Medicine Man* had probably the least enjoyable locale he had ever endured.

McTiernan had scouted locations from Central America to Malaysia in hopes of replicating the Amazon jungle. He knew better than to attempt filming near the actual Amazon, on the basis of the disasters that had befallen the makers of *The Emerald Forest* and *At Play in the Fields of the Lord*. He finally settled on 125 acres of privately owned jungle in sparsely populated Catemaco, Mexico—a full one hundred miles from Vera Cruz. Cameras began to roll in March 1991 after a two-month delay caused by the lack of a suitable location. To ensure accuracy, McTiernan imported trees and undergrowth from the Amazon region, as well as actual Brazilian Indians, although these were city dwellers who had to learn to emulate their brethren who resided in the jungle. Temperatures skyrocketed to 115 degrees, and the humidity consistently approached 100 percent. Virtually everyone on the set succumbed to illness, with the exception of Sean, who confessed he avoided sickness only by "drinking too much vodka." At night, the locale was plagued by millions of insects, and in the day, by boredom. There was nowhere to go and nothing to do. Connery had a satellite dish installed, but it rarely worked.

Tensions on the set grew more pronounced. McTiernan was regarded as affable yet removed—a technically oriented director who would not compromise in his determination to get a specific shot. At one point Bracco was kept hanging on a limb three hundred feet in the air with no safety harness while McTiernan kept reshooting in order to get the proper backdrop. Finally, Connery had the set cleared while he and McTiernan "had it out." According to Sean,

"[McTiernan] was too obsessed with the mechanics of what he was doing. I had bent every actor's dictum and rule to accommodate what he wanted. . . . I shot [a] scene over a period of ten weeks and I shot it under the most adverse conditions. . . . I cleared the set and told him that he had to understand what it entails trying to accommodate all his demands, which were totally mechanical. But that's only his inexperience in understanding what an actor had to live with." Eventually, the director and star settled their differences, and filming resumed.

What is notable about *Medicine Man* is the amount of stunt work performed by the principals, for the most part sans doubles. In a pivotal sequence Connery and Bracco swing on pulleys from the treetops in hopes of finding a rare bromeliad necessary for the cure they are seeking. It's a stunning scene, fraught with both beauty and danger, aided immeasurably by the stars doing their own stunts. Connery and Bracco performed the required action at a height of one hundred and twenty feet by starting at twenty feet and gradually moving higher. It remains one of the most haunting images of the film.

By the time shooting had wrapped in late May, Connery was fatigued, frustrated, and eager to go home. Unlike others on the set, he did not want his concentration disrupted by flying off the locations for long weekends. He managed to shave several days from the filming schedule and departed hastily. This meant the crew did not get the customary wrap party generally given by the lead actor. Some were hurt by this and referred to Connery as a prima donna, while others understood his frustrations and held no grudges. At least one production assistant termed him "a prince."

Considering all the difficulties in filming, it's surprising that *Medicine Man* looks as good as it does. The movie could have been a disaster, and although critic Gene Siskel referred to it as such, this is an offbeat and engaging film that succeeds more often than it fails. Director McTiernan, eager to make a "serious" film in the wake of his *Die Hard* and *Predator* hits, creates a fascinating backdrop to the central story. The locations are unique and filmed with meticulous respect for natural beauty. Many critics complained that the script was more talk than action, but that is precisely why the movie is so engaging. Despite a bang-up finale with a devastating forest fire, the film relies on dialogue, scenery, and performances instead of cheap thrills.

Wearing a gray ponytail and beard, Connery was praised for delivering another larger-than-life performance. Critic David Sheehan encapsulated the feel-

MEDICINE MAN Conferring with director John McTiernan (top) and discussing a scene with Bracco and McTiernan. (Photo credits: Phil Bray, Cinergi Productions, Inc., and Cinergi Productions N.V. All rights reserved.)

253

ings of most reviewers by stating that Connery was at his "charming, crafty best." Hal Hinson of the *Washington Post* took it one step further, referring to Connery as "the greatest actor alive." Bracco, however, suffered the scorn of negative reviews, with some critics stating she had virtually ruined the film. *Variety* referred to her performance as "a lethal job of miscasting" and said, "It's a wonder Connery just doesn't throw her to the crocodiles."

To be sure, many of these criticisms are valid. The attempt to re-create *The African Queen* never fully succeeds because, while Connery is certainly up to the standards of Bogart, Bracco doesn't evoke memories of Katharine Hepburn. In fairness, however, she is merely a reflection of what the script calls for. Why the writers decided to have a brilliant scientist look and sound like a member of a Bronx street gang is not

clear. The cultural differences between the two lead characters do allow for some spirited insults, but at times the script is reduced to one of those *Sanford and Son* episodes with Redd Foxx and his on-screen sister-in-law trading verbal barbs. Nonetheless, the merits of *Medicine Man* far outweigh its shortcomings.

The release of *Medicine Man* was delayed for several months, possibly to avoid the crowded Christmas market. It finally premiered in February 1992, burdened by its uninspired title and negative word of mouth. However, the film topped the charts of box-office hits in its first week and surprised the industry by becoming a modest hit. This is directly attributable to Sean Connery's name above the title, and the loyal following he has built among international moviegoers. Like a fine wine, he seems to get better with age.

RISING SUN   Both the U.S. and Japanese ad campaigns stressed the considerable star power of Connery and Snipes.

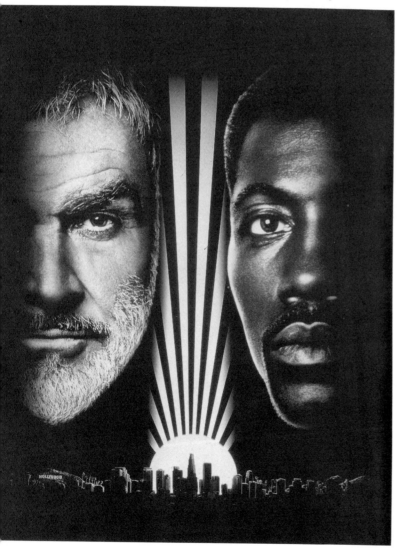

RISING SUN

1993

Released by 20th Century-Fox

CAST:

John Connor: Sean Connery; *Web Smith:* Wesley Snipes; *Tom Graham:* Harvey Keitel; *Eddie Sakamura:* Cary-Hiroyuki Tagawa; *Bob Richmond:* Kevin Anderson; *Yoshida-san:* Mako; *Senator John Morton:* Ray Wise; *Ishihara:* Stan Egi; *Phillips:* Stan Shaw; *Jingo Askuma:* Tia Carrere; *Willy "The Weasel" Wilhelm:* Steve Buscemi; *Cheryl Lynn Austin:* Tatjana Patitz.

CREDITS:

Director: Philip Kaufman; *Producer:* Peter Kaufman; *Executive Producer:* Sean Connery; *Screenplay:* Philip Kaufman, Michael Crichton, and Michael Backes, based on the novel by Michael Crichton; *Director of Photography:* Michael Chapman; *Editors:* Stephen A. Rotter and William S. Scharf; *Production Designer:* Dean Tavoularis; *Music:* Toru Takemitsu. *Running Time:* 129 minutes.

By 1993, Michael Crichton was a triple-threat talent in Hollywood, serving as novelist, screenwriter, and director. Indeed, Crichton was one of the select authors who could command huge advances from publishers merely by announcing he was beginning to work on a new novel (he usually didn't need to provide such mundane details as plot or title). The Crichton name on the cover of a book insured its

254

status as a best-seller. The summer 1993 release of the screen adaptation of Crichton's thriller *Jurassic Park* proved to be one of the greatest success stories in cinema history. With Crichton providing the script and Steven Spielberg in the director's chair, the mega-budget dinosaur epic became the top-grossing film of all time. Expectations were naturally high for the back-to-back release of the film version of another Crichton bestseller, *Rising Sun*.

Unlike *Jurassic Park, Rising Sun* would prove to be a controversial project for all concerned. The novel centers on a murder committed in a Los Angeles office building owned by a Japanese conglomerate. Japanese-Americans griped that the book painted Asians in an unfavorable light, portraying them as devious, sinister, and unwilling to assimilate into U.S. society, while simultaneously using unscrupulous business practices to "steal" the country from under the noses of the American public. Such controversy helped insure that the book maintained a solid stay on best-seller lists. When it was announced that 20th Century-Fox had given the "green light" to a movie version, the protests flared up with even greater intensity.

Sean Connery had established a good relationship with Michael Crichton when the duo collaborated on *The Great Train Robbery*, the 1978 film adventure which Crichton directed, based upon his own novel. The two men had been eager to work together again, and when Crichton wrote *Rising Sun*, he based the lead character—John Connor—on Sean Connery. Under such flattering circumstances, Connery could hardly refuse when Crichton asked him to play the role of Connor in the film. In fact, Connery's enthusiasm for the property was such that he also served as executive producer.

When asked what appealed to him about the project, Connery said, "One's response is always to the writing. There are fewer and fewer writers who can deal with the nuances of character. I was absolutely caught by *Name of the Rose* [by Umberto Eco], even if it was a long read. The same is true of Michael Crichton. I've stayed friends with him ever since we did *The Great Train Robbery*. As soon as I read the galley for *Rising Sun*, I agreed to do the script. There's a dramatic line through different levels of expression. It's a detective story, but it's also a story about black, yellow, and white cultures, and new technology and Japanese-American relations."

In actuality, the novel had nothing to do with black people, but in the interest of dramatic intensity (not to mention maximizing the grosses), it was decided that Connery's costar in the film would be up-and-coming action star Wesley Snipes, who had re-cently made a splash in the surprise box-office hit *New Jack City*. Connery justified this—and other deviations from the source novel—by saying, "I loved the book, but the rhythm of dynamics of a film are much different. I would rather see savage kinds of energies released. We had to make it more filmically complex." To that end, Snipes was cast as Web Smith, the streetwise detective who must form an uneasy alliance with the mysterious John Connor because of the latter's extensive—and perhaps illicit—ties to the Japanese business community in the United States. The two men must join forces to solve the murder of a promiscuous party girl who appears to have been killed by a Japanese executive during a bout of rough sex in an office boardroom.

In the film, much is made of the relationship between the detectives. Connor advises Smith that he should be regarded as the *senpai* (experienced guide or mentor) to Smith's *kohai* (inexperienced pupil). In real life, while Snipes is anything but inexperienced in his profession as actor, he did confess to learning a few things from Connery. This unorthodox teaming of actors resulted in the men forming a mutual admiration society. Snipes, in particular,

RISING SUN   Famed cover girl Tatjana Patitz as Cheryl Austin, the party girl whose murder launches a politically sensitive investigation.

255

sought advice from Connery about how to deal with sudden success. "I asked a lot of questions," Snipes recalled, "as any rookie should do to understand the game. We talked about how to approach the art—and surviving in the business. The primary thing was: Trust your instincts. And never let 'em tell you anything that you don't understand. If they start to throw all these big words at you, tell 'em to break it down. He said, 'If they can't put it in your language, you don't need 'em.' I've been listening ever since. I use his success as an example. It must work. Something he is doing is right."

As for Connery, he was all too happy to share advice with his younger costar. "We talked about a lot of things," said Connery. "I told him he should have a really good confidante and a very good lawyer. Deals that he's making, he should assume the worst of the partner and the partner should assume the worst of him. . . . I was happy to tell him about the mistakes *I've* made." This includes Connery's oft-stated complaint that he's "been screwed more times than a hooker!" Connery also expressed amazement at Snipes's physical prowess, including his karate skills: "He can get his feet in places where I can't even get my hands!"

Rising Sun was directed by Philip Kaufman, who also cowrote the screenplay. Kaufman, a talented filmmaker with a diversified body of work (he wrote and/or directed *The Right Stuff, The Unbearable Lightness of Being,* and *The Outlaw Josey Wales*), was primarily concerned with the thriller aspects of the story as opposed to its observations on race relations. "What I was most interested in making was a murder mystery," he said, "while at the same time exploring the nuances of the business world between the United States and Japan, which is also a very important part of the story. As we move through the nineties into the next century, the collaboration between these two countries is one of the most important globally, economically, politically, and perhaps romantically."

As cowriter and director, Kaufman had a lot of say over how the sensitive issue of U.S.–Japanese relations were depicted in the film. Kaufman decided to head off the anticipated protests from Japanese-Americans by making key changes to the story, most notably switching the identity of the killer from a Japanese to an American. While the script still retained some harsh criticism of Japanese business practices (for instance, executives are show illegally "bugging" their non-Asian business partners, all the while keeping an in-house bordello of leggy blondes for their recreational use), other changes softened the character flaws of several of the Japanese corporate

magnates depicted on-screen. These changes, along with others, caused Michael Crichton to disassociate himself from the movie, citing the oft-used term "creative differences."

Filming took place in and around Los Angeles on the 20th Century-Fox soundstages, the exclusive Sherwood Country Club, and a new fifty-three story high-rise called the California Plaza, where the murder and much of the action takes place. Shooting began on June 22, 1992, and wrapped on October 3. By all accounts, the filming went smoothly and unremarkably, possibly due to the limited location work required.

Casting a critical eye toward *Rising Sun*, one is impressed by the film's glossy look, outstanding production design, and other technical elements. Likewise, the unlikely pairing of Connery and Snipes generally works well. As a thriller, however, the movie opens with a bang (no pun intended) in a highly erotic, stunningly filmed sequence in which a young woman is murdered during a sizzling sexual encounter. The introduction of Connery and Snipes as a team to solve the crime is at first refreshing, with both men trying to upstage the other's knowledge of police work. However, their relationship—like the story itself—quickly degenerates into clichés, and although there are many memorable scenes, the screenplay falls apart precisely when it needs to be strong: during the chaotic scene in which the killer is revealed. The fact that he turns out to be a rather minor character in the story is anticlimactic. The fact that he is Caucasian also seems patronizing and reeks of political correctness—as though the filmmakers could not bear the thought of displeasing Asian movie-goers.

The efforts were for naught. Even before *Rising Sun* was released, Japanese–American groups were protesting across the country. Yes, they acknowledged, the film did tone down the cynicism of Crichton's novel. However, most of the Japanese depicted were still unsavory characters. They overlooked the fact that the movie presented more fully dimensional roles for Asian actors than any hundred other films combined. For example, Cary-Hiroyuki Tagawa plays a playboy with a dubious past, who just might be the murderer. He's funny, intelligent, and sexy—not exactly the qualities Asian actors are usually allowed to display on-screen in American films. Incredibly, even Tagawa bit the hand that fed him and, upon release of the movie, sided with the protesters.

The filmmakers were so distraught at having to deal with the controversy that Michael Crichton actually issued a detailed press release defending the

source novel—including statistical figures indicating how many favorable and unfavorable aspects were presented relating to Japanese characters. Connery, who views press junkets as necessary evils, was ill-tempered through some of the publicity tours as reporters asked him endlessly about the film's "Japan-bashing." He said, "I have enormous respect for Japanese culture and efficiency. In *Rising Sun* I play a mediating character who understands how difficult it is for an outsider to gain acceptance in that culture. The different delineations in Japanese culture are clear. The American concept is much more maverick—there's no country in the world more dedicated to the pursuit of happiness, which makes for a lot of loose cannons. This is why I emphasize that *Rising Sun* is not a movie about Japanese-bashing. Neither was the book—that's the erroneous tag that has followed it around. It shows the shortcomings of both cultures."

Indeed, in the film Connery's character is quick to defend the Japanese "takeover" of American business, pointing out that U.S. corporations willingly sell themselves to Japanese interests. The only anti-Japanese remarks uttered in the film belong to an ignorant L.A. cop played by Harvey Keitel. The role is so two-dimensional and boorish, however, that the only one offended should be the L.A. police department. When *Rising Sun* concentrates on the political and cultural differences between Americans and

RISING SUN   Connery and Snipes at odds over how to handle the investigation.

RISING SUN   As Det. John Connor.

Japanese, it is often an engaging film. When it harkens back to the murder mystery, it becomes unremarkable, predictable, but admittedly never boring. One of the key problems is that most of the action takes place on rainy nights, which gives the film a claustrophobic look despite the opulence of the settings.

Connery has some wonderful moments as the mysterious detective with a fascination for the Japanese lifestyle. He brings both humor and tension to the role, and he commands the screen at all times. Wesley Snipes acquits himself nicely as well, but the screenwriters—not content to deal with U.S.–Japanese culture clashes—go overboard and try to throw in the inevitable black-white conflict, too. The results are some ludicrous and pretentious scenes shoehorned into the film just to make sure we know Snipes's character is not subservient to Connery's. A scene in which he and Connery must rely on some ''brothers'' from the ghetto to help them escape their pursuers is so poorly written as to be laughable. Equally dumb, though admittedly fun, is the tacked-on karate fight at the end, appearing for the most part to allow Snipes to show off his physical prowess. By the time the movie ends, the racial jibes between the two have become wearying. It's like watching *In the Heat of the Night* with kimonos.

Despite its shortcomings, *Rising Sun* is still worthy

of a viewing. It boasts some interesting performances, great music by noted Japanese composer Toru Takemitsu, a few thought-provoking issues, and some truly erotic encounters. (Cary-Hiroyuki Tagawa gets to eat sushi off the bodies of two naked women, and famous cover girl model Tatjana Patitz is simply stunning in her brief appearance as his doomed lover.) It isn't a bad film, just not a very memorable one. Critics gave mixed reviews upon the movie's release in the summer of 1993, and audiences seemed to share this viewpoint. The movie's gross earnings in the United States were adequate but somewhat disappointing—much like the film itself. In short, this *Sun* never rises to the heights it could have.

A GOOD MAN IN AFRICA

1994

Released by Gramercy Pictures

CAST:

Morgan Leafy: Colin Friels; *Dr. Alex Murray:* Sean Connery *Fanshawe:* John Lithgow; *Chloe:* Diana Rigg; *Adekunle* Louis Gossett Jr.; *Celia:* Joanne Whalley-Kilmer; *Priscilla* Sarah-Jane Crutchley; *Hazel:* Jackie Mofokeng.

CREDITS:

Director: Bruce Beresford; *Producers:* John Fiedler and Mark Tarlov; *Screenplay:* William Boyd, based upon his novel; *Director of Photography:* Andrezj Bartkowiak; *Editor:* Jim Clark; *Production Designer:* Herbert Pinter; *Music:* John du Prez. *Running Time:* 95 minutes.

Sean Connery's follow-up to the highly controversial *Rising Sun* was another film dealing with racial tensions—albeit in a humorous way. This time around, Connery would be very much a supporting presence in a relatively big budget ($20 million) social satire titled *A Good Man in Africa*. While Connery's screen time is limited, his role is pivotal to the events that unfold, and his character—like the actor himself—is viewed as larger than life by those around him.

The film is based on a 1981 award-winning novel by William Boyd, who was born in Ghana, the son of

RISING SUN   Connery confers with director Philip Kaufman.

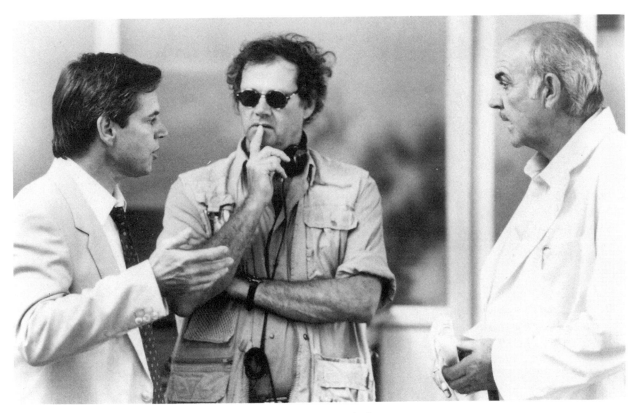

With Colin Friels (left) and director Bruce Beresford.

a Scottish doctor who had made a name for himself locally for his expertise in tropical medicine. Although Boyd spent his school years in England and France, his early upbringing in Africa left him with a fascination for the continent, its people, and most of all, its politics. His book, *A Good Man in Africa*, is a critically acclaimed chronicle of the downfall of Morgan Leafy, an egotistical, manipulative British bureaucrat who is stuck with a largely ceremonial role in the fictitious African country of Kinjanja. The comedy of manners allows Morgan to act as a thinly veiled indictment of colonialism itself. As the last vestiges of British influence are crumbling around him, Morgan finds spiritual renewal through the advice of Dr. Alex Murray, the last "good man in Africa." Murray selflessly helps the local population instead of exploiting them and is sickened by the endless corruption by both European and African officials.

Boyd's novel had caught the attention of director Bruce Beresford, who helmed the Oscar-winning *Driving Miss Daisy*. (Beresford was the subject of controversy when the Academy awarded his film Best Picture of the Year, yet failed to nominate him for Best Director. This caused the film to be referred to as "the movie that directed itself.") Before reading the book, Beresford said that he thought, "No one

will write a book about Africa as funny as the Evelyn Waugh novels, but in fact it *is* as funny as the Waugh novels. I was struck by [it] particularly because I had lived in West Africa—in Nigeria—for two years, and I knew how accurately written it was and how authentically both the Europeans and the Africans were portrayed." Ultimately, Beresford would direct *Mr. Johnson*, another story about racial relations set in Africa, for which Boyd wrote the screenplay. "When I met with Will Boyd in connection with *Mr. Johnson*, I suggested to him that we film [*A Good Man in Africa*]." Boyd agreed and contracted to adapt his own novel for the screen.

In writing the screenplay, Boyd had the unenviable task of editing his own book and eliminating unnecessary events and plot devices, such as the flashback narrative which many readers found enchanting. "Sixty to seventy percent of the average novel can't get into a film," he complained. "It's all about editing, boiling down, looking for essence." Most of the memorable characters from the novel were kept intact, however, and Beresford managed to sign an enormously talented cast to bring them to life. Australian actor Colin Friels has the pivotal role of Morgan Leafy, the horny, excessive diplomat who views the local African population as the "white

261

A GOOD MAN IN AFRICA   As Dr. Alex Murray.

262

man's burden" and constantly schemes to get reassigned to England. His boss is Fanshawe (John Lithgow), a hopelessly prissy snob who berates Morgan for every negative occurrence in the country and seems to be in a race with his subordinate to see who can get transferred from Africa first. Louis Gossett Jr. plays President Adekunle, the U.S.-educated new leader of Kinjanja, who intends to exploit and loot the nation with even more fervor than the British. There are also a number of high-profile female characters, including Diana Rigg as Fenshaw's elegant but sexually frustrated wife, who has eyes for Morgan; the stunningly beautiful Sarah-Jane Fenton as the Fenshaws' sexually frustrated daughter, who also has eyes for Morgan; Joanne Whalley-Kilmer as Adekunle's all-around frustrated wife, who has eyes for Morgan; and Jackie Mofokeng as a "common" black girl, who . . . well you can guess. All of these characters intertwine with each other as their relationships become increasingly frantic and complicated.

The central plot device in this casually paced satire comes when President Adekunle threatens Morgan's life, telling him he must insure that a pending construction project is approved by a planning board. As Adekunle is the silent owner of the company, he will benefit tremendously. Only one obstacle stands in his way: the irritating honesty and principals of Dr. Alex Murray, who has dedicated his life to helping the poor townspeople from his understaffed clinic. Murray sits on the board and knows full well of Adekunle's plans to exploit the nation, and he adamantly refuses to reconsider casting the veto that will negate the construction project. It falls to Morgan to change his mind. He fails in his blatant and awkward attempts to bribe Murray, but in the process finds he has been positively influenced by the only man of true integrity he has ever encountered.

For the supporting role of Alex Murray, no one was better suited than Sean Connery. Upon meeting Connery after the book's publication, William Boyd was pleasantly surprised to hear that the actor had been greatly impressed by the work. According to Bruce Beresford, "Though there are a lot of major roles, the key one, in a sense, is Dr. Murray, who really *is* the 'good man in Africa.' Will was very keen on getting Sean Connery for the role, right from the very beginning, because Will's own father was a Scottish doctor who worked in Ghana and Nigeria, and the character is based on him. Will said, 'We've got to have Connery for this. He is a Scotsman who will understand and it will be perfect.' Connery not only agreed to lend his screen presence to the role of Murray, but also helped fine-tune the screenplay. He made useful suggestions about making the char-

acter much more lighthearted and witty. His most self-serving suggestion was to make Murray an avid golfer. This allowed Connery to act while indulging in his favorite pastime. Artistically, it works marvelously, as Boyd wrote a funny, insightful scene in which Morgan tries to bluff his way through a golf game in order to impress Murray. Connery's skill on the golf course was such that producer Mark Tarlov noted, "He was so good we didn't have to do any editing," jokingly adding, "It was the one reason we cast him!"

Despite the high-profile cast, Beresford wanted to keep the comedy subdued. "It's a fairly naturalistic comedy," he said. "It's not broad, like an old British movie in which everyone is clowning around in the foreign office in countries they don't understand. It's much more straightforward and, in fact, if you've read the novel not knowing very much about Africa, you might think it was rather exaggerated in its conflict and its characters. But if you've lived in Africa, and particularly in an independent African country, you would realize that it's very accurately observed. So I encouraged the actors not to play it too broadly. . . . The film is about cultural conflict and about the lack of understanding of one group of people for another. You have a situation in Africa where countries that were colonies for a century or more are suddenly strong in their own resources. The whites leave or stay on as 'technical advisers,' and suddenly they're subservient to the black government. And then you get all sorts of conflicts, because the whites say, 'Everything should be done this way or that way,' and the Africans are saying, 'We're fed up! You've been telling us how to do these things for a long time, but we want to do it *this* way!' The situations are very, very strong indeed, and for me, that's one of the key factors in making films where people are violently opposed to one another. It can create enormous drama, or, in this case, it creates a lot of funny situations."

A Good Man in Africa was filmed entirely in South Africa in mid-1993, amidst a period of enormous political unrest and violence. During production, the country was plagued by riots and assassinations. Bruce Beresford was directing local people as extras in a scene in which a mob riots and burns the British flag. Beresford relates that he told them, "When you burn the flag, I want you to go on chanting the way I've shown you.' And they said, 'When we burn flags, we usually stamp and whistle and jump up and down.' And I said, 'Oh. I'm sorry, I didn't realize that there was a protocol involved!' So they did exactly what they normally did, which was great. Normally, you're not dealing with people who have experience of the kind of things they're representing. But these guys, unfortunately or fortunately, all did. And they all had a very engaging sense of humor about it.''

A Good Man in Africa is primarily an arthouse film that is masquerading as mainstream entertainment, probably due to Sean Connery's name above the title. Indeed, it was not until Connery agreed to participate that the producers succeeded in raising the required budget. Not surprisingly, however, the ultrasophisticated comedy did not find a wide audience and its theatrical run was an abbreviated one, not only in the United States, but worldwide. Critics were rather savage in their denouncement of virtually every aspect of the film, and one wonders why. In an age in which every film seems prefabricated around how many explosions and murders can be depicted, this emerges as a brave, gentle, little movie that—while undeniably flawed—manages to deliver more good dialogue in ninety-five minutes than can probably be heard in an entire Jean Claude Van Damme film festival. The movie benefits from an exceptional cast, most notably Colin Friels, who is outstanding in the role of the likable cad Morgan Leafy. A major star in Australia, Friels—who is remindful of Pierce Brosnan—remains largely unknown in other countries, despite a winning personality and exceptional comedic skills. *Good Man* should have been a star turn for the actor, but the film's flop at the box office precluded this from happening—at least for now.

Friels gets yeoman support from the seemingly miscast John Lithgow, who is also extremely funny as the priggish British diplomat whose lack of humor is only exceeded by his cowardice. Lithgow, who admitted being intimidated by playing a Brit, masters the accent very well (at least to Yank ears) and has a field day in his scene-stealing sequences with his heavy-weight costars. Louis Gossett Jr. gets a rare chance to show off his comedic skills, and newcomer Sarah-Jane Fenton is wonderfully winning as the girl Morgan tries desperately to seduce. (In one of the film's best scenes, he finally gets the opportunity, only to have to avoid the big moment when he discovers at the last minute that he has contracted a rare venereal disease.) A major complaint is that the two roles played by Joanne Whalley-Kilmer and Diana Rigg are underwritten and do not capitalize on the full talents of the actresses. (Inexcusably, Boyd failed to write any scenes in which Rigg and Connery could appear on-screen together. The chemistry would have been terrific.)

Unsurprisingly, Sean Connery dominates the screen in his few appearances. His scenes are spread throughout the film, giving the impression his participation is more than it actually is, à la John Wayne in *The Longest Day*. For once Connery gets to *underplay* a scene, because he is portraying an everyday man, not a hero or an icon. His low-key mannerisms are a joy to watch, as are his cynical one-liners at Morgan's expense. His unexpected demise at the film's climax is a poignant and very moving moment, and Connery plays it beautifully.

Despite its disjointed plot—which is basically a series of amusing incidents tenuously pasted together—*A Good Man in Africa* has many worthy qualities in addition to the aforementioned performances. Composer John du Prez and a number of African bands contribute a wonderful score, and director of photography Andrezj Bartkowiak's cinematography is a feast for the eyes. All of this has been brought together by Bruce Beresford's sensitive direction. Among the major filmmakers working today, Beresford stands out as a man dedicated to making small, meaningful films. They do not always succeed commercially, or on every artistic level, but they all attempt to deal with real issues and fascinating characters.

Ultimately, however, it is Sean Connery who elevates this film to something more enjoyable than another highbrow arthouse comedy. As one critic astutely noted, ''The best that can be said about *A Good Man in Africa* is that the good man of the title, Sean Connery, plays his part—a giving, practical-minded doctor—with such humility and dignity that he practically stops the movie in its tracks.''

JUST CAUSE

1995

Released by Warner Bros.

CAST:

Paul Armstrong: Sean Connery; *Tanny Brown:* Laurence Fishburne; *Laurie Armstrong:* Kate Capshaw; *Bobby Earl:* Blair Underwood; *Blair Sullivan:* Ed Harris; *Warden:* Daniel J. Travanti; *Wilcox:* Christopher Murray; *McNair:* Ned Beatty; *Evangeline:* Ruby Dee.

CREDITS:

Director: Arne Glimcher; *Executive Producer:* Sean Connery; *Producers:* Lee Rich, Arne Glimcher, and Steve Perry; *Screenplay:* Jeb Stuart and Peter Stone based on the novel by John Katzenbach; *Director of Photography:* Lajos Koltai; *Editor:* William Anderson; *Production Designer:* Patrizia von

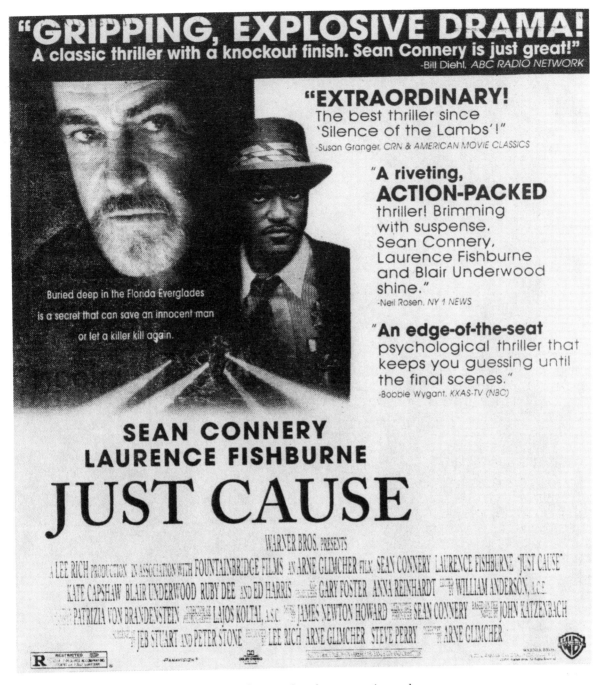

"**GRIPPING, EXPLOSIVE DRAMA!**
A classic thriller with a knockout finish. Sean Connery is just great!"
-Bill Diehl, *ABC RADIO NETWORK*

"**EXTRAORDINARY!**
The best thriller since
'Silence of the Lambs'!"
-Susan Granger, *CRN & AMERICAN MOVIE CLASSICS*

"A riveting,
ACTION-PACKED
thriller! Brimming
with suspense.
Sean Connery,
Laurence Fishburne
and Blair Underwood
shine."
-Neil Rosen, *NY 1 NEWS*

"**An edge-of-the-seat**
psychological thriller that
keeps you guessing until
the final scenes."
-Bobbie Wygant, *KXAS-TV (NBC)*

Buried deep in the Florida Everglades
is a secret that can save an innocent man
or let a killer kill again.

**SEAN CONNERY
LAURENCE FISHBURNE
JUST CAUSE**

WARNER BROS. PRESENTS

A LEE RICH PRODUCTION IN ASSOCIATION WITH FOUNTAINBRIDGE FILMS AN ARNE GLIMCHER FILM SEAN CONNERY LAURENCE FISHBURNE "JUST CAUSE" KATE CAPSHAW BLAIR UNDERWOOD RUBY DEE AND ED HARRIS GARY FOSTER ANNA REINHARDT WILLIAM ANDERSON, A.C.E. PATRIZIA VON BRANDENSTEIN LAJOS KOLTAI, A.S.C. JAMES NEWTON HOWARD SEAN CONNERY JOHN KATZENBACH JEB STUART AND PETER STONE LEE RICH ARNE GLIMCHER STEVE PERRY ARNE GLIMCHER

JUST CAUSE   *Just Cause* presented Connery not only as star but also as executive producer.

Brandenstein; *Music:* James Newton Howard. *Running Time:* 102 minutes.

Sean Connery has always maintained that the success of a film is predicated on its ability to "suspend time for an audience"—to make the viewers so engrossed in the plot that they are unaware of how much time has elapsed and how many lapses in pure logic might exist in the storyline. If these factors are realized, then a film might not succeed entirely on an artistic level, but it may succeed in captivating an audience. Typical of such a film is Connery's *Just Cause*, the first of two major starring releases for the actor in 1995. On one hand, the movie maintains the audience's interest with a very tightly directed story of a man's race against time to prevent a possibly unjust execution. However, it eventually degenerates into a contrived plot that is far murkier than

JUST CAUSE   Ed Harris as a madman who tantalizes Connery with clues to solve the murder.

N-Z-01

267

the Everglades location where the climax takes place. The main virtue of *Just Cause*, however, is that even at age sixty-four, Sean Connery still has the enormous screen presence to make even a flawed film seem dignified.

Just Cause was described by Connery as "an explosive story. I play Armstrong, a renowned law professor who is anticapital punishment; his position being that it's a cruel and capricious system that doles out torture for torture. He discovers that he is capable of things he never thought possible." The plot presents Connery's character, Paul Armstrong, as an attorney who has not tried a case in over a quarter of a century. (Unlike Connery, who makes filing lawsuits his favorite pastime next to golf.) Instead, his time is spent on the lecture circuit debating the shortcomings and racial inequalities of capital punishment. Decades ago, he would be touted as a crusading idealist. Today, however, he would more likely be described as a "knee-jerk liberal."

Armstrong, a happily married father of a nine-year-old girl and the devoted husband to a much younger wife Laurie (Kate Capshaw), finds his world shaken when he is approached by an elderly woman (Ruby Dee) with an impassioned plea to help free her son Bobby Earl (Blair Underwood), a young black man who is on death row in a prison near the Florida Everglades. Despite protests that he is out of touch with courtroom strategies, Armstrong cannot help but be moved by the woman's story—that her son was coerced into confessing to the murder of a little girl by virtue of the torturous methods of the local police chief, Tanny Brown (Laurence Fishburne), himself a black man with a reputation of being an "Uncle Tom."

Armstrong agrees to meet with Bobby Earl in prison and is shocked to find that the young man is quiet, well mannered, and extremely cultured. Bobby Earl tells Armstrong about being beaten within an inch of his life by Tanny Brown and his deputy, and is now about to suffer the ultimate indignity: being executed for a crime he didn't commit. At his wife's urging, Armstrong agrees to try to uncover evidence that will free his new client. On the surface, he appears to have a clear-cut case of pursuing guilt or innocence. As Armstrong digs deeper, however, he uncovers a good deal of dirty laundry among the local population. There are convincing signs that Bobby Earl knows of tainted evidence, and Armstrong intends to pursue these matters with Tanny Brown.

Brown proves to be exactly as Bobby Earl described: arrogant, unstable, and hot-tempered. Armstrong's efforts are further hindered by Bobby Earl's

initial defense attorney, an insipid man (underplayed by Ned Beatty in an all-too-brief appearance), who would sooner see Bobby Earl fry than lose any further clients for having defended him. Armstrong's investigation seems to imply that the real killer is a neighbor of Bobby Earl's on death row: a child molester and serial murderer named Blair Sullivan (Ed Harris). In a tense meeting, Sullivan recounts to Armstrong chilling details of the child's murder spiced with some quasireligious mumbo-jumbo and the hidden location of the undiscovered murder weapon. Much to Tanny's chagrin, the tips allow Armstrong to recover the knife used in the killing. With Sullivan's "confession" and the weapon to boot as evidence, Bobby Earl is set free—only to be taunted and threatened by Tanny Brown, who makes it clear the case is not closed in his eyes.

Up until that point, *Just Cause* is for the most part a solid, respectably intriguing "who-dunnit-if-he-in-fact-didn't-do-it." Then the film takes a 180-degree turn and ceases being an interesting detective story, introducing some fantastic plot twists—sadly, with diminishing returns. A stunning development proves that things are not always what they seem, and Armstrong is made aware of the real killer's identity. It must be said that the authors are divided on this plot device, one of us finding it to be as predictable as yesterday's news, while the other admits to being totally surprised. What is irrefutable, however, is that shortly after this, the film becomes just another potboiler in its last half hour, with Connery dashing wildly around trying to save his wife and child from the killer who has kidnapped them and is planning to torture and murder them based on some fairly unconvincing motives. The grand finale—a convoluted affair set deep in the Everglades (at night, naturally)—is reasonably suspenseful, but comes across as "*Cape Fear* Lite."

Just Cause had a production history almost as contrived as the film's conclusion. In 1991, producer Lee Rich optioned the manuscript of John Katzenbach's novel (in which the Connery character was a news reporter in Miami). Rich elicited the talents of director/producer Arne Glimcher (who had scored some critical acclaim with *The Mambo Kings*). Glimcher was intrigued by a story "where we realize that concrete perceptions [often] dissolve into illusions." This would be Glimcher's second turn as a director. Rich and Glimcher approached Sean Connery for the role of Paul Armstrong.

When it appeared as though Connery would not participate, the rumor was that Dustin Hoffman would sign for the part. Shortly thereafter, however, Connery agreed to star. (William Hurt had at one time been mentioned as a possible costar for Connery, but the deal never materialized.) Eager to exert creative control over the project, Connery also served as executive producer, although he downplayed this status by saying his primary function was to act. Nevertheless, as is his habit of late, Connery also made contributions to the script. According to director Arne Glimcher, "There are a lot of *writers* who don't have the story sense that Sean has. He was able to take a script we'd been having problems with and bring a greater subtlety to it."

A strong supporting cast was signed, topped by Laurence Fishburne, Kate Capshaw, Ed Harris, Blair Underwood, Ned Beatty, Ruby Dee, and—in uninspired, throwaway roles—Daniel J. Travanti, Kevin McCarthy, and Hope Lange. While the cast was rehearsing near Connery's home in Nassau, production designer Patrizia von Brandenstein was scouting many Florida locales, including sites in Ft. Myers (for scenes of the courthouse and police station), Bonita Springs, Copeland (representing Bobby Earl's impoverished home), Naples (doubling as Tanny Brown's home), and Miami, where a studio was used to construct the prison sets. There were also actual sites utilized in the Everglades Babcock Reserve, including an alligator farm (the critters play a grisly but

With Kate Capshaw—the calm before the storm.

predictable role in the climax). Indeed, in addition to the prerequisite heavy boots and insect repellent, the crew was also protected by an armed alligator wrangler. For the night scenes in the Everglades, a nearby airplane hangar was converted into a sound stage resembling a swamp.

By all accounts Connery got along very well with his costars, including Laurence Fishburne, who had an admittedly different style of preparing for a role. "Sean likes to come in, hit it, and go home," he said. "He prepares everything before he comes to the set. I'm a method actor. I like to come in and mess with it. But Sean is quite a guy. It looks like he's doing nothing, and then you look at the screen and he's stolen the scene." Indeed, Connery was actually frisky on the set. Kate Capshaw recalls him teasing her mercilessly when he perceived her fear of working near the alligators. Connery would come up from behind and cause her to scream. On another occasion, Connery was in a car parked near a newsreporter who was standing, doing a broadcast. Connery, noticing the woman was about eight months pregnant, could not resist pinching her behind as he drove by. Infuriated, the woman jumped in her car and caught up with the former 007. Connery turned on the charm, the two laughed, and the reporter promised to forgive and forget—in return for an autograph. Connery was also in a good mood when asked why he didn't wear a toupee in the film. He confessed it was considered, but "the makeup man wasn't particularly gifted and the temperature was too high. . . . I threw the blasted thing in the waste can!" The actor also surprised his director by doing much of the driving for a high-speed car chase.

Connery's happiness on the set came with an expiration date, however. Two weeks before the first press screening of the film, director Glimcher decided that the finale left too many plot holes open. He assembled the cast in London for some reshoots, then sent Warner Brothers' in-house editor Dede Allen to New York with the Herculean job of "fixing" the movie. Working nonstop for days, Allen delivered a "wet print"—literally—for the press show, causing *Variety* to quip they should retitle the movie *Just Finished*. Rumors had it that Connery—who has a short fuse for reshoots—was angered to the point that he considered not promoting the film on its press junket. (Ultimately, he did.)

Upon its release, the film only scored moderately at the box office. Critical reaction to the movie was mixed at best. As usual, Connery emerged relatively unscathed, with most reviewers citing his strong screen presence. Indeed, Connery is more watchable than ever, and although this is his most understated

JUST CAUSE   As Paul Armstrong, diligently racing against the clock to prevent an execution.

starring role in many years, the charisma never fails to shine through. It's especially refreshing to see him in a family setting portraying a regular guy who prefers to spend time with his wife and kid as opposed to engaging in heroics. (The script, however, should call more attention to his May–December romance with Capshaw. When Kevin McCarthy introduces Connery—a man nearly his own age—as "my son-in-law," the moment calls for a wisecrack or witticism that never materializes.)

Among the supporting roles, Kate Capshaw is not used to good effect in the underwritten role of Connery's wife. An engaging actress with a wonderful flair for comedy, she is seen here as the mandatory "woman in jeopardy," bereft of any true personality. Faring much better is Laurence Fishburne, who brings real tension to the complex role of Tanny Brown and matches Connery when it comes to charisma. Equally good is Blair Underwood in a strong performance in the role that is the catalyst for all the action. The Scenery-Chewing Award must go to Ed Harris as the homicidal madman who holds the key to the murder mystery. His performance is so over the top it makes Anthony Hopkins's Hannibal Lechter look like William F. Buckley. Spouting vulgarities mixed with lucid and manipulative clues, Harris literally climbs the walls. His scenes with Connery are brimming with tension. To some critics, Harris was guilty of overacting, but it's doubtful any of them nodded off during his scenes—which are clearly a highlight of the movie.

As director, Arne Glimcher does a respectful job of keeping the action moving. It should be mentioned, however, that for all the location work done in the Everglades, surprisingly very little of the area's unique local flavor shines forth on-screen. The screenplay works well for three-quarters of the film, but its weak and implausible climax prevents *Just Cause* from being a first-rate thriller. Nevertheless, the film remains an enjoyable showcase for Sean Connery's talents. As Glimcher pointed out, "As Sean's gotten older, he's become much more subtle. He can say more with a raised eyebrow than most actors can with a whole paragraph of dialogue."

JUST CAUSE   Celebrating the release of the client he believes is innocent (Blair Underwood), while Ruby Dee looks on.

FIRST KNIGHT

1995

Released by Columbia Pictures

CAST:

King Arthur: Sean Connery; *Lancelot:* Richard Gere; *Guinevere:* Julia Ormond; *Malagant:* Ben Cross; *Sir Agravaine:* Liam Cunningham; *Sir Kay:* Christopher Villiers; *Sir Pavile:* Valentine Pelka; *Sir Mador:* Colin McCormick; *Ralf:* Ralph Ineson; *Oswald:* Sir John Gielgud.

CREDITS:

Director: Jerry Zucker; *Producers:* Jerry Zucker and Hunt Lowry; *Screenplay:* William Nicholson, story by Lorne Cameron and David Hoselton, and William Nicholson; *Director of Photography:* Adam Greenberg; *Editor:* Walter Murch; *Production Designer:* John Box; *Music:* Jerry Goldsmith. *Running Time:* 133 minutes.

Perhaps no major star in recent years has had as many underrated films as Sean Connery. Consider the following: *The Hill, Marnie, Woman of Straw, The Molly Maguires, The Offence, The Wind and the Lion, The Man Who Would Be King, Robin and Marian, A Bridge Too Far, Outland, Five Days One Summer, The Name of the Rose,* and *A Good Man in Africa.* Each of these films was virtually dismissed by the critical establishment upon their initial release, and only in a few cases have they retroactively been reevaluated and received the praise they so richly deserve. The latest Connery film to have the dubious honor of appearing in this group is *First Knight,* a magnificent retelling of the King Arthur legend that was met with shockingly mediocre reviews when it was released in the summer of 1995. In fact, it is one of the best films of Sean Connery's career.

Going into production, it would appear as though every wrong creative decision had been made. The film was to be directed by Jerry Zucker, who gained serious respect in the industry with the surprise success of his first directional effort, *Ghost,* which became one of the greatest smash hits in recent history. However, Zucker was still better known for having brought to the screen such comedy classics as *Airplane* and the *Naked Gun* series through collaboration with his brother David. The idea of Zucker, the ulti-

mate clown, being entrusted with a big-budget epic dealing with the legend of Camelot was viewed by many as akin to having Jim Carrey play Hamlet.

Nevertheless, Zucker's surprising success with *Ghost* gave him clout as a filmmaker. He and his brother signed a high-profile contract with Sony Pictures Entertainment in 1991 to develop new films for the studio. If Sony was expecting *The Naked Gun Part X,* they must have been surprised when the Zuckers announced they wanted to develop films independently of each other and not always work as a team. David Zucker, a self-professed fanatic of the Davy Crockett legend, put his energies into developing a serious biography of the legendary hero. Meanwhile, Jerry had his own legends to concentrate on. It was his goal to completely rewrite the clichéd story of King Arthur, Guinevere, and Lancelot even though the story had already been told many times in film, most notably in the 1967 musical *Camelot.* However, Zucker wanted to show a realistic side of the story, minus dragons, Merlin, and singing and dancing milkmaids. The recent success of Kevin Costner's *Robin Hood: Prince of Thieves* allowed Zucker to get the green light from Sony, whose subsidiary, Columbia Pictures, would release the film.

Zucker commissioned a screenplay written by Lorne Cameron and David Hoselton, whose modest individual credits were *Like Father, Like Son* and *Clarence.* Zucker had already gone into preproduction and was actively scouting locations while the script continued to be fine-tuned by Bo Goldman and Tom Shulman. It had been decided that much of the shooting would take place at Pinewood Studios near London, where the producers could also take advantage of the lush countryside surrounding the studio. The only distant location work would be done in Wales, for sequences in which Lancelot attempts to rescue Guinevere from the evil Malagant, who holds her captive in his underground lair. For these sequences, an abandoned slate mine was deemed eerie and depressing enough to fit the bill. A nearby nonoperational nuclear power plant also served as the exterior of Camelot.

It was intended that production would start in the summer of 1993. However, Zucker felt the script still needed more work. Ultimately, William Nicholson, who had written the screenplay for the highly acclaimed *Shadowlands* was brought on board to rewrite the script in a definitive fashion. Cameron and Hoselton would ultimately be relegated to sharing a "story by . . ." credit with Nicholson.

Zucker then turned to the challenge of casting. He believed that Sean Connery was the most appropriate actor in the world to play the larger-than-life role of King Arthur. Although some cynics felt that Connery was getting too old to portray romantic leading men, it was decided that the role of Arthur required a world-weary, experienced presence, and no one fit the bill like Connery, who in recent years had come to be regarded as somewhat of a majestic presence in the film industry. Connery became the first actor signed for the movie. The role of Guinevere was to be played by Julia Ormond, who had created a sensation in *Legends of the Fall*. The evil Malagant would be portrayed by British actor Ben Cross.

This left the most pivotal role for last—that of Lancelot, who serves as the catalyst for all the events which would unfold. Industry insiders were shocked when it was announced that one of the most famous English legends would be played by . . . Richard Gere! No one was more surprised than Gere to receive the offer, and he admitted having reservations: ''I read the script, and I said, 'It's a beautiful script,' which it was, it was a really well-written, poetic, dramatic script—I was really impressed by it. But I said, 'You've written this for a twenty-two-year-old kid . . . and it's not working. I need some more maturity. So think about it and let's talk about it.''' Gere and Nicholson discussed the actor's concerns, and ''we realized that by changing very little it worked for me, someone of my age and my experience. And it actually did help the story, made it richer.''

After a delay of months to insure the script was satisfactory, production got underway in early 1994. Before actual filming took place, however, Zucker had to insure that all of his sets were ready. *First Knight* would boast some of the most challenging and opulent sets seen in recent years. To oversee this mammoth task, Zucker hired John Box, the Oscar-winning production designer of *Lawrence of Arabia* and *Doctor Zhivago,* among other epics. Box spent five months constructing the sets at Pinewood alone. The *First Knight* team took over the entire studio and became the largest production ever filmed there, much to the chagrin of Eon Productions, Connery's former employers. When production geared up for the first 007 epic in six years—*GoldenEye*—Eon was politely told by Pinewood that there was no room at the studio because of the latest Sean Connery film. Ironically, Connery was still causing Eon frustration—although this time it was hardly *intentional*.

Box succeeded in creating a spectacular world, transporting the viewer back in time. If this is not the way the era of Camelot actually looked, then it certainly is the way we *want* it to look. In addition to magnificent castles and the haunting underground lair of Malagant, special effects supervisor George Gibbs contributed another memorable setpiece: the

medieval gauntlet upon which Lancelot tempts death to win a kiss from Guinevere. A horrific contraption which features spinning boulders, razor-sharp swords, and battle-axes all moving at speeds precisely timed to filet the challenger, the gauntlet is a masterpiece of design. According to Jerry Zucker, ''George Gibbs initially built models of the gauntlet and we would play with them in the office. We were like a bunch of kids sitting on the floor and playing with this thing. . . . I said, 'George, we've got to go all the way with this thing. We've got to make it big!' ''

By the time production wrapped in November 1994, it was apparent that *everything* about *First Knight* was big. The film features brutal, large-scale battles complete with full armies fighting on horse and foot; thrilling chase scenes; eye-popping sce-

FIRST KNIGHT   Arthur (Connery) tries to convince Lancelot (Richard Gere) to join the Round Table.

274

nery, and a deeply engrossing love story that also touches on humility, devotion, temptation, and betrayal.

The plot stays within the framework of the musical *Camelot* in that it depicts Arthur as a truly visionary man trying to encourage human rights, while at the same time barely containing his obsession with his new bride Guinevere. Into this paradise comes two forms of trouble. The most obvious threat comes from the evil Malagant, once one of Arthur's most trusted knights, now a megalomaniac intent on capturing Camelot by force. The other threat is more subdued and is caused by the arrival of Lancelot, a drifter with no allegiances or ties to anyone, but who happens to be a master swordsman. He is immediately obsessed with Guinevere, and when he saves her life, he accepts Arthur's offer to become a knight

of the Round Table. The decision proves to be an unwise one. Despite his devotion to and respect for Arthur, Lancelot cannot resist passionately kissing Guinevere. They are discovered, and a crushed and humiliated Arthur places them on trial, where a guilty verdict will mandate their deaths. Fate, of course, is the great equalizer, and the exciting climax of the film resolves the relationships in a moving but tragic way.

Connery looks as though he were born to play the role of Arthur, and everyone in the production seems to sense this. His entrance in the film—walking proudly through a gauntlet of torches to greet Guinevere—is a stunning moment. The role affords Connery one of the most interesting and multilayered characters he has ever portrayed, and he seems to relish every moment of it. Julia Ormond is also wonderful, playing Guinevere as an intelligent, mannered woman who is blissfully free of the type of nineties one-liners about women's lib that permeate so many costume dramas of recent years. Her classical beauty compliments Connery's ruggedly handsome looks. (Sean decided to wear a toupee this time around, because "I wanted a head that looked like a mixture of Samuel Beckett and Stalin—and that worked. I think of it as an older guy who has a young man's hair." It also happens to be the most flattering "rug" Connery has worn in many a year, and he looks as though he is ten years younger than his actual age.) The screenwriters realize that an adventure is only as good as its villain, and *First Knight* presents us with one of the more memorable bad guys we've seen: Malagant, the dark side of Arthur. Like all good villains, he is witty, occasionally charming, and absolutely ruthless. He is superbly played by Ben Cross.

The most controversial piece of casting remained Richard Gere's Lancelot. At least one critic admitted to virtually salivating over viewing what he felt would be the greatest casting error since John Wayne played Genghis Khan. However, the general consensus was that Gere *was* miscast, but not disastrously so. For better or worse, Gere—like Kevin Costner before him—avoids attempting an accent and uses his natural voice. This prevents the audience from being too distracted, but it does make it glaringly obvious that none but a Frenchman, perhaps, should play Lancelot. In fairness, however, Gere is magnificent in the action sequences, and they are frequent enough to compensate for any shortcomings of his casting. While Gere never soars in anything but the dueling scenes, neither does he embarrass himself or his costars.

In addition to the aforementioned achievements of John Box, the film boasts a great musical score by

Jerry Goldsmith. Adam Greenberg's cinematography makes the most of the gorgeous locations, and Walter Murch's editing is first rate (particularly in the sequence in which Lancelot attempts the gauntlet). The lion's share of the praise, however, must go to Jerry Zucker, who succeeded in bringing this sweeping tale to the screen—thanks also to the intelligent screenplay by William Nicholson. It should also be noted that the film benefits greatly from the work of Gareth Edwards, the digital effects supervisor. While it is true that Gere and his costars did indeed master the art of swordsmanship (and very nearly suffered serious wounds), some of the exciting duels were enhanced by digital effects performed at the Cinesite Digital Film Center. In certain scenes, the actors were using just the handles of the swords—the blades were flawlessly added later. Edwards explained, ''We used motion blur, rotoscoping, and other 3-D techniques that we developed. We had to calculate every detail, including the depth of field, horizons, and the vanishing point. A sword plunges into Malagant's body, and Lancelot pulls it out, and it doesn't look fake. It's believable. There's a definite science to it, but it also requires a gut feeling for what looks right.''

First Knight opened in July 1995 to disappointing domestic grosses that eventually totaled less than $40 million. Although word-of-mouth had it that the film was a box-office disaster, *Variety* would later report that through international grosses and ancillary revenues, such as home video, the movie would ultimately break even. The public's lack of interest could be due to any number of factors: an aversion to literate, costume dramas; the fact that neither Connery nor Gere had had a big hit recently; or, most probably, the film was one of the inevitable victims of the insane policy of releasing a tremendous number of fine movies to simultaneously compete during the summer season. Ultimately, a few score big, while many others that would have attracted big audiences later in the year fall flat during the long, hot summer. (For example, in yet another irony, *GoldenEye* was delayed due to *First Knight's* monopoly of Pinewood, as was explained earlier. This caused the Bond epic's planned summer release to be pushed back to fall. *First Knight* beat Bond to theaters—and grossed less than $40 million. Bond opened in November—sans heavy competition—and grossed over $100 million.)

Regardless of its financial woes, *First Knight* is a film with which everyone associated can be proud. For Connery, it proved that, while technically a senior citizen, he still has enough charisma to again play a man who would be king—this time, literally.

DRAGONHEART

1996

Released by Universal Pictures

CAST:

Bowen: Dennis Quaid; *Einon:* David Thewlis; *Gilbert:* Pete Postlethwaite; *Kara:* Dina Meyer; *Aislinn:* Julie Christie; *Felton:* Jason Issaacs; *Brok:* Brian Thompson; *Young Einon:* Lee Oakes; and Sean Connery as the voice of *Draco.*

CREDITS:

Director: Rob Cohen; *Producer:* Rafaella De Laurentiis; *Screenplay:* Charles Edward Pogue, based on a story by Patrick Read Johnson and Charles Edward Pogue; *Director of Photography:* David Eggby; *Editor:* Peter Amundson; *Production Designer:* Benjamin Fernandez; *Music:* Randy Edelman. *Running Time:* 108 minutes.

Without question, Sean Connery's first of two major film releases in 1996 provided him with the most unusual role of his career. As the mythical Draco, last of the great dragons in *Dragonheart,* Connery never appears on the screen. Instead, his voice dominates the movie with a heartfelt and passionate narration, making an animated creature a flesh-and-blood being, complete with humor, sadness, and irony.

Dragonheart was a troubled production to bring to the screen, and one look at the final cut indicates why. It is a mind-boggling special effects extravaganza that pushes current technology to its limits. The film had been optioned by producer Raffaella De Laurentiis seven years previously, but was deemed too complicated to bring to the screen. De Laurentiis remained adamant that the film could be done, and upon seeing the marvelous computer-generated dinosaurs in *Jurassic Park,* her resolve only increased. Ultimately, the success of that film led Universal to give her the go-ahead. De Laurentiis sent the script to director Rob Cohen, with whom she had previously teamed up for the acclaimed film *Dragon: The Bruce Lee Story.*

The story of *Dragonheart* concerns a knight named Bowen (Dennis Quaid), who is assigned as teacher and sword instructor to young Prince Einon (Lee

DRAGONHEART   Bowen (Dennis Quaid) forms an uneasy alliance with his prey, Draco.

Oakes). The time is the tenth century, and England is a harsh land ruled by a tryrannical king, Einon's father. When the latter is killed during a brutal massacre of rebellious peasants, Einon assumes the crown. His ascension appears to be short-lived, as he is mortally wounded in the battle. Desperate for a miracle, Bowen and Einon's mother, Queen Aislinn (Julie Christie), take the lad to the lair of Draco (the voice of Sean Connery), last of the great dragons. The cynical beast is reluctant to help, as his species has been decimated by dragon hunters such as Bowen. Ultimately, he takes pity on the boy, and upon Einon's swearing to restore adherence to an ancient code which promises to practice peace, love, and tolerance, the dragon makes a sacrifice: he determines to keep Einon alive by donating half of his

heart to the young man. The two will now be inextricably linked. When Draco dies, so too will Einon. As long as Draco lives, the boy will be invulnerable.

Now an adult, Einon (David Thewlis) proves an even worse tyrant than his father, and makes abuse of the peasants a favorite hobby. Among those he torments and murders is the father of Kara (Dina Meyer), a beautiful peasant girl who vows revenge. Enraged that Einon has become a brutal dictator, Bowen blames Draco in the belief that his heart has poisoned the young man's soul. He becomes obsessed with slaying the last dragon. Ultimately, he learns that Draco is innocent, and that Einon always had evil in him. The two forge a strong friendship and team up with Kara to build another uprising to overthrow King Einon. The climactic battle leads to

DRAGONHEART   David Thewlis as the evil Einon.

a "no-win" situation for Bowen: if Einon is to be destroyed, Draco must die as well.

Dragonheart is unique among special-effects-laden epics in that it never loses sight of the humanity of the characters. This includes Draco, who is one of the most intriguing and touching cinematic creatures since E.T. Bringing him to life, however, was anything but fun for the virtual army of technicians who worked for over a year on designing the giant beast. According to Rob Cohen, "The challenge . . . was to pick up where *Jurassic Park* left off, in territory pioneered by Steven Spielberg. Unlike the dinosaurs, Draco is not solely an animal; he's the first CGI [Computer Graphic Imagery] actor. He speaks, he emotes, he has feelings, a soul, and humor."

Cohen would not follow tradition by shooting his dragon in the shadows or in quick cuts. "I wanted to see Draco mythic and glorious in the sun," he insisted. To insure this occurred, Cohen went to the top talent in special effects and CGI. Phil Tippet, the Oscar-winning animator who designed the dinosaurs for *Jurassic Park*, came up with the basic design

for Draco. The dragon was then given to the special effects team at George Lucas's Industrial Light and Magic, the F/X house that is unsurpassed in inventing new technologies to accomplish the seemingly impossible. One of the major obstacles was that Draco was not just window-dressing. He would have to *talk,* as well as *act,* and therefore show a wide range of emotions.

While the special effects work was being mapped out, Rob Cohen began production on the film itself. The voice of Draco would have to belong to a larger-than-life screen presence. Cohen and De Laurentiis agreed there was only one suitable person for the job: Sean Connery. Connery recalls, "It was quite flattering that they would come and ask me. I read the script and adored the idea of it. It's fascinating . . . and very humorous . . . . And I said, 'Well, I'm perfectly happy to do it, but can you tell me something more about the process?' They had not really determined exactly what the dragon would look like." When Cohen assured him that the geniuses at ILM would do the F/X, Connery was immediately confident the concept would succeed.

Ironically, Connery—who recorded his narration in the Bahamas—had virtually completed his duties by the time filming began. In the recording studio, Connery and Dennis Quaid read their own parts, while Cohen read the lines of all other characters. The director admitted he and Quaid were "in awe" of working with the former 007. Connery was filmed from every possible angle during his sessions. Upon completion, the tapes were given to the animators at ILM so they could use the actor's facial mannerisms in their design of Draco. Cohen supplemented their research sources by providing an extensive library of film clips from Connery movies. Animation supervisor James Strauss recalled to *Cinescape* magazine, "The director would say 'I want Draco to act like Sean did in *The Hunt for Red October,* or *The Name of the Rose.'* We went through the tapes together and had video printouts made of key moments in each scene, which the animators put up on the wall around their workspaces so they could look at Sean as they animated." Connery said of the process, "They must be sick of the sight of me, because they have all the cuttings and trims and photographs and pictures and stuff from all the movies. It's quite interesting. One is not conscious of all your gestures until they've been put together like this."

When Connery finished his initial narrative sessions, Cohen convened production in Slovakia, the capital of Bratislava, a small country that borders Austria and Hungry. Here, the filmmakers found unblemished countryside and magnificent castles

278

which could double for tenth-century England. Production designer Benjamin Fernandez built a thirty-foot-high, twenty-foot-wide waterfall, a full-scale castle, and a 250-foot lake. Over 600 authentic period costumes were fashioned and brought to Koliba Studios, where many scenes were to be filmed. Ultimately, Cohen had to give instructions to over 200 crew members from twenty different countries, thus requiring a large number of translators on the set.

Principal photography was completed in November 1994. However, Universal recognized the need to allow sufficient time for special effects work. In essence, while the movie was completed with its flesh-and-blood cast, Draco still had to be superimposed into large portions of the film. This had proven to be an enormous challenge to the cast, particularly Dennis Quaid, who spent most of his time reciting his lines to empty space, or a pair of sticks and balls meant to represent his dragon costar. Ultimately, a partial dragon puppet was created so that Quaid had *something* to inspire his reactions.

Alas, problems ensued. Cohen had already begun filming the Sylvester Stallone movie *Daylight* in Rome. He was simultaneously working on the creation of Draco for *Dragonheart*. Deciding that much of the dragon's dialogue needed to be amended, he persuaded Connery to fly to Rome to redub about twenty percent of his initial narration—a task made all the more complicated by the fact that the dragon animation was still not ready. Connery didn't have the luxury of lip-synching to his scaly, onscreen alter ego. The actor also contributed a series of growls, which would later be blended with animal sounds to double as the roar of the dragon. By the time ILM finished their daunting task, the creation of Draco made the work on *Jurassic Park* pale in comparison. For example, the earlier film had utilized 8,000 matrices (computerized images), whereas *Dragonheart* required over 280,000.

The creative team behind *Dragonheart* can be proud of their accomplishment. The special effects and animation in the film are nothing short of brilliant, and Draco emerges as one of the more memorable creations in recent films. The movie itself offers nothing new in its depiction of the savagery of medieval times. We see the stock characters from "Central Round Table Casting": the tyrannical king and his despicable henchmen, noble peasants, the brave knight who forsakes personal enrichment to fight for a cause, his feisty and brave lady, endless swordfights, and a good deal of bloodletting.

What makes *Dragonheart* unique is that it properly concentrates on the relationship between Bowen and Draco—and a fascinating and touching one it is.

DRAGONHEART   Dina Meyer as the beautiful and brave Kara.

Whether the two are attempting to best one another on the battlefield, or matching sarcastic wisecracks, their scenes together work beautifully. The fact that Draco is given a heart and soul provides the film with its most valuable asset. When the noble but pitiable creature laments the fact that he is the last of his kind and would welcome death if he did not fear it so greatly, you forget you are watching a computer-generated creation. The animated creature is as real at these times as any of the actors on-screen.

Dragonheart has enough action to keep younger viewers enthralled, but director Cohen emphasizes the humanity of the script. The characters are never more than two-dimensional (except for Draco), but Cohen's skill is such that we come to care about each of them. Aside from the Oscar-caliber special effects, the film features a rousing score by Randy Edelman (which is occasionally remindful of John Barry's work), outstanding cinematography by David Eggby, and impressive production design by Benjamin Fernandez. Praise should also go to editor Peter Amundson for keeping the film at a very manageable 108 minutes. In this era of "more is better," Amundson knew when enough was enough. The film flows perfectly at its present length.

The cast performs gamely, although Dennis Quaid

struggles mightily—and reasonably successfully—to overcome the fact that he is glaringly miscast as a tenth-century English dragonslayer. With his all-American good looks and California accent, he is as out of place as Richard Gere was in *First Knight*. Why has Hollywood forsaken ethnic actors to play ethnic characters? In this case, probably because most of the contemporary British stars are not known for action-adventure flicks, as were Connery, Richard Burton, Richard Harris, and others who emerged as leading men in the 1960s. However, like Gere, Quaid manages to never appear embarrassing or laughable. He may not be ideally cast, but his enthusiasm for the role overcomes these drawbacks. (Initially the film had been considered as a starring vehicle for Harrison Ford! The mind boggles at the thought of Ford bandying witticisms with a dragon.)

The supporting cast is a mixed bag. American actress Dina Meyer is suitably pretty and carries her action scenes well enough. The latest tradition appears to be that all damsels in distress can immediately hold their own against their male counterparts. In this case, Meyer's character goes from peasant girl to master swordswoman overnight. Meyer's role of Kara is not particularly interesting or essential to the plot, so the actress has little to do. Refreshingly, however, the expected prerequisite love scene between she and Quaid never occurs. As always, an action film is only as good as its villain, and David Thewlis excels as the evil Einon. Thewlis is neither the "mad as a hatter" demon played by Alan Rickman in *Robin Hood: Prince of Thieves,* nor is he the urbane, sophisticate such as Robert Shaw's Sheriff of Nottingham in *Robin and Marian.* Instead, he is a somewhat pathetic and pitiable monarch who seems to practice brutality because he lacks a love life. The screen lights up when Thewlis emotes. The wonderful Julie Christie pops up as Einon's mother, the queen. Although she looks marvelous, one wonders why Christie chose this role to end a six-year self-imposed retirement. She has little to do or say, and the role might just as easily have been filled by Rosie O'Donnell.

Upon its release in the early summer of 1996, *Dragonheart* received mixed reviews. Negative critics cited a clichéd story, and some felt the film was a bit too violent for family audiences. However, there was virtually unanimous agreement that Draco was a masterful creation. By all counts, reviewers cited Connery as the real star of the film. Most critics went out of their way to mention the dignity which the actor's narration brought to the film, and many said it was the best Connery performance in ages—despite the fact he never appears on-screen.

The movie was expected to flop by insiders, who predicted that Dennis Quaid couldn't "open" a film with Connery appearing only as a voice-over. However, the premiere weekend's gross was a surprisingly hefty $15 million. Sadly, the film quickly fell victim to the simultaneously released likes of *Twister* and *Mission: Impossible,* and its grosses declined substantially. There is a good chance it will find the success it deserves through home video release. As for Sean Connery, by all accounts he enjoyed the experience of bringing a mythical creature to life. He said, "When you're sixty-five and have played as many roles on stage and movies as I have, it's exciting to do something new, *especially* when you can do it without makeup or a wig!"

DRAGONHEART   Connery recording the voice for his on-screen alter ego, Draco, the last dragon.

THE ROCK

1996

Released by Hollywood Pictures

CAST:

John Patrick Mason: Sean Connery; *Stanley Goodspeed:* Nicholas Cage; *Gen. Francis X. Hummel:* Ed Harris; *Womack:* John Spencer; *Baxter:* David Morse; *Paxton:* William Forsythe; *Anderson:* Michael Biehn; *Carla:* Vanessa Marcil; *Hendrix:* John C. McGinley.

CREDITS:

Director: Michael Bay; *Producers:* Don Simpson and Jerry Bruckheimer; *Screenplay:* David Weisberg, Douglas Cook, and Mark Rosner; *Story by:* Weisberg and Cook; *Executive Producers:* William Stuart, Sean Connery, and Louis A. Stroller; *Director of Photography:* John Schwartzman; *Production Designer:* Michael White; *Editor:* Richard Francis-Bruce; *Music:* Nick Glennie-Smith and Hans Zimmer. *Running Time:* 129 minutes.

By the summer of 1996, it had been over six years since Sean Connery had starred in an unqualified box-office hit. (His last film to achieve that goal was *The Hunt for Red October*.) In the ensuing years, the actor had certainly been busy. His body of work during that period consisted of good films that failed to generate substantial heat with audiences (*Medicine Man* and *First Knight*); a small arthouse movie (*A Good Man in Africa*); a big-budget bore (*The Russia House*); films that never lived up to their potential (*Rising Sun* and *Just Cause*) and the proudly inept (*Highlander 2: The Quickening*). It was ironic that the best reviews Connery had received during this time was for lending his voice to the much underrated *Dragonheart*. All of that would change with the release of *The Rock*—a thriller with nothing more on its mind than to make audiences suspend disbelief and munch their popcorn in excited anticipation for what the next whirlwind action sequence would be. It would also do what industry skeptics thought was impossible: restore the sixty-six-year-old Connery to the top of the box-office charts.

The Rock represents Connery's most crassly commercial project in many years (with the exception of the beloved *Highlander* sequel). It also continued the

THE ROCK   *Thunderball* 1996-style: Sean dons a wet suit for *The Rock*.

THE ROCK   Connery with director Michael Bay.

tradition of late of the actor serving as an executive producer. In this capacity, Connery would have more control over the types of filmmaking problems which have perturbed him since the Bond days (such as budget overruns and production delays). Although Connery reportedly had some trials and tribulations with the production, even he must have been pleased that it was completed and released in a time frame that was astonishingly rapid in today's movie industry.

The Rock began as the brainchild of writers David Weisberg and Douglas S. Cook who had been inspired by a real-life story about a woman who served as a park ranger on one of California's Channel Is-

THE ROCK   (top) Spying on the terrorists; (bottom) A tense moment as Cage dismantles one of the rockets.

tation as the director of *Bad Boys*. Bay agreed to helm *The Rock* if the producers agreed to have the script rewritten. They concurred, and writer Mark Rosner was brought on board.

Casting was less of a problem. From the beginning, Bruckheimer and Simpson wanted Sean Connery and Nicholas Cage for the leading roles. The plot finds the Connery as John Patrick Mason, a former British Intelligence agent, who is the only person to have ever escaped from Alcatraz. He has been recaptured and kept in solitary confinement for over thirty years because of his unwillingness to hand over secretive and potentially explosive files to the U.S. government. These sensitive files pertain to a wealth of high-profile and scandalous cases, including that of the Kennedy assassination. When a band of renegade U.S. Marines, led by Medal of Honor winner General Hummel (Ed Harris), take over Alcatraz, the FBI finds itself helpless. Hummel is using missiles loaded with a deadly nerve gas to demand full recognition and benefits for Marines who have died during illegal covert activities ordered by the government. It falls to FBI chemist Stanley Goodspeed to accompany a team of scuba divers into Alcatraz to disarm the missiles. The only man capable of leading the group is the dangerous and unpredictable Mason, who has more than enough reason to distrust his captors (and vice-versa).

Cage and Harris signed on willingly, although the latter did admit that the script had more holes in it than Swiss cheese. Cage considered it refreshing to finally play an action hero and liked the fact that his character starts out as a mild-mannered chemist who is terrified of field duty. As for Connery, however, the task of enlisting his services proved to be more challenging. With characteristic bluntness, he stated that he didn't care for *Bad Boys* and had reservations about the thirty-two-year-old Bay's style of directing. However, after a face-to-face meeting with Bay, enough ice was broken to convince Connery that the two could work together. The actor signed for the role of Mason—certainly the most outrageous and charismatic character he had played in many years.

Problems persisted with the script, however. Bay and Mark Rosner were at odds over the direction of the story. Rosner wanted to stress realism, while Bay insisted on big action set pieces. Rosner left the project, and Jonathan Hensleigh was brought in for the duration of the movie, as rewrites would be an ongoing part of filming *The Rock*. Hensleigh oversaw major changes to the script, and Connery brought in some of his own writers to contribute. (An ugly battle for who would get screen credit had to be arbitrated through the Screenwriter's Guild. Ultimately, Weis-

lands. The writers found the fact that the woman lived entirely alone intriguing. They saw the possibility of turning such a vulnerable person into the catalyst for a screenplay, which somehow led to the grandiose premise that terrorists could take over the relatively isolated prison at Alcatraz in San Francisco Bay. The resulting script resulted in Disney paying $1.2 million in a heated bidding war with other studios.

The film was to be produced by the "boy wonder" team of Jerry Bruckheimer and Don Simpson. The famed team had taken Hollywood by storm years before with movies such as *Top Gun*, only to later falter with disappointing projects. Bruckheimer and Simpson regained their reputations as powerbrokers in 1995 with three big hits: *Bad Boys, Dangerous Minds,* and the terrific thriller *Crimson Tide.* Disney literally handed them *The Rock* as the major summer 1996 release for the studio's Hollywood Pictures subsidiary. The producers approached Michael Bay, a veteran of TV commercials, who had gained a repu-

282

berg, Cook, and Rosner would get the billing, much to the disappointment of Hensleigh.)

With the writing finally under control, attention turned to shooting on Alcatraz Island itself. The former prison is now a part of the National Park Service, a major tourist attraction that draws up to 4,000 visitors a day. The prison, which closed in 1963, had originally been neglected and had fallen into disrepair. However, it eventually dawned on the federal government that a renovated island could pay for itself as a tourist site and by leasing the facility to movie companies. A massive renovation of the prison took place in 1978 for Clint Eastwood's *Escape From Alcatraz,* and the improvements were kept up after the film was shot.

Since Alcatraz is a national park, filming of *The Rock* had to be done during off hours or while visitors to Alcatraz were on site observing the production. Things became more complicated in November 1995 when the U.S. government—caught in a political battle over the federal budget—virtually closed down. Disney immediately placed the park rangers on the studio payroll to insure filming continued. The studio also had to pay for many renovations, including asbestos cleanup to allow filming in otherwise abandoned buildings. The task of duplicating the interiors of the buildings in Alcatraz fell to production designer Michael White, who did a masterful job of seamlessly blending the real prison with studio shots.

Alcatraz is not a pleasant place to shoot a film. It is cold and inhospitable, and all equipment must be transferred by boat to the island. Yet, the cast and crew gamely went about their work and the film's production schedule moved along at a rapid rate.

Then tragedy struck: producer Don Simpson died tragically in his home. The news was a blow to everyone on the film, but not entirely shocking. The fifty-two-year-old mogul had gained a notorious reputation as a boozing, womanizing, drug-user whose excesses had mandated that his partner Jerry Bruckheimer did the bulk of the work on their last few films. Simpson, always a strange and moody man, was concerned about his self-destructive practices, but appeared unwilling or unable to control them. He made only a cursory visit to the set, and his participation had been limited to late-night telephone conferences. Immediately prior to Simpson's death, Bruckheimer—weary of dealing with his partner's problems—had announced this would be their last project together.

Simpson's death was devastating news. Yet, Michael Bay and his cast and crew rallied and completed the movie in an astonishingly short period of time. Disney was so enthused about the movie that they ordered postproduction speeded up so *The Rock* could be an early summer release. Bruckheimer and Bay swallowed hard at that request, but by the movie's opening in mid-June, the final cut was ready. (A lavish premiere was held on Alcatraz, with Connery quipping that at least *this* time he could be off "the Rock" in only two hours.)

The Rock is a marvelous joyride of a movie, but is not without some glaring flaws. First the bad news: the much-troubled script is simply a rehash of other movies. There is the prerequisite car chase in the hills of San Francisco (no one has ever topped the one in *Bullitt,* so why try?), the old chestnut about unstable U.S. military types, and a main story idea that is disturbingly similar to the 1976 Dirty Harry film *The Enforcer* (in which terrorists take over Alcatraz and the hero battles the rocket-firing villain atop the lighthouse).

There is also evidence that Michael Bay's background as a director of TV commercials works against him on occasion. His insistence upon using ultra-fast cuts in the editing process and claustrophobic closeups is wearying and annoying. It also robs the movie of any suspense, because no take lasts longer than a second. Anytime the herky-jerky camera pauses for a minute, it's like a breath of fresh air. In the aforementioned car chase sequence, the editing

THE ROCK   Connery and Cage infiltrate "the Rock."

THE ROCK   (top) Connery maps strategy for the assault on Alcatraz; (bottom) The rock-solid cast: Sean Connery, Nicolas Cage, and Ed Harris.

is so frantic that there is no sense of time or place, and the lack of long shots makes it appear as if it was filmed in a phone booth. Fortunately, these problems become slightly less apparent as the film progresses.

Now for the *good* news. *The Rock* benefits from the wonderful chemistry between Connery and Cage. The "odd couple" of action films works extremely well together, with Connery's old-world cynicism nicely counterbalanced by Cage's nervous energy. Connery has the meatier role, however, and he dom-

inates most of the scenes. When we first see him, he appears to be a caged animal—with Mansonlike dirty hair and a wild look in his eyes. Yet, we find years of solitary confinement have not dulled his intelligence, humor, or unpredictability. It is a small wonder the FBI distrusts him. Shortly after being released, he devises an ingenious method to escape in one of the movie's best sequences. As the reluctant hero, Connery truly shines in this film—none more-so than when he is asked where he learned all of the guerrilla tactics he uses to break back into Alcatraz. "British Intelligence," he remarks, to the shouts of approval from the audience. The sight of Connery donning a black wetsuit and utilizing high-tech underwater contraptions must certainly have been a conscious nod to his *Thunderball* days—and dammit if he doesn't look as fit and ready for action has he did thirty years ago.

Ironically, it is when Connery and Cage actually arrive on Alcatraz that the film disappoints and becomes just another extravagant "shoot 'em up." Until this point, there had been plenty of character development and intriguing subplots. Most of this is tossed out when the duo and their team break back into the prison. Their Marine team becomes predictable fodder for Ed Harris's men, who in turn are transformed from interesting patriots with a political ideology into two-dimensional villains motivated by greed. The exception is Harris, who is allowed some dignity and manages to give yet another first-rate performance.

Although the finale to *The Rock* is nothing we haven't seen before, it is fittingly explosive and entertaining. The sight of Sean Connery wielding a machine gun and mowing down the enemy in between making wisecracks is like manna from heaven for his fans. *The Rock* contains many such small pleasures,

and while Connery has certainly made more thought-provoking films, this is one you'll feel like watching over and over again.

The Rock was not among the more talked-about releases for the summer of 1996. The inside word was that Connery could no longer carry an action film, and even recent Oscar-winner Cage had not been able to translate into a big draw with audiences. The industry was therefore somewhat startled when the movie opened to a huge $25 million weekend and maintained strong "legs" in the following weeks. As of this writing, it has grossed more than $250 million worldwide. For Connery, it proved the charisma that had charmed audiences for four decades was very much in place. Amazingly, the now elder statesman could once again take his place among the top ranks of contemporary action/adventure stars.

Michael Bay revealed a telling moment to *Entertainment Weekly* regarding his initial, tense meeting with Connery. Bay fumbled badly with a bottle of wine in the actor's suite and found he could not open it. Connery nonchalantly picked up the wine and in a second had the cork out. He looked at Bay and smiled, saying, "Bond. James Bond." Thirty-four years after he first said those words on-screen, Sean Connery is still leaving audiences shaken *and* stirred.

Sean's crowning triumph—winning the Oscar for *The Untouchables* (1988).

FREE!
Citadel Film & Television Books Catalog

Now it's easier than ever to receive free information about the Citadel Film & Television books!

For a full-color brochure and a complete listing of every Citadel Film & Television title available, just fill out and return the stamped, self-addressed card below. There's even an extra card so you can have a brochure sent to a friend.

Or for fastest service, call 1-800-447-BOOK and tell the operator you'd like the Citadel Film & Television brochure.

Carol Publishing Group
Dept. 1391
120 Enterprise Avenue
Secaucus, NJ 07094

A tear-out reply card for you...   ...and one for a friend!

Please send me the Citadel Film Series catalog and keep me posted on other books of interest!

Name
Address
City _____ State _____ Zip
Title of this book
Where bought
What other Citadel Film Books do you own
What other Citadel Film Books do you recommend we publish
What magazines/newspapers do you read
Name & address of a friend who would like info

Please send me the Citadel Film Series catalog and keep me posted on other books of interest!

Name
Address
City _____ State _____ Zip
Title of this book
Where bought
What other Citadel Film Books do you own
What other Citadel Film Books do you recommend we publish
What magazines/newspapers do you read
Name & address of a friend who would like info

A Complete Listing of Citadel Film & Television Books

STARS • Alan Ladd • Arnold Schwarzenegger • Barbra Streisand: First Decade; Second Decade • Bela Lugosi • Bette Davis • Boris Karloff • The Bowery Boys • Buster Keaton • Carole Lombard • Cary Grant • Charles Bronson • Charlie Chaplin • Clark Gable • Clint Eastwood • Curly • Dustin Hoffman • Edward G. Robinson • Elizabeth Taylor • Elvis Presley • Errol Flynn • Frank Sinatra • Gary Cooper • Gene Kelly • Gina Lollobrigida • Gloria Swanson • Gregory Peck • Greta Garbo • Henry Fonda • Humphrey Bogart • Ingrid Bergman • Jack Lemmon • Jack Nicholson • James Cagney • James Dean: Behind the Scene • Jane Fonda • Jeanette MacDonald & Nelson Eddy • Joan Crawford • John Wayne Films • John Wayne Reference Book • John Wayne Scrapbook • Judy Garland • Katharine Hepburn • Kirk Douglas • Laurel & Hardy • Lauren Bacall • Laurence Olivier • Mae West • Marilyn Monroe • Marlene Dietrich • Marlon Brando • Marx Brothers • Moe Howard & the Three Stooges • Norma Shearer • Olivia de Havilland • Orson Welles • Paul Newman • Peter Lorre • Rita Hayworth • Robert De Niro • Robert Redford • Sean Connery • Sexbomb: Jayne Mansfield • Shirley MacLaine • Shirley Temple • The Sinatra Scrapbook • Spencer Tracy • Steve McQueen • Three Stooges Scrapbook • Warren Beatty • W.C. Fields • William Holden • William Powell • A Wonderful Life: James Stewart **DIRECTORS** • Alfred Hitchcock • Cecil B. DeMille • Federico Fellini • Frank Capra • John Ford • John Huston • Woody Allen **GENRE** • Bad Guys • Black Hollywood • Black Hollywood: From 1970 to Today • Classic Foreign Films: From 1960 to Today • Classic Gangster Films • Classic Science Fiction Films • Classics of the Horror Film • Cliffhanger • Cult Horror Films • Divine Images: Jesus on Screen • Early Classics of Foreign Film • Great French Films • Great German Films • Great Romantic Films • Great Science Fiction Films • Great Spy Films • Harry Warren & the Hollywood Musical • Hispanic Hollywood: The Latins in Motion Pictures • The Hollywood Western • The Incredible World of 007 • The Jewish Image in American Film • The Lavender Screen: The Gay and Lesbian Films • Martial Arts Movies • The Modern Horror Film • More Classics of the Horror Film • Movie Psychos and Madmen • Our Huckleberry Friend: Johnny Mercer • Second Feature: "B" Films • They Sang! They Danced! They Romanced!: Hollywood Musicals • Thrillers • The West That Never Was • Words and Shadows: Literature on the Screen **DECADE** • Classics of the Silent Screen • Films of the Twenties • Films of the Thirties • More Films of the 30's • Films of the Forties • Films of the Fifties • Lost Films of the 50's • Films of the Sixties • Films of the Seventies • Films of the Eighties **SPECIAL INTEREST** • America on the Rerun • Bugsy (Illustrated screenplay) • Comic Support • Dick Tracy • Favorite Families of TV • Film Flubs • Film Flubs: The Sequel • First Films • Forgotten Films to Remember • Gilligan, Maynard & Me • Hollywood Cheesecake • Hollywood's Hollywood • Howard Hughes in Hollywood • More Character People • The Nightmare Never Ends: Freddy Krueger & A Nightmare on Elm Street • The Northern Exposure Book • The Official Andy Griffith Show Scrapbook • The Quantum Leap Book • Sex in Films • Sex In the Movies • Sherlock Holmes • Son of Film Flubs • Those Glorious Glamour Years • Who Is That?: Familiar Faces and Forgotten Names • "You Ain't Heard Nothin' Yet!"

To order books, or a free full-color catalog, call 1-800-447-BOOK